CLASSICAL HERITAGE
VOL. 5

# HOMER

GARLAND REFERENCE LIBRARY
OF THE HUMANITIES
VOL. 1531

# CLASSICAL HERITAGE

## WARD W. BRIGGS, JR.
*Series Editor*

**OVID**
*edited with and introduction by*
William S. Anderson

**VERGIL**
*edited by*
Craig Kallendorf

**MARTIAL**
*edited by*
J. P. Sullivan

**SOPHOCLES**
*edited by*
R. D. Dawe

**HOMER**
*edited by*
Katherine Callen King

# HOMER

*edited by*

Katherine Callen King

**GARLAND PUBLISHING, Inc.**
*New York & London / 1994*

**Library of Congress Cataloging-in-Publication Data**

Homer / [edited by] Katherine Callen King.
        p.    cm. — (Classical heritage ; vol. 5) (Gar-
land reference library of the humanities ; vol. 1531)
    Includes bibliographical references (p.).
    ISBN 0-8153-0482-X (alk. paper)
        1. Homer—Influence.  2. Literature, Modern—
Greek influences.  3. Classicism.    I. King, Katherine
Callen.    II. Series.    III. Series: Garland reference
library of the humanities ; vol. 1531.
PA4037.H7743   1994
809—dc20                                                    93-37770
                                                                  CIP

Printed on acid-free, 250-year-life paper
Manufactured in the United States of America

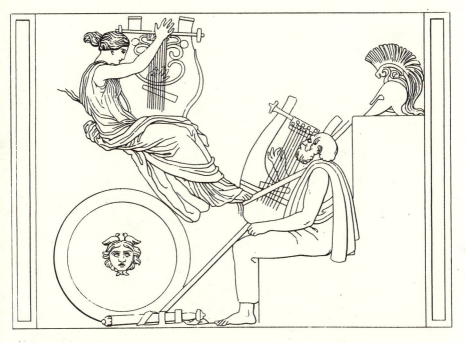

Homer invokes the muse. John Flaxman (*Iliad* series).

# TABLE OF CONTENTS

# EIGHTEENTH CENTURY

# NINETEENTH CENTURY

# TWENTIETH CENTURY

# ILLUSTRATIONS

Frontispiece: "Homer Invokes the Muse." John Flaxman (*Iliad* series, 1804).*

Facing page 1: *Battle at Troy.* Illustration to Canto Decimoquarto of *L'Achille et L'Enea de Messer Ludovico Dolce* (1572). By permission of the Special Collections Library of the University of California at Los Angeles.

Page 30: *Achilles and Hector.* William Hole (1616). Frontispiece to George Chapman's *The Whole Works of Homer, Prince of Poets in his Iliads, and Odysses.* By permission of the Special Collections Library of the University of California at Los Angeles.

Page 48: *Hera Seduces Zeus.* B. Picart (1710). First used as headpiece to Book 14 of Anne Le Fèvre Dacier's French translation of the *Iliad* (1711) and then re-engraved (with attribution to Antoine Coypel) to illustrate Book 14 of the Ozell-Oldisworth-Broome English translation of Dacier's French. Recycled by Alexander Pope to head his own *Iliad* 14 (1720).

Page 72: *The Wrath of Achilles.* Antoine Coypel (1711). Design first used as headpiece to Book I of Anne Le Fèvre Dacier's edition of the *Iliad* (1711) and then re-engraved to adorn Alexander Pope's introductory "Essay on the Life, Writings, and Learning of Homer" (*Iliad*, vol. 1, 1715).

Page 86: *Achilles' Shield.* Jean Boivin and Nicolas Vleughels (1715). Adapted by Samuel Gribelin, Jr. as illustration to Book 18 of Pope's *Iliad* (1720).

Page 104: *The Last Interview of Hector and Andromache*. Angelica Kauffmann (1769). By permission of the National Trust Photo Library, London.

Page 110: *Odysseus following the Wagon of Nausikaa*. Flaxman (*Odyssey* series, 1793).

Page 132: *Council of the Gods*. Flaxman (*Iliad* series, 1793).

Page 142: *Leucothea Saves Odysseus on the Raft*. Flaxman (*Odyssey* series, 1793).

Page 154: Departure of Briseis from Achilles. Flaxman (*Iliad* series, 1793).

Page 176: *Iris Tells Priam to Ransom Hector's Body*. Flaxman (*Iliad* series, 1793).

Page 190: *The Sirens*. Flaxman (*Odyssey* series, 1793).

Page 208: *Descent of Athena to Ithaca*. Flaxman (*Odyssey* series, 1793).

Page 224: *Reunion of Odysseus and Penelope*. Flaxman (*Odyssey* series, 1793).

Page 238: *Achilles Laments over the Body of Patroklos*. Flaxman (*Iliad* series, 1793).

Page 254: *Odysseus Slays the Suitors*. Flaxman (*Odyssey* series, 1793).

Page 264: *Odysseus in Hades*. Flaxman (*Odyssey* series, 1793).

Page 284: *Phemios Sings to the suitors in Odysseus' Palace*. Flaxman (*Odyssey* series, 1793).

Page 310: *Aphrodite and Helen*. Flaxman (*Iliad* series, 1793).

* All Flaxman illustrations are copied from *Homero: obras completas*, trans. Luis Segalá y Estrella (Joaquín Gil: Buenas Aires, 1946).

# SERIES PREFACE

## Ward W. Briggs

With the proliferation in the last generation of courses in Western Humanities or Great Books of the Western World, the need to demonstrate the continuity from ancient to modern culture is ever more pressing. Recent years have seen phenomenal interest in the area of studies known as the Classical Tradition, with at least one major journal well established (*Classical and Modern Literature*) and at least one other in the offing. The Institute for the Classical Tradition at Boston University continues to thrive with conferences and publications both here and abroad. The recent bimillennium of the death of Virgil brought forth a number of volumes in his honor and many of their contributions dealt with his *Nachleben*. Much the same will undoubtedly be true of the bimillennium of the death of Horace. Despite this interest, there have been no volumes designed to survey the influence of various ancient authors throughout European and American history.

This series will present articles, some appearing for the first time, some for the first time in English, dealing with the major points of influence in literature and, where possible, music, painting, and the plastic arts, of the greatest of ancient writers. The editors are published authorities on their authors and they provide introductions that summarize the scope of each author's impact on Western literature and art.

# PREFACE

This volume includes essays on Chapman, Milton, Racine, Pope, neo-classical painter Angelica Kauffmann, Goethe, Keats, Gladstone and Tennyson, Tolstoy, Cavafy, Rilke, Joyce, Yourcenar, Kazantzakis, Seferis, East German poet Erich Arendt, and recent Nobel-prize winner Derek Walcott. Other important figures are briefly discussed both in the introduction, which summarizes and situates the essays in a social or artistic context, and in the essays themselves. The essays are preceded by illustrations (fourteen from John Flaxman's monumentally influential series) that have graced various translations of Homer's texts.

Many important authors who have been influenced by Homer are not represented: William Blake, for example, and Borges, d'Annunzio, Erskine, Giraudoux, H.D., Marivaux, Nabokov, Pound, Yeats. Many more artists, too, would have been welcome: Bryson Burroughs, David, de Chirico, Delacroix, H. Fuseli, G. Hamilton, Ingres, Le Corbusier, Rubens, Max Slevogt, the Tischbeins, Wedgewood—to name only a few. And there is a complete absence of musicians: for example, von Gluck, Offenbach, Saint-Saëns. The reasons for their absence are varied: constraints of space and budget, the unavailability of appropriate essays, the fact that my specialty is literature.

I have selected essays that would show Homer's influence on a wide range of genres—epic, lyric, and dramatic poetry, novels, essays, short stories, and the visual arts—from many countries: England, France, Germany, Greece, Italy, Russia, Spain, United States and the West Indies. I looked for a spectrum of critical approaches—historical, biographical, feminist, formalist, marxist, post-structuralist—in order to demonstrate the interest Homer still holds for a wide variety of important scholars. I hope that most of the essays will not only enlighten readers about the importance of Homer to western culture but will enable new insights into the *Iliad* and the *Odyssey* as well.

I would like to thank the many people who helped me search out and prepare these essays: my two research assistants Caroline Austin and Amy Sapowith; librarians Miki Goral, Tim Strawn, and David Zeidberg; colleagues Albert Boime, Stathis Gourgouris, Thomas Haüssler, Kathleen Komar, Marilyn Manners, Marc Silberman. Thanks, too, to Ward W. Briggs, Jr., the general editor of the Classical Heritage Series, for his patience and support.

# INTRODUCTION

Homer's *Iliad* and *Odyssey* have inspired poetic imitation, been the subjects of paintings and sculpture, supplied quotations to fit contemporary situations, and provided models for contemporary behavior since at least the fifth century B.C. A brief hiatus in the poems' popularity in western Europe during the Greekless thirteenth and fourteenth centuries was quickly ended once Petrarch and Boccaccio persuaded their refugee tutor to translate them into Latin. From then until the present day, European and American artists and writers have continually found the *Iliad* and *Odyssey* relevant to their aesthetic and political concerns. This collection of nineteen essays by modern scholars explores how Homer influenced the expression of those concerns.

## Poets of Medieval Europe and the Italian Renaissance

The first essay, which was written specifically to introduce this collection, offers a brief summary of Homer's fortunes in late antiquity and the Middle Ages and examines in some depth the rebirth of his poems in the Italian renaissance. Available to most readers only in a poor Latin digest and hampered by being on the wrong side of European ancestry, Homer nonetheless remained the Trojan War poet of record until the mid-thirteenth century, when Benoît de Ste Maure's monumental redaction of Darys's version, the *Roman de Troie* (1160), swept away all competition. Homer's influence was at this point nearly extinguished, but not for long. Translations by Leonzio Pilato (1360) and Lorenzo Valla (1444) and an increasing knowledge of Greek among scholars enabled educated fifteenth-century readers to read the originals in all their complexity. The payoff came in the sixteenth century when increasing familiarity bred admiration and imitation: Ludovico Ariosto used Homeric similes and scenes throughout his *Orlando furioso* (1532), and Giovanni Trissino and Luigi Alamanni composed epics about Italian history that were almost translations of Homer. A two-pronged debate ensued: was Homer or Vergil the superior poet and was modern Christian poetry better than pagan classical poetry? Unlike his encomiast Paolo Beni, Torquato Tasso, whose *Gerusalemme liberata* (1575) and prose writings reveal a detailed and sensitive reading of the Greek epics, was unwilling to judge poets or poetry on the basis of religion and found a way thoroughly to integrate both the Homeric and Vergilian poems into his Christian epic.

## George Chapman (1557–1634)

English scholars had begun learning Greek in Italy in the late fifteenth century and had seriously begun to teach it in Oxford, London and Cambridge by the middle of the sixteenth. By the end of the sixteenth century, many translations of the Herodotus and Thucydies, Plato and Aristotle existed to influence the non-scholar's life.[1] But for English writers who, like Shakespeare, had "small Latin and less Greek" Homer was inaccessible until George Chapman produced his translations of the *Iliad* (1608) and the *Odyssey* (1614).[2]

John C. Briggs shows how Chapman used his "preview" translation of Books 1, 2, 7–11 of the *Iliad*, published in 1598 as the *Seaven Bookes of the Iliades*, to convince a prospective patron, the Earl of Essex, that he was Achilles incarnate. Interweaving Elizabethan politics, contemporary views of Homer, and Essex's own tumultuous career as successful soldier and rebellious courtier, Briggs argues that

---

[1]For the coming of Greek to England see J. Churton Collins, *Greek Influence on English Poetry* (London: Sir Isaac Pitman and Sons, 1910) 33-52.

[2]All that was available previously was the Greekless Arthur Hall's 1581 translation of the French verse version of *Iliad* 1-10 by Hugues Salel (1537). For an insightful brief analysis of Hall's translation see Reuben A. Brower, *Hero & Saint: Shakespeare and the Graeco-Roman Tradition* (Oxford: Oxford University Press, 1971) 81-83. See Robert Kimbrough, *Shakespeare's* Troilus & Cressida *and its Setting* (Cambridge: Harvard University Press, 1964) 25-46, esp. 36-38, for what versions of the Troy story Shakespeare did have available and how the appearance of Chapman's *Seven Bookes* might have influenced *Troilus & Cressida*. Brower's chapter on "Achilles Hero," especially pages 50-81, give a splendid analysis of Elizabethan theory of the heroic poem and of Chapman's achievement in his final versions of the *Iliad* and the *Odyssey*.

Chapman modifies and expands his basic text in order "to emphasize and exaggerate specific parallels between Achilles and Essex" and "to temper as well as encourage Essex's rise to greater power." Despite Chapman's belief that his Essex-inspired expansions of the Greek text revealed Homer's true meaning, he removed them from his complete translation of 1608 in response to Essex's execution for treason in 1602.

## John Milton (1608-1674)

Homer is ubiquitous in Milton's *Paradise Lost* (1662): speech and simile, character and scene evoke the *Iliad* and the *Odyssey* as paradigmatic of a fallen world that Christian epic transcends. Mary Nyquist explores the effect of one such evocation on the interpretation of Adam and Eve's behavior in the central passage of book nine, specifically on the interpretation of a simile that compares their post-coital awakening to Samson's awakening in the lap of Delilah. Milton's allusion to Zeus and Hera's lovemaking and awakening in *Iliad* 14 and 15 provides a context in which readers can easily divide Adam and Eve into Zeus-Samson and Hera-Delilah, ignore the logic of the simile that identifies them both with Samson, and obliterate the difference between intellectual temptation and sexual seduction. Such an equation produced the misogynistic misreadings by eighteenth century-critics Joseph Addison (*Spectator*), Thomas Newton (edition), and Pope (*Iliad*) that have been repeated by twentieth-century editors. Nyquist argues, however, that Milton's allusion to Homer here has been mediated by Plato's criticism of the scene in his *Republic*, and that therefore what is at issue is not the "patriarchally structured polarity of male and female but the spiritually structured opposition between the sacred and profane," or between "a divinely created original innocence and its fallen imitation." In Nyquist's post-structuralist terminology, one could say that although the phallocentric (male-supremacist) reading is possible, both text and historical context suggest that the purely logocentric (authoritarian) reading is the more powerful.

## Jean Racine (1639-1699)

In the latter half of the seventeenth century French intellectuals quarreled fiercely over whether Homer should retain his crown as Prince of Poets or be dismissed as a distasteful barbarian. Academics opposed to Homer asked "if this anger of Achilles, this deadly passion

of a hero who was not, except in the Trojan War, either of highest
social rank or morally best among the Greeks, was worth having an
epic poem dedicated to him."[3] They questioned the value of "useless
digressions" and whether Book 24 was a satisfactory ending. Lay
people opposed Homer on Christian grounds, on political grounds
(Agamemnon is a weak and shamed king), and on moral grounds
(Achilles is insubordinate, Odysseus commits adultery with Circe and
Calypso). What united these groups was the idea that Homer did not
conform to current ideas about religious, political and moral *order*.

In the midst of this *querelle des anciens et des modernes*, a few authors remained neutral, keenly aware of the value of Homer but
aware, too, that both social and poetic mores had changed. One such
was Jean Racine. Noémi Hepp, in a short selection from her
monumental book, *Homère en France au XVII<sup>e</sup> siècle*, discusses how
Racine, an avid reader of the *Iliad* and the *Odyssey*, used Homer to
"nourish" his seventeenth-century versions of Euripidean drama even
though he knew that many Homeric values would not be acceptable to
the public for which he wrote. She shows how the early *Andromache*
(1667) evokes *Iliad* 6, 7, 15 and 24 to present a more refined Achilles
who is not only violent but also magnanimous and compassionate, and
a Hector, "knight without reproach," who is strong as well as gentle
and wise. The mature Racine uses Homer even more complexly in
*Iphigenie* (1674), creating an extended imitation of the quarrel
between Achilles and Agamemnon into which he infuses more emotion (specifically that of love), tighter logic, and a nobler tone. Racine
may have declared that "Parisian taste conforms with that of Athens,"
but Hepp shows how his careful changes to Homer belie that affirmation.

## Alexander Pope (1688-1744)

"The Quarrel between Ancients and Moderns" was known in
England as "The Battle of the Books." In her attempt to assess how
well Alexander Pope's *Iliad* (1715-1720) reproduced Homer "within
the semantic and ideological constraints of his time," Kathryn L.
Lynch argues that the "battle" combined with the new "anthropological" scholarship of Bentley and Theobald put unique historical
pressures on the translator. Drawing on comparisons with translations
by Chapman (1608), John Ogilby (1660), Dryden (1700), and Anne

---

[3]Noémi Hepp, *Homère en France au XVII<sup>e</sup> siècle* (Paris: Klincksieck, 1968)
762.

Lefèvre Dacier (1711), she argues that Pope tampers with Homer more than any other translator: his more epigrammatic couplets turn his Jove into a lofty and omnipotent God, his Agamemnon into "a kind of Jacobite hero," and Achilles' soul into a tripartite battleground in which Passion draws Will away from Reason. Why did Pope insist on making Homer's universe into "a mirror and idealized version of his own"? Because he was committed to the unity of Nature, a concept undermined by the new scholarship that posited a vast distance between past and present. Unlike Homer's previous translators, Pope had "to persuade his public that the Greek poet was worth reacting to personally . . . to convince an audience that there was a community of values shared by classical and Christian poets and that the reading of the Greek poet somehow required a commitment of oneself to those values."

## Angelica Kauffmann (1741-1807)

The years 1750-1825, commonly labeled the Neo-Classical period, produced a huge increase in the number of Homeric subjects in art. There seem to have been at least three contributing factors: First, Giambattista Vico's influential *Principii di una scienza nuova* (1725) praised Homer and helped bring him into favor[4]; Second, with the publication of *Tableaux tirés de l'Iliad, de l'Odyssée d'Homère et de l'Eneide de Virgile, avec des observations générales sur le costume* in 1757, the Comte de Caylus started a reform movement to go back to the simpler classical ideals of the seventeenth century[5]; and third, as Albert Boime argues, the English victory in the Seven Years' War (known in the United States as the French and Indian War, 1756-63) encouraged the English ruling class to identify with the heroes of the *Iliad* and the *Odyssey*. Because of this identification, artists such as John Flaxman (1755–1826), the sculptor whose outline drawings of Homeric scenes quickly achieved international fame, and Angelica Kauffmann, a founding member of the Royal Academy of England, could get rich by illustrating Homeric subjects. Boime points out Kauffmann's unique interpretation of her Homeric and other subjects: all are woman-centered, feminine, erotic, which seem to have pleased patrons who wanted their heroic wall-hangings to be decorative rather than tragic.

---

[4]Michael Levey "Tiepolo's Treatment of Classical Story at Villa Valmarana" *Journal of the Warburg and Courtauld Institutes* 20 (1957) 304.
[5]See Dora Wiebenson "Subjects from Homer's *Iliad* in Neoclassical Art," *Art Bulletin* 46 (1964) 25-26, 32.

## Johann Wolfgang von Goethe (1749-1832)

*Wo bist Du hin, Kindheit der alten Welt, geliebte süsse Einfalt in Bildern,*
*Werken und Worten? Wo bist Du, geliebtes Griechenland, voll schöner*
*Gotter = und Jugendgestalten, voll Wahrheit im Truge und Trug voll*
*süsser Wahrheit?–Dein Zeit ist dahin....*[6]

"Where have you gone, childhood of the aged world, lovely sweet
innocence in images, works and words. Where are you beloved
Greece, full of the beautiful forms of gods and youth, full of truth in
illusion and illusion full of sweet truth?--Your time is lost and
gone...." So lamented Johann Gottfried Herder in 1777 in response
to the late Johann Winckelmann's call to turn to the ideals of ancient
Greece for artistic inspiration.[7] Such nostalgia, which pervaded the
second half of the eighteenth century in Germany, encouraged and
was in turn encouraged by the research and writing of the highly
influential *Essay on the Original Genius and Writings of Homer* by
Robert Wood (1775) and *Prolegomena to Homer* by Friedrich A. Wolf
(1795). These works were essentially romantic in mood, making
Homer into the supreme, primitive imitator of Nature and, in Wolf's
work, turning Homer into a collectivity of folk poets. The latter is
apparently what encouraged Johann Wolfgang von Goethe (1749–
1832) to attempt a continuation of the *Iliad* and to create a bourgeois
German equivalent of the *Odyssey*.

David Constantine takes up Goethe's "creative attempt (and failure) to copy Homer" as part of "the whole late eighteenth century's
wish and failure to realize a supreme ideal in the form of Ancient
Greece." He focuses on Goethe's early *Nausikaa* (1787) and his final
Homeric effort the *Achilleis* (1798–99). Through analysis of Winckelmann's, Wood's, and Wolf's writings, the work of other poets and
thinkers of the time, Goethe's letters and other prose, and the fragments of *Nausikaa* and *Achilleis*, Constantine explores the paradoxical
imperative to be both original and imitative. He links what small success Goethe achieved in both abandoned poems to his experience of

---

[6]Johann Gottfried Herder, "Denkmahl Johann Winkelmanns," in *Herders
Sämmtliche Werke* ed. Bernhard Suphan, (Berlin: Weidmannsche Buchhandlung,
1892) vol. 8, 481.

[7]In Winckelmann's *History of Ancient Art* (1764). Rudolf Pfeiffer has called
Winckelmann the initiator of "a true new Hellenism" of which Goethe provided the
consummation (*History of Classical Scholarship: From 1300-1850*, [Oxford: Clarendon,
1976] 170). Martin Bernal prints the relevant passage in *Black Athena: The Afroasiatic Roots of Classical Civilization, Volume I: The Fabrication of Ancient Greece
1785-1985* (New Brunswick, N.J.: Rutgers University Press, 1987) 214.

the "Homeric" landscape in Sicily and in books—that is, to the imaginative potency of landscape that "surviving, links a degraded present with an ideal past."[8]

## John Keats (1795-1821)

In the first decades of the nineteenth century English poets were not so entranced with Homer as was Goethe. William Blake, who had started his life as a fervent neo-classicist, turned against Homer and the classics in 1804 and devoted his subsequent work to counteracting their insidious influence on English culture.[9] Tranquil William Wordsworth mentions learning Homer in school (*Prelude* 5.202) but rarely evokes and never emulates "the great Thunderer" in his own poetry.[10] Percy Shelley's lyrics do not touch on Homer much, though he did translate several Homeric Hymns. Of the Romantic poets, George Gordon Lord Byron, whose genius flowed more toward epic, is the one who uses Homer the most, modelling the structure and many episodes of his mock epic poem on the *Odyssey*[11] and evoking the *Iliad* when bloody battle scenes occur:[12]

> The Russians now were ready to attack;
>   But oh, ye Goddesses of war and glory
> How shall I spell the name of each Cossacque
>   Who were immortal, could one tell their story?
> Alas! what to their memory can lack?
>   Achilles self were not more grim and gory
> Than thousands of this new and polished nation,
>   Whose names want nothing but--pronunciation.
>
> *Don Juan* 7.14

---

[8]For more details of Goethe's experience with Homer see E. M. Butler's highly entertaining *The Tyranny of Greece over Germany* (Cambridge: Cambridge University Press, 1935) 121-35 and Richard Jenkyns, *The Victorians and Ancient Greece* (Oxford: Blackwell, 1980) 22.

[9]See William Richey, *The Covenant of Priam: Blake's Re-Visions of the Homeric Epic*. Ph.D. Dissertation, University of California at Los Angeles, 1990.

[10]Byron's amusing comparison of Homer and Wordsworth is perhaps apt in this context: "We learn from Horace, Homer sometimes sleeps; / We feel without him: Wordsworth sometimes wakes . . ." (*Don Juan* 3.98,1-2).

[11]Hermione de Almeida details the many episodes of *Don Juan* based on the *Odyssey*: *Byron and Joyce through Homer* (London: MacMillan, 1981) 14-16.

[12]See especially 7.78-80.

As this example shows, the irreverent Byron uses Homer as both touchstone and punching bag, to use Hermione de Almeida's apt formulation.[13]

The poet most famous for reading Homer in the early nineteenth century is John Keats. Keats had already experienced Homer in Pope's translation before the exciting night he spent reading aloud with a friend Chapman's translations of the *Iliad* and the *Odyssey*. Bernice Slote brings the magic of that night before our eyes and then shows the various ingredients that went into the creation of "On First Looking into Chapman's Homer" the next morning. Differences between Pope's and Chapman's translations, the contents of mythological handbooks, historical accounts of the exploration of the Americas—all are examined to see why Keats reacted so strongly and why it was natural for him to make his central metaphor "imaginative discovery seen as geographical discovery in Apollo's world." For Keats, Chapman gave access to Homer and the metaphorical gold of Apollo's realm just as the Pacific Ocean gave access to more literal realms of gold for Cortez, Balboa, and Pizarro.

**Alfred Lord Tennyson (1809–1892)**
**William E. Gladstone (1809–1898)**

Greece and Homer gained ascendancy over Rome and Vergil in nineteenth-century England due to a combination of political and intellectual factors. Athenian democracy supplanted the Roman Republic as the political system of record as Britain became more liberal in the 1830's. Robert Wood's late eighteenth-century *Essay*, which had so affected Goethe, and Thomas Blackwell's *An Enquiry into the Life and Writings of Homer* (1735) had located Homer in an historical space and made him worth studying as historian as well as poet. Also, poetic theory veered toward nature as opposed to art and put a new emphasis on originality.[14] In the Victorian period Homer was far from being just an academic subject or object of reading enjoyment. Prominent politicians were intensely interested in his relevance to the proper governing of their polity. Member of Parlia-

---

[13]Almeida argues that if Homer "is the point of direction he is also point of divergence, if he is authority he is also reason for rebellion . . ." (20).

[14]Frank M. Turner, *The Greek Heritage in Victorian Britain* (New Haven: Yale University Press, 1981) 135-186, and "Why the Greeks and not the Romans in Victorian Britain" in *Rediscovering Hellenism: The Hellenic Inheritance and the English Imagination*, ed. G. W. Clarke (Cambridge and New York: Cambridge University Press, 1989) 61-81, esp. 69-71.

ment and Prime Minister William Gladstone, the author of five books and several articles on Homer, continually pointed to the poet as a supporter of his views and wanted the *Iliad* and the *Odyssey*, which he felt were excellent texts for teaching the arts of government, to be a constant in the studies of Oxford undergraduates.[15]

Liberal William Gladstone and Tory Poet Laureate Alfred Tennyson were utterly opposed in politics but united in admiration of Homer. Gerhard Joseph, in "The Homeric Competitions of Tennyson and Gladstone," discusses their "lifelong intellectual competition" over the relevance of the Homeric mythic system to their contemporary world. Gladstone, who felt there was an essential continuity between the classical Greek and nineteenth-century British cultures, read Homer as a secular Bible and precursor of Christianity; Tennyson's poems on classical themes, all of which focus on humankind's relation to ruinous Homeric or Lucretian divinity, reveal a sense of disjunction, of "fundamental irreconcilability."

## Leo Tolstoy (1828–1910)

As early as the seventeenth century there were influential advocates of studying the Greek and Latin classics in Russian schools,[16] and Homer was translated into Russian during the reign of Catherine the Great (1762–96).[17] In the nineteenth century Homer was required reading in the exclusive universities that were intended to prepare aristocrats for their responsibilities as high civil servants.[18] Ancient Greek, however, was not a requirement, and Tolstoy did not learn Greek and read Homer in the original until he was 42, a year after finishing *War and Peace*.[19]

---

[15]Richard Jenkyns (note 8 above) 199-204.

[16]J.L. Black, *Citizens for the Fatherland: Education, Educators, and Pedagogical Ideals in Eighteenth Century Russia* (Boulder, CO: East European Quarterly, 1979) 20-22.

[17]Catherine wrote to Voltaire, who had been urging her to learn Greek, that she would do so but that she could begin her classical Greek education with the translation currently being produced. [Letter 63, as quoted by Chula Chakrabongse, *The Education of the Enlightened Despots: A Review of the Youth of Louis XV of France, Frederick II of Prussia, Joseph II of Austria, and Catherine II of Russia* (London: Eyre and Spottiswoode, 1948) 137].

[18]James C. McClelland quotes a disgruntled conservative as complaining that a new regulation (put into effect in 1809) required high-ranking civil servants to know all sorts of useless things, among them Homer and Theocritus (*Autocrats and Academics: Education, Culture, and Society in Tsarist Russia* [Chicago & London: University of Chicago Press, 1979] 24).

[19]Sophia Tolstoy has recorded in her diary how her husband "suddenly decided he wanted to learn Greek" (December 9, 1870) and how, after immersing

F.T. Griffiths and S. J. Rabinowitz, in "Tolstoy and Homer," explore Tolstoy's claim that *War and Peace* (1869) is like the *Iliad* and conclude that, like Vergil's *Aeneid* and Milton's *Paradise Lost*, its model is the *Iliad* and the *Odyssey* combined. Singularly lacking in Homeric unity of plot and structure, *War and Peace* nonetheless reproduces Homer's vitality and scope. Numerous parallels link Andrei and Achilles as heroes of higher principle and self-immolation, Pierre and Odysseus as earthbound heroes of homecoming, Penelope and Natasha as paragons of chastity, Helene and Helen as scandalous beauties. Tolstoy begins with Achilles and ends with Odysseus, one of his goals being, like Homer's, "to demonstrate at once the appeal and hollowness of military glory." Unlike Homeric epic, *War and Peace* "attains a synthesis of heroic modes when Pierre attains by grace what Andrei sought by force of will." And, like Vergil, Dante and Milton, Tolstoy proclaims his resistance to the epic style at the same time as he uses it: "that gesture of rejection (followed in every case by cease-less cribbing from the same oppressive antecedents) is one of the surest markers of the genre." The article suggests that, finally, Tolstoy achieves a tone of ambivalence by returning to Achillean values in the Epilogues, a return, the authors argue, that is similar to the end of the *Odyssey*.

## Constantine Cavafy (1863–1933)

As the nineteenth century entered its last decade, the symbolist poetics of Baudelaire, Verlaine, Rimbaud and Mallarmé, with its focus on inner life and mood to the exclusion of narrative and politics, began to influence poets outside France. One such poet was the Greek poet Constantine Cavafy. In "Cavafy and *Iliad* 24: A Modern Alexandrian Interprets Homer" Seth L. Schein demonstrates through a close reading of "Priam's Night Journey" (1893) that Cavafy's "imitation" of the Homeric scene is not only symbolist in feeling but also "Alexandrian" in its demands upon the reader. As did the poetry of his fellow Alexandrians who wrote in the Hellenistic period (300-100 B.C.E.), Cavafy's sophisticated intertextuality requires simulta-neous attention to both the new and the "imitated" text. Such atten-

---

himself in it "day and night" for three months, he moved on from Xenophon and Plato to "reading the *Odyssey* and the *Iliad*, which he absolutely adores" (March 27, 1871). Quoted from *The Diaries of Sophia Tolstoy*, edited by O. A. Golinenko, S. A. Rozanova, B. M. Shumova, I. A. Pokrovskaya and N. I. Azarova, translated by Cathy Porter (New York: Random House: 1985) 846.

tion intensifies the reader's penetration of Priam's psychological landscape as he races without end away from the pain of Troy's and his own lamentation.

## Rainier Maria Rilke (1875–1926)
## Franz Kafka (1883–1924)

Clayton Koelb's "Kafka and the Sirens" compares Rilke's "The Island of the Sirens" (1907) and Kafka's "The Silence of the Sirens" (1917). While Rilke "uses the authority of the Homeric text to authorize" alterations to an episode of nearly inexpressible immediate experience, Kafka selects "materials out of which the text is made" and radically reshapes them into a story that "questions the possibility of immediate experience." In Kafka's story, Odysseus's crew disappears, their only trace being the wax that, now in Odysseus's ears, prevents him from either hearing the Sirens silence or perceiving their desire for him. Odysseus, therefore, becomes an unreliable narrator of a non-experience. Koelb argues that the "lethetic" ("forgetful") reading of Homer that created "The Silence of the Sirens" conforms to Kafka's theory of how writers must be unimpeded, "unwounded" by the texts that stimulate their creativity.

## James Joyce (1882–1941)

James Joyce published *Ulysses* in 1922. Before we turn to this remarkable Irish epic, we will benefit from a return to the nineteenth century and a comprehensive look at the interpretations of the *Odyssey* available to Joyce via translations and scholarly writing. In "Homer's Sticks and Stones," Hugh Kenner reminds us that Homer changes as values change, and asks which Homer Joyce had in mind, "which **Odyssey**, which Odysseus." Since Joyce did not know Greek, we know which contemporary Homers he could choose from: the noble, edifying Homer of Matthew Arnold's prescriptions (1860) and Butcher and Lang's translation (1879) or the naturalistic Homer of Schliemann's archeology (1870) and Samuel Butler's theory (1897) and translation (1900). Although Joyce chose the latter as his primary source, he used the former as well--and also included the Homeric committee of F. A. Wolf and the Homer of Stoic exegesis.

Vivienne Koch, in "An Approach to the Homeric Content of Joyce's *Ulysses*," does not take into account the various Homers, but her essay is one of the earliest and best studies to consider what the correspondences between the *Odyssey* and *Ulysses* might mean for interpretation of the Irish text. She argues that Joyce's focus is Ireland through Greece, not the reverse, and sees an ironic counterpoint in the correspondence between Joycean and Homeric characters. She shows how content becomes style in Joyce's transformation of Nausikaa into Gertie MacDowell, how Telemachos' search for his father becomes Stephen's search for a Father (procreative) principle, and how Antinoos, who represents the Most Dangerous Suitor, and Mulligan, who represents Hellenism, function as usurpers of paternity. "Joyce's emphasis," she concludes, "was always on deriving the essential quality from his model rather than on . . . literal parallels."

## Marguerite Yourcenar (1903–1987)

Marguerite Yourcenar, the first woman to be elected to the French Academy in its 300-year history, is well known for her historical novels and for her love of the classical tradition. She is *not* known for feminism. Nonetheless, my essay, "Achilles on the Field of Sexual Politics," examines the production of feminist questions in "Patrocle ou le destin," the second of a pair of short stories originally published by Yourcenar in 1935, just before the outbreak of World War II. The *Iliad*, Western culture's originary war poem, is of paramount concern to these stories' exploration of gender-identification and violence. Interweaving Achilles' post-Iliadic relationship with Penthesileia into Book 24 of the *Iliad*, Yourcenar shuttles back and forth between war as literal social event and war as an image for conflict between male and female in society, masculine and feminine in the psyche. She ends by producing a feminist critique of the power relations and cultural ideals that were perhaps responsible for the authoritarian fascism that was erupting in Europe.

## Nikos Kazantzakis (1882–1964)

Nikos Kazantzakis began his *Odíssia* in 1924; he completed the eighth and final draft in 1938 (three years before starting *Zorba the Greek*). During the fourteen years in which he worked on successive drafts, he was briefly arrested for communist activity, changed wives, visited Spain, Italy, Egypt, and Sinai as a newspaper reporter, spent several months touring in the Soviet Union before becoming disillusioned about its government, lived in Czechoslovakia, published a two-volume history of Russian literature, translated French children's books into Greek, translated Dante's *Divine Comedy* into Greek *terza rima*, wrote elementary school textbooks, travelled to Japan and

China in order to write travel articles, wrote a novel in French (*Le Jardin des rochers*), translated a play by Pirandello and part one of Goethe's *Faust*, spent two months in Spain as a war correspondent, and wrote two original plays.[20] Given this history, which shows Kazantzakis at home in many venues, it is not surprising that his epic hero turns out to be "a revolutionary, possessed by his ambition for a remade world,"[21] who shows no nostalgia for a physical home. Portraying a quest for freedom rather than a return home, Kazantzakis's epic might well seem to have been inspired more by Dante and Tennyson than by Homer.[22]

The *Odíssia* had been long awaited, but was not popular in Greece. Its 33,333 lines—nearly three times the length of Homer's *Odyssey*—are composed in an unfamiliar metre and with a vocabulary more comprehensible to Cretan peasants than to Athenian intellectuals.[23] It has been much more popular in Kimon Friar's English translation *The Odyssey: A Modern Sequel*,[24] and it is specifically this English version that Morton P. Levitt addresses in the pages from his book that are excerpted here.

Levitt shows how Kazantakis rewrites books 23 and 24 of Homer's *Odyssey* and starts Odysseus on a new journey, one that takes him away from Ithaka to the Antarctic, away from the flesh and towards the spirit. The characters at the beginning are those of the *Odyssey*, but they are there only to be abandoned—Penelope and Telemachus on Ithaka, Menelaus on Sparta, Helen on Crete—as Odysseus, radicalized in stages as he moves further and further from Homer, moves on toward a mystical vision informed by all the philosophies that have molded the twentieth century. Kazantzakis's Odysseus, Levitt argues, "impels us to be the masters of our own myths, to make of our lives a work of art that is worthy of belief."

---

[20]My source is Peter Bien's most useful chronology on xx-xxi of his *Kazantzakis. Politics of the Spirit* (Princeton: Princeton University Press, 1989). Bien also has an excellent chapter on the *Odíssia*.

[21]Paul Merchant, "Children of Homer: The Epic Strain in Modern Greek Literature," *Aspects of the Epic*, ed. Tom Winnifrith and K. W. Gransden (London: Macmillan, 1983) 93.

[22]As indeed it seemed to W. B. Stanford, *The Ulysses Theme* (1963; Ann Arbor: University of Michigan Press, 1968) 235-36.

[23]Morton P. Levitt, *The Cretan Glance* (Columbus: Ohio State University Press, 1980) 111

[24]New York: Simon and Schuster, 1958.

## George Seferis (1900–1971)

Although neither Kazantzakis nor his hero were particularly concerned with the idea of homecoming, this was a subject that would recapture the energies of the next generation of Greek intellectuals and writers. For this generation, among whom was George Seferis, home meant the tradition of Hellenism as it had survived in the West after Greece had succumbed first to Rome and then to the Turks. Seferis's early poem *Mythistorema* has been described as a search "both for the life in his poetic 'fathers' and for his home: that is, the right place for him to be within the Greek tradition."[25] But "home" also meant Greece as a territorial nation. Artemis Leontis in "Seferis's Myth of Return and Hellenism's Suspended Homecoming" shows how, in the midst of the intolerable chaos of the Greek Civil War, Seferis's *Thrush* (1946) unites the Neohellenic project, which attempted to bring Hellenism home to Greece to be resurrected in a modern Greek culture, with the modernist project of reconnecting with the past through fragmentation and recombination.

## Erich Arendt (1903–1983)

World War I had already disillusioned those who went off to fight with the *Iliad* sounding in their hearts.[26] World War II, in addition to proving that war cannot end war, brought Nazi extermination camps and the atomic bomb. Like Byron 130 years earlier, Anglo-American poet W.H. Auden, to whom as a youth "Hector and Achilles were as familiar as his brothers,"[27] turned to Homer to express his horror at these atrocities and at the world that lived after them. The tone of "The Shield of Achilles," title poem to the volume Auden published in 1955, is, however, not in the least Byronic. No trace of satire allows readers to smile as they watch with Thetis the creation of a world-encompassing shield that smashes all their expectations. At first reading, the poem might seem merely to counterpoint the glorious heroism of the Homeric Achilles with the inglorious mass passivity and mindless violence of modern times. But in fact the poem does not

[25]Ruth Padel, "Homer's Reader: A Reading of George Seferis," *Proceedings of the Cambridge Philological Society* n.s.31 (1985) 94.

[26]Jenkyns beautifully describes this process in England ([note 8 above,] 338-43).

[27]W. H. Auden, "Editor's Introduction" to *The Portable Greek Reader* (New York: Viking Press, 1948) 1.

look back to the classical past with nostalgia. A closer reading reveals that Auden portrays the heroic age as containing, in the words of Claude Summers, "the seeds of modern dehumanization."[28]

Other poets too found Homer relevant to what they experienced during and after the war. One of these was Erich Arendt. Forced to leave Germany when Hitler came to power, Arendt was one of the more important among the older generation of emigré poets who returned to East Germany after World War II. A dissident both in his life and his poetry—he refused to write in the socialist-realist model promoted by the government—he was a mentor to and protector of younger poets. He was also the most important translator of Cuban poet Pablo Neruda and the main conduit through which both East and West Germany received Latin American literature.

Ernest Wichner, in "Homer, Odysseus, and the 'Angel of History'," gives a full account of how Arendt used Homer in his poetry. His earlier status as exile caused him to identify uncritically with Odysseus in the 1950s, but in the 1960s discontent with the historical situation of the twentieth century broke down his optimistic concept of Odysseus. He identifies with Homer as a poetic force occupying an autonomous position between art and history as we move toward the future, looking back at Auschwitz and Hiroshima.

## Derek Walcott (1930–    )

It is quite another "war" that has shaped Derek Walcott's poetics: African-Americans look first for atrocities to the over sixty million killed by the "middle passage" of the slave trade and only second to Auschwitz and Hiroshima. Now a Nobel-Prize winning poet and visiting professor at Boston University, Walcott was born in the British West Indies to a middle class family that contributed to his make-up equal shares of European and African genes and somewhat less than equal portions of European and Afro-Carribean culture. His formal schooling and immediate family fostered a love of European literary and artistic traditions; an aunt and the people of more purely African descent who make up the vast majority of St. Lucia's population taught him to love also the oral traditions of the islands.[29] Having

---

[28]Claude J. Summers, "'Or One Could Weep because Another Wept': The Counterplot of Auden's 'The Shield of Achilles'." *Journal of English and Germanic Philology* 73,2 (Apr 1984) 220.

[29]See Edward Baugh: *Derek Walcott* (London: Longman group Limited, 1978) 9-11.

been deeply influenced by these two cultures, which competed within a colonialist society segregated by race and class, and having finally given his political allegiance to the oppressed majority, it should come as no surprise that his poetic vision is marked by a tension between conflicting aesthetics and histories.

In Walcott's poem *Omeros* (1990) such tension surfaces in two ways: as an Ovidian refusal to choose between, for example, "Hephaestus or Ogun" (LVIIIi)[30] and as denial, denial of the poem's epic status and denial of being inspired by the *Iliad* and *Odyssey*. Oliver Taplin explores this denial (by the narrator within the poem and Walcott without) in conjunction with the poem's being, as he argues in detail, "infused and suffused with Homer all the way from its title page to its final section." Taplin demonstrates that Walcott's "spurning embrace" of Homer has contributed importantly to the creation of "a new and great epic."

## Supplementary Note on the Illustrations

In 1572 Lodovico Dolce published a gigantic work in Italian ottava rima that combined the *Iliad* and the *Aeneid* with supplements from Statius' *Achilleid* and the redactions of Darys and Dictys. The woodcut illustration printed here (Figure 1) was used twice: first to introduce Canto 14 (p. 132), which contains the duel of Ajax and Hector, and then to introduce Canto 24, which describes Achilles return to battle.

Royal Painter Antoine Coypel (1661-1722) produced three versions of "La Colere d'Achille," a painting for the Duc d'Orleans, a tapestry cartoon (1718), and the design for this engraving (Figure 4). First engraved by Charles Simmoneau for Dacier's translation of the *Iliad* (1711), the design was engraved anew by M. von Gucht for use in Pope's translation. Coypel also provided the design for Dacier's *Odyssey* (*Odysseus Slaying the Suitors*) and painted a *Farewell of Hector and Andromache* that hung in the Duchess of Orleans' apartments.[31]

John Flaxman (1755-1826), English sculptor and designer for Wedgewood pottery, was privately commissioned to draw designs illustrating the Homeric epics in 1792. An additional eleven designs were added to the original sixty two in 1805. First published in Italy

---

[30]Derek Walcott, *Omeros* (New York: Farrar Straus & Giroux, 1990) 289.

[31]See Nicole Garnier, *Antoine Coypel (1661-1722): peintre du roi* (Paris: Arthena, 1989) 176-178, 222.

(where they were drawn) in 1793, the outline drawings quickly reached an international audience through editions published in England, France and Germany. Flaxman had clearly surpassed what he believed to be the duty of the artist: "to convert the beauty and grace of ancient poetry to the service of the morals and establishments of our own time and country,"[32] for his drawings continued to inspire artists of many different countries well beyond Flaxman's own time.[33] They eventually supplanted the original illustrations in Pope's translation and have continued to grace translations into the twentieth century. His influence on other artists, too, has continued, though by the mid-twentieth century one might not want to call it inspiration: the reprinting of his drawings to illustrate Paul Mazon's French translation (1954) provoked Le Corbusier, who felt that neither Flaxman nor Mazon interpreted Homer correctly, to superimpose his own twenty-four crayon designs to the *Iliad* over Flaxman's originals (1955–1964).[34]

---

[32]Quoted by Roberk Essick and Jenijoy La Belle in their introduction to *Flaxman's Illustrations to Homer: Drawn by John Flaxman, Engraved by William Blake and Others* (New York: Dover Publications, 1977) xii.

[33]See Sarah Symmonds, *Flaxman and Europe: The Outline Illustrations and their Influence*, (New York and London: Garland, 1984).

[34]*Le Corbusier: L'Iliade Dessins.* Edited and Introduced by Mogens Krustrup (Copenhagen: Borgen, 1986).

# ACKNOWLEDGEMENTS

"*Chapman's Seaven Bookes of the Iliades*: Mirror for Essex" first appeared in *Studies in English Literature* 21 (1981) 59–73.

"Textual Overlapping and Delilah's Harlot Lap" is reprinted from *Literary Theory / Renaissance Texts*, eds. Patricia Parker and David Quint. Baltimore and London: Johns Hopkins University Press, 1986. 352–372.

"Homeric Themes in Racine's l'*Andromache* and l'*Iphigenie*" appeared in *Homère en France au XVII<sup>e</sup> siècle*, Paris: Librairie C. Klincksieck, 1968). 494–504. Trans. K. King and P. Faria.

"Homer's *Iliad* and Pope's Vile Forgery" appeared in *Comparative Literature* 34,1 (Winter 1982) 1–15.

"Angelica Kauffmann" is reprinted from *Art in an Age of Revolution*. Chicago: University of Chicago Press, 1987. 109–115.

"*Achilleis* and *Nausikaa*: Goethe in Homer's World" appeared in *Oxford German Studies* 15 (1984) 95–111.

"Of Chapman's Homer and Other Books" is reprinted from *College English* 23,4 (Jan. 1962) 256–260.

"The Homeric Competitions of Tennyson and Gladstone" appeared in *Browning Institute Studies* 10 (1982) 105–115.

"Tolstoy and Homer" is reprinted from *Comparative Literature* 35,2 (Spring 1983) 97–125 (101–12, 114–22).

"Kafka and the Sirens: Writing as Lethetic Reading" is reprinted from *The Comparative Perspective on Literature*, eds. C. Koelb and Susan Noakes. Ithaca and London: Cornell University Press, 1988. 300–314.

"An Approach to the Homeric Content of Joyce's 'Ulysses' " is reprinted from *Briarcliff Quarterly* 1 (1944) 119–130.

"Homer's Sticks and Stones" appeared in *James Joyce Quarterly* 6 (Summer 1969) 285–98.

"Achilles Awash in Sexual Politics" is reprinted from *Lit* 3 (1991) 201–220 (201–2, 209–220).

"Kazantzakis' *Odyssey*: A Modern Rival to Homer" is reprinted from sections ii and vii of Chapter Six, *The Cretan Glance*. Columbus, OH: Ohio State University Press, 1980. 115–118, 135–38.

"Homer, Odysseus und der 'Engel der Geschichte' " appeared in *Text + Kritik* 82/83 (1984) 90–110. The text was translated by Michael Armstrong, the selections from Arendt's poetry by Nicholas Vazsonyí.

"Derek Walcott's *Omeros* and Derek Walcott's Homer" appeared in *Arion* 1,2 (Spring 1991) 213–226.

# CONTRIBUTORS

Albert Boime, Professor of Art History at the University of California at Los Angeles, is the author of *Art in an Age of Revolution* (Chicago: University of Chicago Press, 1987) and has written extensively on 18th- and 19th-century art in its political context. His most recent book is *The Magisterial Gaze: Manifest Destiny and American Landscape Painting, c. 1830–1865* (Washington: Smithsonian Institution Press, 1991).

John Channing Briggs, Associate Professor of English at the University of California at Riverside, is the author of *Francis Bacon and the Rhetoric of Nature* (Cambridge: Harvard University Press, 1989).

David Constantine, Fellow in German at Queens College, Oxford, is the author of *Early Greek Travellers and the Hellenic Ideal* (Cambridge: Cambridge University Press, 1984) and several essays concerning English, French, German, and classical literature. He has also published two volumes of poetry and a novel.

Frederick T. Griffiths, Professor of Classics at Amherst College, is the author of *Theocritus at Court* (Leiden: Brill, 1979) and, with Stanley J. Rabinowitz, *Novel Epics: Gogol, Dostoevsky, and National Narrative* (Evanston, IL: Northwestern University Press, 1990). He has written on assorted topics in classical and comparative literature.

Noémi Hepp, Professor at L'Université de Strasbourg II, France, is author of *Homère en France au XVIIᵉ siècle* (Paris: Klincksieck, 1968) and is a coauthor of *Précis de littérature Francaise du XVIIᵉ siècle*

(Paris: Presse de l'Université de France, 1990). She has also written several articles on both French and classical literature.

Gerhard Joseph, Professor of English at Lehman College in New York, is the author of *Tennyson and the Text: The Weaver's Shuttle* (Cambridge: Cambridge University Press, 1992) and many other articles and books on English literature, many of which focus on Tennyson.

Hugh Kenner, Professor Emeritus of English at Johns Hopkins University in Baltimore, Maryland, has written extensively on Irish, English, and American literature. His most recent book is *Historical Fictions: Essays* (San Fransisco: North Point Press, 1990).

Katherine Callen King, Associate Professor of Comparative Literature and Classics at the University of California at Los Angeles, is the author of *Achilles: Paradigms of the War Hero from Homer to the Middle Ages* (Los Angeles and Berkeley: University of California Press, 1987) and several articles on classical and modern literature.

Vivienne Koch is the author of *William Carlos Williams* (Norfolk, Conn.: New Directions, 1950) and *W.B. Yeats, the Tragic Phase: A Study of the Last Poems* (London: Routledge & Kegan Paul, 1951).

Clayton Koelb, Professor of Comparative Literature and German at the University of North Carolina at Chapel Hill, is the author of several books on literary theory and criticism. His most recent book is *Kafka's Rhetoric: The Passion of Reading* (Ithaca: Cornell University Press, 1989).

Artemis Leontis, Instructor of Greek in the Department of Judaic and Near Eastern Languages and Literatures at Ohio State University, is the author of *Territories of Hellenism: Neohellenic Modernism, Nationalism, and the Classical Tradition*, Ph.D. thesis, Ohio State University 1991.

Morton P. Levitt, Professor of English at Temple University, is the author of *The Cretan Glance* (Columbus: Ohio State University Press, 1980) and *Modernist Survivors: The Contemporary Novel in England, the United States, France, and Latin America* (Columbus: Ohio State University Press, 1987).

Kathryn L. Lynch, Associate Professor at Wellesley College in Wellesley, Massachusetts, is the author of *The High Medieval Dream Vision: Poetry, Philosophy, and Literary Form* (Palo Alto: Stanford University Press, 1988) and many articles on Medieval and Renaissance literature.

Mary Nyquist, Associate Professor of English and Women's Studies at New College, University of Toronto, is the author of essays on feminist and anti-racist theory, popular romance, female novelists from Jane Austen to Edith Wharton, and Wallace Stevens. Besides publishing several articles on Milton, she has co-edited (with Margaret Ferguson) *Re-membering Milton: Essays on the Texts and Traditions* (New York: Methuen, 1987).

Stanley J. Rabinowitz, Professor of Russian at Amherst College, is the author with F. T. Griffiths of *Novel Epics: Gogal, Dostoevsky, and National Narrative* (Evanston, IL: Northwestern University Press, 1990). He is an authority on the work of the symbolist poetry and prose of Fedor Sologub.

Seth Schein, Professor of Comparative Literature and Classics at the University of California at Davis, is the author of *The Mortal Hero: An Introduction to Homer's Iliad* (Berkeley & Los Angeles: University of California Press, 1984) and articles concerning classical literature. He has most recently edited a book *Reading the Odyssey: Selected Interpretative Essays*, forthcoming from Princeton University Press.

Bernice Slote, who was Professor of English at the University of Nebraska, is a poet and the author of *Keats and Dramatic Principle* (Lincoln: University of Nebraska Press, 1958).

Ernest Wichner, poet, literary critic, and translator, is the author of *Stensuppe. Gedichte* (Frankfurt am Main: 1988), editor of *Ein Pronomen is verhaftet worden: die frühen Jahre in Rumänien*—Texte der Aktionsgruppe Banat (Frankfurt am Main: Suhrkamp, 1992) and *Das Wohnen ist kein Ort* (Bremerhaven 1987) The translator, Michael Armstrong, is Assistant Professor of Classics at Hobart and William Smith Colleges, Geneva, NY.

Oliver Taplin teaches Greek literature at Oxford University, where he has been a fellow and tutor at Magdalen College since 1973. He has tried to keep a constant eye on the reception of ancient Greece and has tried to reach beyond the academy, especially to theatre and radio. He translated books 5 and 12 of the *Odyssey* for performance at the J. Paul Getty Museum in Summer 1992. His publications include *Greek Fire* (1989) on the presence of ancient Greece in the contemporary world, and *Homeric Soundings* (1992) on the poetic constructions of the *Iliad*.

Figure 1. Battle at Troy. Illustration to Canto 24 of Ludovico
Dolce's *L'Achille et L'Enea.*

# INTRODUCTION:
## Homer in the Middle Ages and Italian Renaissance

*Katherine Callen King*

A study of Homer's influence on post-classical artists might be thought properly to begin in fourteenth-century Italy, when, thanks to Petrarch's and Boccaccio's insistence, the *Iliad* and *Odyssey* were born again in the Latin translation of Calabrian monk Leonzio Pilato.[1] In western Europe from the sixth century until Boccaccio's Greek teacher produced his literal prose rendition in 1360, the only access to Homer for the Greekless reader (99.9% of the population)[2] was through the first-century Latin abridgement of the *Iliad*, the *Ilias Latina*.[3] This miserable summary, which reduces Book 9 to ten hexameters, eliminates the reconciliation between Achilles and Priam in Book 24, and centers the quarrel in Book 1 around *caecus amor* ("blind love"), stripped the work and its hero of all tragic resonance

---

[1] Howard Clarke terms this translation a "crude paraphrase" *Homer's Readers: A Historical Introduction to the Iliad and the Odyssey* (Newark: U. of Delaware Press, 1981) 57.

[2] See Gilbert Highet, *The Classical Tradition: Greek and Roman Influences on Western Literature* (New York and London: Oxford U. Press, 1949) 5-6; L.D. Reynolds and N.G. Wilson, *Scribes and Scholars*, (Oxford: Oxford U. Press, 1974) 105-107, 240, and R.R. Bolgar, *The Classical Heritage and its Beneficiaries* (Cambridge: University Press, 1954, rprt. 1977) 122-123.

[3] For some reason, the complete translations of Livius Andronicus (*Odyssey*, third century B.C.E), Cnaeus Matius and Ninnius Crassus (*Iliad*, both first century B.C.E.) did not survive.

and left Homer vulnerable to two competitors who wrote alternative accounts of the Trojan War under the pseudonyms "Dares" and "Dictys."

The "History" of Trojan Dares and the "Journal" of Greek Dictys, supposed participants in the Trojan War,[4] claimed and achieved an authority superior to that of Homer, for, as the letter appended to the Latin translation of Dares says, the translation was done "so that readers may know how the events happened: either they may judge to be truer what Dares the Phrygian committed to memory, he who lived and was a soldier during the time the Greeks besieged Troy, or they may decide that Homer is to be believed, he who was born many years after this war was waged."[5] There were three other reasons many readers preferred to believe these belated fictions rather than Homer's: First, the pagan gods were eliminated. Second, by more nearly equalizing the heroism of the several participants, they provided an opening for later revisions in the relative merit of Hektor, Trojan ancestor of most European peoples, and Achilles and Odysseus,[6] proleptic enemies of the Holy Roman Empire and representatives of the somewhat suspect Eastern half of Christendom. Third, they tied Achilles' death to an overwhelming love for Priam's daughter Polyxena, thus making it possible to fit him into the roles of chivalric knight and Christian sinner desired by medieval authors and allegorists.[7] And lastly, Dares makes Achilles' love for the enemy woman the sole cause of his withdrawal, thus making an exculpated Agamemnon more pleasing to those at the top of strict feudal hierarchies.

However, despite the poor quality of the *Ilias Latina* and the

---

[4] For full accounts of Dictys' *Ephemeris Belli Troiani* (*Journal of the Trojan War*) and Dares' *De Excidio Troiae Historia* (*History of the Fall of Troy*) see W.B. Stanford, *The Ulysses Theme: A Study in the Adaptability of a Traditional Hero*, 2d ed. (Ann Arbor: U. of Michigan Press, 1968) 152-156; Clarke, 24-32; and Katherine Callen King, *Achilles: Paradigms of the War Hero from Homer to the Middle Ages* (Berkeley and Los Angeles: U. of California Press, 1987) 139-143, 195-201.

[5] "Ut legentes cognoscere possent, quomodo res gestae essent: utrum verum magis esse existiment, quod Dares Phrygius memoriae commendavit, qui per id ipsum tempus vixit et militavit, cum Graeci Troianos obpugnarent, anne Homero credendum, qui post multos annos natus est, quam bellum hoc gestum est." (Prologue to *Daretis Phrygii De Excidio Troiae Historia*, ed. Ferdinand Meister [Leipzig: Teubner, 1873] 1.9-14.) All translations are my own unless otherwise noted.

[6] In Dictys, Achilles kills Hector in a night ambush; in both authors Achilles is capable of being severely wounded. Troy is taken by Greek trickery, but only with the collaboration of two Trojan nobles.

[7] For a brief account of the allegorists' use of Achilles' love affairs, see King (note 4 above) 201-203.

competing claims of Dares and Dictys, Homer managed to remain the Trojan War poet of record until the mid-thirteenth century. Not only do there survive several medieval Latin poems obviously influenced by the *Ilias*,[8] but the author of one of them, Pierre de Saintes, pauses to declare "I will be another Homer, or greater than Homer himself, / when I am able to describe so many misfortunes.[9] The earliest vernacular redaction of the *Ilias Latina* confirms that Homer was still the poet to surpass—though from quite a different angle than Pierre's. The *Libro de Alexandre*,[10] which includes this 1712-verse Spanish *Iliad* as part of a Trojan War digression within its larger story about Alexander the Great, makes it clear that the Trojan War in general and the career of Homer's Achilles in particular is the standard by which Alexander's achievements can be judged and which they can be seen to surpass.[11] This poet does not need to undermine Homer's authority in order to convey a different message about the events at Troy and the proper end of human heroism; instead, under cover of that authority, s/he alters context and detail to suggest that Achilles won his immortal fame by damning his immortal soul and that what Alexander truly lacked was not another Homer but Christian ethics.

Alexander narrates the Trojan War events while his army takes a rest-stop at Achilles' tomb *en route* to attack Darius, his purpose being to inspire his men by proving that deeds do ensure one's immortal survival (stt. 328, 764–765). The Achilles of his story is motivated, like Alexander himself, by a desire for *preçio* "glory" and recognized *mejoría* "superiority" (compare Achilles in st. 614 with Alexander in stt. 52d, 70–71, 85, and 2575d). This Achilles is more violent·than the original--he attacks and kills quantities of his fellow Greeks when

---

[8] Three poems survive from the eleventh century: Godfrey of Rheims's "Hektor and Achilles" (incomplete at 481 verses), an anonymous "Lament for Hektor" (24 couplets), the 25-verse summary of Odo of Orleans's several-hundred-verse poem. Two survive from the twelfth century: Pierre de Saintes's "Viribus, arte, minis" (124 verses) and three versions (the last amplified to nearly a thousand verses) of Simon Chevre d'Or's *Ilias*. For a fuller description and analysis of these poems see King (1987) 143-158.

[9] "Alter Homerus ero vel eodem major Homero, / tot clades numero scribere si potero." "Viribus, arte, minis" 83-84, as printed by M.E. du Méril, ed. *Poésies populaires latines antérieurs au douzième siecle* (Paris: Brockhaus and Avenarius, 1843) 404. All translations are my own unless otherwise noted.

[10] There is a general consensus that this 10,700-verse Spanish poem, whose main source is the Latin *Alexandreis* (1180), was written in the first decade of the thirteenth century (see Jesús Cañas Murillo, "Introducción," *Libro de Alexandre* [Madrid: Editora Nacional, 1978] 19-25).

[11] See Ian Michael, *The Treatment of Classical Material in the Libro de Alexandre* (Manchester: Manchester U. Press, 1970) 261.

Agamemnon dishonors him by taking his *amiga* (st. 419)—and more arrogant, but the most substantial difference occurs in the description of the shield.[12]

After Achilles has lamented Patroklos "as if he were his father or his grandfather" (st. 647b) and vowed revenge, he orders new arms made by a *maestro* who paints the shield so skillfully that merely looking at it would make a scholar out of an ignoramus (st. 659). The scholar's education would consist of an abbreviated version of the shield in the *Ilias*: the sea, with ships and fishes (st. 654); the earth, with mountains, lakes, and cities, and birds and beasts (st. 655); the sky, with wind and storm (st. 656); the four seasons, which are here personified (st. 657); and the sun, stars, and seven planets (st. 658). As Ian Michael notes, the pagan nymphs, Nereids, and deities are omitted (1970, 200). But something Christian is also added: in stanza 655, which closely translates *Ilias* 875–876, the poet inserts the Tower of Babel so that instead of "high-walled cities in which quarreling people go to law" (876–877), we have "walled towns and the tower which the traitorous folk built" (655bc). The poet shifts from the cooperative legal system humans constructed to save themselves from bestial violence to the impious tower that was constructed to achieve godhood but instead caused eternal noncommunication and noncooperation. Achilles carries this prime Christian symbol of spiritual blindness[13] into his battle with Hektor, who now, for the first time in the poem, is portrayed in good Christian terms: Hector asks God to do with him as He will (st.677d), he commends his soul to "el Padre Santo" (st.678c) before turning to face Achilles, and he stops to pray in a most Christian fashion in the middle of the battle (stt. 685–688). The battle between the angry self-confident bearer of the tower and the humble suppliant of God comes very close to being an allegorical battle between Pride and Christian humility.

The tower is a minor element in the shield, but because it is the only Christian element its symbolism is significant, all the more so because it is a significant symbol in Alexander's career. Its most neutral appearance in this career is as part of a long Biblical sequence on the tomb Alexander had built for Darius's captured wife (st.

---

[12] For illustrations of these changes and others see King (note 4 above) 150-158. What follows was printed in substantially the same form on pp. 156-158 of the above.

[13] See, for example, Otto of Friesing, *Two Cities*, ed. A.P. Evans & C. Knapp, trans. C.C. Mierow (New York: Columbia U. Press, 1928) 14, and Hugo of St. Victor, "Sermon 38," in *Patrologiae Cursus Completus* (Paris: J.P. Migne, 1857-1866) vol. 77, cols. 994-999.

1241d), where its significance is religious in a general sense. Most often it is associated with Alexander's enemy Darius, who claims descent for himself and all Persians from the giants who built it (stt. 948ab, 1369ab), and whose pride in this descent makes him confident that he will conquer Alexander (stt. 948cd, 1369cd). Darius, like Achilles, carries a picture of the tower and its builders on his shield (st. 990cd), along with those of several other great sinners. When Alexander takes possession of the Babylon he takes possession of the tower, the folly (*locura*) of whose builders is now explicitly condemned by God (st. 1506), just as Alexander's will be later. The tower appears one last time just before Alexander is killed. After he has completed his mad ventures to conquer the air and the sea and has thereby prompted offended *Natura* to secure his condemnation for pride (*sobervia*, st. 2330a), the conqueror takes possession of a wonderful tent, the ceiling of which depicts Biblical scenes of punishment for the great sinners: Lucifer, Adam and Eve, the tower builders (st. 2552), and victims of the Flood, and ends with a holy man in one of his more fallible moments: the drunken Noah (stt. 2550–2553). On the walls of the tent are painted the greatest human achievements to date: the labors of Hercules, the Trojan War, and Alexander's own deeds. We must, I think, agree with Michael that the pictures are meant to be interconnected and that they signify the "futility and fleetingness of human achievement and the vanity of human ambition *sub specie aeternitatis*" (1970, 268). We must further understand that Alexander's possession of the tower emblem, like Achilles' possession of his more abbreviated version, symbolizes the overweening pride that earns his early death by poison.

Like Alexander, the Achilles of the *Alexandre*'s version of the *Ilias* is killed shortly after he takes possession of the tower emblem. Like Alexander, too, he is killed by poison with the aid of *el peccado*, "the devil." It is perhaps to the very end of making their deaths as similar as possible given their differing traditions that the *Alexandre* poet uses the story of Achilles' invulnerability, a story absent both from the *Ilias Latina* and from the redactions of Dares and Dictys.[14] The invulnerability, which is announced at the beginning of Achilles' story (st. 411ab), is mentioned twice more before it figures in the death scene. It appears first in Hektor's fight with Patroklos, whom he

---

[14] E. Bagby Atwood and Virgil K. Whitaker believe that the provenance of this story in medieval redactions is the *Excidium Troiae* (*Excidium Troiae* [Cambridge, Mass.: Mediaeval Academy of America, 1944], xlv-xlvii), but the poet could as well have gotten the story directly from Hyginus (second century C.E.) or Servius (fourth century C.E.).

thinks is Achilles and whom he thinks he may have to poison when he remembers "the story that he was enchanted and that no iron could harm him in any way" (*que le dixieran que encanto era, / que nol farié mal fierro por ninguna manera*; stt. 643cd–644ab). It is mentioned again during Achilles' arming, which the poet remarks is taking place despite the hero's being "enchanted" (st. 660ab). This latter instance is perhaps motivated by a desire either to appear consistent and logical or to lessen any admiration we feel for Achilles' boldness in the ensuing battle with Hektor. The motivation of the earlier instance is clearly to foreshadow the final poisoning by Paris and to emphasize that poison is the only means possible to kill Achilles. As the poet will stress later, poison is also the only means of killing Alexander (stt. 2332, 2431).

Achilles' arrogant killing of Hektor, which we can relate directly to the desire for *mejoría* that sent Patroklos into battle in his stead, is made his last action in the poem and the direct cause of Paris's vengeance. When, therefore, Paris, who is at a loss as to how to kill Achilles, is reminded by *el peccado* of Achilles' vulnerability in the soles of his feet (stt.722d–724b), we can view this diabolic intervention in the same way that Michael interprets Satan's participation in the death of Alexander: as "the outer or allegorical presentation of Alexander's inner state. . . . On one plane the devil brings him down; on the other, he brings himself down by succumbing to pride" (155–156). In Alexander's case this interpretation is reinforced by the poet's comment that Alexander's *sobervia*, "pride," is as great as Lucifer's (st. 2327d); in Achilles' case it is reinforced by the devil's reminder that the hero's invulnerability was a factor in his facing Hektor so boldly (st. 723d) and by the poet's reminder that the devil's presence is gratuitous as far as Paris is concerned (st. 724cd).

That Achilles presents his soles to the poisoned arrow while praying (st. 725cd) does not destroy the case for his deadly pridefulness. It merely creates another parallel with Alexander, who in one breath is explicitly condemned for the sin of pride (st. 2330) and in the next is called "a great light to the world" (st. 2457a). Both of these men are great heroes and are basically to be admired; only thus can the lesson be made clear about the dangers of centering one's hopes in the world. Desire for immortal fame is set in subtle opposition to Christian immortality and is identified with the major deadly sin of Pride (see st. 2406). Anger, which here as in every version of Achilles' story is associated with winning this glory, is also a deadly sin (see st. 2356). The *Libro de Alexandre* portrays the Homeric Achilles as being at the zenith of the kind of human power and achievement that will send one straight to Hell.

The *Libro de Alexandre* is the last extant major medieval work on the Trojan War directly to rework Homer. Some fifty years earlier, in 1160, Benoît de Ste. Maure had chosen Dares' and Dictys' already reworked accounts as the basis for his monumental *Roman de Troie*, saying that although Homer was a "marvelous scholar, wise and knowledgeable" (*clers merveillos / E sages e esciëntos*), his account could not be trusted since he was not present at the events.[15] His 30,000-verse romance, full of love affairs and battles in which not one but two sons of Priam prove themselves superior to Achilles, was soon translated into Spanish and German, condensed into moralized French prose, and used as the basis for an Italian poem.[16] When Guido delle Colonne translated this work into Latin prose in 1287, thus making it available to vernacular redactors throughout Europe, he also transmitted his own more censorious judgment of Homer, condemning him as vile (*miser*) for having praised Achilles, a man who "never killed any strong man except by deceit" (*numquam . . . virum strenuum nisi proditorie interfecit, Historia Destructionis Troiae*, fol.100).[17] At this point Homer's influence on the Trojan War tradition was nearly extinguished.

At this point also, however, an increasing number of scholars were reading classical Latin texts at the universities that had begun to spring up all over Europe. Since some of the most important of these texts, like Cicero's essays, Horace's *Ars Poetica*, and Juvenal's *Satires*, certify Homer as a Very Important Poet, and since no Latin translation of the *Odyssey* had survived and the abridgement of the *Iliad* was clearly inadequate, these readers increasingly felt the need to learn Greek. Petrarch apparently tried in 1339, employing as teacher a monk who may have been a secret agent of the Byzantine empire. He was unsuccessful, but as a second-best he prevailed upon Boccaccio's tutor to translate the two epics into Latin some 21 years later.[18]

Which brings us back to where we, and Homer's true influence on European creative artists, began.

---

[15] I. 45-56. The text is printed by Léopold Constans, ed. *Le Roman de Troie*, 6 vols. (Paris: Firmin Didot, 1904-1912).

[16] See King (note 4 above) 303, notes 17-19, for more on these redactions.

[17] Printed in *Historia Destructionis Troiae*, ed. N. E. Griffin (Cambridge, Mass: Medieval Academy of America, 1936) 206.

[18] For the revival of classical Latin see C. H. Haskins, *The Renaissance of the Twelfth Century* (Cambridge, Mass.: Harvard U. Press, 1939); for Petrarch's failed first attempt, see Highet (1949) 16.

The fifteenth century saw more translation into Latin as well as increased opportunity for learning Greek and reading Homer in the original. Lorenzo Valla's translation of the *Iliad* in 1444 became very popular, replacing Guido as the primary source of new vernacular versions of the Troy Story after 1500. When Byzantium fell to the Turks in 1453, many Greek scholars fled to Italy to become teachers, and one of them, Demetrios Chalcondyla, edited a Greek text of Homer (*Iliad, Odyssey, Batrachomyomachia,* and *Hymns*), published in Florence in 1488, that greatly improved accessibility for those happy few who succeeded in learning Greek.[19]

Ludovico Ariosto, author of the *Orlando furioso* (1532), was not one of those happy few, but he apparently did take advantage of the Latin translations. The "Ferrarese Homer" (so named more in recognition of his excellence than for his poetic affinities with the Greek poet[20]) dipped into the *Iliad* and the *Odyssey* for similes to image his warriors[21] and for scenes and patterns that would link his heroes—sometimes parodically—to Homer's. Thus Rodomonte, the enemy hero of the *Orlando furioso*, is like Achilles in his wrath and superlative prowess among the pagans; and the central hero, Ruggiero, is like Achilles in his martial superiority and fated early death in battle. Ruggiero is also like Odysseus in the broad movement of his career through far-flung adventures, both martial and sexual, to the consummation of his marriage with Bradamante and the subsequent defeat of the irredeemably anti-social Rodomonte.[22] Ariosto's poetry

---

[19] On the struggles of many Italians to learn Greek under these improved but still difficult conditions, see L.D. Reynolds and N.G. Wilson, *Scribes and Scholars* (Oxford: Clarendon Press, 1974) 131-32.

[20] Richard Lansing points out that when Tasso calls Ariosto the Ferrarese Homer he was following an established convention that lasted "well into the nineteenth century" (Richard H. Lansing, "Ariosto's *Orlando Furioso* and the Homeric Model" *Comparative Literature Studies* 24 [1987], 313).

[21] See Denis Fachard "L'Immagine dell'eroe: reminiscenze omeriche nell' *Innamorateo* e nel *Furioso,*" *Études de Lettres* 6 (1989) 5-40. Fachard compares Ariosto's use of Homeric similes with Boiardo's, whose *Orlando innamorato* was published in 1483. Ariosto uses many more similes and uses them more Homerically, that is, more often in battle scenes and more complexely.

[22] Lansing argues for a similar correspondance between Ruggiero and Odysseus and includes the contest set by Bradamante (318-319). Lansing also sees a stronger parallel betwen Orlando and the Homeric Achilles (318). David Marsh argues, unconvincingly, for Iliadic inspiration for the reconciliation between Trojan-Italian Ruggiero and Greek Leone near (but not at) the end (David Marsh, "Ruggiero and Leone: Revision and Resolution in Ariosto's *Orlando Furioso*" *MLN* 96 [1981] 149); although its transcendent ending is indeed inspirational in a general sense, reconciliation and higher morality are not unique to the *Iliad*. We could equally well see the *Furioso*'s reconciliation, which is brought about through the chivalric code of courtesy, as a revision of the ending of the *Odyssey* where the opposing camps form a new social compact under the aegis of Zeus-enforced codes of hospitality.

is not, I think, truly inspired by Homer's, nor is it an imitation of Homer. Instead, the similes and scenes of the *Iliad* and the *Odyssey* function as immediately recognizable vocabularly to express the epic heroism that Ariosto playfully manipulates throughout his epic romance.

Other epic poets, who could read Greek, *were* inspired—but not always in felicitous ways. Giovanni Giorgio Trissino (1478–1550), who had studied Greek with Chalcondyla and published a paraphrase of Aristotle's *Poetics*, intended his epic to express Aristotelian *precetti* and Homeric *idea*.[23] The result was the *Italia liberata dai Goti* (*Italy Freed from the Goths*) (1547–48), which did neither successfully. In addition to similes and archaic modes of fighting, the major Homeric element seems to reside in an episode that stretches from Canto 11 to Canto 22 (out of a total of 27) in which the valiant young Corsamente, along with his friend Achille, abandons the army insulted and angry at being denied the hand of Elpidia, returns when she is abducted by the Goths, kills her abductor, and then is killed by treachery. Renaissance mores affect the central action to the degree that King Belesarius is mostly exculpated in the quarrel, the major blame being deflected onto one of Corsamente's peers. Although this deflection of blame will be imitated by subsequent Italian redactors of the quarrel,[24] and Torquato Tasso will re-create Elpidia in his *Gerusalemme liberata*,[25] Trissino's epic was neither a critical nor popular success. As Torquato Tasso testifies in his *Discourses on the Heroic Poem* (1594), this unmodernized unimaginative tribute to Aristotle and Homer died a swift death and was entombed unread in the libraries of scholars.[26]

---

[23] The Homeric "ideas" include speeches, descriptions, similes and such like. Giovanni Trissino, LA ITALIA LIBERATA DA GOTHI DEL TRISSINO (Roma: Valerio & Luigi Dorici A petitizione di Antonio Macro Vincentino, MDXLVII, di Maggio). F. i.v - iii.r. UCLA Special Collections Library.

[24] See John M. Steadman's excellent discussion of scenes surrounding the Homeric Achilles figure in Trissino, Alamanni, and Tasso: "Achilles and Renaissance Epic: Moral Criticism and Literary Tradition" in *Lebende Antike* (Berlin: Erich Schmidt Verlag, 1967) 145-152. The reader should be warned, however, that Steadman's arguments about the *Iliad* itself are flawed.

[25] Salvatore Multineddu analyzes Tasso's use of Trissino's quarrel over Elpidia in *Le fonti della Gerusalemme liberata* (Torino: C. Clausen, 1895) 58-64.

[26] Tasso gives this information while comparing Trissino to Ariosto, who broke all the rules and whose poem is beloved. Torquato Tasso, *Discorsi della poema eroico*, libro terzo, in *Torquato Tasso: Prose*, ed. Ettore Mazzali (Milan and Naples: Riccardo Ricciardi, n.d.) p.573. The *Discorsi* have been translated by M. Cavalchini and I. Samuels (Oxford: Clarendon Press, 1973).

The less rigid Luigi Alamanni (1495–1556) achieved more success, perhaps because his *Avarchide* (1554, published posthumously in 1570) mingled Homeric inspiration with chivalric romance. The plot reproduces the main episodes of the *Iliad* with new names: King Arthur besieges King Clodasso in Avarco, which Clodasso has taken by force from King Ban, the father of Lancilotto. After a disagreement with Arthur (and his envious nephew) that involves honor, insubordination, and a woman, Lancilotto leaves the camp with his friend Galealto. When Arthur is near defeat, Galealto returns in Lancilotto's armor and is killed by Segurano; whereupon Lancilotto returns, avenges his friend by killing Segurano, and then defeats the army of Clodasso. If this plot summary is not enough, the poem's opening stanza will show how close the imitation was meant to be:

> Canta, O Musa, lo sdegno, e l'ira ardente
> Di Lancilotto del Re' Ban figliuolo,
> Contra 'l Re Arturo, onde si amaramente
> Il Britannico pianse, e'l Franco stuolo;
> E tante anime chiare afflitte, e spente
> Lasciar le membra in sanguinoso duolo,
> D'empi uccelli, e di Can rapina indegna;
> Come piacque a colui, che muove, e regna.[27]

> ("Sing, Muse, the hate and burning anger
> of Lancilotto son of King Ban
> Against King Arthur, whence so bitterly
> the army of Britain and France wept;
> And so many famous spirits left behind limbs
> Broken and worn in bloody affliction,
> Shameful spoil for impious birds and dogs;
> Such was the will of him, who moves and reigns.")

Although Tasso faulted the *Avarchide* on *invenzione* because its plot is identical to the *Iliad*'s, he nonetheless judged it "the most perfect in the Italian language" ("é la più perfetta che si legga in questa lingua").[28] He does not remark what some Homerists might see as major inventions: Lancilotto's offer to spare his defeated enemy's life

---

[27] *LA AVARCHIDE DEL S. LUIGI ALAMANNI*, (Florence: Stamperia di filippo Giunti, e Fratelli. MDLXX). University of California at Los Angeles Special Collections Library.

[28] *Discorsi della poema eroico*, libro secondo, pp. 532-33.

and his excellent treatment of the body after he is forced to kill him. These changes, as John Steadman points out, helped convert the Achilles figure "into an *exemplum* of the characteristic vices and virtues of the magnanimous man" and made him acceptable as a sixteenth-century hero.[29]

Humanist poets like Trissino and Alamanni apparently now considered Homer's epic equal to or superior to Vergil's, Greek Achilles on a par with Roman Aeneas. The relative value of the two epics, however, was not a settled question. If, under the influence of the ever more influential *Poetics* of Aristotle, academics like Sperone Speroni wrote treatises proving Homer's aesthetic superiority to Vergil on the grounds of plot and diction, others like Bartolomeo Maranta wrote treatises proving just the opposite.[30] For critics who felt it was necessary to rank the poets, there were, in addition to whether one might prefer one poet's language or the construction of his plot, two non-literary phenomena that urged preference for Vergil: first, the Italians were descendants of Achilles' victims, and second, Aeneas' *pietas* was more comparable to the behavior dictated by contemporary state religion than was Achilles' *ira*. Also, if one were a good Roman Catholic Christian, or at least believed strongly in the hierarchies that governed Renaissance spirituality and politics, the great-man ideology of the Roman epic was far more congenial than the *Iliad*'s tragic focus on slippage between political power and personal worth. Such socio-political phenomena made it impossible for some sixteenth-century readers to appreciate the complexity and significance of Homer's tragic hero.

A good example of the interpretation of Homer that such ideological underpinnings often produced in the late sixteenth century occurs in Paolo Beni's encomiastic commentary to Tasso's *Gerusalemme liberata*—an encomium that would, I think, have made Tasso, who did not feel he had to choose between two beloved poets, wince. To illustrate what Tasso was up against in his own attempt to imitate his predecessors, I here offer several passages and summaries from Beni's oft-cited but never translated work, *Comparison of Homer, Vergil, and Torquato* (c. 1600).[31]

---

[29] 149-150. Steadman argues that all the Renaissance poets who "imitated" Homer moralized the motif of the quarrel and eliminated "the more objectionable aspects of Achilles' conduct" as they transformed "the Homeric into the chivalric *éthos*" (152).

[30] See Bernard Weinberg, *A History of Literary Criticism in the Italian Renaissance* (Chicago: U. of Chicago Press, 1961; Midway Reprint 1974), vol. 1 pp. 169-174.

[31] The full title includes: *And to whom of these should go the palm of the Heroic Poem: precepts for which must now be recognized; with a comprehensive account*

"FIRST DISCOURSE: Torquato Tasso in his Goffredo has represented a more noble and perfect model of a worthy (*valoroso*) Captain and Hero, than Homer or Vergil. [After some introductory words and praise of Tasso's Goffredo, Beni offers apparent praise of both Homer and Vergil:] "No one doubts that Homer in the *Iliad* intends to represent therein a strong and worthy captain and hero: just as it is also certain that in the *Odyssey* he intends to depict a knight and hero of singular sensibility (*accortezza*) and skill (*sapere*), who must be the image of prudence and valor (*virtú*)to his grand princes and captains. And thus if Achilles is manifestly the most valiant (*valoroso*) and strong of the Greek warriors and Odysseus the wisest (*il più saggio*) and most prudent, it will therefore seem that the *Iliad* of Homer, which sings the extraordinary feats of Achilles, should be an example and model to the best warriors and captains of strength and courage (*valore*), while the *Odyssey*, which celebrates Odysseus, must of course represent, as on a stage, the life and habits of a prudent and sage man, who, as much in adversity as in prosperity, shows himself constant and perfect.

"Since true strength and invincible resolution (*animo*) cannot be found in anyone without prudence and counsel, nor is it any less impossible to conclude difficult enterprises if prudence is unaccompanied by strength and courage, wisely and intelligently did Vergil conjoin in his Aeneas both the valor (*valore*) of Achilles and the prudence of Odysseus, so that both in peace and in war he would be revealed as a perfect example to every man, a Prince and Hero to whom supreme power is entrusted not less in war than in peace.

"Also, because all virtues must look upwards and (as much as is allowed) at celestial and divine purpose, he adorned his Aeneas with rare piety (*pietà*) and religion. Which virtues I cannot see easily expressed in Achilles or Odysseus, insofar as the former shows himself angry (*iracondo*) and harsh (*acerbo*) and puts all his reason in his sword, and the other reveals that he is marvelously clever and cunning (*sagace*) beyond everything, not to mention ready for fraud and deceit.

---

*of Heroic Poets, Greek as well as Latin and Italian: and in particular an opinion of Ariosto.* I base my translations and summaries on the text of *Comparazione di Omero, Virgilio, e Torquato* printed in *Opere di Torquato Tasso colle controversie sulle GERUSALEMME*, vols. 21-22 (Pisa: Nicolò Capurro, 1821). Beni's treatise is also an example of another contemporary quarrel: that between the ancients and the moderns. As will be evident, Beni prefers the moderns. Citations are to one of the ten "Discorsi" followed by the page number in either volume 21 (Discorsi 1-4) or 22 (Discorsi 5-10).

"The prince of Latin poets lacks only one thing: that is, the piety and religion of Aeneas is superstitious and empty, as was the religion of the wretched and blind Gentiles. And lo! the prince of Italian poetry, Torquato, has collected in his Goffredo all the virtues that were found in Achilles or Odysseus or even in pious Aeneas, joining therein the perfection of Christian virtue. So that no example of heroic life and virtue can be represented as more perfect than that which in this grand captain and Christian champion is seen." [I, 146–147].

Beni adduces several quotations from other characters and from Goffredo's own speech to show how wise, constant, pious, and Christian Goffredo is and how his actions back up his speech [I, 148–152]. "In sum, anyone who will attentively consider this noble poem in detail will find that a more noble idea of a perfect captain cannot be imagined or represented. Even Aeneas cannot easily attain to this perfection, much less Achilles or Odysseus; not to mention Agamemnon or any other person to whom Homer gives a scepter or governance.

"But already I seem to hear someone who opposes me in favor of Vergil arguing: 'I don't wish to deny, for now, that Goffredo has been made a more noble model of a strong and wise captain than Achilles, who is represented by Homer as not only subject to amorous passion, and (as they say) as inexorable and harsh and one who seems often enough to make all his justice (*ragion*) depend on force, but also as avaricious, cruel, and proud. So he shows himself when he savages Hektor's corpse and when finally he sells it to the afflicted father. Besides this, he sheds copious tears when he laments the lost Briseis and leaves the noble martial enterprise for a feeble woman, not for anything worthy of a strong knight and hero. Another example is his complaining in fear to the Goddess Thetis lest flies (I will say it though not without some blushing) outrage the dead Patroklos or rather (to keep to his own words) lest they enter his wounds and breed worms so that the corpse might become putrefied and deformed; this feeling and thought seem to me to be base and lightweight, and unbecoming to a generous and well-bred (*costumato*) knight.

"I am content to believe the same of Odysseus, since—to pass in silence over how shamefully (*bruttamente*) he forgot his fatherland, his son and his modest wife for the insidious and immodest Circe; to omit also the tricks and lies of which he was the most remarkable and noble fabricator; to conceal finally with what indignity, even infamy, to his royal state he exposed himself, like a base person or a very young athlete, to the way of life of the meanest sort, coming even to a challenge and duel with Iros the meanest vagabond—since he sheds tears in such quantity, and with such groans, and (to put it most succinctly) in a feminine manner, that this alone is sufficient to remove the name of strong captain and hero. In addition, during his voyage from Phaiacia to Ithaca, not only does he not give any sign of prudence and valor, but he sails always in a deep sleep or lethargy. He is sleeping when the sailors put him aboard the ship, he sleeps while sailing, and he sleeps still when the sailors put him ashore, thereby showing himself stupid and drunk (*ebro*) and displaying neither sense nor fortitude (*fortezza*).

   " 'These things I'll concede to you about Achilles and Odysseus. I will also concede that Achilles seems at one time like a weak and tender maiden, all effeminate and soft (partly because of his love-affairs and withdrawal, but much more because of his quantity of sighs and tears), and at another time like a savage hungry lion, totally angry, implacable, haughty and proud (*iracundo, implacabile, superbo, fiero*); which he shows himself at the end against Hektor and in battle. And [I will concede] that Odysseus shows himself composed of tricks, tears and sleep, seldom or never very far from sleeping or complaining (*pianti*) or weaving deceptions (*tesser inganni*).

   " 'What more? I am willing to be persuaded that Torquato with great care depicted the Ambassadors of the Egyptian King, I mean Alete and Argante, with the insignia and colors (so to speak) of Odysseus and Achilles, in order to show, *pace Omero,* that these insignia and colors are not those of a wise and true hero but are instead those of a clever messenger and haughty champion.

> Parlar facondo, e lusinghiero, e scorto,
> Pieghevoli costumi, e vario ingegno,
> Al finger pronto, all ingannar accorto;
> Gran fabro di calunnie, adorne in modi
> Novi, che sono accuse, e paion lodi
>
>                                   (*G. L.* ii. 58, 4–8)

("A ready, charming, and clever speaker, with an adaptable character and versatile nature, quick to invent, shrewd to deceive, great fabricator of lies in a new form: he accuses in the guise of praise.")

Such is Alete, formed exactly like Odysseus.

L'altro è il Circasso Argante, uom che straniero
Sen venne alla Regal Corte d'Egitto;
Ma de' satrapi fatto è dell' impero,
E in sommi gradi alla milizia[32] ascritto:
Impaziente, inesorabile, fero,
Nell' arme infaticabile, ed invitto,
D'ogni Dio sprezzatore, e che ripone
Nella spada sua legge, e sua ragione

(*G. L.* ii.59).

("The other is the Circassian Argante, a man who
came to the royal court a foreigner, but became
Imperial Satrap and achieved highest military rank.
Impatient, inexorable, fierce, untiring in arms and
unconquerable, despiser of God, he made his sword
his law and his reason.")[33]
This also represents Achilles to the life.' " [I, 152–155].

Here Beni's fictional interlocutor draws the line. He will not
concede similar faults to Aeneas, despite the fact that the Latin poet
was an idolater, but argues by many examples that he was the perfect
leader in both peace and war [I, 155–157]. Beni then returns to his
own voice to attack Aeneas for his disgraceful affair with Dido, and he
compares him unfavorably with Goffredo, who is not in the least
swayed by the far greater beauty of Armida [I, 157–162]. He cites
Holofernes, Hannibal and Marc Antony as examples of how love and
leadership do not mix, and then cites Scipio and Alexander as
examples of continent and therefore successful leaders [I, 162]. In this
context he gives some grudging praise to Odysseus: "Odysseus's
principal virtue seems to me to be continence; for although he showed
himself unchaste with Circe, at least he endured Kalypso's love with
grief" [I, 162–163].

Beni proceeds to attack Aeneas for his false religion and his
Achillean cruelty at Pallas's funeral, and then brings up, though he

---

[32] The 1784 text (Florence: Stamperia di S. A. R. per li Tartini e Franchi) has
*malizia* "wickedness" instead of Tasso's *milizia* "warfare"–a Freudian slip perhaps?
Tasso's verse is printed correctly in the 1826 text.

[33] Readers familiar with Greek and Roman tradition and with Vergil, will
recognize that Argante is in fact a mixture of Achilles as interpreted by Horace (*Ep.*
2.3.120-122) and two famous god-scorners:  Vergil's Mezentius (*Aeneid* 7.647-648)
and Statius's Capaneus (*Thebaid* 3.602-603).  Multineddu, of course, gives both
references (note 25 above, 36-37).

says he does not believe it, the rumor that Aeneas betrayed his country.[34] But even if the rumor is not true and Aeneas is the best of heroes, he argues, Goffredo is still better. Goffredo is further praised for his constancy, virtue, purity, *caritas*, humility, zeal, faith—in all of which Aeneas falls short. [I, 164–166.]

Near the end of his First Discourse, Beni uses a metallic metaphor reminiscent of Plato to compare the three poets: "Although Tasso has used Homer and Vergil extensively, nonetheless he has with his judgment and style given marvelous perfection to the *concetti* and *invenzioni* of others: he has composed with such grace, delight (*vaghezza*), gravity and majesty that the copper (so to speak) of Homer and the silver of Vergil seem in Torquato to be the finest brightest gold" [I, 181–182]. This metaphor will reappear in alchemical form in the succeeding nine "Discourses" as Beni proceeds to argue that not only are Tasso's heroes better than Homer's and Vergil's but that Tasso's poem fulfills all of Aristotle's precepts better than do the poems that gave rise to those precepts.

In Discourse Nine, for example, Beni writes as follows: "Someone might happen to challenge me, arguing that I have shown that Torquato is linked to Homer and that the actions and progressions as well as the episodes . . . of the *Gerusalemme liberata* are similar to those of the *Iliad*. I certainly would not deny this, but would respond that what might be considered less than perfect in the *Iliad* is improved and perfected in the *Gerusalemme*, so that copper is changed to silver, and silver to gold. Good God! (may I only be strong enough to respond adequately to this challenge) Homer makes Helen, the adulteress and sole cause of the Trojan slaughter and ruin, sit side by side with Priam in a high tower above the walls watching the battle and describing the most valiant knights. Now who would not scorn and rebuke such behavior in an adulteress? And how is this scene not totally lacking in verisimilitude, since Helen is to blame for what Priam and Hecuba, together with many daughters-in-law and an infinite number of Trojans, witness: sons and husbands bleeding to death and the whole kingdom put in enormous danger. How much more properly does Torquato present Erminia, the noble and modest queen who, when deprived of her kingdom of Antioch, took refuge in the court of the aged Aladino: she quite properly sits beside Aladino in the high tower above the walls, whence (for she has had previous contact with the Christian host in the siege of Antioch) she points out the strongest

---

[34] This rumor first appears in print in Dictys, which was perhaps composed in the first century C.E. See note 4 above.

and most valiant knights!" [9, 226–227]. After a further comparison of the unmerciful, mercenary Achilles (savaging and selling Hector's body) with the merciful and generous Goffredo (sparing Altamoro without ransom), he concludes this argument and this Discourse with yet another version of the metaphor: "This will suffice . . . to respond to the proposed quarrel and to show that Torquato truly knew how to change copper into gold and how, to speak more clearly, to make what is unrealistic in others both realistic and decorous. [9, 227].

Despite his early attempt to slough off Achilles onto the ferocious Argante, Beni admits that, like Vergil, Tasso models good characters as well as bad on Homer's: "Torquato has also his Agamemnon and his Achilles, but more illustrious and excellent by far, to wit the great Goffredo and Rinaldo, just as he also has his Nestor and Calchas, that is Raimondo and Pietro the Hermit, with other personages and outstanding ministers who resemble Homer's personages. In Vergil's epic it is obvious that Aeneas takes the place of Agamemnon and Achilles and Ulysses and other princes and captains, although [he is] much more elevated" [6, 45–46]. Only once does Beni discuss Tasso's "alchemy" with regard to the Achilles-Rinaldo pairing. While discussing unity of plot in "Discourse Two" he writes that although Tasso's opening line—*Canto l'armi pietose e'l capitano* ("I sing the holy arms and the leader" I, 1.1)—might seem to indicate a double plot, in fact "he meant by 'holy arms' Goffredo's holy enterprise and by 'the leader' he meant Goffredo himself. Whence in Tasso the proposition is singular and the execution is singular. . . . Thus Rinaldo, Raimondo, Tancredi and all the others are dependent on and subordinate (so to speak) to Goffredo, a situation no one could fear finding in Homer, who makes Achilles so eminent that it is impossible to tell who, Achilles or Agamemnon, the story is about. Homer can, as he pleases, make Achilles imperiously call the army to council, challenge Agamemnon (*venga a contesa con*) and despoil him of Chryseis, spurn his gifts as well as his friendship; and at the end, without Achilles' submission, have Agamemnon reconcile with him. Tasso never makes his Achilles, I mean Rinaldo, equal to Goffredo, but always places him in a lower, subject position. It is for this purpose that Hugo reasons as follows in a vision from Heaven:

> Perchè se l'alto providenza elesse
> Te dell' impresa sommo capitano,
> Destinò insieme ch'egli esser dovesse
> De' tuoi consigli esecutor soprano:
> A te le prime parti, a lui concesse

Son le seconde: tu sei capo, ei mano
Di questo campo; e sostener sua vece
Altrui no puote, e farlo a te non lece
                              (*G. L.* xiv, 13).

("When high Providence elected you supreme
leader of this enterprize, it destined him at the
same time to be supreme executor of your counsels;
To you it gives the first part, to him the second: you
are the head, he the hand of this army; and others
may not take your place, nor you his") [2, 195].

Beni proceeds from this to argue that Tasso's poem, which presents all
the actors conjoined in a firm hierarchy under a single leader,
exemplifies the most perfect unity, more perfect than the *Aeneid* and
far more perfect than the *Iliad* and the *Odyssey* [2. 195–215].

Beni's literary criticism exemplifies the problems that stood in the
way of appreciating Homer and clarifies John Steadman's observation
that Italian writers in the sixteenth century had to come to grips with a
"tension between ethical and literary norms" that "was nowhere more
evident than in criticism of Homer's warriors."[35]  To a gifted Christian
poet like Tasso, who, unlike his pedantic commentator, possessed
both a synthesizing genius and a literary sensitivity that could distinguish between defects in religion and defects in art,[36] the tension was
a creative one.  His "alchemical" poetics in his epic about the First
Crusade go far deeper than what Beni proposes.  But before I look at
Tasso's solution to the problem of including (and paying homage to)
Homer within a Christian poem, I would like to digress briefly to discuss how Vergil had responded to a similar tension in 19 B.C.E.

---

[35] Steadman (note 24 above), 140. Beni's *Comparazione* is one of the texts
Steadman cites to support this observation.

[36] Tasso says that we should not judge classical poets defective just because
they depict something *empia* and *crudele* like human sacrifice: "*Ma questa no è colpa
de l'arte poetica, ma de la religione; laonde se pur è difetto ne' poeti, par difetto non per
sé, ma* per accidens" (*Discorsi del poema heroico*, III, Mazzali p. 613).  Later in the
same work he judges Homer and Vergil equal as poets, though their strengths lie in
different areas: Homer's excellence is that of the poetic art in general, Vergil's excellence is that of the heroic poem in particular, "which maintains decorum and sustains
grandeur (*grandezza*) beyond all other things" (VI, Mazzali 715).  Unlike Beni, he
thinks that the *Iliad* is perfectly unified and that both the *Iliad* and the *Aeneid* are
"perfect" epics (*Apologia in defesa della Gerusalemme liberata* [July, 1585], Mazzali
439-40, 446).

Vergil uses Achilles initially as the exemplar of traditional epic heroism at its most violent. In the first two-thirds of the *Aeneid* he skews the reader's recollections of the Homeric original by interjecting details that evoke the least favorable non-Homeric traditions (for example, Achilles dragging Hector around Troy *alive*, 1.483, 2.273). The Trojan past in which Aeneas can no longer participate is specifically Iliadic, and Achilles' type of passionate heroism, characterized by *furor*, is set up as something diametrically opposed to the new *pietas* that Aeneas must learn. Achilles also provides the archetype for Aeneas's opponent Turnus, who, as the *alius Achilles* predicted by the Sibyl in Book 6 is—like the Homeric Achilles—young, beautiful, wrathful, and brutal in war. Achilles thus functions as a foil to Aeneas's forced Romanization in Books 1–8.

But then when Aeneas battles the new Italian Achilles, he himself becomes Achilles with all the passion and cruelty of that warrior at his worst. Meanwhile Turnus, who has been given the character of Achilles, is made to play the role of Hector, Achilles' victim. In the final battles of Book 12, identification with Achilles and Hector spreads to identification with many Homeric heroes until at last the two opponents are united in representing Homeric heroism in general. This heroism is in turn reduced by means of similes to the equivalent of animal passion. Then, in the denouement, role finally fixes character as Aeneas becomes solidly identified with Achilles, supreme symbol of that heroism in victory, and Turnus becomes identified with Hector, supreme symbol of that heroism in defeat.

The civil war in Italy between Trojans and Latins, both of whom are destined to become future Romans, is reflected in the psyche of Aeneas as a kind of civil war between the old Homeric and the new Roman components of heroism. And just as Juno wins at last the obliteration of her old enemy, Troy, except for the *morem ritusque sacrorum* (12.836), so Homeric heroism bliterates all of its new enemy Roman *pietas* except for ritual sacrifice. When Aeneas kills Turnus and says that Pallas "sacrifices" him, the worst of two epic worlds combine in an act that is personal vengeance conceived as religious duty. This synthesis of Achilles and *pietas* helps create a world view that has disturbingly little clarity, the "darkness visible" of W. R. Johnson's thesis.[37] Vergil has set it up so that *furor pius* is not a viable

---

[37] *Darkness Visible* (Los Angeles and Berkeley: U. of California Press, 1976). For a fuller exposition (with bibliography) of Vergil's use of Achilles see my article "Foil and Fusion" *Materiali e discussioni per l'analisi dei testi classici* (1985) 31-57.

concept, and the ending is a dramatic illustration of the prediction that even under the enlightened sway of the Roman empire *furor impius* will always exist. The best the Romans will be able to do is keep it chained (*Aeneid* 1.294–96).

Vergil's synthesis helps us more clearly to understand Tasso's. In the *Gerusalemme liberata*[38] Tasso attempts a task similar to Vergil's: he attempts to integrate the established classical heroic components of the epic tradition with the newer conception of Christian epic. He has, of course, more authors to work with: most importantly for my purposes here, he has Vergil's own problematic synthesis of clashing Homeric and Roman virtue, especially his two Homeric Achilles's, Aeneas and Turnus. Tasso's complex use of Aeneas and Turnus together with Achilles and Hector produces a synthesis far more optimistic than Vergil's—one that supports rather than subverts the epic's overt message of faith in the power of the Christian religion.

In Tasso's work, classical heroism is definitely suspect. As Judith Kates has shown, nearly all direct classical allusions image pagans, and the devils who oppose the Christian forces are presented as debased versions of classical heroes.[39] A pagan ambassador tries to seduce Goffredo away from Jerusalem by stressing honor and renown (ii. 62–79), the supreme goals of most Homeric heroes, including Achilles—but, as Kates has pointed out, Goffredo responds "to the assumptions behind Alete's oratory by asserting a completely different set of motives for their warfare" (Kates 74). A seditious Christian Achilles figure, Argillano (8.57–71), who in addition to Achilles is modelled both on the Homeric Thersites (*Iliad* 2.211–242) and on the Vergilian Turnus at the moment when he is transformed into an Achilles figure by Allecto (*Aeneid* 7.435–470), has also a third, equally unsavory source: a contemporary murderer and pirate who operated in papal lands in defiance of the Pope's authority and later became a mercenary in a Ducal army.[40]

Nonetheless, Iliadic heroism does not produce the disquiet we find in Vergil. Argillano, punishable stand-in for Rinaldo,[41] is Gof-

---

[38] Citations and quotations will be to the edition of the *Gerusalemme liberata* edited and annotated by Lanfranco Caretti, (Torino: Einaudi, 1971).

[39] Judith A. Kates *Tasso and Milton: The Problem of Christian Epic* (London and Toronto: Associated University Presses, 1983) 68-88. The pagan seductress Armida, for example, is compared to Circe, Medea, Venus, the Sirens, Proteus, Narcissus, and Cleopatra (Kates 68).

[40] David Quint makes a good argument for this idenfification in his superb article, "Political Allegory in the *Gerusalemme Liberata*," *Renaissance Quarterly* 43 (1990) 8.

[41] See Quint 10-11.

fredo's enemy only insofar as he is an *altered* Achilles: debased to
Thersites, maddened like Turnus. The other Achilles in the poem
shows that Achillean heroism is in and of itself not the problem.[42]
Tasso, who appears to have been a careful reader of Homer, distinguishes between the heroism of the complex Homeric Achilles and
that of his one-dimensional wrathful successors, and he distinguishes
between the tragic violence of the Iliadic hero and the hubristic
violence of a hero like Capaneus. Achillean heroism may have been
superseded by Christian, but it need not be either obliterated or kept
chained. Tasso finds a happy solution in the principle of hierarchy:
Achillean epic heroism must be subordinate to Vergillian, which must
be subordinate to Christian. This *literary* hierarchy is expressed
implicitly through the relationship of Goffredo and Rinaldo to each
other and to the epic heroes of Homer and Vergil.

It will be well, I think, before I continue my analysis of the
*Gerusalemme liberata*, to offer Tasso's own interpretation of the relationship between Goffredo and Rinaldo as he presents it in his
"Allegory of the Poem."[43] The last section, which focuses on Tasso's
Achilles, Rinaldo, and recapitulates much of the epic's action, will
help to orient the reader who has not read the poem and to set the
stage for the poet's deployment of characters from classical epic:

> But since Rinaldo is one of the two characters who
> hold the principal place in the poem, it will perhaps
> be welcome to readers if I repeat some of the things
> I have already said and exhibit in detail the allegori-
> cal sense that hides beneath their actions. Gof-
> fredo, who holds the principal place in the story, is
> in the allegory nothing else than the intellect, which
> is indicated in a few places in the poem, as in this
> verse: *Tu il senno sol, tu sol lo scettro adopra* ("You
> employ wisdom alone, you alone wield the sceptre,"

---

[42] See King (1987) 127-128 for Achilles as equivalent to war insanity in the
*Aeneid.*

[43] Tasso published his "Allegoria del poema" in 1581. I translate from the
text printed along with the poem in *La Gerusalemme liberata. Poema di Torquato
Tasso* vol. 1 (Florence: Giuseppe Molini e Comp., 1818) xxxiii-xlvi. The portion translated can be found on pp. xlii-xlvi. I have divded the text into paragraphs, which do
not exist in the original. The first complete modern English translation of the
"Allegory" will be published soon by Lawrence F. Rhu in *The Genesis of Tasso's Narrative Theory. English Translations of the Early Poetics and a Comparative Study of
Their Significance,* forthcoming from Wayne State University Press.

7.62.7) and more clearly in this other one: *L'anima tua, mente del campa, e vita* ("Your soul, mind and life of the host," 11.22.7). . . . Rinaldo, then, he who holds the next rank of honor in the action, must also be placed in a corresponding rank in the allegory. What this power of the spirit (*animo*) is that holds the second rank in worth will now be made clear.

The Irascible power is that which among all the soul's other powers comes closest to the nobility of the mind, and in fact it appears that Plato, in some doubt, explored whether it was different from reason or not. It is such in the soul as are warriors in a gathering of men, and just as it is their job to fight against enemies in obedience to the princes who know the art of commanding, so it is proper for the irascible part of the spirit, warlike and robust, to arm itself with reason against concupiscence, and with the vehemence and ferocity proper to it, to fight off and drive away everything which can be an impediment to happiness. When, however, it does not obey reason, but allows itself to be carried away by its own impulse, it happens sometimes that it fights not against concupiscence but *for* conscupiscence, in the manner of a wicked watchdog who bites the herds instead of robbers.

This violent, vehement and invincible virtue, although it cannot be entirely represented by a single knight, is nonetheless principally signified by Rinaldo, as is well indicated in that verse where it is said concerning him: *Sdegno guerrier della ragion feroce* ("Wrath, ferocious soldier of reason," 16.34.4). This wrath passes the bounds of civil revenge while he is fighting Gernando, and while he serves Armida it may denote anger not governed by reason, and when he disenchants the Woods and battles the city and routs the enemy Army, [it may denote] anger directed by reason. The return, then, of Rinaldo, and his reconciliation with Goffredo signifies simply the obedience that the irascible power makes to the reasoning power. And in this reconciliation two things are pointed out. The first, that Goffredo shows himself superior to Rinaldo with civil moderation, which teaches us that reason commands anger not as a subject but as a citizen. By contrast, when Goffredo imperiously imprisons Argillano he puts down sedition, which gives us to understand that the power of the mind over the body is royal and lordly. The second thing worthy of consideration is that, just as the reasoning part ought not (in which the Stoics much deceived themselves) to exclude the irascible power from actions, nor to usurp its offices, because this usurpation would be against natural justice, but ought to make it her companion and minister; so may Goffredo not attempt the adventure of the wood nor take upon himself the offices proper to Rinaldo. . . .

But to come finally to my conclusion, the Army in which Rinaldo and all the other knights have, by the grace of God and human wisdom, returned to be obedient to the captain signifies the man who has returned to the state of natural justice in which the superior powers command, as they ought, and the inferior obey; and beyond this [it signifies being] in a state of divine obedience: at this point the wood is easily disenchanted, the city easily taken, and the enemy army easily defeated, that is, with all external impediments easily overcome, the human being achieves political happiness. But because this civil blessedness ought not to be a Christian's ultimate goal, but he ought to gaze higher at Christian happiness, therefore Goffredo does not desire to take the territory of Jerusalem simply to have earthly dominion, but so that in it divine worship may be celebrated and the liberated Sepulchre may be visited by the pious and by dedicated pilgrims. The poem closes with Goffredo's praying in order to demonstrate that the intellect, wearied from civil action, must finally come to rest in prayer and in the contemplation of the goods of the other most blessed and immortal life.

This allegory should make it clear that in one sense all the Christian heroes of the *Gerusalemme liberata* are like Aeneas: all must learn to subordinate passions to the purpose of God. One, however, is singled out and cast in the role of a perfected Aeneas, the wise, pious, and enduring leader Goffredo. Although Goffredo has another identification as well—three scenes: Erminia on the wall (3.58–59 cf. *Iliad* 3.178–180), the quarrel with Rinaldo (5.37, 59), and the recalling of Rinaldo (14.21–26 cf. *Iliad* 9.92–172), are clearly meant to suggest that he is an improved version of the *Iliad*'s Agamemnon[44]—the more persistent and overriding identification is with Aeneas. Goffredo, like Aeneas, is the privileged recipient of messengers from god—Gabriel in Canto 1 (15–17), Hugo in Canto 14 (1–19); like Aeneas he is wounded in the leg in Canto 11 and healed by dittany plucked from Ida and delivered by his guardian angel (54–56, 68–76); and, as Venus did for Aeneas, Michael in Canto 18 (93–96) permits Goffredo to see divinity itself—in this case angels and dead Christian heroes—at work destroying the city. Like Aeneas, too, Goffredo is weighed down by his responsibilities, is never very cheerful.

Subordinate to Goffredo is Rinaldo, who is like the Homeric Achilles not only in *ira*, the wrath that had become the mark of Achilles, but also in being, unlike the eternally fierce Argante and Solimano, *dolcemente feroce*, "gently ferocious" (1.58). This phrase, which Giovanni Getto has termed "refined chiaroscuro,"[45] would in fact be a good description of Homer's complex hero, the hero who sings and heals as well as kills. Rinaldo is like Achilles in youth (1.60), beauty and swiftness (3.37, 4.8);[46] in his characterizing wrath[47] and focus on honor (1.10, 5.13), in his quarrel and withdrawal over honor (5.26–52); in supernatural greatness and ferocity during battle

---

[44] Quint (note 40 above) notes the resemblance to Agamemnon and also points out another identification: Lucan's Julius Caesar, antagonist of the *Pharsalia*. Quint comments: "The identification of Goffredo with Caesar, Lucan's enemy of Republican liberty, suggests just how authoritarian is the political thought of Tasso's poem" (p. 4, n.3).

[45] *Nel mondo della "Gerusalemme"* (Rome: Bonacci Editore, 1977) 67. Getto feels that Rinaldo's combination of strength and beauty, ferocity and gentleness, youth and virility, makes him unique and utterly superior to all the poem's other heroes. I would argue the same for Homer's Achilles.

[46] Non-Homeric characteristics come from Statius's *Achilleid*: upbringing by a foster parent (1.59), Apollordorus's *Bibliotecha*: Achilles was fifteen years old when the Greeks first gathered to go to Troy (3.16), the same age as Rinaldo when he heard the trumpet of war and ran off to join (1.60).

[47] There are too many references to Rinaldo's anger to list them in the text. Some examples: Erminia tells Aladino that he should fear Rinaldo's "angry right hand" (*la sua destra irata*) more than any seige engine (3.39); Goffredo has to restrain Rinaldo's martial wrath (*sdegno, ire*) in the first battle after his group captain is killed (3.50, 52, 53).

in Cantos 18–20;[48] and in taking vengeance on an avowed personal enemy (Solimano) whose death marks the fall of the besieged city (20.107–108). The last three motifs, however, have already been filtered through Vergil, and indeed Rinaldo is given more Aeneas nuance than any other character in the *Gerusalemme liberata* except Goffredo.

Rinaldo withdraws from the Christian army strictly because of honor and wrath. Goaded into fighting a forbidden duel because of insults to his honor, he turns his anger on Goffredo when he is called to account. Persuaded by Tancredi not to attack Goffredo but to leave the army until Goffredo realizes how much he needs him, he goes off to win glory on his own. So far, he is blatantly a re-born Achilles. But after leaving the army he falls into another kind of error, love, which causes him to forget his purpose just as Aeneas forgot his purpose while he stayed with Dido. Just before he disappears into Armida's garden, Tasso begins Rinaldo's secondary identification with Aeneas by making Pietro the Hermit prophesy the future greatness of Rinaldo and his descendants (10.74–76). This prophecy ends with the prediction that these descendants, generation upon generation, will have as "their special art to suppress the proud and raise up the weak, to defend the innocent and to punish the guilty" (*Premer gli alteri e sollevar gli imbelli / difender gli innocenti e punir gli empi, / fian l'arti lor*, 10.76.5–6). This passage is clearly meant to evoke Apollo's prophecy to Aeneas at *Aeneid* 3.97–98 and Anchises' famous pronouncement to Aeneas at 6.852–853.[49] It casts Rinaldo into the role of Aeneas, a role he will maintain simultaneously with that of Achilles throughout his reawakening to his martial purpose,[50] his leavetaking of Armida (16.42–62),[51] his receiving an emblematic shield (17.58–80), and even into his final battle with Solimano (20.105–108).

---

[48] At 20.53-54 Rinaldo moves into battle like an earthquake and thunderbolt (*tremoto e tuono*) and his bloodlust (*l'appetito del sangue e de le morti*) soon rouses him to perform "incredible, horrible, monstruous deeds" (*cose incredibili, orrende, e monstruose*).

[49] Both passages are of course noted by Caretti.

[50] This scene in which Carlo and Ubaldo shock Rinaldo back into his warrior identity (16.30-35) conflates the Aeneas of *Aeneid* 4.260-81 with the Achilles of Statius's *Achilleid* 1.852-71. Statius had already mined the Vergilian scene for his own, so the merger of Achilles and Aeneas is quite thorough.

[51] Kates (note 39 above) discusses Rinaldo as an improved Aeneas in the leavetaking scene (119). For a brilliant analysis of Armida as Dido/Ariadne see Fredi Chiappelli, *Studi sul linguaggio del Tassso epico* (Florence: F. Le Monnier, 1957) 25-32.

The scene in which Rinaldo receives his new armor and shield on the way back to the Christian camp offers a good example of Tasso's syncretic rather than oppositional use of his predecessors' heroes. Before Rinaldo receives the shield, he is lectured by the aged wizard (*mago*) who has made it. The wizard tells him that anger (*ire*) is natural and proper in a man, but that it must be used for its natural and proper purpose. Nature, he says, "gave you quick and ready anger" (*ti die l'ire ancor veloci e pronte*) not to serve civil brawls and personal pursuits contrary reason (17.62),

> ma perché il tuo valore, armato d'esse,
> piu fero assalga gli aversari esterni,
> e sian con maggior forza indi ripresse
> le cupidigie, empi nemici interni.
> Dunque ne l'uso per cui fur concesse
> l'impieghi il saggio duce e le governi,
> ed a suo senno or tepide or ardenti
> le faccia, ed or le affretti ed or le allenti.
>
>                                        (17.63)

> ("but in order that your valor, armed with it, might assault more fiercely external adversaries and that sensual desires might be repressed with greater force, impious internal enemies. Wherefore the wise leader employs it in the use for which it was given, and governs it, and in his breast makes it now lukewarm now hot, now speeds and now stays it.")

Although this focus on the usefulness of anger is most un-Vergilian,[52] the shield the wizard has made to incite Rinaldo's valor (17.65.5–6) seems at first much like Aeneas's, for its scenes are almost all martial and its protagonists are part of history. In a reversal of Vulcan's depiction of Aeneas's descendants, however, the wizard has painted Rinaldo's ancestors rather than descendants. The shield's ancestral deeds are, of course, a more personal version of the "famous deeds of old" (*chiari antichi essempi* 1.10.8) that Rinaldo was

---

[52] Its being useful comes closer to the Homeric battle sequence (sorrow, anger, revenge), but, like the "Allegory of the Poem," it is, in fact, Platonic. The best analysis I have found of Tasso's manipulation of Plato's tripart soul (*Republic* 439-442) is James T. Chiampi, "Tasso's Rinaldo in the Body of the Text," *Romanic Review* 82,4 (Nov. 1990) 487-503.

portrayed as hearing from Guelfo when he was first introduced as the Achilles figure of the poem.[53]

Rinaldo's reaction to the shield confirms the dominance of his identification with Achilles but continues a lesser contribution from Aeneas. Unlike Aeneas's uncomprehending admiration and happy shouldering of Rome's future (*Aeneid* 8.730–31), Rinaldo is fired up like Achilles:

> Rinaldo sveglia, in rimirando, mille
> spiriti d'onor da le natie faville,
> e d'emula virtú l'animo altèro
> commosso avampa, ed è rapito in guisa
> che ciò che imaginando ha nel pensiero,
> citta abbatuta e presa e gente uccisa,
> pur, come sia presente e come vero,
> dinanti a gli occhi suoi vedere avisa;
> e s'arma frettoloso, e con la spene
> già la vittoria usurpa e la previene.
>
> (17.81.7–83.8)

> ("As he beholds it, Rinaldo awakens a thousand
> spirits of honor from his inbred sparks of fire, and
> his proud spirit blazes, stirred by emulous virtue,
> and he is so ecstatic that what he imagines—the city
> pulled down and conquered and its people killed—
> he seems to see as if it were truly there before his
> eyes; he arms in haste and in his hope already
> snatches victory before the fact.")

The blazing spirit and eagerness to get into battle is Achilles' (*Iliad* 19.15–17), but the brutal vision of the destroyed city comes by way of Aeneas—Aeneas at one of his problematic Achillean moments in *Aeneid* 12. Frustrated by his inability to find and duel with Turnus, Aeneas focuses on the Latins' city, "an image of a greater battle suddenly fires him" (*continuo pugnae accendit maioris imago*, 12.560), and he immediately decides to end the war by burning the city (which we know is full of women and children) to the ground (*urbem hodie . . . ni frenum accipere . . . eruam et aequa solo fumantia culmina ponam*,

---

[53] The *chiari antichi essempi* are almost certainly meant to recall the *kléa andrôn* of Homer's Achilles (*Iliad* 9.189) and the *virum honores* of Statius's (*Achilleid* 2.158).

567–69). Tasso incorporates Aeneas' destructive vision into Rinaldo's Achillean mood with no hint of competing systems of value. The inspiration for Rinaldo's anger is neither grief nor frustration; it is purely the reasonable desire to emulate the exemplary deeds of his ancestors. When Carlo next gives him Sveno's sword and asks that he avenge its previous owner by killing Solimano, Tasso again evokes a Homeric motif that has been filtered through Vergil. Achilles vowed and carried out vengeance for Patroclus in a blaze of inhuman wrath; Aeneas avenged Pallas in an Achillean *furor*; Rinaldo's vengeance will be equally furious, but Tasso smoothly subordinates the personal motive (Rinaldo has never even met Sveno) to one of true Christian piety: in the same breath that Carlo asks him to use Sveno's sword for vengeance he urges him to "use it, no less justly and piously than strongly, solely on behalf of the Christian faith" (*e solo in pro de la critiana fede / l'adopra, giusto e pio non men che forte*, 83.5–6). Since it is governed not by grief but by reason, Rinaldo's vengeance, unlike Aeneas's, will spring from truly righteous wrath.

Because of the context Tasso creates in this scene, no Vergilian tension attends Rinaldo's brutal furious fighting in the final battle—fighting in which Rinaldo is described as a "cruel avenger" (*fero vincitore*) with an "appetite for blood and death" (*l'appetito del sangue e de le morti*, 20.54.5–8) and for which Tasso creates similes modelled on those used for Achilles, Turnus, and Aeneas before him.[54] When Rinaldo finally attacks Solimano with *furore* (20.107.4) after Solimano's status as the tragic "Turnus" figure of the poem[55] has been newly invoked by a dream-running simile (20.99),[56] it is clear that Tasso is re-creating the end of the *Aeneid* as well as Achilles' killing of Hector. But the action of Tasso's Achillean Aeneas does not darken the reader's vision. Rinaldo's *furor* is good because it is subordinate to reason and to the Christian god; it is because Solimano's refuses subordination that it and he must be eliminated.

---

[54] For example, the wolf simile at 19.35.1-4 has antecedents in the *Aeneid* (Turnus: 9.59-64; Aeneas: 2.355-58), but two ingredients are left out of Rinaldo's simile: *rabies* and *improbus*. Rinaldo's hate and fury are not "mad" and "evil."

[55] As many have noted, Solimano's helmet at 9.25 is like Turnus's at *Aeneid* 7.785-88, he recieves a wolf simile (10.2) closely modeled on Turnus's at *Aeneid* 9.59-66. Giovanni Getto has an excellent chapter on Solimano as a tragic figure (73-107); Kates (note 39 above), who offers some excellent pages in English based on Getto (note 45 above, 83-86), says that "Through him Tasso expresses most fully in the poem the classical heroism of both the exterior sphere in martial action and the interior sphere of contemplation and tragic awareness" (86).

[56] Compare *Aeneid* 12.909-12 and *Iliad* 22.100-200.

As I said earlier, Tasso is able to make unproblematic use of Homer by creatively employing the principle of hierarchy that governed so much of Renaissance life. He creates an implicit double identification for both Goffredo (Aeneas/ Agamemnon) and Rinaldo (Achilles/Aeneas), which is in turn subservient to their explicit roles as Christian leaders. That they share identity with Aeneas makes the allegory of the poem come literally (and literarily) alive: the Christian army is one body of which Goffredo is the head or heart, Rinaldo is the hand. Passionate Achilles, pious Aeneas, and the Christian God finally co-exist in an epic world that allows the "virtues" of Aeneas and Achilles to complement each other.

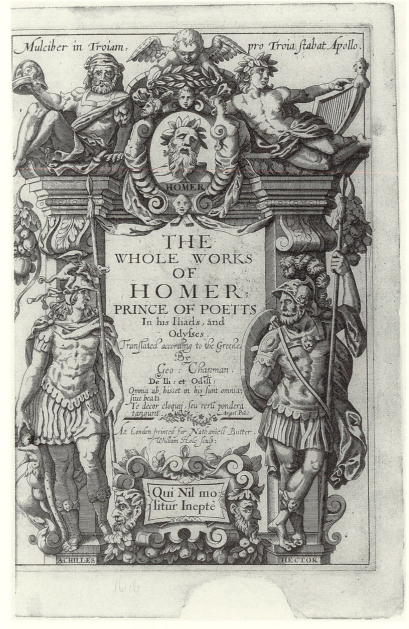

Figure 2. Achilles and Hector. Frontispiece to George Chapman's *Iliads* and *Odysses*.

# Chapman's Seaven Bookes of the Iliades:
# Mirror for Essex

*John Channing Briggs*

The 1598 translation of books 1, 2, and 7-11 of the *Iliad* is George Chapman's extraordinary attempt to discover contemporary topical meaning in a text he seems to have worshipped. In his preface, his enthusiasm for "Homericall writing" compels him to claim not only that Homer rescues and preserves the fame of ancient heroes but that the *Iliad* prefigures a living Elizabethan hero in its characterization of Achilles. The Earl of Essex, the man Chapman tried to make his patron, is the "now living instance of the Achileian vertues," a man "whom by sacred prophecie Homer did but prefigure in his admirable object."[1] Statius, in his dedication to the *Achillead,* also likens Achilles to the poet's patron, the Roman emperor Domitian; but Chapman's gesture is more ambitious. In the *Seaven Bookes of the Iliades* he seems determined to make good his hyperbolic flattery, to prove that Essex can discover himself in Homer's story of Achilles.

In order to understand the difficulties— and possibilities for success— in Chapman's endeavor, it is helpful to recall the ambiguities in Achilles' reputation during the Renaissance. Viewed from one per-

---

[1] George Chapman, dedication to Seaven Bookes of the Iliades (London: John Windet, 1598), title and lines 60-61. Chapman's translations are most accessible in Allardyce Nicoll's two-volume edition *Chapman's Homer* (Princeton: Princeton Univ. Press, 1967); Nicoll's line numbers will be used throughout. I use the traditional book numbers of Homer, not Chapman's misleading enumeration in the 1598 edition. Chapman's books 1-7 are Homer's books 1,2,7 11 respectively. Where I quote from Chapman's prefaces and dedication, I will use page numbers in Nicoll's edition.

spective, Chapman's championing of Achilles runs counter to a long-standing English distrust of Homer and dislike of Greek character.[2] Expressions of distrust are ample, though not clearly dominant, in the dialogue of Greene's *Euphues, His Censure to Philatus* (1587). The traditional Roman jibes at levity and double-dealing among the Greeks are apparent in Udall's Mathew MerryGreek (*Roister Doister*, ca. 1553). Commonplace references to faithless, shameless Greeks occur in Juvenal, and Paul's condemnation in *1 Corinthians* must have been a continuing influence upon later opinion.[3] Anthony Gibson's damning praise of Homer in *A Woman's Worth* (published 1599) rekindles the medieval hatred of Achilles for his killing of Hector; following Lydgate, Gibson singles out Achilles as an incontinent bully and an enemy to order.[4]

On the other hand, there is evidence of a contrary Renaissance estimation of Homer and his hero which would have complemented Chapman's intention. Achilles does receive occasional admiring glances even in Lydgate's *Troy Book*,[5] and in Chapman's own time there were significant, positive reactions to Achilles' character. The 1595 edition of *A Myrrour for English Soulders* makes a typical comparison: "Homer in his Achilles, Virgil in his Aeneas, and Xenophon in his Prince, all sought but to pourtrayt a perfite soulder."[6] Sidney makes a similar comparison in his *Defense,* as does Thomas Heywood in his *Apology for Actors:* "[Achilles, Theseus, and Hercules] bred in them such hawty and magnanimous attempts, that every succeeding age hath recorded their worths, unto fresh emulation."[7]

The competition between different appraisals of Achilles' active virtues is perhaps tacitly recognized in Shakespeare's description of

---

[2] T.J.B. Spencer, " 'Greeks' and 'MerryGreeks': A Background to *Timon of Athens* and *Troilus and Cressida*" in *Essays on Shakespeare and Elizabethan Drama in Honor of Harden Craig*, ed. R. Horley (Columbia, Mo.: Univ. of Missouri Press, 1962), pp. 223-33.

[3] Ibid., p. 225.

[4] Anthony Gibson, *A Woman's Worth* (London: J. Wolfe, 1599), pp. 16–16v: "[Homer established] a contempt for royalty, duty and obeyance, in the person of Achilles (a mere brothel hunter) who preferred a brutish kinde of affection, before the love of his country, and his owne peculiar hate before the general welfare of his followers.

[5] John Lydgate, *Lydgate's Troy Book,* ed. Henry Bergen, 3 vols. (London: Kegan Paul, Trench, Trubner and Co. Ltd., 1906, 1908, 1910) 1:390 (Book 11, 8590 601).

[6] *Myrrour for English Soulders* (London: for N. Ling, 1595), sig. Cl.

[7] Philip Sidney, *The Defence of Poesie* (London: for William Posonby, 1595), sigs. Flv, G3v; Thomas Heywood, *Apology for Actors* (London: N. Okes, 1612), p. 19.

Achilles in *The Rape of Lucrece* (1594). There he is an enigmatic shape on a tapestry:

> For much imaginary work was there;
> Conceit deceitful, so compact, so kind,
> That for Achilles' image stood his spear,
> Griped in an armed hand; himself behind
> Was left unseen, save to the eye of the mind:
> A hand, a foot, a face, a leg, a head
> Stood for the whole to be imagined.[8]

The ambiguous portrait elicits awe as well as fear, an effect enhanced by its position in the poem between the more positive descriptions of the Greek heroes and the extremely negative picture of Sinon, the Greek of arch deceitfulness.[9]

The fairly mixed contemporary picture of Achilles allows Chapman to take advantage of the positive view of Achilles in order to flatter and instruct the Earl of Essex. Since Achilles himself would have been "most happie to have so firme an Eternizer as Homere" (p. 504), Chapman offers Essex a similar service with the aid of Chapman's own "Homericall writing." At the same time, however, the translator cannot escape taking into account Achilles' reputation for insurrection, and the wrath with which he nearly destroys the Greeks. The task of making Achilles an admirable mirror for Essex, and yet remaining true to Homer, informs the 1598 edition of the *Iliades*.

Political conditions in England around the time that Chapman registered his work would have made a complex view of Achillean virtue especially pertinent, for from late 1597 and throughout 1598 important trends in Elizabethan foreign policy and politics were converging toward a crisis catalyzed by Essex. In fact, history had conspired to make prominent certain analogies between Essex and Achilles; the opening books of the *Iliad* apparently struck Chapman in 1598 as preternatural reflections and foreshadowings of Essex's career.

During what Chapman calls "this tumultuous season" (p. 506), England was embroiled in a debate over war policies, a debate in which Essex advocated more aggressive action against Spain while diplomats led by Burghley and Cecil urged caution. The Queen

---

[8] William Shakespeare, *Complete Works,* ed. Alfred Harbage (Baltimore: Penguin Books, 1969), p. 1434, lines 1422-28.

[9] Ibid., pp. 1433-34, lines 1394 1421.

wavered. After the first major Elizabethan expeditions to the Nether-
lands in the 1580s, which received her measured consent, and the
defense against the Armada, after which she disbanded most of the
English forces, she had given Essex command of an attack on Cadiz
(1596) and the Azores (mid-1597). Nevertheless the Queen's reaction
to Essex's pressures was variable, especially after 1597. She avoided
large-scale preparation for war as much as possible, and, instead of
elevating Essex upon his return from the Azores voyage (autumn
1597), she recognized a rival of Essex—a man who had not sailed in
that last raid—by naming him to a military rank exceeding that of
Essex. The Earl's soldierly expectations of reward were bitterly dis-
appointed, and he angrily withdrew from the court for an entire
month, an Achillean gesture that drew a reprimand from an unnamed
advisor: "There are many different censures about my Lord of Essex's
absence from the Parliament, some earnestly expecting his advance-
ment, others that daily make use of his absence confess his worth but
wish him well only in words. Yet is my Lord for all his good parts least
perfect in working his own good, for his patience continually giveth
way to his crosses, and upon every discontentment he will absent himself from court."[10] It was not until the Queen's changeable temper
relented and she appointed Essex Earl Marshall, the highest military
rank among the earls, that Essex's anger abated and he returned to
her company (ca. mid December, 1597).[11]

The quarrels of this period spurred Essex to write his *Apology,*
probably written in 1598 though not printed until 1603. Defending the
naval raids as necessary acts of war, he ridicules those who believe
there is a chance for negotiation with Spain, and blames policy-
makers rather than soldiers for the low reputation of active, martial
virtue: "I know great scandal lieth upon the profession of Armes, as if
it were a schole of dissolutenesse: but that groweth by commandment
and charge given to dissolute chiefs, and it is a fault of the professors
not of the profession."[12]

Like Barnaby Rich, who defends the profession of arms in his
*Allarme to England,* Essex uses the well-known story of Troy to make

---

[10] G.B. Harrison, *The Elizabethan Journals,* 3 vols. (London: Routledge and
Kegan Paul, Ltd., 1955) 2:235. Harrison's source is *State Papers Domestic,* 265:10.

[11] For a summary of these events, see the DNB, 5:880b, 881a, and G.B. Harrison, *The Life and Death of Robert Devereux, Earl of Essex* (London: Cassell and Co.,
1937).

[12] Robert Devereux, *An Apologie of the Earl of Essex* (London: R. Bradocke,
1603), sig. B3.

his point. The history of the old city is a lesson to the new Troy that its
military should not be neglected:

> But do they [the Spaniards] offer entreate, and
> meane no peace? What is then their meaning? If
> you will have me to interprete, I will tell you: Their
> first maine attempt against *England* was in 88. From
> that time to this present is full tenne years, the just
> time of the siege of *Troy*. And now they see open
> force cannot prevaile, they have prepared a *Sinons*
> horse, which cannot enter if we cast not down our
> walls. But because we are thought more credulous
> then the Trojan were, the bare letter of a base beg-
> gerly traitorous fugitive, assuring us that good faith
> is meant, is the uttermost strategem they use to
> deceive us with.[13]

Waverings between schism and reconciliation characterized
Essex's history in the court, especially after his rise to political prominence in 1596. He quarreled frequently with fellow soldiers like
Raleigh over precedence of command and with diplomatic councillors
such as Cecil over the planning of policy. The Queen herself was
involved. After the raid on Cadiz, Essex argued violently with her over
his personal right to the ransoms of his prisoners, an incident Chapman could capitalize upon when he translated the *Iliades*. Home from
the Azores, he broke with her again over his rivalry with Raleigh during the expedition. Such disputes were serious political arguments
since Essex's potential powers as a popular courtier-soldier had
immense influence on the imagination of the general populace, the
court, and apparently the Queen herself. His claims to royal ancestry
and his leadership in the mourning for Sidney by means of his role in
the annual Accession Day pageant[14] made Essex an increasingly
dominant, if unpredictable, champion of English arms.

Tensions surrounding Essex's role in Elizabeth's government were
at their peak in the few months after he was named Earl Marshall, the
three months preceding the registration of Chapman's first version of

---

[13] Devereux, sig. B4. See Paul A. Jorgenson, "Theoretical Views of War in
Elizabethan England," *JHI* 13 (October 1952):469-81

[14] William Camden, *History of the Most Renowned Princess Elizabeth*
(London: M. Flesher and J. Tonson, 1688), p. 568. Camden reports that Essex
claimed he was an heir of Edward III. Frances Yates, "Elizabethan Chivalry," *Journal
of the Warburg and Courtauld Institute 20 (January 1957):25.*

the *Iliades* in April, 1598. England was engaged in very limited hostilities on the Continent at that time, and Elizabeth was relying upon the diplomatic skills of Cecil to shore up the English position. Since October, 1597, however, the state of English affairs in Ireland, with all the attendant dangers of Spanish interference, had been cause for increasing concern. In the last months of 1597, both commanders of the English forces fighting the rebel Tyrone had died, and the English garrisons were led by a temporary commander. Some negotiations with Tyrone were begun by February, 1597/98, but it was clear that Tyrone would not accept the English conditions. The English commander gave Tyrone one last truce, until April 10, in which to agree to the treaty. The news of this arrangement was received by Elizabeth's skeptical and increasingly impatient council sometime around mid-March. England's traditional wariness of Irish independence in a period when Spain might use the rebel's animosity for its own purposes was thus forcing a decision to intervene. With the abatement of fighting on the Continent, the conflict in Ireland assumed a higher priority, and a large military action in Ireland was becoming more and more likely.

The opportunity for Essex to take a more powerful position in such matters was clearly perceived by Francis Bacon during these crucial weeks, since he counseled Essex to take advantage of Cecil's absence in France (February and March, 1597/8) as well as the new turn of events in Ireland: "[Ireland] is one of the aptest particulars for your Lordship to purchase honour upon. . . . the world will make a kind comparison between those that have set it out of frame and those that shall bring it into frame; which kind of honour giveth the quickest kind of reflexion. . . . being mixt with matter of war, it is fittest for you."[15] Another letter written soon afterward endorses the threatening of an aggressive war if Tyrone breaks the treaty: "because he [Tyrone] may well waver upon his own inconstancy as upon occasion (and wanton variableness is never restrained but by fear), I hold it necessary he be menaced with a strong war, not by words, but by musters and preparations of forces here, in case the accord proceed not."[16] These messages were of course secret, but there were also public urgings for greater militancy and for Essex's leadership. The appearance of Spenser's *A Vewe of the Present State of Irelande*, registered only weeks after Bacon's letters were written and in the

---

[15] James Spedding, *The Letters and the Life of Francis Bacon* (London: Longmans Green and Co., 1890), pp. 95-96.
[16] Ibid., p. 99.

same month as the registration of Chapman's *Iliades*, seems to indicate the growing prominence of the issue in the spring of 1598. Spenser's call for armed intervention is accompanied by his special praise for an unnamed nobleman, almost certainly Essex, who can lead the English army to success. That nobleman is in fact the only bulwark against Irish secession; the rebels wait for the death of "one noble persone whoe beinge himself most steadfaste to his Souvraigne Quene his Countrye . . . stoppethe the ingrate at his back [Ireland] with the terrour of his greatness and the Assurance of his Imoveable loyalltye."[17]

Later in the year, Spenser published a more specific argument which laid the blame for English reversals in Ireland on England's lack of both unity and strong martial leadership, qualities a man like Essex could presumably resurrect.

> After . . . the chaunge of government succeeding the death of noble Lord Burrowes [the English commander who died in late 1597] ensewing the sundrie altercations of Councils and purposes following together with the division and partaking of those themselues of your Councill here haue since brought thinges to that dangerous condition they now stand in. ffor from this head through tolleracion and too much temporizing the euell is spred into all partes of the Realme and growne so vniversall a contagion that nothing but a moste violent medecyne will serue to recoueryt.[18]

Essex was himself uncertain of the merits of leading a huge army into the bogs[19] but he also would not allow his rivals to supersede him by taking command of the forces in Ireland. By the end of 1598 it was clear that a martial impulse was overcoming the earlier wariness of the court, and by October 1598 Essex was actively seeking command. Thus the dedication to Chapman's *Achilles Shield*, the translation of Homer's book 18 registered separately from the *Seaven Bookes* in 1598, anticipates the "expected president" of Essex, by which the Earl

---

[17] Edmund Spenser, *A Vewe of the Present State of Irelande*, in *Spensers Prose Works*, ed. R. Gottfried (Baltimore: Johns Hopkins llniv. Press, 1949), p. 147. See also p. 228.

[18] Ibid., pp. 237-38.

[19] Devereux, sig. Elv.

will propagate the true meaning of Homer throughout England: "But the chiefe and unanswerable meane to his [Homer's] generall and just acceptance must be your Lordship's high and by all men expected president, without which hee [Homer] must, like a poore snayle, pull in his English hornes" (p. 545). Nevertheless, Elizabeth's long delay in raising a large army and giving its command to Essex indicates that Essex could be a dangerous presence as well as an aid to his queen. Elizabeth, like Agamemnon, needed a heroic warrior in a time of danger, and yet if she granted the temperamental Earl an army, she might give him the power to menace the sovereign he was to protect. More than anyone, Essex seemed capable of exploiting the immense power about to be granted him, either by armed force, or by surpassing his queen in popularity.

In order to forestall such fears, Spenser argues for the Earl's appointment by carefully stressing the "imoveable loyalltye" of the Queen's champion. For similar reasons, Bacon urges not that Essex lead a military expedition, but that he argue in the council for "musters and preparations of forces here," presumably to strike fear into the Irish from a distance. Indeed, in Bacon's later *Apologie* for his role in the career of Essex, he claims that he explicitly asked Essex not to go to Ireland, that his major concern during the late 1590s was to dissuade Essex "from seeking greatness by a militarie dependance, or by a popular dependance, as that which would breed in the Queene iealousie, in him presumption, and in the state perturbation. . . . I did vsually compare them to Icarus two wings which were ioyned on with waxe, and would make him venture to soare too high, and then faile him at the height."[20] Although the subtle counselor may have colored the facts to absolve himself after the execution of Essex in 1602, his description of the Queen's fears in the late 90s is plausible. To control those fears Bacon claims to have warned the Earl that "[Essex's] absence in that kind [in Ireland] would exulcerate the Queens mind, whereby it would not be possible for him to carrie himselfe so, as to give her sufficient contentment: nor for her to carie her selfe so, as to giue him sufficient countenance, which would be ill for her, ill for him, and ill for the State" (p. 23). In Bacon's view, Essex was indeed "the fittest instrument to do good to the State" (p. 12), but an instrument which should have been "obsequious" and "observant" (p. 17). Tensions increased because Essex "had a settled opinion, that the Queene

---

[20] Francis Bacon. *Sir Francis Bacon His Apologie* (London: printed by R. Field for F. Norton, 1604), p. 19.

could be brought to nothing, but by a kind of necessitie and authority" (p. 18).

Working in the first months of 1598, Chapman would not have been able to ignore the dilemma Essex posed for the Queen. The Earl's desire to achieve military victory could easily have been called unalloyed ambition, as could his desire to take popular command over a huge army. On the other hand, Chapman, like Bacon, was not blind to the extraordinary opportunity, in early 1598 especially, for Essex to become an "instrument to do good to the State." The 1598 *Iliades,* like *Achilles Shield* published later in the year, therefore attempts to temper as well as encourage Essex's rise to greater power.

Evidence of poor printing and Chapman's later apologies lend credence to the notion that, despite the delicacy of his rhetorical task, Chapman worked quickly early in 1598 to ride the Essex crest, attempting to reveal Homer's meaning for the Earl's purposes. He was later to maintain that he could translate twelve books of Homer in fifteen weeks (p. 15), but in 1598 he could only present the public with seven nonconsecutive ones and a separate edition of book 18. He tells the reader to "peruse the pamphlet of errors" in the meantime and to tolerate the unadorned first volume as a preview of a later translation (p. 508).

Moreover, his choice of books in his first edition of Homer seems to have been made from topical as well as aesthetic considerations. The seven books (1, 2, and 7-11) highlight the story of Achilles in a way which amplifies its applicability to Essex in 1598, while it also focuses the action for an effective abbreviation of Homer. Achilles' original dispute with Agamemnon and subsequent withdrawal (1) is followed by a display of Greek indecision and Agamemnon's apology (2); Chapman excludes books 3 to 6, which cover indecisive matters such as the duel between Paris and Menelaus, politics among the gods, the momentarily successful Greek attack led by Diomedes (4-6), and Hector's leavetaking (6). Books 7 to 9 are prominent, however, since Hector's counter-attack obliterates Diomedes' successes. The consequences of Achilles' withdrawal from the battle can no longer be ignored, and indeed his absence is most painfully felt by the Greeks at this point. Chapman thus includes this section with the first two books, linking the withdrawal of Achilles to the overwhelming Trojan counter-attack (7). By the end of book 9 the Trojans have driven the Greeks in panic back to their ships, and Agamemnon must make the humiliating embassy to Achilles. Although book 10 (Chapman's penultimate book) tells of a Greek success, the spy mission of Ulysses and Diomedes, and the Greeks' belated plans for a new attack, the

*Seaven Bookes* ends at the moment of greatest disaster for the Greeks: in book 11 all the prominent Greeks fighting in the battle are wounded, and Nestor begs Patroclus to petition Achilles for help one last time.

Chapman's shortened format exposes and emphasizes Greek powerlessness without Achilles, and it uses the narrative structure of the *Iliad* to build toward this last embassy as though it were the climax of the translation. Nestor's last appeal to Achilles at the conclusion of the *Seaven Bookes* duplicates the avowed intention of Chapman's translation: to stir the Achillean Essex with an account of an ancient war.

Chapman's organization results in a convenient correspondence between the Greeks' desperate need for Achilles and England's need for the Achillean Essex. It is probably no accident that Chapman's later publication of *Achilles Shield* features not only the grandeur of Hephaestus's handiwork but also the increasing excitement of Achilles' imminent entry into the battle. As the year progressed, the story of the forging of Achilles' armor would have been more and more appropriate to Essex's preparations for the Irish expedition.

Chapman's tendency to modify and expand his basic text enables him to emphasize and sometimes exaggerate specific parallels between Achilles and Essex. One of the clearest instances of Chapman's delight in cultivating these associations occurs in book 1, where he freely revises the references to Achilles' divine ancestry by mentioning "Royaltie" as well. Chapman's Achilles castigates Agamemnon for being "sencelesse of all Royaltie" (line 166), a remark Chapman invents. Homer's epithet, "son of Peleus" (πηλείδη),[21] becomes in Chapman's line 288 "a king's heire," emphasizing the tie to royal blood which Chapman uses to flatter Essex in one of his dedications (p. 546.143-44). Whereas in the Greek text Agamemnon grants that Achilles is "valiant" (καρτερός—Loeb 1.280), Chapman says Achilles is "better borne" (290). Likewise, whereas Agamemnon grumbles in the Greek that Achilles is "minded to hold sway and to be king among all" (Loeb 1.288), Agamemnon concedes in Chapman's version that Achilles' dominance is already an established fact: "All in his power he will conclude" (298). In the *Seaven Bookes* in general, Achilles' power and privilege are presented much more explicitly than in the ancient text.

---

[21] *Homer, The Iliad,* trans. A. T. Murray. 2 vols. (Cambridge, Mass.: Harvard Univ. Press, 1960) book 1, line 277. This edition will hereafter be called "Loeb."

Although Chapman does not identify Agamemnon with Elizabeth, he emphasizes the striking correspondence between Achilles' dispute over his right to Briseis and Essex's argument with Elizabeth over prisoners he took at Cadiz. Thebes, the town from which Briseis was taken, Homer calls a "sacred" (ἱερὴν) city (Loeb 1.366), whereas Chapman, pointing to a parallel with Cadiz, calls it a "wealthie" town (383). Chapman's adjective is most fitting for the rich, treasure-laden Cadiz Essex had raided––a town profane in the eyes of the English soldiers because it was filled with Spanish Catholics. Chapman makes Essex's prize a byword for wealth in *Hero and Leander,* registered in the same year; Cadiz is

> Th' *Iberian* citie that wars hand did strike
> By English force in princely *Essex* guide,
> When peace assur'd her towres had fortifide;
> And golden-fingred *India* had bestowd
> Such wealth on her, that strength and Empire flowd
> Into her Turrets; and her virgin waste
> The wealthie girdle of the Sea embraste.[22]

Chapman's topical modifications are less a barrier to the modern reader of the *Seaven Bookes* if the conjunction of Chapman's strong interest in contemporary political life and his extreme enthusiasm for "Homerical" truth is fully appreciated. If Chapman believed his own vehement claims that his translation somehow captured the essence of Homer, then the topical and "Homerical" meanings of his text were, in his own eyes, more than artificially related. Thus one of the most significant topical alterations in the 1598 translation both exaggerates and enforces Achilles' vilification of Agamemnon:

> O thou possest with Impudence, that in command of men
> Affectst the brute mind of a Fox, for so thou fill thy denne
> With forced or betrayed spoiles thou feelest no sence of
>       shame!
> What souldier can take any spirite to put on (for thy fame)
> Contempt of violence and death, or in the open field
> Or secret ambush, when the heyre his hie desert should yeeld
> Is beforehand condemnd to glut thy gulfe of avarice?
>       (154-60)

---

[22] George Chapman and Christopher Marlowe, *Hero and Leander* (London: Felix Kingston, 1598), sig. Gl.

(Ah me, thou clothed in shamelessness, thou of
crafty mind, how shall any man of the Achaeans
hearken to thy bidding with a ready heart either to
go on a journey or to fight amain with warriors?
(Loeb 1.149-51)).

Chapman's expansion of the ancient text draws attention both to
the degree of Achilles' rage and the topical relevance of the warrior's
confrontation with his king. The complaint of the unrewarded soldier,
spoken with such force by Homer's Achilles and augmented by Chapman, would also have special application to the period after the
Armada year, when whole-hearted support for the English military
radically diminished. The soldiers' resentment is touched upon in
Greene's *Euphues His Censure to Philatus*[23] where Achilles criticizes
the illiberality of commanders and predicts disaster if armies are not
properly rewarded. At the end of the 1590s, Shakespeare's Achilles
makes the similar complaint that Agamemnon enjoys using "policy"
which is no more than "bed-work, mapp'ry, closet-war" and
"cowardice" (I.iii.205, 197).[24]

Chapman's addition to Achilles' accusation also seems to focus on
a particular contemporary target; by changing Homer's χερδαλέοφρον
("crafty minded") to "Fox" and emphasizing Agamemnon's "avarice,"
the translator invokes the slur Spenser had coined for Burghley in the
*Mother Hubbard's Tale*.[25] The Queen's diplomatic councillors,
Burghley and his son, Cecil, had in fact been accused of avarice by the
Essex faction.[26] In the eyes of Essex, those who influenced policy at
court while he was in the field profited far more than he.

While Chapman directs attention to parallels between Achilles
and Essex, he confronts the crucial problem of reconciling Achilles'
boundless wrath with the delicate exigencies of Essex's role in the
political life of England. The problem is particularly difficult because
Chapman tries to magnify Achilles' stature—including his capacity for

---

[23] *The Life and Complete Works of Robert Greene,* ed. Alexander Grosart, 15
vols. (London and Aylesbury: printed for private circulation, 1881-1886), vol. 6. See
also I.O., *Lamentation of Troy for the Death of Hector* (London: Peter Short, 1594).

[24] *Complete Works,* ed. Harbage, p. 986.

[25] Edmund Spenser, *Poetical Works,* ed. J. C. Smith and E. De Selincourt
(London: Oxford Univ. Press, 1970), pp. 504-508, lines 938-1384. For this and other
reasons, Spenser's work was suppressed. See Tucker Brooke, *The Renaissance* (New
York: Appleton-Century Crofts, 1967), p. 488.

[26] See Simon Harward, *The Danger of Discontentment* (London: W. White,
1598), sig. C2v.

anger—to win attention for Essex's "Achillean" virtues. To resolve the dilemma, the translator attempts to enhance and justify opposite sides of Achilles' character that are perhaps ultimately related: his capacity for showing extreme outrage over injury to his honor, and his extraordinary restraint—aided by higher powers or wisdom—which seems so powerful because Achilles sees himself as the victim of the most extreme of provocations. Hence several passages doctored by Chapman in book 1 show Achilles to be more clearly in the right in his dispute with Agamemnon, while other passages are designed to show that Achilles displays an absolute rational control in order to protect the common good.

Chapman adds a clause to undercut Agamemnon when Nestor warns both Agamemnon and Achilles to temper their conflict: "Obedience better is than rule, *where rule erres in his sway.*" (Chapman's addition is italicized [285]; see Loeb 1.274.) Conversely, he exaggerates evidence in Homer for Achilles' self-control, even as he gives the hero more license to revile Agamemnon. A brief, forceful statement by Achilles to Agamemnon gives way in Chapman's 1598 *Iliades* to a passage combining execration and self-denial:

> tis more safe, *with contumelious breath*
> To show thy manhood gainst a man that contradicts thy lust
> And *with thy covetous valour* take his spoiles *with force unjust,*
> *Because thou knowest a man of fame will take wrong ere he be*
> *A general mischiefe, nor shamst thou though all the armie see*
> (Chapman's addition is italicized [233-37]; see Loeb 1.228–32.)

Chapman later prompts Achilles to emphasize that he would "reforme" Agamemnon's "insolence" were it not for the "common good" which is more important than Achilles' "owne delight" (304-308; see Loeb 1.295-96).

Accordingly, when Agamemnon takes Briseis from Achilles, Chapman inserts a passage to focus on the power of Achilles' passionate anguish, and then to praise the hero for subduing that passion with an even more powerful fortitude guided by "wisedome":

> Shee wept and lookt upon her love- he sigh't and did refuse.
> O how his wisdome with his power did mightilie contend—
> His love incouraging his power and spirite, that durst descend
> As far as Hercules for her, yet wisedome all subdude,
> Wherein a high exploite he showd, and sacred fortitude.
> (360-64; see Loeb 1.345-46.)

Chapman thus confines and yet fires the hero's essential fury, so that the later publication of *Achilles Shield* fittingly presents Homer's adjacent images of peace and war, ambiguously prefaced with the translator's claim that Essex is the man to champion Homeric "wisedome" in England.

The problematic nature of Essex's Achillean role is again evident in the poet's pronouncement that the Earl should use Homer as the "wealthy ornament to [kings'] studies" as well as "the main battayle of their armies" (p. 546). As a patron of true scholarship, Essex is asked to protect the new translation of Homer from "five-witted censors" who would profane it with their ignorance and "puritanical" biases (p. 544); but the language of Chapman's appeal often points toward martial rather than philosophical ends. He requests that the Earl reform the "unmanly degeneracies" prevailing in England (p. 546) by displacing the ballad and sonnet with the epic (p. 549), purging all corruption from England by defending "Homerical wisdom" with "armed garrisons" (p. 546). "Intellectual blood" has already been shed for the cause; Essex must "stirre [his] divine temper" (p. 504) to "forge out of that holie knowledge" of Homer the "darts" for victorious combat (p. 503).

Chapman's translation never explicitly urges the Earl to use his popularity and power in ways that would antagonize the Queen and her council. Still, the 1598 translation risks appealing to Essex's interests and advising him, if only indirectly, to take a more active, if dangerous, part in public life. By highlighting the analogies between Essex and Achilles, Chapman emphasizes the explosive potential in the relationship between Achilles and Agamemnon and presents that potential in a way that shows Chapman's concern to excite as well as caution the Earl's ambition. The translation and its prefaces consequently call for intellectual devotion to Homer, while sometimes seeming to declare active war on all forms of foreign and domestic corruption, be they in Ireland, England, or even proximate to the Queen.

We can see in retrospect that Chapman's sense of danger and opportunity was well-founded. Once he possessed the Irish command, Essex indeed terrified the Queen, first by breaking off in Ireland and rushing home to confront his enemies in the council, and then by leading an abortive rising in 1601, after military frustration in Ireland. Even after his arrest, Essex apparently attempted to call down Mountjoy's army upon London, confirming others' fears that his armed forces would impose themselves on English political life.

When Chapman began to prepare his second, larger edition of the *Iliades,* he most probably recognized that history had made his topical translation of Homer a liability. He worked in later years to mute the specifically political implications of the *Seaven Bookes,* and though he did not explicitly retreat from his earlier defense of Homer, his revealing apology in the 1608 preface to books 1–12 seems to admit that his 1598 work was "following the common tract": "if in some place (especially in my first edition, being done so long since and following the common tract) I be somthing paraphrasticall and faulty—is it justice in that poore faulte (if they will needs have it so) to drowne all the rest of my labour?" (p. 17). Whether or not Chapman here refers to the 1598 book as a kind of political tract, there is evidence in his 1608 edition that the "paraphrasticall and faulty" parts of the 1598 text included the topical references cited earlier. Those passages are almost all obliterated in a judicious revision of books 1 and 2, in which Chapman omits most of the modifications inspired by Essex.

The most telling alteration in the new book I occurs in Achilles' speech to Agamemnon. Where the hero calls the king an avaricious fox in the 1598 version, his language in 1608 is much milder:

1598:

> O thou possest with Impudence, that in command of men
> Affectst the brute mind *of a Fox, for so thou fill thy denne*
> *With forced or betrayed spoiles thou feelest no sence of shame!*
> What souldier can take any spirite to put on (for thy fame)
> Contempt of violence and death, or in open field
> Or secret ambush, when the heyre his hie desert should yeeld
> Is beforehand condemnd to glut *thy gulf of avarice?*
> For me, I have no cause t'account these Ilians enemies.
> (Italics mine.)
>                               (154–61)

1608:

> O thou impudent! of no good but thine owne
> Ever respectfull but of that with all craft covetous—
> With what heart can a man attempt a service dangerous,
> Or at thy voice be spirited to flie upon a foe,
> Thy mind thus wretched? For my selfe, I was not injur'd so
> By any Troyan.
>                               (150–55)[27]

---

[27] All citations of the 1608 translation are from Nicoll's edition.

The reference to the fox and the vindictive phrases with no basis in the Greek are omitted.

Likewise, where Achilles calls Agamemnon "Thou sencelesse to all Royaltie," meaning the king is not sensitive to Achilles' royal blood (166), the 1608 version uses the more accurate phrase "thou dog's eyes" (161). Reference to Achilles as "a king's heire" (288) in 1598 is replaced by the phrase "Great sonne of Peleus" in 1608 (275). Similarly, "though better borne thou bee," Agamemnon's concession to the hero's better birth in 1598 (290), is replaced by the observation that Achilles has "strength superior" (277). Missing entirely is Chapman's compliment to Achilles for his restraint when Briseis is given to Agamemnon.[28]

In 1598, Agamemnon also refers to Achilles' powers as though they were granted by the state, as the command of the forces in Ireland was soon to be granted to Essex: "What if the ever-being state to him such strength affordes? / Is it to rende up men's renownes with contumelious wordes?" (300–301). The 1608 version replaces "state" with a more accurate translation of Homer's word Θεòι: "If the Gods have given him the great stile / Of ablest souldier, made they that his licence to revile / Men with vile language?" (287–89). A general perusal of the new books 1 and 2 shows that these books in the old 1598 text were completely rewritten.[29] Vocabulary and phrasing were altered everywhere, producing an English version closer to the Greek.

Although it is not as clear as some have concluded that Chapman's later revision indicates a rejection of his idealization of Achilles, it can be said that specific, topical material which was appropriate to the 1598 edition was no longer functional in the later work. Essex's rise to power had ended in his execution, and Chapman's contemporary, Daniel, had discovered that a literary plot which too closely resembled the history of Essex was politically dangerous. For his *Philotus* he was forced to face an official inquiry in 1605.[30]

Despite Chapman's obliteration of much of the 1598 text, however, the *Seaven Bookes of the Iliades* is not reduced to a document of mundane political circumstance. Chapman does indeed twist the ancient text in 1598 so that it images even more strikingly the

---

[28] Compare lines 349-50 in the 1608 version.

[29] Chapman's 1598 translation of books 7-1 I seems to have been left virtually intact in later versions, whereas books I and 2 underwent drastic revisions.

[30] For a summary of the plot that caught the censor's eye, and for Daniel's apology, in part a defense of Essex, see Samuel Daniel, *The Complete Works of Samuel Daniel*, ed. Alexander Grosart, 5 vols. (London: Hazell, Watson and Vinney, 1885). 3:180-81.

career of Essex in the late 1590s; but his first translation of Homer also is an attempt to absorb the career of Essex into the epic of Troy. The audacity of the translator's topical imagination is matched only by his belief that he was revealing Homer's true meaning. For Chapman the 1598 translation was the true story of Essex precisely because it aspired to capture what Chapman considered to be the essence of nobility and wisdom. He was convinced that in "Homericall writing" "the soules of al the recorded worthies that ever liv'de become eternally embodyed even upon earth and, our understanding parts making transition in that we understand, the Iyves of worthilie-termed Poets are their earthlie Elisummes" (p. 503. 24–28).

The Battle still Continuing advantageous to ÿ Trojans, Juno makes use of Venus's Girdle to charm Jupiter, & of Somnus to lay him to sleep, in ÿ mean time Neptune spirits up ÿ Greeks, & ÿ Trojans are Repuls'd in their turn. B.14;

Figure 3. Hera seduces Zeus. Antoine Coypel?

# Textual Overlapping and Dalilah's Harlot-Lap

*Mary Nyquist*

So said he, and forbore not glance or toy
Of amorous intent, well understood
Of Eve, whose Eye darted contagious Fire.
Her hand he seiz'd, and to a shady bank,
Thick overhead with verdant roof imbowr'd
He led her nothing loath; Flow'rs were the Couch,
Pansies, and Violets, and Asphodel,
And Hyacinth, Earth's freshest softest lap.
There they thir fill of Love and Love's disport
Took largely, of thir mutual guilt the Seal,
The solace of thir sin, till dewy sleep
Oppress'd them, wearied with thir amorous play.
Soon as the force of that fallacious Fruit,
That with exhilarating vapor bland
About thir spirits had play'd, and inmost powers
Made err, was now exhal'd, and grosser sleep

Bred of unkindly fumes, with conscious dreams
Encumber'd, now had left them, up they rose
As from unrest, and each the other viewing,
Soon found thir Eyes how op'n'd, and thir minds
How dark'n'd; innocence, that as a veil
Had shadow'd them from knowing ill, was gone,
Just confidence, and native righteousness,
And honor from about them, naked left
To guilty shame: hee cover'd, but his Robe

Uncover'd more. So rose the *Danite* strong
*Herculean Samson* from the Harlot-lap
Of *Philistean Dalilah,* and wak'd
Shorn of his strength, They destitute and bare
Of all thir virtue: silent, and in face
Confounded long they sat, as struck'n mute,
Till *Adam,* though not less than *Eve* abasht,
At length gave utterance to these words constrain'd.
*O Eve,* in evil hour thou didst give ear
To that false Worm, of whomsoever taught
To counterfeit Man's voice, true in our Fall,
False in our promis'd Rising.

(9.1034-70)[1]

* * * * * *

*Nyquist explains her intent to examine the intertextuality of the above passage from* Paradise Lost *"in ways that open up, rather than delimit, the discursive space it inhabits." Her starting point in Part I is the simile that compares the waking of Samson "from the Harlot-lap / of Philistean Dalilah" (1060–61) with the waking of post-lapsarian Adam and Eve from "Earth's freshest softest lap" (9.1041): Samson "Shorn of his strength, They destitute and bare / Of all thir virtue" (1062–63). Traditional critics almost unanimously ignore the "They" of verse 1062 and discuss the passage as a comparison between Samson and Adam, both men betrayed by women. Bringing the discourse of Protestant theology to bear, Nyquist argues that the simile illustrates not betrayal of man by woman but the couple's joint "retrospective discovery of loss"—the loss of God's Word or divine grace. She links modern misogynistic misreadings not only to critics' failures to historicize the context but also to cultural codes (as revealed especially by St. Augustine and Milton editor J.M. Evans) which make Samson's loss of strength equivalent to detumescence or castration—conditions which exclude Eve.*

*Part II seeks to establish "the complex network of signs into which the simile has inserted itself" in order to "explain why the simile might be incapable of communicating" the non-misogynistic theological message of its Protestant context. Drawing mainly on Spenser, but also on artists*

---

[1] Quotations from Milton's poetry are from John Milton, *Complete Poems and Major Prose*, ed. Merritt Y. Hughes (New York, 1952).

*Mantegna and Rubens, Nyquist examines an iconographic tradition that places slumbering disarmed men in the laps of women lying on the ground in shaded bowers. The allegorical reading is clear: "the unconsciousness of the victim illustrates the complete subjection of the reason or will to desire or, in the Pauline sense, the flesh." In Milton's own* Samson Agonistes, *all the familiar features of the* topos *are present: "female deceit and female seductiveness, their well-to-do half-sister Luxuria, the female lap, and its treacherous capacity to unman and disarm its victim."*–Ed.

* * * * * *

So far, we have been dealing with laps that are representationally and anatomically grounded by an individual female temptress figure. Like the Latin *gremium*, the Anglo-Saxon "lap" can refer either to the bosom or to the area between the waist and the knees on which, most commonly, a child is held. Yet in Renaissance England, the substantive "lap" may have had a more explicitly sexual connotation than we now suppose, one of the obsolete meanings of "lap" cited by the *O.E.D.* being the female pudendum.[2] This is, presumably, one reason

---

[2] Further evidence of the pervasiveness of this *topos* and of the currency of the sexual connotation of "lap" can be found in act 3, scene 2 of *Hamlet*, where the following well-known exchange takes place:

*Ham.* (lying down at Ophelia's feet) Lady, shall I lie in your lap?
*Oph.* No, my lord.
*Ham.* I mean, my head upon your lap.
*Oph.* Ay, my lord.
*Ham.* Do you think I meant country matters?
*Oph.* I think nothing, my lord.
*Ham.* That is a fair thought to lie between maids' legs.
*Oph.* What is, my lord?
*Ham.* Nothing.

The several sexual innuendos here have frequently been remarked. Harold Jenkins, editor of the Arden *Hamlet*, refers the reader to a piece by Marie Collins, who mentions four English morality and interlude plays in which a young hero is portrayed lying or sleeping in a deceitful lady's lap. Collins concludes that Hamlet, knowing this dramatic iconography full well, employs it to cast Ophelia in the role of the dangerous temptress and to suggest that he is, in relation to her, "a vulnerable morality hero" ("Hamlet and the Lady's Lap," *Notes and Queries*, n.s., 28 [1981], 130–32). Yet if we see *Hamlet* alluding here more generally to the *topos* I have been tracking (Spenser's *The Faerie Queene* had of course been published by this time), another reading suggests itself. With reference to this *topos*, the allusion might indicate that there is, possibly, something rather unheroic about Hamlet's substitution of dramatic for revenge action; that, having already, as it were, laid aside his arms, the hero might just as well go all the way and lie in his lady's lap.

that Dalilah's lap can be described as "lascivious." The very *topos* we have been discussing, however, turns the lap into what is also metaphorically a lap of pleasure or a lap of luxury—a phrase that is, interestingly, still current. Even when not literalized by a female body, this lap of luxury is always associated with women and thus, from a masculinist perspective, with effeminacy. For example, when Britomart boasts to Guyon about her martial upbringing, she states "Sithence I loathed have my life to lead, / As Ladies wont, in pleasures wanton lap" (3.2.6.6–7).[3] The verbal form of "lap" can similarly invoke this figure, as it does when we learn that Adonis lies with Venus "Lapped in flowres and pretious spycery" (3.6.46.1.5). More obviously sinister is Comus's description of the practice of his mother Circe and the three sirens, "Who as they sung, would take the prison'd soul / And lap it in Elysium" (256–57). Not unrelated, as a final, more ambiguous, example, are the lines "And ever against eating Cares, / Lap me in soft *Lydian* Airs" from Milton's "L'Allegro" (135–36).

Although all laps inviting retreat or associated with rest are undoubtedly enervating female laps, it does not follow that laps can play only this single psychosocial role. For nature, too, has a lap, a fertile lap that in its capacity to bring forth flowers and vegetation would seem to be both innocent and blessed. Even when presented as relatively inactive, as it is when *Paradise Lost* says in describing paradise that "the flow'ry lap / Of some irriguous Valley spread her store" (4.254–55), the innocence of nature's lap is not called into question. And its more actively procreative character seems just as virtuous, as we can see by the way Milton's "May Song" celebrates "The Flow'ry May, who from her green lap throws / The yellow Cowslip, and the pale Primrose" (3–4); or by the way that in Book 4 of *The Fairie Queene* the song that bursts forth in praise of Venus stresses the responsiveness of nature's lap: "Then doth the daedale earth throw forth to thee / Out of her fruitful lap aboundant flowers" (4.10.45.1-2). Passages such as this, which so abound as to not need instancing, would suggest that nature's bounteous lap is in Renaissance texts sharply differentiated from the lap of the temptress or of luxury. But because like Luxuria, nature or the *hortus conclusus* is symbolically female, there is always, inevitably, the possibility of slippage. That Acrasia's victim is named Verdant gives some indication of the direction of this slippage; so does the conjunction, in the examples cited above, of literalized female laps and flowers and grassy grounds.

---

[3] Quotations from *The Faerie Queene* are from J.C. Smith's edition (Oxford 1909; rpt. 1964).

Perhaps the most powerful example of this potential ambiguity appears in Milton's Fifth Elegy, which has the earth call out passionately, and perhaps seductively, to her desired partner, the sun, "Huc ades, et gremio lumina pone meo" (1.95) ["come hither and lay your glories in my lap"]. Is this, or is this not, a lascivious lap?

It should by now be evident that a similar question could legitimately be asked of "Earth's freshest softest lap" in the passage from *Paradise Lost* to which we can now return, having situated it in the context of the iconographic and literary conventions on which it undoubtedly draws. The adjective "fresh" certainly suggests a natural innocence. And one could argue that the superlative forms of "fresh" and "soft" convey the kind of poignancy associated with imminent loss, in part by recalling the language used to describe the initial appearance of "delicious Paradise" in *Paradise Lost* (the "loftiest shade," "stateliest view," "goodliest Trees loaden with fairest Fruit" in 4.132-47). But the adjective "soft" is without question implicated in the *topos* of the regressive lap. Viewed retrospectively, from Adam and Eve's awakening as if from a "harlot-lap," both superlatives therefore do more than hint at a potential excess, or even looseness, in this lap's freshness and softness. On the other hand, perhaps a backward glance of this sort is not so useful to an understanding of the operation of this simile as would be an analysis of its dynamic forward movement. If due weight is given to the way a fully dramatized action unfolds between "Earth's freshest softest lap" and "Dalilah's harlot-lap," then it becomes possible to see that the action itself resolves the initially ambiguous or doubtful innocence of nature's lap. Earth's freshest softest lap in effect *becomes* a kind of harlot-lap because while lying on it Eve and Adam experience a dying into a fallen sexuality. Where Nature initially groaned in response to the forbidden acts of Eve and Adam, it now, more passively, simply lies there, becoming somehow embedded in the final stages of their fall. Its lap—or rather the two laps here becoming one—thus signals by means of this passive participation a general lapse, *lapsus*, a fall, the Fall.

It is of course only the English language that makes possible this particular theological pun, which is interestingly appropriate, even central, to the masculinist biblical and doctrinal story *Paradise Lost* here enacts. If Adam and Eve bring death into the world, it is supposed to be because death becomes inseparably a part of the process of reproduction. But in the Judeo-Christian tradition as well as in *Paradise Lost,* the sign of this inseparability becomes woman. Nature's simple there-ness in "Earth's freshest softest lap" for this reason signals the falling movement into a new and emergent maternity, now

associated with death. In his lengthy soliloquy in Book 10, Adam
protests the deferring of the death penalty, associated with the
Father's thunderous Word, by crying:

> why do I overlive,
> Why am I mockt with death, and length'n'd out
> To deathless pain? How gladly would I meet
> Mortality my sentence, and be Earth
> Insensible, how glad would lay me down
> As in my Mother's lap! There I should rest
> And sleep secure; his dreadful voice no more
> Would Thunder in my ears, no fear of worse
> To mee and to my offspring would torment me
> With cruel expectation.
>
> (10.773-82)

We might think we are to take this extraordinary desire for his
Mother's lap and its accompanying construction of an oedipal past to
be merely a sign of Adam's fallen warpedness of mind. But in Book 11
Michael describes the process of dying naturally in exactly the same
symbolic terms: "So may'st thou live, till like ripe Fruit thou drop /
Into thy Mother's lap, or be with ease / Gather'd, not harshly pluckt,
for death mature" (11.535-37). Together these remarkable passages
suggest that in *Paradise Lost*, when Eve and Adam lapse by falling
away from the Father's Word and then into "Earth's freshest softest
lap," not only death but the (paradigmatically masculine) subject's
desire become associated inescapably with nature, mothers, harlots,
their laps.

### III

Read against this *topos*, the Samson simile's "laps" obviously lose
their character as neutral ground, the solid basis of a poetic theology
elaborating an unproblematically egalitarian downfall. Yet while symbolically and to some degree threateningly female, "Earth's freshest
softest lap" and its counterpart "Dalilah's harlot-lap" do not in themselves call into question the innocence of *Paradise Lost*'s heroine, Eve.
If we turn, next, to what eighteenth-century commentators on *Paradise
Lost* considered the most noteworthy feature of the entire passage—
beginning with line 1029, Adam's "For never did thy beauty," and
extending through the opening lines of Adam's "O Eve in evil hour"—
this is precisely what we find happening, however. Writing in the *Spec-*

*tator* in 1712, Addison is the first to draw attention to the intertextual relation between the scene of Adam and Eve's love-making and the scene in Book 14 of the *Iliad* in which Hera, adorned with the enchanting zone of Aphrodite, comes upon Zeus, who greets her by proposing they make love and by declaring that he has never before so intensely desired any goddess or woman, including Hera herself. Adam's "converse" with Eve after he has eaten of the forbidden fruit—in lines immediately preceding the lengthy passage quoted above—is said by Addison to be an "exact Copy" of Zeus's passionate declaration to Hera:[4]

> But come, so well refresh't, now let us play,
> As meet is, after such delicious Fare;
> For never did thy Beauty since the day
> I saw thee first and wedded thee, adorn'd
> With all perfections, so inflame my sense
> With ardor to enjoy thee, fairer now
> Than ever, bounty of this virtuous Tree.
>
> (9.1027-33)

Although a similar invitation to love-making is uttered by Paris in Book 3 of the *Iliad*, the scene in Book 14 in which Zeus responds sexually to Hera's artificially heightened attractiveness is clearly the principal source of Milton's "copying," which in this instance takes the form of what we would now call an overt allusion. That the allusion is unquestionably overt is established by Milton's imitation of other features of Homer's scene, such as the way the lovers' verbal exchanges come to an end when Zeus takes Hera in his arms and they make love on a peak of Mount Ida, which, as Addison notes, produces underneath them a bed of flowers they fall asleep on when sexually satisfied.

It is not only Zeus's invitation and the love-making itself that Milton imitates, however. As Thomas Newton points out in his 1749 edition of *Paradise Lost*, in an annotation modern editors pass on to their readers, Adam's postdiscovery speech, "O Eve, in evil hour," is based on the passage in Book 15 of the *Iliad* in which Zeus lashes out verbally at Hera upon awakening from a postcoital slumber to discover that he has, through her, lost control of the battle. Newton construes the Samson simile correctly: "As Samson wak'd shorn of his

---

[4] Joseph Addison, *The Spectator*, no. 351 (April 12, 1712), ed. Gregory Smith (London, 1945; rpt. 1973), 100-1.

strength, they wak'd destitute and bare of all their virtue."[5] Yet the
awakening he is really interested in is Adam's postcoital verbal
awakening to an outrage that resembles Jupiter's. The intertextual
reading Newton produces tells the story of the progress in the two
patriarchs of an emasculating or effeminate desire: "As this whole
transaction between Adam and Eve is manifestly copied from the
episode of Jupiter and Juno on Mount Ida, has many of the same circumstances, and often the very words translated, so it concludes
exactly after the same manner in a quarrel. Adam awakes much in the
same humor as Jupiter, and their cases are somewhat parallel; they
are both overcome by their fondness for their wives, and are sensible
of their error too late, and then their love turns to resentment, and
they grow angry with their wives; when they should rather have been
angry with themselves for their weakness in hearkening to them."[6] By
suggesting an ironic dimension, Newton here modifies Pope's openly
misogynistic comments in his edition of this book of the *Iliad*, where
he states that both Adam and Zeus, whose "Circumstance is very
parallel," awaken "full of that Resentment natural to a Superior, who
is imposed upon by one of less Worth and Sense than himself, and
imposed upon in the worst manner by Shews of Tenderness and
Love."[7] Newton's reading is less stridently masculinist, for he implies
that far from being the legitimate expression of patriarchal
self-righteousness, the anger verbalized by Zeus and Adam merely
indicates, ironically, the defensive self-deception that results when
patriarchal superiority becomes unsettled. Where the emphasis of
Pope's discussion falls on the evil consequences of female duplicity,
Newton's stresses the instability of male superiority. But in spite of
this, by concentrating, like Pope, on the similarities or parallels
between Adam and Zeus, Newton contributes to a masculinist reading
of the passage in *Paradise Lost* we are here considering. Granted,
Newton generously remarks that the positions of the two patriarchs
are "somewhat" rather than "very" (Pope's choice) parallel. Yet even
a qualified parallelism seems the product of a decidedly phallogocentric* structure of thought. For it tends to obliterate the difference between the scene of sexual seduction which Hera consciously
designs, with an intent to deceive Zeus, and the scene of Adam's

---

[5] Thomas Newton, ed., *Paradise Lost* (London, 1749), 2.201.

[6] Newton, *Paradise Lost*, 202.

[7] Alexander Pope, *The Iliad of Homer*, ed. Maynard Mack, vol. 7 of *The Poems of Alexander Pope*, Gen. Ed., John Butt (London and New Haven, 1967), 193.

* "Phallogocentric" = both masculinist and authorial.–Ed.

transgression against the Father's Word, a scene in which *Paradise Lost* has Eve participate only ambiguously since she is herself deceived. The critics' parallelism also erases the narrative or temporal difference between Book 9's two scenes of temptation against the Word and the scene of the fallen Eve and Adam's love-making on "Earth's freshest softest lap." That even Newton's modest parallelism ends up conflating verbal or intellectual temptation and sexual seduction can be seen in his statement that both Jupiter and Adam "should rather have been angry with themselves for their weakness in harkening to them," a statement that unmistakably, even if unintentionally, echoes the patriarchal Lord's judgment of Adam; the phrase echoed appears both in Genesis 3:17,[8] "Because thou hast hearkened unto the voice of thy wife," and in *Paradise Lost*, 10.198.

But is this difference-denying parallelism generated solely by masculinist commentators or is it implicit in *Paradise Lost*'s overt allusion to the *Iliad*? It is of course impossible to imagine on what grounds such a question might be given a definitive answer. One could argue, against the neoclassical commentators cited above, that the allusion functions ironically and that it intends to mark the *difference* between Zeus's anger at his seductress Hera and Adam's, which is "fallen" or inherently and therefore illegitimately self-exculpating. Yet *Paradise Lost* makes any rigorous pursuit of this line of thought rather difficult, since the narrator has already, officially, remarked that Adam was "not deceiv'd, / But fondly overcome with Female charm" (9.998-99). If in referring to the parallel weakness of Zeus and Adam in "hearkening" to their wives Newton echoes both Genesis and Milton's epic, in stating that "they are both overcome by their fondness for their wives" he echoes these very lines from *Paradise Lost*. Newton's echo therefore draws attention to the way the narrator's interpretive intervention itself conflates spiritual fall and sexual seduction, thereby sanctioning a reading of the overt allusion to the *Iliad* which concentrates on the parallels between Zeus and Adam.

If parallelism, thus overcoming difference, can be seen to inform both commentaries and to some degree text, then we must conclude that the allusive context *Paradise Lost* creates for Eve and Adam's postcoital awakening clearly complicates matters considerably, perhaps to the extent of calling into question the notion that the Samson simile has been misogynistically *misread*. To safeguard the reading of the simile I have been proposing, it would seem necessary either to

---

[8] Biblical quotations are from the King James version.

suppress or to make light of this context, for it forcibly reintroduces the very hierarchical polarization of the sexes that that reading has shown to be basically irrelevant. Instead of illustrating, unequivocally, Adam and Eve's mutual recognition of a mutual change, the simile now appears significantly and inescapably expressive of the deeply sexist attitudes that its context, with its exclusively patriarchal spokesmen (Book 9's narrator, Adam, Zeus, and then Addison, Pope, Newton), makes explicit. If Hera is to Zeus what Eve is to Adam, then the Samson simile suggests, in spite of itself, that Eve has the same relation to Adam as her temptress daughter, Dalilah, has to Samson. The sexes become related just as our phallocentric cultural tradition would lead us to expect they would be: the (either "somewhat" or "very") righteously aggrieved Zeus, Adam, and Samson are aligned against the beguiling and deceitful Hera, Eve, and Dalilah.

But what are we to make of the contradictory possibilities for meaning our discussion has so far opened up? The question is tricky precisely because the contradictions have not before been exposed. Dwelling only on Milton's copying of the *Iliad*, eighteenth-century commentators registered no difficulties with the passage. More recently, J.M. Evans simply posits a noncontradictory relationship between allusive context and simile. Referring to Milton's allusive use of the *Iliad*'s scene of immortal love-making in Book 9 of *Paradise Lost* and in its innocent counterpart in Book 4, Evans says: "The point of the allusion is that Hera had deliberately set out to distract Zeus's attention while his rival, Poseidon, assisted the Greeks. The love-making was a political manoeuvre on the wife's part; the husband was the dupe. Hence the balancing allusion to the biblical story of Samson's betrayal by Dalilah, the 'harlot' who sold her body for his secret. . . . The combined effect of these references, internal (to Book 4) and external (to the *Iliad* and Judges), is to make Adam and Eve's erotic siesta seem guilty and to confirm Eve's role as seductress."[9] Evans, author of *Paradise Lost and the Genesis Tradition*, the major scholarly treatment of this subject, here suppresses altogether *Paradise Lost*'s allusion to Genesis, which the Samson simile explicates; and it is obviously suppressed precisely because far from "balancing," the Genesis allusion, with its unequivocal "they," topples the whole structure. Aligning Hera, Dalilah, and Eve, Evans thus mediates a decidedly patriarchal construction of the text, while by minimizing its

---

[9] J. Martin Evans, ed., *John Milton, "Paradise Lost": Books IX-X* for the *Cambridge Milton for Schools and Colleges*, gen. ed. J. B. Broadbent (Cambridge, 1973), 173.

contradictions he also, simultaneously, produces a stabilizing, or phallogocentric, discourse.

Setting aside previous attempts to master this passage's allusive meanings, however, let us ask again what we are to make of the way the Samson simile's allusive context undermines its ostensible meaning. We could, if we wished to use New Critical terms, talk about the "tension" between the "correct" reading of the Samson simile and its error-inducing context. Invoking the figure of the author, and the psychological determinants the use of this figure sanctions, we could then refer this tension back to Milton's own ambivalence about the relations of the sexes. But we could also, much more appropriately, see in this remarkable instance of intertextuality the signs of an historically, not psychologically, determined ambivalence. In this case, the text would testify to the success with which a dominant patriarchal ideology, here represented by the overt allusion to the *Iliad*, is able to contain and defuse egalitarian sentiments, the limited expression of which might be encouraged, historically, by an emerging bourgeois family structure. To put this another way, the allusive context exposes what will increasingly become the merely formal or juridical status of the equality of the sexes in bourgeois society, an equality here elaborated in the Samson simile. The simile therefore acknowledges that both Adam and Eve are, technically, guilty; it defers to Genesis, signifying, according to the letter of the text, that the eyes of them both have been opened. But it does so in a context that indicates clearly that this does not really matter; that what *really* counts is what has happened to Adam, father of mankind, Man. That in *Paradise Lost* it is a patriarchal figure, Samson, to whom both Adam and Eve are compared is thus of crucial importance, ideologically; the syntactical priority of Samson to the "they" for whom he is a figure suggests that "Samson" functions in the slippery and misleading way the generic masculine still continues to do in our culture. *Paradise Lost* would thus seem to generate the counterpart in poetic discourse of the sexist linguistic practice that codes the word "man" equivocally to mean the generic humankind at the same time that, in context, it most often means exclusively the representative or exemplary male being. If we focus on the context that the allusion to the *Iliad* seems to provide, we find the ostensibly generic "man," as it were, being canceled by the masculine pronoun "he," which thereby undoes the equality *Paradise Lost* appeared, in the briefly enlightened simile, to endorse.

## IV

Up to this point, we have confined our discussion of Book 9's allusive use of the *Iliad*'s scene of immortal love-making to the ways in which *Paradise Lost* re-represents those features of Homer's representation that are basically dramatic, such as Zeus's verbal invitation to make love and his angry awakening, undeceived, into a verbal outburst. But there is another feature of Homer's representation of equal importance to *Paradise Lost* as well as to our discussion of the Samson simile's context: that is the descriptive passage in Book 14 of the *Iliad* in which the earth is presented as responding sympathetically to the sexual embrace of the two gods. The passage follows upon the concluding speech of the dialogue between Zeus and Hera:

> So speaking, the son of Kronos caught his wife in his arms.
> There underneath them the divine earth broke into young, fresh
> grass, and into dewy clover, crocus and hyacinth
> so thick and soft it held the hard ground deep away from them.
> There they lay down together and drew about them a golden
> wonderful cloud, and from it the glimmering dew descended.[10]

This very passage is cited by Comes, who points out that the sexual embrace as presented here by Homer is interpreted by allegorists as transferring generative heat from fire or ether, associated with the superior god, Zeus, to air, the lower but desirous element associated with Hera, thereby producing the fertile rains that can in their turn bring forth spring flowers.[11] In a different but related allegorical equation, not by any means regularly tied to this particular passage, Hera is thought to represent the earth itself. As one mythographer puts it: "and oftentimes also they take Juno for the earth, and in that respect acknowledged as the wife of Jupiter, in that (say they) there falleth from above a certaine powerfull and engendring seed on the earth, by whose strength and vertue it receiveth means and abilitie to bring forth, maintaine, and nourish what we see here produced."[12] The larger masculinist context for this equation is of course the

---

10 *Iliad*, trans. Richmond Lattimore (Chicago and London, 1951), 303. All further quotations from the *Iliad* are from this edition.

11 Natalis Comes, *Mythologie*, trans. J. de Moutlyard, rev. and ed. by Jean Baudouin (Paris, 1627; rpt. New York and London, 1976), vol. 1, 97-98. See also vol. 2, 1048-49.

12 Vincenzo Cartari, *The Fountaine of Ancient Fiction*, trans. R. Linche (London, 1599; rpt. Amsterdam and New York, 1973), l-lii.

etymological association of *materia* with *mater*, an association that lands us right back in the female lap. Developed philosophically, this equation permits Ficino to state that latent forms "ex materiae eruit gremio" [are brought forth from the lap of matter];[13] reassigned to a mythical figure, it enables Spenser to refer to Love's creative awakening in "Venus lap."[14] In a simpler, more directly mythic form, the lap of the sky-father's spouse appears in lines from Virgil's *Georgics* quoted by Comes and by modern editors of a passage from *Paradise Lost* to which we will now be turning: "tum pater omnipotens fecundis imbribus Aether / coniugis in gremium laetae descendit et omnis / magnus alit magno commixtus corpore fetus" ["Then Heaven, the Father almighty, comes down in fruitful showers into the lap of his joyous spouse, and his might, with her mighty frame commingling, nurtures all growths"].[15]

Although both of Juno's cosmological roles—air to Jupiter's ether or earth to his sky—are potentially present in a simile developed by Book 4 of *Paradise Lost*, it would seem that the former is more directly relevant. The simile self-consciously mythologizes the relation between Adam and Eve, who, having completed the first exchange that has been presented, ceremonially, to the reader, continue their conversation in an erotic embrace:

> hee in delight
> Both of her Beauty and submissive Charms
> Smil'd with superior Love, as *Jupiter*
> On *Juno* smiles, when he impregns the Clouds
> That shed May Flowers; and press'd her Matron lip
> With kisses pure.

(4.497–501)

As has frequently been remarked, the comparison would seem to want to elevate the already-elevated Adam and Eve, as well as to dignify the aggressively hierarchical nature of their relationship. Yet one of the reasons it can attempt these effects is that it does not function either overtly or covertly as an allusion to the scene of immortal

---

[13] Cited from *De Immortalitate Animorum*, 15.2, by John Erskine Hankins, *Source and Meaning in Spenser's Allegory* (London, 1971), 257.

[14] "Hymne in Honour of Love," ll. 57-63, in Spenser's *Minor Poems*, ed. Ernest De Selincourt (London, 1910; rpt. 1960), 438. Also cited by Hankins, *Source*, 258.

[15] Vergil, *Georgics*, 2.325-27; cited, for example, by Fowler in an annotation on *Paradise Lost* 4.499-501, *Milton*, 652.

love-making in the *Iliad*. Instead that scene is, as it were, veiled by the allegorical equations only tenuously related to it. It is true that in Book 14 of the *Iliad* and here in *Paradise Lost* the epic couples embrace after concluding a dialogue, and that in both the embrace is associated with the production of flowers. Yet this simile's flowers do not spring forth to provide Eve and Adam with a couch, but are quite clearly figurative flowers. And they are figurative perhaps because they testify to a creative potency that is not in any literal sense here enacted, Adam and Eve's embrace being an erotic not a fully sexual or potentially generative embrace (even though reproductive sexuality is clearly a part of *Paradise Lost*'s prelapsarianism).

As editors since Pope have pointed out, there are, however, two different passages where flowers clearly related to those in the *Iliad*'s scene of immortal love-making do make their appearance in the Edenic landscape of *Paradise Lost*. The more striking occurs in Book 8 where Adam tells the story of his courtship of Eve and of their marriage:

> To the nuptial Bow'r
> I led her blushing like the Morn: all Heav'n,
> And happy Constellations on that hour
> Shed thir selectest influence; the Earth
> Gave sign of gratulation, and each Hill;
> Joyous the Birds; fresh Gales and gentle Airs
> Whisper'd it to the Woods, and from thir wings
> Flung Rose, flung Odors from the spicy Shrub.
> (8.510–17)

Pope relates these lines to the *Iliad* by stating, "The Creation is made to give the same Tokens of Joy at the Performance of the nuptial Rites of our first Parents, as she does here at the Congress of *Jupiter* and *Juno*."[16] Closely associated, though not so vividly linked to the moment of sexual intercourse--which, significantly, does not actually get represented--is the following passage from the narrator's description of the "blissful bower" in Book 4:

> each beauteous flow'r,
> *Iris* all hues, Roses and Jessamin
> Rear'd high their flourisht heads between, and wrought

---

16 Pope, *Iliad*, 181.

Mosaic; underfoot the Violet,
Crocus, and Hyacinth with rich inlay
Broider'd the ground.
                                          (4.697–702)

Of these lines Pope says that they "are manifestly from the same Original;" and that "the very Turn of *Homer*'s Verses is observed, and the Cadence, and almost the Words, finely translated."[17]

Though Pope's delight in Milton's praiseworthy translation of Homer's verses is not communicated by modern editors, the relevance of Book 14 of the *Iliad* to these two passages in *Paradise Lost* is generally noted. Yet neither Pope nor subsequent editors ventures to explore the possible relations of these floral passages to the scene of love-making in Book 9 of *Paradise Lost*. Fowler alone mentions that the flowers making up Adam and Eve's "couch" in Book 9 "have *hyacinth* in common with those of the couch prepared by Earth for Zeus and Hera," pointing, besides, to the flowers of the nuptial bower in Book 4. But this is the extent of his commentary.[18] Tillyard actually criticizes the "insertion of the flowery bank" in Book 9's scene of love-making, calling it "strangely inept,"[19] while R. E. C. Houghton, who notes the allusion to the *Iliad* together with the contrast *Paradise Lost* sets up between Book 4 and Book 9, nevertheless can say that "the introduction of flowers here as well as there seems unsuitable, unless it is designed to set the change in the human pair against unchanging nature."[20]

Our earlier discussion of female laps alone suggests the utter inadequacy of these comments. Yet if we are to explore further the filiations of this gathering of epic flowers, we will need to look at some of the competing hermeneutical principles the scene of immortal love-making (not necessarily this Homeric scene alone) has been associated with. Although popular and many-lived, cosmological allegorizations such as those mentioned above have frequently been criticized. Both Plutarch and Origen, for example, mockingly reject such allegorical interpretations, but on grounds that are significantly different. Plutarch, speaking for an ethically based criticism, confidently assumes that the Homeric scene of lovemaking requires no

---

[17] Ibid., 182.

[18] *The Poems of John Milton*, ed. John Carey and Alastair Fowler (London and Harlow, 1968), 916.

[19] E.M.W. Tillyard, *Paradise Lost: Books IX and X* (London, 1960) 140.

[20] R.E.C. Houghton, *Paradise Lost: Books IX and X* (London, 1969), 171.

allegorization because its moral significance is transparent. The lesson that in his view it teaches is very much the one that Addison, Newton, and Pope are interested in, and which is implicit in the reading given the Samson simile by modern commentators, namely, that deceitful wives bring short-lived pleasure.[21] Yet Origen, writing from the more beleaguered position of an early Christian, is not at all sure that pagan texts are so innocent as this, singling out for special scorn a cosmological reading the Stoic Chrysippus gives a pictorial representation of Hera "performing unmentionable obscenities with Zeus" (presumably fellatio). According to this reading, which Origen clearly finds ludicrously defensive, Hera represents matter that is in the position of receiving the generative principles of Zeus or God.[22] Although Origen does not refer to the *Iliad*'s scene of divine love-making, Pope does in a remark that is not so confident of the innocence or moral purity of Homer's representation as the comments by him we have so far mentioned would seem to be. Comparing the scene in the *Iliad* with its counterpart in *Paradise Lost*, Pope praises Milton's imitation of Homer in the following manner: "But it is with wonderful Judgment and Decency he has used that exceptionable Passage of the Dalliance, Ardour, and Enjoyment: That which seems in *Homer* an impious Fiction, becomes a moral Lesson in Milton; since he makes that lascivious Rage of the Passion the immediate Effect of the Sin of our first Parents after the Fall."[23] The contrast Pope sets up here reveals the continuity of the Christian tradition's official disapproval of pagan scenes such as Homer's. It also suggests without explicitly saying so that Milton's copying is not mere copying but an appropriation and transformation.

But it is possible that Homer's scene of immoral immortal love-making has been transformed even more radically than Pope's comfortable moralizing of Milton's moralization of Homer supposes. Although Pope elsewhere in his annotations refers to Plato, in commenting on the story of Hera and Zeus he does not. Nor, for that matter, does any more recent critic, so far as I know. Yet it would certainly not be merely fanciful to suggest that the most influential and moralistic of commentators on Homer has mediated Milton's own

---

[21] Plutarch, "How the Young Man Should Study Poetry," *Moralia*, vol. 1, trans. Frank Cole Babbitt (Cambridge and London, 1927; rpt. 1960), 100-3. I am indebted for these references to Jean Pépin's discussion in *Mythe et Allégorie* (Paris, 1958), 181-84, 349, 454.

[22] Origen, *Contra Celsum*, trans. Henry Chadwick (Cambridge, 1953), 223.

[23] Pope, *Iliad*, 182.

appropriation. In Plato's critique of imitation in Book 3 of the *Republic*, Socrates, as is well known, takes Homer to task for representing the gods falsely, in ways unworthy of them and potentially dangerous to his audience. Among the numerous passages from Homer that Socrates singles out for censure is the sexual scene in Book 14 of the *Iliad*, of which he asks, is it really appropriate for young people to hear "how Zeus lightly forgot all the designs which he devised, awake while the other gods and men slept, because of the excitement of his passions, and was so overcome by the sight of Hera that he is not even willing to go to their chamber, but wants to lie with her there on the ground and says that he is possessed by a fiercer desire than when they first consorted with one another"?[24] What Plato is referring to here is that specific moment in the exchange between Hera and Zeus preceding their love-making in which Hera pretends to be reluctant to sleep openly on the peaks of Ida and proposes that they go to the "chamber" Hephaistos has built. In response, Zeus assures her they will not be seen where they are, for he will gather a "golden cloud" about them. It is at this point that he embraces her and that the earth reacts by breaking forth in floral vegetation. In the passage just quoted from the *Republic*, Plato gives the content of this exchange-as-foreplay (and, on Hera's part, as-cunning) a definite moral significance, yet one that does not save Homer's text, constructing an ethically coded contrast between making love in a "chamber" and casually, "on the ground," in order to stress the shameful shamelessness Homer has here, casually, depicted.

If Plato's moralization indeed structures Milton's allusive use of the *Iliad* in the passage from *Paradise Lost* we are here examining, then its intertextual complexity is even greater than our discussion has so far suggested. Critics have frequently commented on the carefully structured opposition between prelapsarian eroticism and Book 9's postlapsarian lust, and it has also been noted that in Book 9 Adam and Eve do not make it into their "blissful bower." As Fowler has remarked, the indefinite article "a" in "a shady bank" (9.1037) underlines the causal randomness of their choice of place.[25] Further, although this has not ever specifically been remarked, the passages in Books 4 and 8 that can be referred back to their "original" in Homer both have specific reference to the "blissful bower." The passage in Book 8 spiritualizes Homer's scene by having the Earth give "sign of

---

[24] Plato, *The Republic*, 3.390, B-C, trans. Paul Shorey, The Loeb Classical Library (Cambridge and London, 1953), 216-17.

[25] Fowler, *Milton*, 916.

Gratulation" at the nuptial union of Adam and Eve in their "nuptial Bow'r;" the passage in Book 4 describes, specifically, the floor of the bower that the "Sovran Planter" has set apart for his creatures: "underfoot the violet, / Crocus and Hyacinth with rich Inlay / Broider'd the Ground." In Book 9, however, the earth neither ceremonially participates in the love-making nor displays the signs of the artistically arranged naturalness making the ground of the blissful bower a different kind of "Couch." Although nature has participated sympathetically in the falls of both Eve and Adam, it is as if nature here is losing its capacity for response; rather than spontaneously gratulating their sexuality, nature is somehow, seductively, in a potentially ensnaring manner, simply there: "Flow'rs were the Couch, Pansies, and Violets, and Asphodel, / And Hyacinth, Earth's freshest softest lap."

Read in this way through Plato's mediating commentary, the main point of the Homeric allusions in Book 9 of *Paradise Lost* would now seem to be *not* the patriarchally structured polarity of male and female but instead the spiritually structured opposition between the sacred and the profane. The blissful bower, "a place / Chos'n by the sovran Planter" and consecrated for prelapsarian love-making, is the polar opposite of "a shady bank, / Thick overlaid with verdant roof embowr'd."[26] That it is specifically a "shady" bank clearly establishes its affinity with the *topos* of the regressive lap, but this *topos* now seems to have a new context, one that turns Adam and Eve's *al fresco* love-making on "Earth's freshest softest lap" into the polar opposite of the divinely sanctioned activity of making love on the "Broider'd" ground. Indeed, it is tempting to think that the figures of Samson and Dalilah with her "harlot-lap" were initially generated by the profane role played in this structure of oppositions by "Earth's freshest softest lap," the "lap"—rather the two laps—here signifying a lapse.

If this passage shows us Milton reading Homer through Plato's eyes, it probably also suggests a set of oppositions overlapping with that of the sacred and the profane. For Plato the sacred is of course associated with the realm of ideas, with the originals of which the realm of appearance and, *a fortiori*, artistic products are the profane and debased copies. Appropriated by *Paradise Lost*'s Christian Platonism, this becomes the opposition between a divinely created or

---

[26] John Hollander discusses the echoing relations of this "shady bank / Thick overlaid with verdant roof embowr'd" with the subsequent "Pillar'd shade / High overarch't" (9.1103-7), both, as he says, "imprinted with the shadowy type of death," and with Book 1's famous "where th' Etrurian shades / High overarch't imbower" (1.302-3), in *The Figure of Echo* (Berkeley and Los Angeles, 1981), 49.

original innocence and its fallen imitation. But the difference between original and copy, which gets translated into the difference between Book 4's prelapsarian sexuality and its fallen counterpart in Book 9, is a difference produced in *Paradise Lost* by Book 9's imitation of Homer's scene of immortal love-making in the *Iliad*. It is also produced by a kind of unveiling of the Homeric scene as the literary site of a sexual act that is simply and unquestionably just that. The allegorizing tradition invoked by the allusion to Jupiter and Juno in Book 4's simile is in Book 9 stripped away to reveal the representational literality of Homer's mimesis. This is a literality that Plato himself associates with drama and that Book 9 would also seem to mark as essentially dramatic, since it presents its generically tragic central *peripeteia* and *anagnorisis* in the context of an overt allusion that relies, for its overtness, on the likeness of dramatic situation and speech in the cases of Adam and Zeus. Yet as we have seen, Milton's imitation of the scene of immortal love-making in the *Iliad* is ultimately mediated by Plato's critique of representation. What Book 9 of *Paradise Lost* would therefore appear to give us is an imitation of a scene in the *Iliad*, which, subjected by Plato to an attack on its shameful debasing of its divine originals, is itself presented by *Paradise Lost* as a debased or fallen version, bringing forth shame in its actors, of its literary "original" in Book 4. To say, as eighteenth-century commentators do, that Milton here imitates or copies Homer, is thus entirely to miss the kind of logocentric critique of imitation that the scene, in this context, seems to constitute. Book 9's profane and self-implicated dramatic mimesis is radically dialectical, in that, by casting a Platonic doubt on the simple there-ness of its own mimesis, it attempts to preserve its moralizing discursive distance from the Fall.

It is possible to take this even further, and to argue that the dramatic imitation's two laps, by acknowledging their status as the fallen mimetic ground of the action represented, could really both be considered harlot-laps, since in the only two instances in Milton's poetic works besides this one where the term "harlot" is used, it is firmly associated, in good antitheatrical fashion, with a fallen and imitative status. (Obviously relevant here is the derivation of "meretricious" from "meretrix," prostitute or harlot.) In Book 4, in the hymn to "wedded love" sung when Adam and Eve enter their blissful bower to make love, the narrator contrasts this sacred original—an original that, as the narrator's very presence in phrases such as "I ween" reminds us, is *not* represented—with its profane and fallen copies:

> Here Love his golden shafts imploys, here lights
> His constant Lamp, and waves his purple wings,
> Reigns here and revels; not in the bought smile
> Of Harlots, loveless, joyless, unindear'd,
> Casual fruition, nor in Court Amours,
> Mixt Dance, or wanton Mask, or Midnight Ball,
> Or Serenate.
>
> (4.763–69)

Even more suggestively, in *Paradise Regained* the Son defends himself against Satan's temptation to devote himself to learning the wisdom of the Greeks by declaring:

> That rather Greece from us these Arts deriv'd;
> Ill imitated, while they loudest sing
> The vices of thir Deities, and thir own
> In Fable, Hymn, or Song, so personating
> Thir Gods ridiculous, and themselves past shame.
> Remove thir swelling Epithets thick laid
> As varnish on a Harlot's cheek, the rest,
> Thin sown with aught of profit or delight,
> Will far be found unworthy to compare
> With *Sion*'s songs.
>
> (4.338–47)

We are apparently not to notice that the Son articulates this Judaic version of the opposition between original and copy by drawing on Plato's critique of Homer, just as *Paradise Lost* does in representing, against its better knowledge, not deceived, Adam and Eve's lapse into a merely mortal lust.

But what do we do with the Samson simile now? This Platonic turn suggests a way of reading *Paradise Lost*'s allusions to the *Iliad* that leaves intact a nonsexist reading of the simile. If the *Republic* mediates Milton's use of Homer, then it would seem to provide us with a genuine *tertium quid*, one that permits us to acknowledge the presence of the potentially sexist allusive context but does not require that it signify as it has been thought to do. It could even be argued that Genesis and the *Republic*—or rather theology and philosophy— work together to effect a transformation (or *Aufhebung*) of the phallo-centric intertext established by the *Iliad*, Judges, and our fallen symbolic order, emptying the allusions of their representational and patriarchal content, and raising from the representational laps(e) a complex of abstract and spiritual significations.

Relying on Milton's Platonic (and therefore logocentric) critique of representation, such a reading would be able to lay claim to stable grounds for the Samson simile's intelligibility. It could do so, however, only by suggesting that theological, philosophical, and poetic discourses join forces in this passage to carve out a space in which abstract meanings appear as if in their original or unfallen transparency. And since the only guarantor of such a neutral, nonsexist transparency would be the textual self-consciousness posited by critical discourse, it is really critical discourse itself that would finally have to be the unacknowledged fourth partner in the work of saving the text. Both textual or authorial self-consciousness and the critical discourse that seeks to posit such consciousness by effacing itself are, of course, ultimately phallogocentric constructs. So while it might be tempting to argue that *Paradise Lost* is not only fully awake to the implications of its masculinist codes but knowingly and subtly transforms them, to do so would be to posit a textual self-consciousness as transhistorically vigilant as the Father's all-seeing eye.

As a quintessentially phallogocentric turn, this reading would also seek to sever the grounds of the simile's intelligibility from its troublesome laps. The misogynistic misreading of the Samson simile obviously needs to be challenged or corrected. But I would like to argue, in conclusion, that the challenge should not dress these laps up in modern, unisex wear. It is not just because they are irreducibly figurative that these laps should be permitted---in good poststructuralist fashion---to disturb the grounds of the text's intelligibility. It is also because, being irreducibly female, they bear the traces of the very same anonymous and nondiscursive forces that have played such a crucial role in the critical discourses mediating *Paradise Lost*'s reception.

That the commentators who have actively misread the Samson simile are near-contemporaries is evidence that we are not in any position to begin pretending we can transcend this reception's history. Further evidence can be found in *Ulysses*, a text that is to contemporary debates about the relations of the sexes and the nature of authorship and authority what for generations *Paradise Lost* has been. Molly Bloom's monologue concludes (in what some modernist and postmodernist theorists are happy to think of as a "feminine" refusal of closure) with recollections of a sexual experience which, like that of Zeus and Hera in the *Iliad*, and that of Adam and Eve in *Paradise Lost*, takes place outside the domestic enclosure, on a mountaintop (here, in a realist mode, the hill of Howth), amidst flowers (not hyacinths but rhododendrons). In a deeply ambiguous gesture, Molly gives Bloom "a bit of seedcake" out of her mouth: she both appropriates a kind of Zeus-like procreative activity and reenacts Eve's passing of the apple to Adam.[27] *Ulysses* ends here, with Bloom's "mountain flower" (the text's "Gea-Tellus," Joyce's "Ewig-Weib-liche") rehearsing the scene of seduction while responding, as if end-lessly, in the affirmative. Since *Ulysses,* then, too, in a way overlaps with Book 9's central passage, a feminist critical discourse could just decide that for the time being *Paradise Lost* might as well occupy that discursive space or *lapsus* that is intertextuality itself.

---

[27] Richard Ellmann comments on the possible correspondence between Molly and Eve here in *Ulysses on the Liffey* (New York, 1972), 168-69.

МНИС АХІΛΗΟС

Figure 4. The Wrath of Achilles. Antoine Coypel.

# Homeric Themes In Racine's Andromache and Iphigenia

*Noémi Hepp*
*Translated by Katherine King and Paul Faria*

It is with less perplexity, since we know his *Notes on the Odyssey* and his annotations on the *Iliad*, that we approach the dramatic transposition of Homer that Racine has done in *Iphigenia*.[1] But one should recall beforehand how the young dramatist—still an undistinguished novice, who had just reread the *Iliad*—balanced numerous Homeric echoes in his first brilliant tragedy, *Andromache*. Uniquely among the works that concern us here, *Andromache*'s plot strictly speaking has nothing to do with the Trojan War, although it is animated by the Trojan myth and strengthened by Homer. Thus we speak of echoes, or better yet, reflections: the story of Troy lives in the heart of each of the heroes and is there reflected in accordance with what each one is. It therefore presents very diverse aspects that together form a tableau of numerous planes, with hues that are warm, deep, intense and at the same time always distant. For Hermione, powerless, humiliated, the Trojan War is the triumph of one woman:

> What! without her having to entreat a single time,
> My mother armed all of Greece in her favor.
> In ten years of combat for her sake, her eyes
> saw perish twenty kings whom they knew not . . . (V,2).

---

[1] The author has devoted the preceding pages to Fontaine's utilization of the *Iliad* in his uncompleted *Achille*.

To the inert Orestes, who does nothing but "drag from sea to sea (his) chains and troubles" (I,1), the war is action, a clash through which privileged people managed to escape emptiness, failure, oblivion:

> Yes, let us go, madame;
> Let us once more set all Greece in flames;
> Let us take, blazoning my arm and your name,
> You, Helen's place, and I, Agamemnon's;
> Let us awake Troy's miseries in this country
> And may one speak of us as well as of our fathers (IV, 3).[2]

To Andromache, who has buried her heart in Hector's tomb, the Trojan War is the end to all hope and ambition, both national and personal. She says to Pyrrhus, who enables her to glimpse Astyanax's restoration to his forefathers' throne

> Sir, so much greatness touches us no longer,
> I held out such hopes only while his father lived.
> Nay, no longer expect to see us again,
> Sacred walls that my Hector failed to keep! (I,4)[3]

But Troy is to her also a legion of beloved and venerated dead, with whom she mysteriously keeps in contact:

> Did you think Andromache unfaithful enough
> To betray a husband who thinks to live again in her,
> And that, with so many dead awaking pain
> Care for my own repose would make me trouble theirs? (IV,1).

So she confides to Cephissa.

In the story of the Trojan War, two heroes are prominent, Achilles and Hector. Achilles, victim of Agamemnon's injustice, figures in Pyrrhus's discourse to Orestes:

> May they search for a second Troy in Epirus:
> May they confound their hate and distinguish no longer

---

2 Perhaps here Racine recalls those strange words Helen says to Hector: "Zeus has reserved for us an evil fate, so that later we might serve as poetic inspiration to future men" (*Il.* 6.357-358).

3 Pyrrhus comes around to this way of thinking when, before Orestes, he adopts Andromache's cause (I,2.197-204).

The blood that made them conquer from that of the vanquished.
This is as well not the first injustice
With which Greece has paid Achilles' service.
Hector profited from it, Sir, and some day, too,
His son might well profit in his turn (I,2).

Achilles, arbiter of the destiny of the Greeks, is exalted by Hermione in the brief moment when she believes she will marry his son:

Do you think that Pyrrhus fears? And whom does he fear?
People who for ten years fled before Hector,
Who a hundred times, frightened by Achilles' absence,
Sought asylum in their burning vessels,
And whom one would see still, without help from his son,
Demanding Helen from the unpunished Trojans? (III,3).

By unleashing his fury on Hector, Achilles left Andromache an indelible memory:

Ought I to forget Hector deprived of a funeral
And dragged without honor about our walls? (III,8).[4]

But she also remembers the way Achilles, soothed by Priam, returned the body he had desecrated, and, side by side with the image of a furious Achilles, she retains another of a different sort, of a great-souled hero:

Once a humbled Priam was respected by Achilles:
I expected of his son yet more kindness . . .
In spite of himself I did believe him magnanimous (III,6).

And also:

to respect the misery of an enemy,
To spare the unfortunate, return a son to his mother . . .
Sir, these are cares worthy of the son of Achilles (I,4).

Pyrrhus is to Andromache, and not only to Andromache, a kind of image of Achilles himself. She recognizes in him strengths and

---

[4] A detail here has Vergilian and not Homeric origin: in fact, in the *Iliad*, Achilles drags Hector's body only around Patroclus's tomb (*Iliad* 24.14-18), but in the *Aeneid* he drags it around the walls of Troy (*Aeneid*. 1.483).

weaknesses similar to his father's: "I know what Pyrrhus is: violent but
sincere" (IV,1).[5]

Orestes addresses him as the son of Achilles, as the worthy rival
of that hero (I,2); Hermione, as we have already seen, thinks that
Pyrrhus fears the Greeks no more than Achilles did (III,3). Pyrrhus
remains loyal to his father and his behavior sometimes subtly evokes
Achilles. Does not his indignation at the attempt to reclaim Astyanax,
who has fallen to him as part of his share of the booty, evoke Achilles'
outrage at Agamemnon's seizure of Briseis?

> Has Greece any further right upon his life?
> And alone of all the Greeks, is it not permitted me
> To dispose of a prisoner whom fate has assigned me? (I,2).[6]

In the sudden and sadistic flash of joy that traverses him at the
thought that Andromache will die of grief at his destruction of her
son, does one not see a replay of Achilles' pursuing Hector?

> I turn over her son. How many tears shall flow!
> By what name shall her grief call me!
> What a sight is arranged for her today!
> It will kill her, Phoenix, and I shall be the cause.
> It is as if I thrust a dagger to her bosom (II,5).[7]

Thus an Achilles humiliated yet all-powerful, an Achilles blood-
thirsty yet open, at least once, to pity, appears by turns in *Andromache*, in a way that is all the more striking in each circumstance
because intense emotion animates those who speak of him and
because past actions of the dead hero are resuscitated, as it were, by
the ardor of those who evoke him.

Next to awe-inspiring Achilles, there is the strong, gentle, wise
Hector. No longer gentle and wise in the eyes of all, he too offers var-

---

[5] As for Achilles' sincerity, compare *Iliad* 9.312-313. Many critics have
already pointed out the psychological kinship between Pyrrhus and his father, particu-
larly R. C. Knight, *Racine et la Grece*, pp. 275-276, and K. Wais, *Racine, der Achilleus
Helens Kontrast . . . in Franzoesische Marksteine . . .* Berlin, 1958, gd in-8th, pp. 1-32.
Mr. Wais's thesis is that not only does Achilles live again in Pyrrhus, but so does
Helen in Hermione, her daughter, and Hector in Andromache, his widow. Entirely
constructed in relation to the *Iliad*, *Andromache*, which must lead to the reign of
Astyanax in Epirus, will mark the reconciliation between Greece and Troy. We find it
difficult to follow Mr. Wais in the whole of his thesis.

[6] Compare *Iliad* 9.335-336.

[7] Compare *Iliad* 22.269-272.

ious visages and remains, in the memory of the Greeks, a redoubtable warrior.

> Do you not remember, Sir, who Hector was?
> Our weakened peoples remember him still.
> His name alone makes tremble our widows and daughters . . .
> And who knows what his son might accomplish one day?
> Perchance we shall see him descend on our ports,
> Such as we saw his father scorch our vessels
> And, torch in hand, pursue them over the seas (I,2).[8]

This is how the Greek spokesman argues before Pyrrhus. Yet still more often it is Hector's widow who speaks of him. To Pyrrhus she recalls his heroism:

> His death alone has rendered your father immortal,
> He owes to Hector's blood all his martial glory (I,4).

To Hermione she evokes his benevolence:

> Alas! when weary after ten years of misery
> The Trojans in wrath threatened your mother,
> I was able to get my Hector to help her (III,4).

To Cephisa she speaks of his marital tenderness, never belied even in his heroic ardor:

> Alas, I recall the day when his courage
> Made him seek Achilles, nay, his death.
> He asked for his son, then *took him in his arms:*
> Dear wife, he said *as he dried my tears,*
> *I know not what fate awaits my arms;*
> I leave you my son as pledge of my faith:
> Should he lose me, may he have me in you—
> If you hold dear the memory of a happy marriage,
> Show your son to what point you cherished his father (III,8).[9]

---

[8] Compare *Iliad* 12.440ff and 15.718ff. The scene that Orestes describes here of setting fire to the vessels does not exactly conform with Homer's version. As Mr Knight writes, "The vessels which Hector had attacked , quite small and easy to tow, were drawn up on the shore. Racine seems to have in mind, perhaps for the pleasure of his public, moored galleys like those of the French navy" (*op. cit.* p. 282).

[9] We highlight what is borrowed from *Iliad* 6.474, 485, 487-89. The rest is Racine's creation.

And it seems to her that she and her son have nothing more beautiful or necessary to accomplish than to prolong Hector's presence on earth: "Should he lose me, may he have me in you" she sings to herself from the bottom of her heart. Because Racine did not wish to make her the pathetic widow of the *Iliad*, to whom the husband before dying said no πυκινόν ἔπος, a close word to be remembered night and day amid her tears (*Iliad* 24.744–745), he has fulfilled the hope that Homer had left forever frustrated. Similarly, he has replaced the mother's fears for the orphan vulnerable to any and all insult with the hope Andromache expresses of regaining Hector in his son: "He would have taken the place of a father and a husband" (I,4).[10]

The unsullied hero who thus appears "a fearless irreproachable knight" is himself quite vivid in *Andromache*, although the light shed over him is one of nostalgia, of profound and loyal love, in complete opposition to the rough and disturbing glints shed by the memory of Achilles. More specifically, if the fidelity to Homer is not without flaw—especially in the final verses cited above where Racine, in his desire to give harmony and serenity of heart to his heroine, takes her well beyond the tragic mood of the life proposed for her in the *Iliad*—there is no doubt that the dramatist has aptly transposed in this work much of the real atmosphere of Homer's poem, particularly of the contrast between the hero of the Danaans and that of the Trojans. This is a unique accomplishment in the French theater of the seventeenth century, one which Racine himself will not repeat when he comes to extract from the *Iliad* the quarrel between Achilles and Agamemnon. Yet there is no great mystery in this. It was for all practical purposes impossible to give Homer's heroes substance, to display them on stage, to make them talk, to give them the full dimensions of a living and effective human being during a time when tastes were so far removed from anything that is primitive and when so many constraints, conscious or otherwise, were imposed. The few verses of *Andromache* in which Racine has given Hector speech reinforce this view. On the other hand, it was possible to render these heroes recognizable by playing with veils, to give them an existence that was filtered through the consciousness of others without displaying them directly. By so doing—at least if one was a Racine—it was possible to return them to the realm of poetry. Racine knew the *Iliad* very well, having read it with an eagle's eye, yet he shows in *Andromache* little more than phantoms of Troy, of Achilles, of Hector, taking only

---

[10] This verse is in total opposition to *Iliad* 22.485-507.

certain traits of theirs and not delineating their contours. A great shadow, or perhaps a luminous mist, never ceases to envelop them. That is why this tragedy seems so accomplished in respect to the usage of Homer, as in all other respects. All that is derived from the *Iliad*, magnified by absence and death and vivified by the emotions of the survivors, is harmonized in true and profound agreement with the grandeur of the ancient poem.

\* \* \*

Racine rejected for his *Iphigenia* the strange Achilles that Euripides offered him. What to do with this character who is prudent, contemplative and minimally active, who himself judges it inopportune to intervene with Agamemnon in order to save Iphigenia, and who, at the moment when the young girl decides to submit to sacrifice out of love for Greece and respect for the gods, admires her soul's nobility and envies her? For once, one of Homer's heroes seemed to behave in a way that was appropriate to the Court and the city, and it is in the *Iliad* that Racine searches for his Achilles in defiance of Euripides.

Reminiscences of the *Iliad* abound in *Iphigenia*: for example, the nightly dreams sent by the gods to Agamemnon (*Iphigenia* I,1),[11] the role given to Ulysses to prevent the disbandment of the army by its chief (I,1),[12] the affirmation that the Greek triumph over Troy will become "An eternal topic of discussion for future generations (I,5).[13] One might add allusions to Patroclus, one in particular that reworks an idea explicitly expressed in the *Iliad*: Achilles is so eager to conquer Troy that he declares to Agamemnon: "And even though I might have to beseige her alone, / Patroclus and I, Sir, shall avenge you" (I,2).[14] There are also the allusions to Achilles' fate: "The choice is given me between many years without glory, / Or limited days followed by lasting fame" (I,2).[15] None of these appears in *Iphigenia in Aulis*.

---

[11] *Iliad* 2.1-40.

[12] *Iliad* 2.110-211. In Euripides, it is Menelaos who opposes abandoning the expedition.

[13] On the subject of *Andromache* we earlier cited *Iliad* 6.357-358, the lines Racine has in mind here.

[14] *Iliad* 16.97-100; the other allusion to Patroclus is in V,2.

[15] *Iliad* 9.410-416. In the same scene, I,2, right before Achilles pronounces the quoted verses, Agamemnon had alluded to this prediction.

Racine's most important borrowings, however, have to do with Achilles' character and his quarrel with Agamemnon. The great scene 6 of Act IV is obviously essential in this respect, but the quarrel can be said to cast a kind of radiance over the tragedy. Before it takes place, Eriphile wishfully evokes it:

> Oh Doris, what joy! . . .
> (If) I could arm Agamemnon against Achilles,
> If their hatred, forgetting their quarrel with Troy,
> Would turn against themselves the iron they sharpen against
>      her (IV,1).

After it becomes reality, the quarrel constitutes a new reason for Agamemnon to allow his daughter to meet the sacrificial knife:

> little watchful of my glory
> Must I grant victory to proud Achilles?
> His fearsome pride, which I shall redouble,
> Will believe that I yield, that he makes me tremble (IV,8).

Achilles is likewise stiffened to the utmost by his clash with the king of kings; Arcas describes his behavior to Clytemnestra as follows:

> The fated sacrifice is still suspended.
> They threaten, they run, the air moans, the iron shines,
> Achilles positions around your daughter
> All those friends ready to die for him...
> He himself wishes with his own hand, steaming with
> Blood, to return his beloved to your arms (V,5).

Let us now concentrate on this Homeric "core" that constitutes scene 6 of Act IV, or at least its second part. It is certainly Homeric on several counts. The situation is analogous: the point is, in both cases, to determine whether Achilles or Agamemnon has rights over a young girl or young woman whom Achilles loves. The proportion of forces is analogous: Achilles has all the power, and in both cases he prevails, but he may end up having to pay since his adversary has right on his side and is furthermore by character a more consistent man. The movement is analogous: Achilles attacks, threatening to retire if his cause is not heard; Agamemnon replies by raising a challenge: "Flee then . . ."; he has others to count on and cares little about Achilles' threats. In defeat, Achilles refuses to give free reign to his wrath, and a more powerful force makes him still respect his detested chief. On the level of details, too, one can find a significant number of points borrowed from the *Iliad,* from books 1 and 9 both: Achilles has no personal grievance against the Trojans, and his only reason for going to war against them is his espousal of Agamemnon's cause;[16] Agamemnon dreads his subordinate's upsetting pride;[17] Agamemnon has promised his daughter to Achilles;[18] Achilles will perish under the wall of Troy;[19] and since the war takes place to return his wife to Menelaos, it is illogical to force from Achilles the woman he loves.[20] Never has Racine set himself to imitate to such length a scene from Homer, and his imitation is careful. Nevertheless, once we set up this list of borrowings, the most striking thing is not how Homeric this scene is but to what extent it is not.

Indeed, if in both cases a woman is the object of the quarrel, only Racine's Achilles can be considered in love, love is truly a motive only for him. Love not only motivates his current anger—while Homer's Achilles is angry only because of wounded pride—but before this it had motivated his joining the forces on their way to beseige Troy— while his model had come in order "to please Agamemnon" and especially, it would seem, for love of war—and, at the end of the scene it is what motivates his respectful behavior ("Be thankful for the single knot that restrains my anger, I still respect Iphigenia's father") instead of the religious feeling that stays the arm of the *Iliad*'s offended warrior. Whatever this Achilles does is inspired by his love for Iphigenia; the hero he most resembles is not the Achilles of the *Iliad* but Artamenes of the *Great Cyrus.*

One may also note that Racine has brought many more emotions into this scene than existed in the scene he imitates. A simple glance at our references makes this fact apparent, for Racine's dialogue includes an idea taken from Book 1 that goes farther than the imitated passage and, in addition, three elements that in the original are in Book 9 and therefore do not figure in the quarrel between Achilles and Agamemnon. But Racine has added elements beyond these obvious ones. Thus, not only does Achilles go to seek death in Troy, but also, in so doing, he shows himself "Deaf to the voice of an

---

[16] Compare *Iliad* 1.152-160.

[17] Compare *Iliad* 1.286-289.

[18] Compare *Iliad* 9.283-288.

[19] Compare *Iliad* 9.410-417.

[20] Compare *Iliad* 9.337-343.

immortal mother / And heedless of his dismayed father's wishes,"
which the *Iliad* does not intimate. Achilles recalls not only martial but
also diplomatic activity: "You whom I helped name both their chief
and mine, / You whom my arm avenged in burning Lesbos," a passage which has no source, at least for the first verse, either in Homer
or Euripides. He evokes a covenant with Iphigenia: "Your daughter
pleased me, I aspired to please her. / She is the sole repository of my
oaths"—while Homer's Achilles refuses Agamemnon's daughter (*Iliad*
9.386–391), and Euripides' Achilles had never considered marrying
the young woman whose name he barely knew. On his part, Agamemnon evokes the oracle according to which Troy could not be taken
without the aid of Achilles:

> Plenty of others will submit to my orders,
> Cover themselves with laurels promised you.
> And, forcing destiny with successful exploits,
> Will forge for Ilium its day of doom.

All this creates a text that is extremely dense, dramatically very effective, and totally opposed to Homer's spirit.
    Simultaneous with this gain in affective density there is a clear
gain in logic. In order to weave a plot more weighted with ideas as
well as to enrich the gamut of emotion, the dramatist resorts to
Homeric passages that are foreign to the quarrel—for example, since
the war is waged to revenge insulted love, Achilles says that those who
wage it cannot allow one of their own to be mocked in his love (compare *Iliad* 9.337–343); and Agamemnon replies that pride in subordinates is what a chief detests most (compare *Iliad* 1.286–289).
Elsewhere he eliminates a development in the *Iliad*. Thus in *Iphigenia*
Agamemnon's tirade begins and ends on the same idea:

> Flee then. Return to your Thessaly. . . .
> Flee, I fear not your ineffectual wrath,
> And I sever all bonds that tie me to you,

while in Homer this idea recurs two times but the tirade does not end
with it.[21] In addition, Racine feels obliged to eliminate all that is
somewhat vague in Homer, all that gives the impression of being

---

[21] This idea is expressed in *Iliad* 1.173, then in 179-180, but Agamemnon's
tirade continues until verse 187.

dreamlike, as he also eliminates all that smacks of familiarity in order to create an aura of consistent nobility. We saw above Racine's description of the Cyclops' kids and bowls; here, prevalent taste forces him to suppress all that deals with material things. How could his Achilles speak of booty and of the manner in which it was distributed among the Greeks following each battle (*Iliad* 1.166–168)? How could he explain that never in fertile Phthia had the Trojans stolen from him either cows or mares or harvest (*Iliad* 1.154–156)? Racine will never make mention of booty; as for the goods which the Trojans never attempted to seize, the passage must become "Did ever in Larissa a dastardly abductor / come to take either my wife or my sister?" (*Iliad* 1.149).[22] More important than these details, however, is the ennobling transformation of the relationship between Achilles and Agamemnon. Granted, *Iphigenia*'s Achilles detests Agamemnon as much or more than that of the *Iliad*, and yet he does not insult him. "Oh truly, profit-seeker clothed in arrogance" (*Iliad* 1.149) becomes "Fair heavens! Can I hear and suffer this language? / Can he thus add insult to injury?" The emotion is no weaker but the tone is much different. Anaphora and rhetorical questions throughout the scene give it a perfect decorum, and Achilles shows himself constantly aware of his powers and obligations. The warrior's wrath has been cloaked in courtly habits.

If the fundamental motivation of Achilles' behavior is different, if the dramatic atmosphere has been powerfully concentrated, if the logical rigor has strongly increased at the same time as the nobility of tone, will the transformations not end up weighing more heavily than the borrowings? This is an interesting question, although our personal answer is not doubtful. But what remains certain is that Racine instituted all these arrangements in full awareness; the same question that we posed with La Fontaine without being able to answer, with Racine we find enough clues to arrive at an answer: he knew and appreciated quite well the values of the Homeric universe, and he was equally aware that those values were not transmittable to the audience for which he wrote. He substituted other values for use by this public. We could say of him as Hermione did of Pyrrhus: "He wills all that he does." He does not, however, believe all that he says when he writes the preface to *Iphigenia*:

---

[22] The Homeric Achilles speaks of Phthia but names no villages. It is in Vergil that Racine finds the expression "Larissaeus Achilles" (*Aeneid* 2.197).

I gladly recognized from the effect produced on our
theatre by all that I have copied from Homer and
Euripides that good taste and reason were the same
in all centuries.  Parisian taste conforms with that of
Athens.

No, Paris and Athens definitely have not the same taste, and Racine
knew that better than anyone.

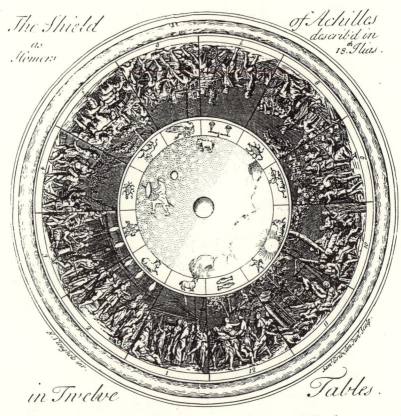

Figure 5. Achilles's shield. Jean Boivin and Nicolas Vleughels.

# Homer's Iliad and Pope's Vile Forgery

*Kathryn L. Lynch*

What is the purpose of a translation? Should it, as Matthew Arnold contends, reproduce "the movement and general effect" of its original?[1] Or should it, in Douglas Knight's words, merely maintain "some ordered relation" to its text?[2] Undoubtedly the aims of translation differ from age to age. Vladimir Nabokov, perhaps the most extreme advocate of the modern "servile path," concedes that he forfeits elements of form to achieve "total accuracy and completeness of meaning."[3] This sacrifice of form would have seemed a "pedantic" aberration to Pope and his contemporaries. Even Richard Bentley's famous attack on Pope's *Homer* did not fault it for the level of its diction or for its heroic couplets; as Richmond Lattimore observes, "Neither Bentley nor Pope would have considered any verse form more appropriate."[4] For the Augustans, form was a necessary component of meaning.

There are, of course, many other differences between the twentieth century attitude toward the translator's role and the Augustan viewpoint. While Pope might count on his public for some small familiarity with Homer's Greek, a modern translator can no longer depend on his reader's classical knowledge. The kind of his-

---

[1] "On Translating Homer," in *Essays Literary and Critical* (New York and London, 1906) p. 271; hereafter cited in the text.

[2] *Pope and the Heroic Tradition* (New Haven, Conn., 1951), p. 4.

[3] "The Servile Path," in *On Translation,* ed. Reuben Brower (1959; rpt. New York, 1966), p. 97.

[4] "Practical Notes on Translating Greek Poetry," in *On Translation, p. 54.*

torical scholarship prevalent in the last two hundred years has distanced us from Homer; current linguistic theory has made the pre-
sent-day translator skeptical about his ability to capture Homer's
"Poetical Fire." Pope works within the unbroken heroic tradition of
Virgil and Milton, certain that nothing less than the idiom of the Latin
and English epics will approximate Homer's "Rapture."

Despite these changes, Pope's aspirations as a translator are basically closer to Arnold's desire for a "reproduction" than to Knight's
for an "ordered relation." Most translators, whether Augustan or
modern, believe they are doing more than allowing their world and
that of the original "a mutual or shared life."[5] In his Preface to his
*Iliad*, Pope writes, "It is certain no literal Translation can be just to an
excellent Original in a superior Language: but it is a great Mistake to
imagine (as many have done) that a rash Paraphrase can make
amends for this general Defect . . . I know no Liberties one ought to
take, but those which are necessary for transfusing the Spirit of the
Original, and supporting the Poetical Style of the Translation" (VII,
17). Although Pope's prefatory comments are not the last word on his
intentions as a translator, this goal of "transfusing the Spirit of the
Original" is consistently expressed in his letters and notes on the *Iliad*.

Undoubtedly his understanding of the "Original" as well as his
approach to style are Augustan rather than modern. Even as moderns,
we have no guarantee that our own vision is correct. Twentieth-
century scholars, attempting to be "fair" to Pope, have unanimously
avoided any evaluative judgment of his *Iliad*. We now have evidence
that Pope's Greek was adequate to his task.[6] There is no reason why
we cannot assess his translation for its success in reproducing Homer
within the semantic and ideological constraints of his time. Pope's
conception of Homer's poem and many of his stylistic devices differ
widely from those of his contemporaries. To see Pope's *Iliad*, as
Knight does, solely as representative of the "Augustan mode" of
translating is to miss its unique aspects.

The Augustan impulse is to alter Homer in the direction of
generalization. All of Homer's translators, Pope included, "misunder-
stand" the function of the simile in the Greek epic. Influenced by the

---

[5] Douglas Knight, "Pope's *Iliad*," in *The Iliad, Books I-IX*, trans. Alexander
Pope, ed. Maynard Mack, Vol. VII of the Twickenham Edition of the *Poems of
Alexander Pope* (New Haven, Conn., 1967), p. cxciii. Unless noted otherwise quota-
tions from Pope, cited in the text, are from this edition.

[6] Among other evidence, see Norman Callan, "Pope's *Iliad*: A New Document," in *Essential Articles for the Study of Alexander Pope*, ed. Maynard Mack (Ham-
den, Conn., 1964), pp. 593-610.

*Aeneid* and by *Paradise Lost*, the similes of translators in the seventeenth and eighteenth centuries had the effect of defining the poem's action against a background of similarities and oppositions; as Arnold says, "Where Homer marks separation by moving away, Pope marks it by antithesis" (p. 219). Modern scholarship suggests that Homer's similes create a pause in action meant to intensify description by providing contrast, but the earlier translator finds in the simile a means of understanding the specific by its relation to the general. The simile becomes an allusive technique, a way of placing action by deepening its resonance—discovering, for example, what Menelaos' wound has in common with a horse's ornamental "cheek piece"; as Pope reveals in a note, "this implies that the honourable wounds of a Heroe are the beautiful Dress of War" (IV.170n).

Pope epitomizes this characteristically Augustan allusiveness, this impulse to generalize by seeing events in their larger context. Standing at the culmination of an allusive tradition, Pope's poetry is stronger and more extensive in its generalizing force than any previous verse. He reflects this quality in the construction of his couplets and in the structure of his entire translation. Pope's couplets, for instance, are the most balanced and epigrammatic of his age. Arnold notes that while couplets duplicate the rapidity of Homer's hexameter, the "rhyme inevitably tends to pair lines which in the original are independent, and thus the movement of the poem is changed" (p. 218). Not all rhymed couplets, however, halt the reader as do Pope's. Compare these lines from Book I of Pope's *Iliad* with Lattimore's translation and with Dryden's version, also in heroic couplets:

> Thus *Chryses* pray'd: the fav'ring Pow'r attends,
> And from *Olympus'* lofty Tops descends.
> Bent was his Bow, the *Grecian* Hearts to wound;
> Fierce as he mov'd, his Silver Shafts resound.
> Breathing Revenge, a sudden Night he spread,
> And gloomy Darkness roll'd around his Head.
>                              (I.61–66)

> So he spoke in prayer, and Phoibos Apollo heard him,
> and strode down along the pinnacles of Olympos, angered
> in his heart, carrying across his shoulders the bow and the
> hooded quiver; and the shafts clashed on the shoulders of the
> god walking angrily. He came as night comes down and knelt
> then apart and opposite the ships and let go an arrow.[7]

---

[7] Homer, *Iliad*, trans. Richmond Lattimore (Chicago, 1951), I.43-48; here-

He pray'd, and Phoebus, hearing, urg'd his flight,
With fury kindled, from Olympus' height;
His quiver o'er his ample shoulders threw,
His bow twang'd, and his arrows rattled as they flew.
Black as a stormy night, he rang'd around
The tents, and compass'd the devoted ground.[8]

Dryden's lines include more of the circumstantial detail present in the Greek than do Pope's. In addition Pope's couplets do more violence to the movement of Homer's poetry. Pope structures these lines carefully; the caesura always falls after the second beat and marks the change from description to action ("Bent was his Bow, | the Grecian Hearts to wound"). Each couplet has a self-sufficiency that forces the reader to pause at its close. Dryden moves with a narrative energy similar to Homer's. In this passage, the enjambment in Dryden's first and third couplets requires the reader to move past the first line in order to complete the syntax. We do not feel each rhyme "resound" but are rather "urg'd" forward in the poetic "flight." This is not to say that Dryden's poetry is better; he simply provides a contrast against which to judge Pope's form more clearly.

The balance typical of Pope's couplets derives from his use of a kind of linguistic parallelism. Richard Ohmann notices in the prose of George Bernard Shaw a similar quality which he discusses in his essay "Modes of Order": "A kind of axiom for interpreting human artifacts might go, 'Things are not placed together without reason,' or 'Proximity implies similarity' . . . tight parallelism, through the juxtaposition of identical linguistic frames (grammatical forms) whose slots are filled with different words, clearly signals a collation of meanings."[9] Pope structures his couplets by balancing semantic units. The first two lines in our selection from Pope end with "attends" and "descends." The rhyming words occupy an identical linguistic frame, both grammatically and in their location in the line. Pope exploits this positional similarity to stress that in order for Apollo to hear or "attend" Chryses, he must "descend." In other words, the gods are dis-

---

after cited in the text. Lattimore's translation is quite literal. For references to the original Greek, I follow The Oxford Classical Text Edition, ed. David Monro and Thomas Allen (Oxford, 1902).

8 John Dryden, "The First Book of Homer's *Ilias*," in *The Poetical Works of John Dryden*, ed. George R. Noyes (Cambridge, Mass., 1909), I.67-72.

9 "Modes of Order," in *Linguistics and Literary Style*, ed. Donald C. Freeman (New York, 1970), pp. 215, 217.

tant from men. Not only is there no authority in the Greek for either word, there is no precedent for this emphasis on the remoteness of the gods. By comparing these two words Pope suggests, even on the syntactical level, a "collation of meanings" that more severely distorts the text than Dryden's juxtaposition of "flight" and "height."

Each line of one of Pope's couplets comprises a linguistic frame, the second commonly restating the first. However, "gloomy Darkness" not only rephrases "sudden Night" but also generalizes it. The specific motive, "Revenge," is breathed first into "Night" and widens finally into the more universal "Darkness." Even the couplets whose second lines do not expand the meaning of the first progress to their own brand of generalization. "Bent was his Bow" parallels the succeeding "Fierce as he mov'd." In the Greek there is no syntactical association of Apollo's anger with his bow and arrows. In Pope's version, Apollo's bow becomes implicitly the instrument of wrath and is raised to the generic weapon. Any linguistic comparison necessarily requires of the reader a search for common ground. One thing is like another; we are forced to uncover underlying similarities. Although as Knight rightly observes, this generic contest enriches Pope's verse and is partly responsible for the rapidity of his couplets, Dryden's less resonant lines are in this respect more Homeric.

Achilles' distress when Agamemnon steals away Briseis becomes in Pope a kind of "Rage," which only the generalized "Reason" can oppose. The movement is away from Achilles' specific anger and toward the hero's "strong and ruling Faculty" (Preface, p. 5).

> *Achilles* heard, with Grief and Rage opprest,
> His Heart' swell'd high, and labour'd in his Breast.
> Distracting Thoughts by turns his Bosom rul'd,
> Now fir'd by Wrath, and now by Reason cool'd:
> That prompts his Hand to draw the deadly Sword,
> Force thro' the *Greeks,* and pierce their haughty Lord;
> This whispers soft his Vengeance to controul,
> And calm the rising Tempest of his Soul. (I.251–58)

> So he spoke. And the anger came on Peleus' son, and within
> his shaggy breast the heart was divided two ways, pondering
> whether to draw from beside his thigh the sharp sword, driving
> away all those who stood between and kill the son of Atreus,
> or else to check the spleen within and keep down his anger.
> (Lattimore, I.188–92)

Achilles then with extream greif opprest,
Felt mighty struglings in his manly Breast;
Whether he should draw forth revengefull Steele,
Break through them all, and Agamemnon kill;
Or else himself compose, and wrath asswage.[10]

Pope's couplets are here contrasted with Ogilby's (1660). Although Ogilby's "revengefull Steele" is at least as foreign to Homer as Pope's "deadly Sword," in other ways Pope is again farther from the original than his seventeenth-century predecessor. The μὲν . . . δέ construction in the Greek ("on the one hand . . . on the other hand") partially justifies the symmetry of Pope's translation; Achilles' heart, as the Greek idiom διάνδιχα μερμήριξεν suggests, hesitated between two opinions. Yet though separated by three hundred years, Ogilby and Lattimore find a more satisfactory solution, closer to the spirit of Achilles' internal debate, with their looser "Whether . . . Or else." Thoughts do not rule Achilles' bosom "by turns." No mention is made in the Greek of any equivalent to the abstract "Reason." The impulse, rather, is to emphasize Achilles' individual ἄχος 'distress' not the universality of his struggle. Yet by dramatizing Achilles' anger through the generalized dialogue between Reason and Rage, Pope reverses the direction of the Greek. He stresses the universal qualities that lie behind Achilles' emotions.

This generalizing force is felt not only in style but also in the overarching structure of Pope's poem. Reuben Brower justly points out that Pope transforms Homer's Zeus into a Christian God, a "more uniformly majestic and impersonal deity."[11] While Homer's Zeus suffers the pangs of a father when his son Sarpedon is killed in Book XVI, Pope's Jove never deviates from his Olympian detachment. In inventing similarities between Homer's god and his own, Pope recreates his own theology in Homer. As Brower observes, "The historical past lives for us mainly by virtue of analogies with the present, and we reach our understanding of its sameness and difference by a series of analogical approximations."[12] To generalize is not necessarily to idealize; yet by extracting the generic essences that he felt to be lying beneath Nature, for Homer and for his own generation alike, Pope forges a new poem that does both. Pope makes of Homer's universe a mirror and idealized image of his own.

---

[10] John Ogilby, *Homer's Iliads* (London, 1660), p. 11.

[11] *Alexander Pope: The Poetry of Allusion* (Oxford, 1956) , p. 124.

[12] *Alexander Pope*, p. 107.

In a letter written to Henry Cromwell in 1710, before beginning the major work on his translation, Pope expresses his "Dislike" of Cromwell's use of the word "Paradise" in a rendering of Ovid, "who will be thought to talk too like a Christian in your Version at least, whatever it may have been in Latine or Greek."[13] Yet in trying not to do "Violence to the [English] Ear or to the receiv'd Rules of Composition" (Preface, p. 19), Pope makes Zeus' dwelling, Χαλκοβατὲς δῶ, a "Brazen Dome." No matter how similar in sound, the Homeric and Augustan words do not mean the same thing; far from suggesting the dimensions of a dome, δῶ or δῶμα is merely a house—or even more comfortably and modestly, part of a house or a household. In this passage, Thetis promises her son Achilles that she "will go" (εἶμι) for his sake to Zeus' home, "and take him by the knees and I think I can persuade him" (Lattimore, I.427). In Pope this tearful intimacy is much elevated: "Then will I mount the Brazen Dome, and move / The high Tribunal of Immortal *Jove*" (I.560–61). Jove becomes the "Omnipotent" Latinized Deity; even the other gods "confess'd their awful Lord" (I.528), a phrase with no lexical equivalent in the Greek line, echoing Christian language just as Cromwell does.

Jove's exalted sovereignty is reflected in Agamemnon's kingship. We learn in Book I that Agamemnon inherits his scepter from God; in Pope's rendition he also inherits Jove's unfaltering majesty. At the beginning of Book IX, we discover that King Agamemnon even "griev'd above the rest; / Superior Sorrows swell'd his Royal Breast" (IX.12). Not only is there no authority in the Greek for the regal distinction of Agamemnon's grief; neither Ogilby nor Pope's contemporary Madame Dacier makes such claims for the king's "Sorrows." Not since Chapman's "But Agamemnon most of all was tortur'd at his heart"[14] had the king been idealized so far above the rest of his men.

In Nestor's speech to the assembled heroes later in Book IX, Pope describes in detail Agamemnon's relationships and responsibilities with respect to his subjects. Nestor's speech is significantly longer in Pope's version than it is in the original. (The entire *Iliad* is almost twice as long in Pope's translation.) The additional lines place Agamemnon in an Augustan social and political context:

[13] Letter of August 21, 1710, in *Correspondence,* ed. George Sherburn (Oxford, 1956), I.96.

[14] George Chapman, *The Iliads of Homer,* ed. Richard Hooper (London, 1865), IX.9.

Curs'd is the Man, and void of Law and Right,
Unworthy Property, unworthy Light,
Unfit for publick Rule, or private Care;
That Wretch, that Monster, who delights in War:
Whose Lust is Murder, and whose horrid Joy,
To tear his Country, and his Kind destroy!
                                              (IX.87–92)

Again, neither Ogilby nor Madame Dacier makes such additions.
Even Chapman, whom Pope criticizes for "frequent Interpolations,"
renders these sentiments in two lines, following the Greek closely.
Pope, as he himself tells us, translates this passage "with Liberty"
(IX.87n), expanding generously upon the Greek punishments for
fighting among one's fellows. As Nestor warns, the man who turns
against his own people will end up alienated from brotherhood, law,
and home—ἀφήτωρ ἀθέμιστος ἀνέστιός. These are indeed
undesirable eventualities, but they are not emphasized and nothing is
made of the distinctions between them. The opposition between
"publick Rule" and "private Care" is Pope's own, as is the parallelism
of "Law," "Right," "Property," and "Light." These last words suggest
the concerns of Pope's world, not of Homer's. In idealizing the king
whose just and temperate rule nourishes such benefits, Pope creates
in Agamemnon a general type, a kind of Jacobite hero.

Nothing could be further, as Pope himself realizes, from the
intention of the Greek. As H. Munro Chadwick observes, "The form
of government truly characteristic of the Heroic Age . . . is an
irresponsible type of kingship, resting not upon tribal or national
law—which is of little account—but upon military prestige."[15] And
Pope concurs: "Those Persons are under a Mistake who would make
this Sentence [II.243] a Praise of Absolute Monarchy. *Homer* speaks it
only with regard to a General of an Army during the time of his Com-
mission. Nor is *Agamemnon* styl'd *King of Kings* in any other Sense,
than as the rest of the Princes had given him the supreme Authority
over them" (II.243n). In spite of the validity of this perception, Pope
insists on balancing Agamemnon's kingly "Pride" with "Magnanimity"
(I.155n) in order to accentuate his noble struggle against Achilles,
who is "a Mind suay'd with unbounded Passions, and entirely regardless of all human Authority and Law" (XVI.283n).

---

15 *The Heroic Age* (Cambridge, 1912); quoted in Brower, *Alexander Pope*, p.
89.

Just as Pope pictures an image of the paradigmatic Rule of Jove in Agamemnon's earthly reign, he constructs a microcosm of the universe in the little world of man's mind. In his description of Achilles' internal debate as a battle between the ruling faculties of "Reason" and "Rage," he imposes a generalized schema of the microcosm on the Greek epic. As Martin Battestin observes. Pope divides the inner faculties of man into Reason, Passion, and Will: "Like the universe, the microcosm was comprised of warring elements, the passions, which though essential to life, required a higher agency, the reason, to distinguish their proper functions and to direct them to suitable ends."[16] The human will, like the corresponding "Will of Jove," or the kingly will of God's "Scept'red Sons," is the reconciling force, acting out the final compromise between Reason and Passion.

Such a tripartite organization of the soul causes great difficulties for Pope in his translation. The Greek word for "soul," θυμός, is also the word for "passion" and for "heroic courage." θυμός was for the Greeks ultimately positive. While they recognized that it could get out of control, it was the source of all heroic values. As Pope realizes in his translation of Diomedes' speech at the beginning of Book IX, bravery is derived from it. Here he renders θυμός as "a brave and virtuous Soul" (IX.56). Yet θυμός is also the root of Achilles' wrath. In Book I, when Achilles tries to control his urge toward regicide, θυμός is dubbed "the rising Tempest of his Soul" (line 258). It is a testimony to the seriousness of Pope's attempt to be "faithful" to Homer in this instance that he retains the word "Soul," representing as it does the inherently troubling θυμός. As in Homeric psychology, the mind for Pope is also inspired by a single principle, instead of θυμός, Nature. But Nature as a kind of equivalent to Will brings together for a common good distinctly *disparate* faculties: "Two Principles in human nature reign; / Selflove, to urge, and Reason, to restrain" ("An Essay on Man," II.52–53).

Pope cannot disguise the uneasiness that the univalent and excitable Greek "soul" causes in him. In a footnote to Achilles' internal debate Pope asserts, "The Allegory here may be allow'd by every Reader to be unforc'd: The Prudence of *Achilles* checks him in the rashest Moment of his Anger . . . and no sooner is Wisdom gone but he falls into more violent reproaches for the Gratification of his Passion" (I.261n). Rather than being "unforc'd," the allegory fits here only under great compulsion. When compared to Ogilby's and Lat-

---

[16] Martin C. Battestin, *The Providcnce of Wit: Aspects of Form in Augustan Literature and the Arts* (Oxford, 1974), pp. 87-88.

timore's renderings, this passage, with its fragmentation of the soul into three generalized divisions, does violence to the original. Of the θυμός of Diomedes, Pope writes, "This is the Language of a brave Man, to affirm and say boldly, that Courage is above Scepters and Crowns" (IX.13n). In what sense is Diomedes' indignation really different from Achilles'? Here the text is clearly subordinated to Pope's preconceptions. Rather than show us a Greek world in which Achilles' passion and Diomedes' have the same source, Pope sacrifices the "Spirit of the Original."

If we fail to find fault with Pope, we treat him with less respect than did the writers of his time. Bentley has a point when he condemns Pope's *Iliad* for not being Homer. Johnson is also right in observing that " 'necessitas quod cogit defendit,' that may be lawfully done which cannot be forborne."[17] Yet Pope's distortions of Homer are not wholly dictated by the age in which he lived. Regardless of the quality of Pope's poem as art in its own right, his *Iliad* tampers with Homer more than other translations do. For this he must be held responsible. In a letter to Addison, Pope describes his approach to the *Iliad*: "I think there may be found a method of coming at the main works by a more speedy and gallant way than by mining under ground, that is, by using the Poetical Engines, Wings, and flying over their heads."[18] At times his "Poetical Engines" carry him so far over Homer's head that Pope loses sight of his way. Perhaps he would have done better as a translator if he had applied some of the "pedantic" scholarship he found so distasteful.

Ever since men first crowned Homer "Prince of Poets," they have been trying to reconcile the excellence of his poetry with what seem in him the primitive and insidious intrusions of a tribal past. In *The Republic* Plato writes, "Once more, then we shall ask Homer and the other poets not to represent . . . gods as lamenting, or at any rate, not to dare to misrepresent the highest god by making him say: 'Woe is me that Sarpedon, whom I love above all men, is fated to die at the hands of Patroclus.'" In Pope's contrasts between Homer and Virgil in his Preface to his *Iliad*, he struggles to come to terms with this wildness in Homer's magnificent powers of "Invention": "Our Author's Work is a wild Paradise, where if we cannot see all the Beauties so distinctly as in an order'd Garden, it is only because the Number of them is infinitely greater . . . If some things are too luxuriant, it is

---

[17] Samuel Johnson, *Lives of the English Poets,* ed. George Birkbeck Hill (Oxford, 1905), III.238.
[18] Letter of January 30, 1714, in *Correspondence,* I.208.

owing to the Richness of the Soil; and if others are not arriv'd to Perfection or Maturity, it is only because they are over-run and opprest by those of a stronger Nature" (p. 3). Pope is fond of the image of the untamed garden, but he longs to bring it under control. In "An Essay on Man," he pictures the "Paradise" cultivated:

As fruits ungrateful to the planter's care
On savage stocks inserted learn to bear;
The surest Virtues thus from Passions shoot,
Wild Nature's vigor working at the root.

(II.181–84)

Pope, it may be said, similarly domesticates Homer. I think we can see in his translation an ordering of the wildness of the past, a censoring of Homer, passing him "through a literary and rhetorical crucible" to eliminate his threat (Arnold, p. 221). In the strangeness of the past Pope finds a menace to his vision of a universal Nature. Exactly what Pope means by Nature is obscured by all the contradictions that the concept is pressed into service to reconcile; it is, at least, a force that orders history by unifying it. Pope's translation of the *Iliad* tries to convince us that we are not different from Homer. In the Greek epic there should be no contradiction to Pope's Nature, only her own "vigor working at the root": "But when t'examine ev'ry Part he came, / *Nature* and *Homer* were, he found, the *same*" ("An Essay on Criticism," lines 134–35).

Pope transforms Homer more thoroughly than his predecessors partly because of the unique historical pressures operating on him, though this is not to say that he is determined by them. In the Introduction to the Twickenham Edition of Pope's *Iliad,* Norman Callan suggests that "Pope's *Homer* (1715–26), falls in the period just before the great awakening of Homeric scholarship which took place towards the close of the eighteenth century. This historical position is not without significance, for, in a sense, Pope's translation is the end of an old Homer and F.A. Wolf's *Prolegomena ad Homerum* (1795) the beginning of a new . . . But these came after Pope's time, and belong essentially to another world."[19] While it is true that Pope's *Homer* is the "culmination of what may be called the 'Prince of Poets' tradition," it does not follow that Pope was not significantly influenced by the new atmosphere of scholarship, represented long before Wolf

---

19 "Pope's Homer and the Greek Learning of his Time," in the Twickenham Edition, VII, lxxi and lxxiii.

by Bentley and Theobald. The period marks not just the end of an old Homer and the birth of a new, but the death of a personal involvement with the literature of the past in favor of a more distanced and anthropological approach. Pope is the last translator of Homer to have a stake in the ancient world. His *Iliad* is a corrective to the Bentley school, an argument for our relationship to the past, for the unity of nature. The anthropological viewpoint is heresy to Pope unless it reveals the underlying similarities between men. Even in the "poor Indian," Pope discovers a "simple Nature" and a dream of a "humbler heav'n" ("An Essay on Man," I.99, 103–04).

The desire to assimilate Homer into a broad and unifying concept of Nature is nowhere more clearly seen than in Pope's rendering of Zeus' lament on the fated death of his son Sarpedon in Book XVI. Brower's careful analysis of this passage illuminates many of the assumptions that govern it, e.g., the metamorphosis of Zeus, the personalized father-god, into a lofty and omnipotent Jove. The question remains, why? More than previous translators, Pope idealizes Jove. In making Homer's Zeus like his own Christian God, Pope affirms the sameness of the Greeks and the Augustans. This altering can be seen most dramatically in a comparison of Pope's translation with Lattimore's more literal rendering.

> *Jove* view'd the Combate, whose Event foreseen,
> He thus bespoke his Sister and his Queen.
> The Hour draws on; the Destinies ordain,
> My godlike Son shall press the *Phrygian* Plain:
> Already on the Verge of Death he stands,
> His Life is ow'd to fierce *Patroclus'* Hands.
> What Passions in a Parent's Breast debate!
> Say, shall I snatch him from impending Fate,
> And send him safe to *Lycia,* distant far
> From all the Dangers and the Toils of War;
> Or to his Doom my bravest Offspring yield,
> And fatten, with celestial Blood, the Field?
> Then thus the Goddess with the radiant Eyes:
> What words are these, O Sov'reign of the Skies?
> Short is the Date prescrib'd to mortal Man;
> Shall Jove, for one, extend the narrow Span,
> Whose Bounds were fix'd before his Race began?
> How many Sons of Gods, foredoom'd to Death,
> Before proud *Ilion,* must resign their Breath!

Were thine exempt, Debate would rise above,
And murm'ring Pow'rs condemn their partial *Jove.*

(XVI.528-48)

And watching them the son of devious-devising Kronos
was pitiful, and spoke to Hera, his wife and his sister:
"Ah me, that it is destined that the dearest of men, Sarpedon,
must go down under the hands of Menoitios' son Patroklos.
The heart in my breast is balanced between two ways as I
    ponder,
whether I should snatch him out of the sorrowful battle
and set him down still alive in the rich country of Lykia,
or beat him under at the hands of the son of Menoitios."
In turn the lady Hera of the ox eyes answered him:
"Majesty, son of Kronos, what sort of thing have you spoken?
Do you wish to bring back a man who is mortal, one long since
doomed by his destiny, from ill-sounding death, and release
    him?
Do it, then; but not all the rest of us gods shall approve you.
And put away in your thoughts this other thing I tell you;
if you bring Sarpedon back to his home, still living,
think how then some other one of the gods might also
wish to carry his own son out of the strong encounter;
since around the great city of Priam are fighting many
sons of immortals. You will awaken grim resentment among
    them.

(Lattimore, XVI.431-49)

This passage is crucial to Pope because of the evidence he
claims to find here that Jove is superior to Fate. In a footnote, he
deduces an elaborate theology from these lines:

> [Homer] assigns three Causes of all the Good and
> Evil that happens in this World, which he takes a
> particular Care to distinguish. First the *Will of God,*
> superior to all . . . Secondly, *Destiny,* or *Fate,* mean-
> ing the Laws and Order of Nature affecting the
> Constitutions of Men, and disposing them to Good
> or Evil, Prosperity or Misfortune; which the
> supreme Being, if it be his Pleasure, may over-rule
> (as he is inclin'd to do in this Place) but which he
> generally suffers to take effect. Thirdly, our own

> *Free-will,* which either by Prudence overcomes
> those natural Influences and Passions, or by Folly
> suffers us to fall under them. (XVI.535n)

This hierarchy, Pope observes, is "very clear, and distinctly agreeable to Truth."

In fact, it is not at all clear from Homer's poem; Pope wrenches the sense of the original to fit his theology. This tampering is particularly evident at two points. In line 535, "Say, shall I snatch him from impending Fate," Pope substitutes "Fate" for the Greek μάχης δακρόεσσης 'tearful battle.' Zeus does not debate whether he can thwart Sarpedon's "Fate," but merely whether he should lift him out of his present danger. Hera reminds him immediately that mortals are ruled by αἶσα 'Destiny' (XVI.441), over which Zeus has no ultimate control. Pope omits the word "Fate" from this line, translating simply, "Short is the Date prescrib'd to mortal Man" (XVI.542).

Pope also excludes Hera's warning to Zeus that if he saves Sarpedon, all the other gods will wish to do the same for their favorites (XVI.542). The threat of rebellion undermines Jove's authority. It is a reminder not only that this kind of insurrection is possible but that it is the way the son of Kronos himself originally assumed power: "The gods, it will be remembered, have not created the universe but only taken possession of a world which existed before they came on the scene. As natural forces they form part of the order to which they conform."[20] Pope eliminates the background of Homeric religious myth, replacing it with his own Christian context. Pope attacks Hobbes's translation for omitting "whole Similes and Sentences,"[21] Yet when it serves his purpose Pope is guilty of the same fault.

As Pope points out in his note to Jove's speech, "Mr. *Dryden* . . . contends that *Jupiter* was limited by the Destinies" (XVI.535n). In fact, the rest of Homer's translators shared Dryden's opinion. Neither Chapman, Ogilby, nor Madame Dacier elevates Zeus above Fate. Where Pope interpolates "Fate" for "tearful battle," Chapman writes simply "fight" (XVI.413), Ogilby "bloody Battell" (p. 360), and Madame Dacier (more elaborately but just as accurately) "au danger qui le menace dans cet affreux combat."[22] None of Pope's predecessors eliminates Hera's warning to Zeus that the other gods may follow

---

[20] Erland Ehnmark, *The Idea of God in Homer* (Uppsala, Sweden, 1935), pp. 84-85.

[21] Quoted in Knight, *Pope and the Heroic Tradition, p. 25.*

[22] Anne Dacier, *L'Iliade d'Homere* (Paris, 1741), pp. 449-50.

his lead. In a marginal gloss to his translation of Jove's lament, Ogilby "justly taxeth the vanity of the Heathens for subjecting their greatest God to the power of Fate" (p. 360). This was the first version of Homer that Pope ever read; perhaps the memory of Ogilby's interpretation of this scene stayed with him until his own rendering of it. At last he found an opportunity to vindicate Homer, to assert that the Greek pagans were motivated by the same theological instincts as are Christians.

Pope was subject to different cultural and historical pressures from those which influenced Dryden, Ogilby, Chapman, or even his contemporary Anne Dacier. She was embroiled in a feud between supporters of the Ancients and proponents of the Moderns, which while perhaps explaining certain distortions in her translation presupposes a personal involvement with literature. None of Homer's previous translators had to persuade his public that the Greek poet was worth reacting to personally; hence no other translator found himself obliged to convince an audience that there was a community of values shared by classical and Christian poets and that the reading of the Greek poet somehow required a commitment of oneself to those values. None of their cosmologies was threatened in the way that Pope's faith in an overriding Nature was being called into question by the probing scholarship of his culture. I think we can see in Pope's translation of the *Iliad* an attempt to impose traditional patterns of meaning on experience in a society where an old order is falling apart, in what Leo Spitzer calls the "epoch of dechristianization" or "the great caesura in occidental history."[23]

Linguistic parallelism, according to Ohmann, arises from such a need to create order. In an author's use of what he calls "equivalence categories," Ohmann finds the effort to "*order* experience as we order language, by clustering things (or words) along the axis of similarity and difference."[24] As we have seen, Pope's couplets manifest this kind of parallelism; in their very structure they call attention to lexical and conceptual similarities. By placing selected details in parallel structure with generalized concepts, Pope tries to organize Greek experience under Augustan categories. Even in his shaping of epic action, Pope imposes a new order on Homeric theology, psychology, and politics. He idealizes them as he restructures them to reflect the values of his own age rather than the earlier one. He searches always for what we

---

[23] *Classical and Christian Ideas of World Harmony,* ed. Anna Granville Hatcher (Baltimore, Md., 1963), p. 76.

[24] Ohmann, p. 226.

have in common with Homer, hoping at every point to find evidence for the unity of Nature.

The translation of the values of the past into the terms of the present becomes a kind of ruling passion in Pope's work. On its success ride all of his most precious assumptions. It is not surprising that his final mock epic, *The Dunciad,* grew out of a dispute with Theobald over Pope's edition of Shakespeare. The new scholars denied that Genius has any privileged insight into Nature. As Pope announces righteously in a note to *The Dunciad,* Theobald was willing to admit Shakespeare's "terrible *Anacronisms,* or low *Conundrums*" (I.162–63n). This comment seems to imply that Pope believed either that Shakespeare is incapable of bad poetry or that his lapses should be concealed. Why is Pope forced into this extreme and untenable position?

Just as Pope is unwilling to concede contradictions between Homer's theology and his own, so, too, he resists the suggestion that any Genius might fall away from aesthetic Truth ("Nor is it Homer nods, but we that sleep," "An Essay on Criticism," I.180). Regardless of what he insists in letters, notes, and prefatory remarks, in practice Pope operates under the assumption that the role of an editor or translator is to enhance the agreement of Art and Nature. "Mining under ground," "pedantic" study can only interfere with Pope's desired communion with Homer. As Parnell writes, "There is something in the Mind of Man, which goes beyond bare Curiosity and even carries us on to a Shadow of Friendship, with those great Genius's whom we have known to excell in former Ages."[25] Pope felt that this "something" was menaced. The driving force of his *Iliad* is not to translate or to transfuse "the Spirit of the Original" but to transform it. In order to establish his affinity with Homer, he is willing finally to make the Greek poet over in the image of the Augustan one.

---

[25] Thomas Parnell, "An *Essay* on the Life, Writings, *and* Learning of Homer," in the Twickenham Edition, VII, 26.

Figure 6. *The Last Interview of Hector and Andromache.*
Angelica Kauffmann.

# Angelica Kauffmann

*Albert Boime*

Few painters of either sex could have been more commercially successful than Kauffmann; her classical compositions and portraits were eagerly sought after by the English aristocracy and could be found in most of the major collections including those of George III and other members of the royal family. Kauffmann's work was engraved and reproduced in every conceivable medium including fans, furniture, flower vases, snuffboxes, wine coolers, tea sets, porcelain groups, ceiling and interior decorations. Her *Cleopatra Adorning the Tomb of Mark Antony* was engraved twice, showing the demand for her work, and was reproduced in such varied media as a watch case and a tea wagon. Another indication of her popularity was the patronage of the industrialist Matthew Boulton, who developed a secret method for the mechanical reproduction of pictures at his Soho firm around 1780.[1] Through his transfer process (a variation of aquatint engraving) he planned to "mass produce" neoclassical ceiling decorations for Adam's burgeoning market. While he employed several designers, his favorite was Angelica Kauffmann, who executed nearly thirty pictures for the project. Indeed, it is likely that her decorations for the Montague House at 22 Portman Square were carried out with Boulton's process. During her fifteen years in England (1766–1781), she earned 14,000 pounds—no small sum in that period for a female artist. Her career attests to the vast market

---

[1] E. Robinson and K.R. Thompson, "Matthew Boulton's Mechanical Paintings." *Burlington Magazine*, 112 (1970) 504.

for neoclassicism and her ability to satisfy demands of her elite clientele.

Angelica Kauffmann was born at Chur in 1741. As she was the only child of his two marriages, Josef centered all his interest on her, and she developed precociously. Less tyrannical than the father of Mengs, Josef was nevertheless a strict master and drove her to the utmost of her unusual abilities. As a result of his program, she became a practicing professional at eleven years of age. Hoping to exploit her talents for profit, he looked for more urban prospects and took her first to Como, then Milan, and finally they made their way to Rome in 1763. They then sought out Mengs who was out of town at the moment, but his wife introduced them to Winckelmann. The antiquarian informed them of the great prospects in Rome and stimulated her participation in the neoclassical movement. Winckelmann commissioned her to do his portrait, an important document of the year in which he published his *History of Ancient Art*.

Kauffmann's first compositions show the influence of Batoni, Mengs, and Gavin Hamilton. She established a close association with the circle of Hamilton, Clérisseau, the abbé Peter Grant (whose portrait she also painted), and Thomas Jenkins who acted as her banker when she returned to Rome in 1782. Kauffmann soon attached herself to the English community and became an instant hit among the Grand Tourists. Gifted linguistically, she spoke English fluently and received her most profitable commissions from British visitors in Rome, Naples, and Venice where she traveled. Winckelmann noted in a letter to a friend that "she paints all the English who visit Rome."[2] Their orders for portraits and classical subjects encouraged her to move to England and set up shop.

Her arrival in England coincided with a period of peace and relative prosperity. The war had brought England vast possessions both in the East and in the West, and the heady sense of Empire sought expression in the "classicalities" (as contemporaries called Kauffmann's works) offered by enterprising architects, painters, and sculptors. Symptomatic are her decorations for the Home House and Harewood House, whose owners derived their wealth from colonial investments. Within 6 months of her arrival, Kauffmann was well established. She took a large house in Golden Square in 1767 where she received her aristocratic sitters. Even her previous apartments were located in a fashionable area of London and run by a servant;

---

2 V. Manners and G.C. Williamson, *Angelica Kauffmann* (London, 1924), 14.

she claimed this was necessary because she could not receive persons of rank in a mean place and under mean conditions. During her first year of independent activity, she received visits from Lord Baltimore, the Princess of Wales, and Princess Augusta of Brunswick (the king's sister), and she was introduced to Queen Charlotte who became a close friend. The next year (1768) she was elected as one of the founding members of the new Royal Academy—an astonishing record for the twenty-seven-year-old painter! (Until 1936 only one other woman, Mary Moser, who was also a founding artist, had been elected a full member.)

Her meteoric career may be understood only in the context of her patrons' demands. At the first exhibition of the Royal Academy in 1769 she exhibited four pictures, all of them Homeric and Virgilian subjects: *The Last Interview of Hector and Andromache, Achilles Discovered by Ulysses amongst the Attendants of Deidamia, Venus Showing Aeneas and Achates the Way to Carthage* and *Penelope Taking Down the Bow of Ulysses for the Trial of Her Wooers*. The aristocracy, many of them just returned from service in the Seven Years' War, now looked upon the Trojan War as its ancient counterpart and identified with the heroes of the *Iliad* and the *Odyssey*.[3] This series had been commissioned by John Parker (later Lord Boringdon), a staunch member of the king's party in Parliament, to decorate Saltram House. The *Hector and Andromache* depicts graciously poised figures without drama and emotional tension, a style akin to Mengs and Gavin Hamilton. One of the most pathetic scenes in the *Iliad* is reduced to a restrained image of wifely and maternal solicitude. But Kauffmann reveals her personal point of view in the transformation of Hector from the stalwart hero who rejects the entreaties of his wife to a wistful juvenile who wears his helmet uneasily. Kauffmann's emphasis is on Andromache's tender gesture and the nurse who cradles the child in her arms. The picture tells less about masculine courage than about domestic concerns which Hector repudiates. The following year Kauffmann painted *Andromache and Hecuba Weeping over the Ashes of Hector*, which was exhibited in 1772. Andromache leans listlessly upon the funeral urn, while young Astyanax tries to comfort the inconsolable Hecuba, Hector's mother. As opposed to Gavin Hamilton's scene of male sacrifice, the emphasis here is on feminine grief and mourning.

---

[3] For the quantum leap in Homeric subjects after mid-eighteenth century see D. Wiebenson, "Subjects from Homer's Iliad in Neoclassical Art," *Art Bulletin* 46 (1964), 23-37. The comte de Caylus recommended a series on the subject in 1757: *Tableaux tirés de Iliad, de l'Odyssée d'Homère et de l'Enéide de Virgile avec des observations générales sur le costume* (Paris, 1757).

Following the Seven Years' War there were many images in England and France of grieving widows, but Kauffmann's commitment to a feminist position is consistent throughout her career. This pleased her aristocratic patrons who wanted to decorate their houses with Greco-Roman allusions to a heroic age but not in a heavy-handed Spartan or tragic mode .

Women occupy the central place in Kauffmann's work, if not always the formal center. Her *Venus Showing Aeneas and Achates the Way to Carthage* relegates the two male protagonists to the far left and in shadowy profile, while Venus is shown frontally, brightly illuminated, and totally in command of the pictorial field. Generally, her male figures resemble the Hector and appear weaker than the female, with a boyish face and demeanor. The masculine hero of *Zeuxis Selecting Models for His Picture of Helen of Troy* is located centrally and strategically, but his stiff presence is overwhelmed by the sharply lit and lively women he inspects for his grand synthesis. Curiously, at the far right is a woman grasping a brush before the canvas as if on the verge of painting; her head is modeled upon Kauffmann's own features.

Kauffmann expressed in her neoclassical works fundamental feelings about sexual relationships and male-female roles, but her peculiar approach satisfied the taste of her English patrons. Her friend Dr. John Wolcot, a satirist who wrote under the name of Peter Pindar, parodied this approach in his *Lyric Odes to Royal Academicians*:

> Angelica my plaudits gains—
> Her art so sweetly canvas stains!—
> Her Dames so Grecian! give me such a delight!
> But were she married to such gentle Males
> As figure in her painted tales—
> I fear she'd find a stupid wedding night.[4]

Indeed, her love relationships with men were unsuccessful, and while wild rumors perpetually plagued her she seems not to have had an active sex life. Her first husband turned out to be a swindler, and her second marriage to Zucchi, a much older man, was one of convenience. Their nuptial settlement stipulated that her assets were not to be touched by him and that he was responsible for his own debts. Nevertheless, they worked well as a team for Robert Adam and other contemporary architects.

---

[4] J. Wolcot, *The Works of Peter Pindar, Esquire*, 2 vols. (London, 1794) 1:45.

Kauffmann veiled her classical women and never painted entirely nude people except for children, perfectly appropriate for the boudoir ceilings of the homes she and Zucchi decorated. Her effeminate males and gracefully poised women fit the pattern of the pioneer neoclassicists and underscore their primarily decorative function. Here she had no peer and was much more in demand than they as an interior designer. Her style was admirably suited for Adam's light, somewhat playful, and delicate interiors. Like him, she also drew her inspiration from the classical repertoires published by Sir William Hamilton, the comte de Caylus, and the Royal Herculaneum Academy.

Sir William Hamilton commissioned several pictures from Kauffmann, including a *Penelope* for which she waived her customary fee. Their relationship clarifies her appeal to the aristocracy. In 1782 William Beckford (another heir to a Jamaican fortune) wrote Sir William: "As for Angelica, she is my Idol; so say everything that can be said in my name and tell her how I long to see Telemachus's Papa and all the noble Family."[5] Beckford here refers to her stock of subjects centering on Ulysses, king of Ithaca, the hero of Homer's *Odyssey* (including the *Penelope* she did for Sir William). As mentioned earlier, her patrons evidently identified with the Greek chiefs returning to their families after the end of the Trojan War. Beckford's comment about the "noble Family" shows to what extent Kauffmann managed to create an appealing environment of domesticated, playful, erotic deities for lords and ladies who looked upon them as their antique counterparts.

---

[5] L. Melville, *The Life and Letters of William Beckford of Fonthill* (London, 1910), 163, 113–114, 122.

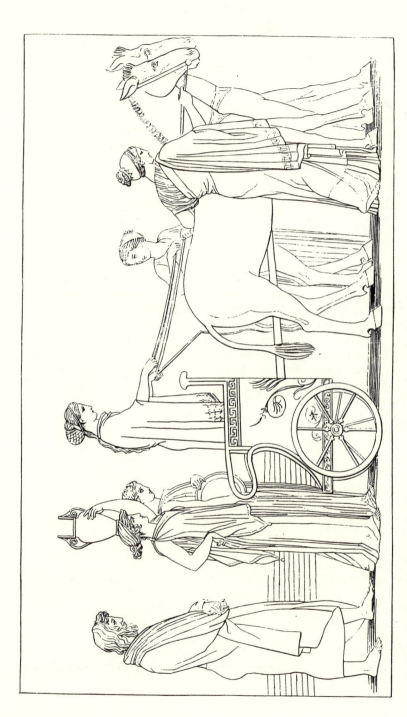

Figure 7. Odysseus follows the wagon of Nausikaa. Flaxman (*Odyssey* series).

# Achilleis and Nausikaa:
# Goethe in Homer's World

*David Constantine*

> Das Unzulängliche ist produktiv.
> Goethe

The two works in the title are fragments. Goethe wrote rather more about *Nausikaa* than he did of it; and the *Achilleis,* conceived as an epic to fit between the *Iliad* and the *Odyssey,* he advanced no further than line 651.

My main purpose is to discuss not so much the works themselves as a more general endeavour of which they are instances. I shall have quite a lot to say about locality, about the sense and spirit of place—what Johnson called 'local emotion'—in the two fragments; but also my theme will be Goethe's wish, characteristic throughout his career, to root what he wrote in real life; and place—particular place with its own forms and spirit—is one kind and an important one of substantiality in a literary work. Further, since these works were unfinished and must in that sense be considered failures, I shall say what I can about this kind of failure. There can be no doubt that in both cases Goethe's conception of the work was very intense and clear, and the falling short of it in execution, the leaving off unfinished, is surely of interest—in Goethe himself, and in the whole late eighteenth century's wish and failure to realize a supreme ideal in the form of Ancient Greece.

*Nausikaa* was begun and abandoned in 1787, the *Achilleis* in 1798–99, the two works, unfinished, marking thus the beginning and almost the end of Goethe's so-called classical period. But the real matter under discussion here—how to give substance to a conception, form to an ideal—is something which occupies all poets, and Goethe very intensely from the moment he found his own voice in the early 1770s in *Sturm und Drang*.

At the heart of *Sturm und Drang*, Goethe its foremost exponent, is the insistence that all forms of life, including of course the forms of art, must be infused with vital energy, and if they are not capable of that they must be smashed, discarded and replaced with others that are:

> Schon tönet's aber ihm in der Brust. Tief quillt's,
> Wie damals, als hoch oben im Fels er schlief,
> Ihm auf. Im Zorne reinigt aber
> Sich der Gefesselte nun, nun eilt er
>
> Der Linkische; der spottet der Schlaken nun,
> Und nimmt und bricht und wirft die Zerbrochenen
> Zorntrunken, spielend, dort und da zum
> Schauenden Ufer und bei des Fremdlings
>
> Besondrer Stimme stehen die Heerden auf,
> Es regen sich die Wälder, es hört tief Land
> Den Stromgeist fern, und schaudernd regt im
> Nabel der Erde der Geist sich wieder.
>
> Der Frühling kömmt. Und jedes, in seiner Art,
> Blüht.

That is not a *Sturm und Drang* text of course, but Hölderlin's 'Ganymed' thirty years later. I quote him because he is close to much of what I have to say about Goethe, here in the urgent question of how life may be rescued from under the weight of dead tradition.

You are familiar with the models that young Germans took for themselves in the early 1770s as polemical and inspirational antitheses against the exhibits in the mausoleum of contemporary German culture. Folksong and ballad, the Bible, Ossian, Jean-Jacques Rousseau, Strasbourg Cathedral, Homer, 'Shakespeare und kein Ende!' In a word (or two): 'Natur! Natur!' Homer concerns us here.

That mysterious Greek (or amalgam of Greeks) excited and fascinated Goethe throughout his writing life. It might help subvert the categories we sort his career into if we remember that. Homer was the hero of his *Sturm und Drang* and the unreachable ideal of his classicism. 'Geniale Naturen erleben eine wiederholte Pubertät', said Goethe, knowing that to be his own experience. But continuity and constancy are hallmarks of his genial character too. Many-sided Homer was both an abiding and a various inspiration.

The young Goethe was helped towards a clearer enthusiasm for Homer as were many of his fellow countrymen—by an English work: the *Essay on the Original Genius of Homer*, by Robert Wood. Wood was for a large part of his life an adventurous and scholarly traveller of a kind not uncommon in the eighteenth century. He was born around 1717 in County Meath, and wherever he got his education it fitted him to be a travelling-companion and tutor to English aristocrats abroad. He toured Greece, one of the first to do so extensively and usefully; but was chiefly famous in his day as the discoverer of the desert cities of Palmyra and Balbec. With two companions, John Bouverie and James Dawkins, he landed in the Troad in 1750 and located, wrongly but to his own satisfaction, Priam's city. When he returned to England he entered upon a diplomatic career, became Pitt's Under-Secretary of State, and produced the book which Goethe read only in his spare time, of which he had very little.

By a curious route the *Essay* became quite widely known in Germany before it had any circulation in England. In 1769 Wood, still not able to find time to finish the work, had half a dozen copies of a provisional version privately printed. One of these, via a friend, reached the classical scholar C.G. Heyne in Göttingen. He reviewed it enthusiastically and at some length in his *Gelehrte Anzeigen* on 15 March 1770; and rights of translation were eagerly sought. Wood, anxious to finish the work properly, never gave his permission before he died, in 1771; but then J.D. Michaelis, in Göttingen, went ahead and a translation of that provisional version, which however contains all the essentials of argument and illustration, did appear in Germany in the spring of 1773. It was two years before a full version, put together from Wood's notes, came out in England.

Wood's thesis, not entirely original but advanced by no-one so persuasively before him, was that Homer's peculiar genius was truthfulness to Nature. That is, Homer faithfully depicted what he saw around him, in landscape and in manners. Homer was, in Wood's view, a writer rooted in real time and place, and he believed he could prove this, as a traveller, by adducing what he had observed himself in Homer's supposed localities.

It seemed then an inestimable advantage to read Homer in situ: 'the Iliad has new beauties on the banks of the Scamander, and the

Odyssey is most pleasing in the countries where Ulysses travelled and Homer sung'.[1] One's pleasure in the text was powerfully enhanced by seeing its truthfulness proved at every turn. Features of landscape survived, and could be checked the original and the faithful copy:

> Not only the permanent and durable objects of his description, such as his rock, hill, dale, promontory etc. continue in many instances to bear unquestionable testimony of his correctness, and shew, by a strict propriety of his epithets, how faithfully they were copied; but even his more fading and changeable landscape, his shady grove, verdant lawn, and flowery mead, his pasture and tillage, with all his varieties of corn, wine and oil, agree surprisingly with the present face of those countries.[2]

Likewise in manners. Homeric manners survive, and Wood studied them with interest when he was in the East. Among the Bedouin tribesmen, for example, heroic, patriarchal manners survive: violent, as in the *Iliad*, but also hospitable, as in the *Odyssey*. The men appreciate wiliness, Odysseus' chief quality; they accord their women, as do the Homeric heroes, a less than European respect. As a corollary to this last observation Wood notes, both in Homer and among these latter-day Homeric tribes, the absolute absence of sentimental love; which is interesting when we consider what Goethe hoped to make of Homer's Nausicaa.

Truthfulness to particular time and place, together with the potent idea that out of a fabulous Greek past into our debased modern times landscape survives and traces of manners remain: that is my main interest here. But I should like to indicate another of Wood's important insights and emphases. In an admirable chapter on Homer's language this Under-Secretary of State to William Pitt said things which must have gladdened the heart of German *Sturm und Drang*.

Wood examines Homer's epics as primitive song, as oral poetry; in a most pragmatic and perceptive way he examines the nature and

---

[1] Robert Wood, *Ruins of Palmyra*, London 1753, the Preface.

[2] Robert Wood, *An Essay on the Original Genius and Writings of Homer*, London 1775, p. 75. All subsequent references to this work are incorporated into the text, together with the German version of 1773 (deriving from Wood's provisional text of 1769) whenever I have thought it helpful to show what German readers read.

conditions of such poetry, drawing on his own observations in those countries where it still survives. Those exciting new notions, soon commonplaces, but still exciting, in the latter half of the eighteenth century concerning the primacy of poetry over prose—that poetry is the natural first language of man, that prose is a fall from Nature—those are the criteria he brings to his study of Homer. He is engaged, perhaps without knowing it, in the polemics against sophistication, over-civilisation, politeness, artificiality, when he praises 'that noble simplicity of language', p. 246 ('eine edle Simplicität der Sprache'), that 'simplicity, without meanness', p. 291 ('Simplicität . . . nie aber Niedrigkeit und grober Ausdruck') by which Homer is graced. Unobtrusively—but how the Germans must have seized on this—he is anti-French; for in the chapter on Manners he remarks: 'our polite neighbours the French seem to be most offended at certain pictures of primitive simplicity, so unlike those refined modes of modern life, in which they have taken the lead', p. 144 ('unsere zu feinen Nachbarn, die Franzosen, scheinen sehr durch gewisse Gemälde der ersten Simplicität beleidigt zu werden, die von den erkünstelten Moden der neuern Zeit, darin sie anderer Nationen Muster seyn wollen, so sehr verschieden sind . . .'). Homer has 'that genuine cast of natural simplicity', p. 145 ('jene ächte naturliche Simplicität') which the Bible has. And his language exactly suits his own simplicity and that of his times. It is a language concrete and unambiguous; easily intelligible when listened to; sonorous, dignified and expressive. In short, a language supreme

> in the province of Poetry, where the most finished efforts of artificial language are but cold and Languid circumlocution, compared with that passionate expression of Nature, which, incapable of misrepresentation, appeals directly to our feelings, and finds the shortest road to the heart. (p. 284)

> wo die künstliche Sprache, hätte sie auch den höchsten Grad der Vollkommenheit erreicht, doch gegen den feurigen Ausdruck der Natur immer nur kalte und matte Umschreibung bleibt. Er ist keiner Misdeutung fähig, greift gerade unsere Empfindungen an, und bahnt sich den kürzesten Weg zu unserm Herzen.

In *Dichtung und Wahrheit* Goethe acknowledged what he and his generation owed to Robert Wood:

> Glücklich ist immer die Epoche einer Literatur,
> wenn grosse Werke der Vergangenheit wieder ein-
> mal auftauchen und an die Tagesordnung kommen,
> weil sie alsdann eine volkommen frische Wirkung
> hervorbringen. Auch das homerische Licht ging uns
> neu wieder auf, und zwar recht im Sinne der Zeit,
> die ein solches Erscheinen höchst begünstigte: denn
> das beständige Hinweisen auf Natur bewirkte
> zuletzt, dass man auch die Werke der Alten von
> dieser Seite betrachten lernte. Was mehrere
> Reisende zu Aufklärung der Heiligen Schriften
> getan, leisteten andere für den Homer. Durch Guys
> ward man eingeleitet, Wood gab der Sache den
> Schwung. Eine Göttinger Rezension des anfangs
> sehr seltenen Originals machte uns mit der Absicht
> bekannt, und belehrte uns, wie weit sie ausgeführt
> worden. Wir sahen nun nicht mehr in jenen
> Gedichten ein angespanntes und aufgedunsenes
> Heldenwesen, sondern die abgespiegelte Wahrheit
> einer uralten Gegenwart, und suchten uns dieselbe
> möglichst heranzuziehen.[3]

The emphasis in this appreciation falls on the new understanding of Homer, to which Wood materially contributed, as the product of a particular time and place. It is an unclassical view of those classics the *Iliad* and the *Odyssey*. They are retrieved from a vacuum of timelessness and the Absolute, and planted in life again, in a particular age, climate, people and culture. This does not lessen their greatness, nor their inspirational potency; but it does radically alter the manner in which any subsequent age should try to emulate or imitate them. The more general application is the one Herder makes in his doctrine of palingenesis. This is Hölderlin's formulation of it: 'wie der Frühling, wandelt der Genius/Von Land zu Land.' It is an encouraging notion for each and every culture; especially for Germans who, in the early 1770s, were engaged in one of their periodic struggles to discover or create their own identity. 'Werde, der du bist!' is not such an easy mat-

---

[3] Goethe, *Werke, Hamburger Ausgabe*, ix, 537-38. Goethe's works are referred to throughout in this edition. All subsequent references are incorporated in the text.

ter. In Herder's hopeful view every people was capable of its own florescence; every nation's spirit should find its own proper form. Forms wrongly applied or mistakenly submitted to would need to be cast off, like the ice in Hölderlin's 'Ganymed', if the proper spring were ever to come. To imitate or submit to another nation's culture, however excellent, was the way of ossification and death. It is easy to see that the Germans could well do without the debased merely nominal classicistic traditions of France. But the issue becomes more acute when they feel themselves to be going under the spell of the Thing Itself—Greece, Homer. Still the law is: mere imitation, of however excellent a predecessor, is the way of death.

There is more in this topic than I can possibly present here. But the crux, for a national culture and for the individual artist, is: imitation, its nature and practice. Winckelmann's injunction seems quite categorical: 'Der einzige Weg für uns, gross, ja, wenn es möglich ist, unnachahmlich zu werden, ist die Nachahmung der Alten . . .' But in that statement are contained both the way of life and the way of death, and Winckelmann himself, though he strove with body and soul for the former, has sometimes encouraged the latter. How is it possible that imitation should be a creative and productive enterprise? Robert Wood, though he was no aesthetician, had doubtless read Winckelmann's first work (which was translated into English by Fuseli in 1765) and when he calls Homer 'the most constant and faithful copier after Nature' p. 5—('der getreueste Maler der Natur') and praises his 'mimetic powers' (viii-ix) clearly he means nothing slavish or dull by that, and nearly always when giving such praise he couples with the notion of 'copying' the notion, apparently paradoxical, of originality: 'In the great province of Imitation he is the most original of all Poets'—p. 5—('in dem grossen Felde der Imitation unter allen Dichtem am meisten Original'); and the essay is entitled *On the Original Genius of Homer.* Wood is speaking of Homer vis-a-vis Nature; I am speaking (or should be) of Goethe vis-a-vis Homer. Winckelmann urged contemporary sculptors to copy not from Nature but from Greek statues, because in them Nature was, so to say, crystallized out and more clearly to be perceived. (Nature herself, he gloomily believed, was in his own day, north of the Alps at least, debased or, in the form of beautiful boys, inaccessible.) But in either undertaking, whether 'copying' Nature in the real world around us, or 'copying' her in a great classical work (Homer or the Cnidian Venus) there is a way of slavery and a way of creation. For this latter way, which alone really concerns us, we had better replace the word 'nachahmen' with Büchner's word 'nachschaffen'. We are interested here in Goethe's creative attempt (and failure) to copy Homer.

In adducing evidence to prove the 'mimetic powers' of Homer, Robert Wood drew attention, almost incidentally, to the fact that of the real Greece, where the ideal was once reality, much survives. It would be hard to exaggerate the imaginative potency of this single simple truth. I mean chiefly landscape: those elemental constituents, the sea, its bays, the mountains, plains and rivers which we used to think not just lasting but eternal. That Parnassus exists, still, is, even now, an idea of peculiar power. Landscape, surviving, links a degraded present with an ideal past. For Hellenists like Byron, optimistically and politically disposed, a landscape surviving in unlessened beauty acts as an incitement to recreate *in situ* in the same localities the ideal. For the more elegiac it makes for a permanent poignant discrepancy between past and present. Ruins of the great past, those unequivocal proofs that the ideal was once real, continually remind the Hellenist of an irrecoverable loss. Attempts *really* to recover the ideal past, for example, in the rising of 1770, end in the bitterest disappointment. Hölderlin, by nature elegiac, almost wills his hero Hyperion to failure in that locality where it will hurt most—at Mistra, ancient Sparta.

If physically beautiful Greece were gone from the face of the earth that would be the end of the matter; but she survives, as a reminder, and an incitement. The landscape then is that part of the whole ideal which is *actually* recoverable; it is, so to speak, there for our re-possession. Hölderlin's poetry is luminous with the physical beauty of Greece. At the same time, he knows that the gods have gone out of it. Presence and absence co-exist. Then, in the landscape, ruins and works of art are recoverable; in the eighteenth century the travellers and first archaeologists were bringing more and more to light. Such discoveries and, more generally, all increasing scholarly knowledge about Ancient Greece might be thought a way to recover the ideal. The more we know, the better? Perhaps. Hyperion looks with cold contempt at a couple of British archaeologists grubbing through the debris below the Acropolis. Hölderlin spoke with horror of all attempts at what he called: 'positives Beleben des Todten'. Once the spirit has gone antiquarian knowledge may not satisfactorily replace it. Scholarship is not the kiss of life. The corpus of learning is a corpse.

The awareness and admission of absence, despite the persuasive beauty of the surviving places, is a creative, perhaps *the* creative factor.

Goethe never went to Greece, though he was offered a very favourable opportunity. But he did go to Sicily, home of the western

Greeks, which with its marvellous sites, climate and landscape, is a very good second best. In Sicily, though he does not mention him, Robert Wood's perceptions really became his own. Herder, even less of a traveller than Goethe, had caught the spirit of Wood's idea as soon as the book came out. He was quite carried away:

> . . . zu den Schotten! zu Macferson! Da will ich die Gesänge eines lebenden Volks lebendig hören, sie in alle der Würkung sehen, die sie machen, die Örter sehen, die allenthalben in den Gedichten leben, die Reste dieser alten Welt in ihren Sitten studiren! eine Zeitlang ein alter Kaledonier werden. . .

in fact to read Ossian as Wood had read Homer:

> Wood mit seinem Homer auf den Trümmern Troja's, und die Argonauten, Odysseen und Lusiaden unter wehendem Segel, unter rasselndem Steuer: Die Geschichte Uthals und Ninathoma im Anblick der Insel, da sie geschahe; wenigstens für mich sinnlichen Menschen haben solche sinnliche Situationen so viel Würkung. Und das Gefühl der Nacht ist noch in mir, da ich auf scheiterndem Schiffe, das kein Sturm und keine Fluth mehr bewegte, mit Meer bespült, und mit Mitternachtwind umschauert, Fingal las und Morgen hofte. . .[4]

There is some poetic licence in this. Herder's voyage in 1769 from Riga to Nantes took him nowhere near Ossian's fabulous coasts; still less did the return journey from Antwerp to Amsterdam. But the sentiments are exactly right.

'Sinnliche Situationen': that is when all the senses are in play, when one's awareness of real circumstances is keen, both in the appreciation and in the production of a work of art. Goethe, once he had met Herder and been sorted out by him, rooted his life's work of poetry in 'Sinnlichkeit'. This wants no proof: we have only to think of Italy.

---

[4] J. G. Herder, *Sämtliche Werke* ed. Suphan, reprinted Hildesheim, 1967, v, 167, 169.

Much came to fruition there; and it came, as Goethe himself said many times, with the force of *recurrence*. Things in him like seeds since childhood (the Mignon images from his father's travels) flowered. Things known but not central moved to the very middle of his being—like Winckelmann, whose letters and works Goethe only read when he got to Rome. It is a marvellous and mysterious faculty this, the storing of experience for assimilation and full appreciation at the right time. In that sense Goethe is a poet continually coming into his own. The psyche has her own sense of timing, of *kairos*, which Goethe intuitively obeyed. Then once fortunate circumstances have come about, as they did for him in Rome, how everything pours in to confirm their rightness. Goethe in Italy radiates poetic confidence. In that mood, which lasted blessedly long, almost anything can be turned to poetic good.

Reading Winckelmann in Rome, where *he* (after what miseries) *became what he was*, is not at all like reading him in Leipzig or Weimar. In Rome the effect is heightened, the reading has a nearness, an appropriateness and necessity. Still, reading Winckelmann in Rome is, as an experience, left standing by the experience of reading Homer in Palermo. Nietzsche suggested that it ought always to be possible to distill a man's biography into three anecdotes. One of them, in Goethe's case, must surely be that of his sudden need, his being taken short we might almost say, for a copy of Homer in the public gardens in Palermo:

> Aber der Eindruck jenes Wundergartens war mir zu tief geblieben; die schwärzlichen Wellen am nördlichen Horizonte, ihr Anstreben an die Buchtkrümmungen, selbst der eigene Geruch des dünstenden Meeres, das alles rief mir die Insel der seligen Phäaken in die Sinne sowie ins Gedächtnis. Ich eilte sogleich, einen Homer zu kaufen, jenen Gesang mit grosser Erbauung zu lesen und eine Übersetzung aus dem Stegreif Kniepen vorzutragen (HA xi, 241).

The landscape puts him in mind of the *Odyssey*, more particularly of the island of Phaeacia, where the shipwrecked Odysseus was so hospitably received first by the princess Nausicaa, then by her father Alcinous. Thereafter, 'uberzeugt, dass es . . . keinen besseren Kommentar zur *Odyssee* geben könne als eben gerade diese lebendige Umgebung' (HA xi, 299), on his tour of Sicily Goethe read Homer. In so doing he was following Lady Montagu, Pierre-Augustin Guys and Robert Wood, but the experience of course was all his own. The truth and beauty of the *Odyssey* were revealed to him with new intensity in the places in which, so he believed, the poem was set:

> Was den Homer betrifft, ist mir wie eine Decke von den Augen gefallen. Die Beschreibungen, die Gleichnisse etc. kommen uns poetisch vor und sind doch unsäglich natürlich, aber freilich mit einer Reinheit und Innigkeit gezeichnet, vor der man erschrickt. Selbst die sonderbarsten erlogenen Begebenheiten haben eine Natürlichkeit, die ich nie so gefühlt habe als in der Nähe der beschriebenen Gegenstände.
>
> Nun ich alle diese Küsten und Vorgebirge, Golfe und Buchten, Inseln und Erdzungen, Felsen und Sandstreifen, buschige Hügel, sanfte Weiden, fruchtbare Felder, geschmückte Gärten, gepflegte Bäume, hängende Reben, Wolkenberge und immer heitere Ebnen, Klippen und Bänke und das alles umgebende Meer mit so vielen Abwechselungen und Mannigfaltigkeiten im Geiste gegenwärtig habe, nun ist mir erst die Odyssee ein lebendiges Wort. (HA xi, 323)

And more than ten years later, preparing to attempt the *Achilleis*, he said this to Schiller:

> Uns Bewohner des Mittellandes entzückt zwar die Odyssee, es ist aber nur der sittliche Theil des Gedichts, der eigentlich auf uns wirkt, dem ganzen beschreibenden Theile hilft unsere Imagination nur unvollkommen und kümmerlich nach. In welchem Glanze aber dieses Gedicht vor mir erschien, als ich Gesänge desselben in Neapel und Sicilien las! Es war als wenn man ein eingeschlagnes Bild mit Firnis überzieht, wodurch das Werk zugleich deutlich und in Harmonie erscheint. Ich gestehe, dass es mir aufhörte ein Gedicht zu seyn, es schien die Natur selbst (*Briefe*, ii, 331)

Of that insight and excitement, there on the spot in Sicily, came a response which Wood, a traveller, scholar and statesman, could not give, but which Goethe, a poet, could. Goethe's response to Homer's 'creative imitation' of Nature, there for all to see in the *Odyssey*, was the wish to create, to imitate Homer: 'auf und aus diesem Lokal eine Komposition zu bilden' (HA xi, 298). In that blessed place he had before him Nature herself, the unspoilt original, and Homer's faithful copy. No poem ever sprang from clearer sources than *Nausikaa*. It was the real Sicilian landscape which drove him to read Homer, and out of Homer's lines—almost literally: the pencil marks are still there to be seen in the margins of his copy—out of Homer's own words Goethe began to draw his *Nausikaa*. Those two elements, Greek landscape and Greek poem, are the ground itself.

He added a third constituent, a discrepant one: sentimental love. He wanted to make of the Nausicaa episode, beautifully elusive in Homer, a five-act tragedy of sentimental love. In the *Odyssey,* in the sixth and seventh books, all that happens, of 'sentimental' interest, is this: the shipwrecked Odysseus, naked and salty, crawls out of the bushes where he has been asleep and, covering his manhood with a branch, appeals to Nausicaa, who has come down to the rivermouth with her maids to do the washing, for clothing, food, shelter and a passage home. When he has bathed and dressed, still on the beach, she does indeed admire him and wishes she might find a husband like him. She asks that he should not be seen with her when they return to the town, for fear that she might be compromised. This is a very delicate speech, and it might be the young girl's shy and subtle courtship of the stranger. Her father Alcinous is just as impressed and says, though not in her hearing, that he would be glad to have Odysseus for a son-in-law. But Odysseus wants to go home to Penelope and always says so. Having stayed three days with the happy Phaeacians, regaled them with his adventures and distinguished himself at their games, he leaves. There is only one exchange between him and Nausicaa after their meeting on the beach. She says:

> Stranger, goodbye. And may you in your own country
> Remember me, since to me first you owe your life.

And Odysseus replies:

> Nausicaa, daughter of generous Alcinous,
> May Zeus the Thunderer, husband of Hera, give
> Me safe return to my country. But there

I will always think of you in gratitude and reverence.
For you restored me to life, lady.

In Goethe's version the young girl was to have fallen in love with
the stranger and admitted it, so compromising herself—'was die Situation vollkommen tragisch macht' (HA xi, 299). Odysseus himself was
to have been 'halb schuldig, halb unschuldig' (HA xi, 300). Quite
simply, Goethe, full of himself as he invariably was, identified with the
salty Odysseus, 'der Bettgenoss unsterblich schöner Frauen' (HA V,
69)—he was fresh from Calypso—and so hoped to add to the Nature
of the Sicilian landscape and the Nature of Homer's poem his own
Nature, in the form of his experiences as an 'homme fatal'. As he said:
'Es war in dieser Komposition nichts, was ich nicht aus eignen
Erfahrungen nach der Natur hätte ausmalen können' (HA xi, 300).
Goethe wrote only 156 lines of his five-act tragedy, and of those
many are incomplete and disconnected. In details, turns of phrase,
imagery and tone there is a great deal of very close allusion to the
Homeric original. Odysseus' soliloquy, when he wakes hearing
Nausicaa's maids, is a compendium, in 38 lines, of 'Odyssian' details.
For the remainder, the best by far are those sketches towards an
evocation of the landscape. The *Odyssey* has a greater variety of place
than does the *Iliad*, and the books Goethe read and re-read 'mit
unglaublichem Anteil' (HA xi, 299) for his projected play have perhaps a keener sense of place than any others in Homer: where the
girls bring the washing, for example, at the rivermouth; or the grove of
Athene outside the town, where Odysseus hides to allow Nausicaa to
precede him; and, best of all, the garden of Alcinous. This last, a most
beautiful and famous evocation, Goethe recreates:

> Dort dringen neben Früchten wieder Blüten,
> Und Frucht auf Früchte wechseln durch das Jahr.
> Die Pomeranze, die Zitrone steht
> Im dunklen Laube, und die Feige folgt
> Der Feige. . . beschützt ist rings umher
> Mit Aloe und Stachelfeigen. . . ,
> Dass die verwegne Ziege nicht genäschig (HA v, 71 )

Further on, unconnected, there are two lines of his own immediate
observation:

> Ein weisser Glanz ruht über Land und Meer,
> Und duftend schwebt der Äther ohne Wolken.

That is to say: what is best realized in the *Nausikaa* fragment are Homer and Nature ('das Lokal')—in the lines on Alcinous' garden, the two together.

Goethe dwelled on (or in) his project throughout his tour of Sicily, and it died away to nothing when he left the island. The account of his 'excited reverie' contained in the *Italienische Reise* was written some thirty years later.

Love such as Goethe wished to depict in *Nausikaa* is quite un-Homeric. That is obvious, and he must have known it perfectly well. And yet it was his intention to try the same again in the *Achilleis*, the same three ingredients: Homer (this time the *Iliad*), Homeric landscape (this time the plain of Troy), and sentimental love (that of Achilles for Polyxena).

Were the projects undermined by their modern ingredient? In both sentimental love was intended actually to constitute the story, and in neither was Goethe able to proceed with it. The question becomes a more general one than I can answer or even broach satisfactorily here. But in my view, very briefly, discrepancy of this kind may indeed be fatal to the project, but it is nevertheless necessary, in some measure and form, if imitation is to be creative, if 'Nachahmung' is to become 'Nachschaffen'. 'Nachschaffen', if we abide by the insights of *Sturm und Drang, must* mean reproduction and re-creation *in our own form*. It must mean the playing off of our own cultural and personal needs against the imitated tradition. That tension or discrepancy constitutes the dynamic life of the true work of art. Consider the discrepancy between *Faust* and its Christian framework; or, more pertinent here, that between Iphigenie's Weimar humanism and the bloody myth of the House of Tantalus.

It is the question of tradition and the individual talent—of 'Aneignung', appropriation, of 'das Fremde' and 'das Eigne', in Hölderlin's terms. Always an issue for every artist, but of an almost deadly urgency to eighteenth-century Hellenists. Goethe resolves it triumphantly in his lyric poetry, in the *Romische Elegien* especially, and it would be interesting to study why success was so much more likely there than in his *Nausikaa* and his *Achilleis*.

Very reluctantly Goethe came back from Italy to Weimar, and never went anywhere near Homer's physical world again. His *Achilleis* then was composed, so far as it went, in circumstances lacking the immediacy of those in which *Nausikaa* was begun and abandoned. Circumstances in fact, it must be said, altogether more academic. In the 1790s, in close association with Schiller, Goethe was again intensely preoccupied with Homer. He re-read the works, often aloud in company; he wrote a full synopsis of the *Iliad*, book by book; he struggled to understand the nature of epic. His *Reineke Fuchs* (1793) and *Herrmann und Dorothea* (1797) are attempts to appropriate Homeric form. Form, as a surface matter, is certainly imitable, and both works are in that sense successful. The *ethos* of these two finished epics is of course quite un-Homeric; and it was towards that ethos, as something not at all easily appropriated, towards Homer himself, that Goethe was, in the late 1790s, irresistibly drawn. In that *rapprochement* he used all the guidance he could get. He read widely in recent and contemporary scholarly work on Homer, and especially the *Prolegomena* of Friedrich August Wolf (1795).

Wolf was important in that, developing ideas in Wood and others, he saw the Homeric epics as both oral poetry and an amalgam of works by various bards and rhapsodes finally collected together under the common denominator Homer. This thesis, though it offended Goethe's characteristic love of wholeness, did attract and for a time persuade him for the curious personal reason that it broke down the wholly inaccessible genius Homer into numerous smaller and thus more imitable component parts:

> Denn wer wagte mit Göttern den Kampf? und wer mit dem
> Einen?
> Doch Homeride zu sein, auch nur als letzter, ist schön.
>
> (HA i, 198)

Homerids were, strictly speaking, a guild of poets on the island of Chios who claimed descent from Homer and a hereditary property in the Homeric poems, which they recited publicly; but as Goethe uses the word here it means rather that group of anonymous poets by whom the two great epics were composed. Goethe's passionate wish was to be one of their number, albeit in Weimar in 1798.

His intention was quite specific: to place between the *Iliad* and the *Odyssey* a worthy link. Pursuing this rather gradually unfolding but intense desire Goethe had recourse to a great deal of 'background reading'. He read those expansions of Homer's work which were composed in late antiquity by Dictys Cretensis, Quintus Smyrnaeus and Statius. He read scholars on the Homeric texts; travellers and topographers on the Homeric localities; he discussed with Schiller whether such a work as he had in mind was even in *theory* possible.

This is not the sudden inspiration experienced on an April day in Sicily, but a steadily growing fixation on one great purpose. The poem does not emerge from the Mediterranean sea, nor out of Homer's own verses acquired and read on the spot. It is worked towards. Both *Nausikaa* and the *Achilleis* are, in conception, intensely imagined. But the latter is the more ambitious. *Achilleis* is a titanic wish, hubristic; like Faust reaching after Helena.

Nobody would deny, certainly not in Goethe's case, that a programme of reading, study, immersion in 'secondary literature', might contribute to imaginative production. But the course is always a risky one. What *can* be given life by sheer scholarship? It smacks more of coercion than creation, as though a work might be brought into existence by main force of assembled facts. That is 'positives Beleben des Todten'. The accumulation and assembling of information, learning, facts, what Coleridge calls 'fixities and definites', is something a poet might be drawn into if an intensely imagined conception refuses to materialize.

The *Achilleis* was to tell the story, in eight cantos, of Achilles' unhappy love for the Trojan girl Polyxena. It is, I think, significant that both these passionately conceived but unfinished works have as their subjects unhappy love. The plot itself is an analogue of the whole abortive undertaking. Likewise the youthfulness of the two tragic figures. Both were to die, Achilles on good authority, Nausicaa by Goethe's invention; and as a focus of longing there is nothing quite like the young dead, in their unfinishedness:

> Aber der Jüngling fallend erregt unendliche Sehnsucht
> Allen Künftigen auf, und jedem stirbt er aus neue.
> *Achilleis*, 524-25. (HA ii, 532)

After more than a year's preparation Goethe finally began to compose his epic on 10 March 1799. He worked steadily at it throughout that month and sent the nearly completed first canto to Schiller on April 2. No more got written. It is more substantial than *Nausikaa* but still, compared with what was projected, only a small fragment.

The *Achilleis* begins exactly where the *Iliad* ends, with the obsequies of Hector, tamer of horses. Achilles, still grieving for Patroclus, watches the flames of Hector's funeral pyre and turns then at once to thoughts of his own death, which he knows to be imminent, and of his own monument, a barrow on the headland over the Hellespont. The building of this great mound is already under way. In standard Homeric fashion the scene then shifts, at dawn, to Heaven, where the gods, after the deaths of Patroclus and Hector, are continuing to be interested in Achilles. Goethe spends 150 lines in the Homeric heaven, describing the immortals and having them speak their opinions. This is, in my opinion, only an antiquarian and mythological achievement, *essentially* not worth doing, but part of the whole form into which Goethe had put himself, and something which could only be done picturesquely. He composes a *tableau*, such as the comte de Caylus loved to discover in the *Iliad* (quite mistakenly, Lessing thought). Goethe did have a painter's eye for the 'picturesque' in Homer and having worked on the *Achilleis* he set subjects from the *Iliad* and the *Odyssey* in Weimar's annual art competition. But his own tableau, in the wrong medium, is a museum piece. He then further undermines its validity by ascribing to his Zeus a most un-Homeric inclination to soften Fate. Zeus comforts Thetis, the already grieving mother of Achilles, with the old adage: where there's life there's hope. Who knows what might turn up? But of course what makes the *Iliad* so unrepeatably grand is precisely the inexorable hold of Fate. Nothing is more poignant in all the literature of the world than the meeting of Achilles and Priam, when both weep. They are both under implacable Fate. At heart, Goethe shied away from such an ethos. He told Schiller: 'ich muss mir zu eigen machen, was mir selbst nicht behagt' (*Briefe*, ii, 344). Goethe's goddess Athene descends from Olympus quite simply to cheer Achilles up. And back on earth again the poem improves and is magnificent until, 300 lines later, it breaks off.

The opening of the *Achilleis* and the last three hundred lines are successful poetry, I think, because they have a secure footing in real locality. Goethe never saw the Hellespont and the Plain of Troy, but he read Robert Wood and his successor in those fabulous localities, an unscrupulous and self-advertising Frenchman by the name of Lechevalier; also Richard Chandler, and Carl Gotthold Lenz's compendium volume *Die Ebene von Troja nach dem Grafen Choiseul Gouffier und anderen neuen Reisenden.*[5] He went to some pains to get the topography of the Troad by heart. Then, with great sureness of poetic imagination, he concentrated, among the many details, on the barrows above the Hellespont.

Homer himself says enough about these tumuli to tantalize readers and travellers for all ages to come. Knowing that before long he will be dead himself Achilles raises over the ashes of Patroclus only a relatively modest mound, to be increased, he orders, once the ashes of both of them are mingled there together. In Hades then the ghost

---

[5] Published Neu-Stretlitz, 1798. Lenz actually supplies diagrams of the supposed tomb of Achilles.

of Agamemnon reports to the ghost of Achilles that this was duly
done:

> Burning like a forge when the flames had consumed you
> At dawn we collected your white bones Achilles
> And laid them in pure wine and oil. Your mother gave us
> A golden urn, the gift, she said, of the god Dionysus,
> The work of great Hephaestus. Therein we placed your bones,
> Famous Achilles, together with those of Patroclus,
> Son of Menoetius, who died before you. The bones of
>           Antilochus,
> Whom you loved above all others when Patroclus was dead,
> We placed close by and over all we soldiers raised
> A colossal mound on a high headland above
> The Hellespont where the waters widen so that in our
> Generation and in all generations to come
> Men at sea will mark it from a great distance.
>
> *(Odyssey* xxiv, 71–84)

In antiquity the Achilleion was confidently identified by sailors
approaching the Sigean headland. Alexander the Great, who regarded
Achilles as his ancestor and tutelar spirit, adorned the tomb with flowers, anointed its stone with perfumes and danced around it naked, as
he passed through the Troad eastwards on his campaigns. His
favourite, Hephaestion, sacrificed particularly to Patroclus, in order to
indicate that he was to Alexander what Patroclus had been to
Achilles.

The tomb was one of the holy places of the cult of heroic friendship, and for that reason Hölderlin's Hyperion and Alabanda are
drawn there:

> Da ich die Wälder des Ida mit ihm durchstreifte,
> und wir herunterkamen in's Thal, um da die
> schweigenden Grabhügel nach ihren Todten zu
> fragen, und ich zu Alabanda sagte, dass unter den
> Grabhügeln einer vielleicht dem Geist Achills und
> seines Geliebten angehöre, und Alabanda mir
> vertraute, wie er oft ein Kind sey und sich denke,
> dass wir einst in Einem Schlachtthal fallen und
> zusammen ruhen werden unter Einem Baum . . .[6]

---

[6] Hölderlin, *Sämtliche Werke, Grosse Stuttgarter Ausgabe*, iii, 36. Such places
have considerable aphrodisiac power. Homer's Grotto is another one in the same
novel.

Modern sentimental travellers found the desire to identify Achilles' tomb, and that of Ajax on the northern shore, quite irresistible. The by no means 'enthusiastic' Richard Chandler states simply and categorically:

> After walking eight minutes we came between two barrows standing each in a vineyard or inclosure. One was that of Achilles and Patroclus; the other, which was on our right hand, that of Antilochus, son of Nestor . . . We had likewise in view the barrow of Ajax Telemon. . .[7]

Lechevalier, no less definite, is more expansive:

> Diese sonderbare Erdmasse, welche die Griechen hier aufführten, ist noch vorhanden. Sie ist nicht mehr, wie ehedem, von Ulmen umgeben. Aber die hohen Pappeln, und die klagenden Cypressenbäume, die ihre Stelle einnehmen, vermehren das melancholische Dunkel dieser Gräber.[8]

When Goethe's Athene descends to earth she joins Achilles, in the form of his friend Antilochus, *in the half-finished tomb itself.* He is standing in his own huge grave whilst his Myrmidons heap up the terrific walls outside. Lechevalier opened one of the numerous tumuli on the land overlooking the Hellespont. Digging away the earth he discovered two broad stones leaning together and beneath them a statuette of Athene and a metal urn containing cremated human bones. Goethe must have had this in mind when he has his Achilles give these instructions to Antilochus (alias Athene):

> dir sei empfohlen
> In der Mitte das Dach, den Schirm der Urne, zu bauen.
> Hier! zwei Platten sondert ich aus, beim Graben gefundne
> Ungeheure; gewiss der Erderschüttrer Poseidon
> Riss vom hohen Gebirge sie los und schleuderte hierher

---

[7] Richard Chandler, *Travels in Asia Minor*, Oxford 1775, p. 42.

[8] J.B. Lechevalier, *Beschreibung der Ebene von Troja*, Leipzig 1792, pp. 220-21. This is the German version of a paper Lechevalier delivered in French to the Royal Society in Edinburgh in the spring of 1791.

Sie, an des Meeres Rand, mit Kies und Erde sie deckend.
Diese bereiteten, stelle sie auf, aneinander sie lehnend
Baue das feste Gezelt! Darunter möge die Urne
Stehen, heimlich verwahrt, fern bis ans Ende der Tage.
                                              (11.432–40)

That Athene stands in the grave with Achilles—one of the poem's
finest touches—was, I am sure, suggested to Goethe by Lechevalier's
discovery of the statuette. That is: he gave an archaeological detail
poetic life.

Soon, as part of her wish to console him, Athene suggests to
Achilles that they walk on the ramparts of the tomb; and there, having
a view over the Hellespont and beyond, she expands on those lines in
the *Odyssey*—'so that in our / Generation and in all generations to
come / Men at sea will mark it [the tomb] from a great distance'—and
offers Achilles the only consolation he can have: eternal fame. His
tomb will always be seen. And in a characteristically Goethean manner this fame, incorporated in the physical landmark, the tomb,
becomes a focal point for good human enterprises, it becomes a
daymark for sailors going to and fro across the seas trading. Achilles'
fame thus lives for ever, in human activity. That is an ethical colouring
which the Homeric idea of fame never had.

Nothing else is so good in the fragment *Achilleis* and perhaps, had
Goethe continued, nothing else would have been so good. The personal, poignant plot—that Achilles forgets his imminent fate and falls
for the Trojan hostage Polyxena—would not have sorted very well with
the grand consolation on the ramparts of the tomb at the outset. The
Homeric localities are persuasively evoked in the *Achilleis*, recreated
by force of imagination out of the travellers' accounts. Prominent on
the headland the unfinished tomb may, in Goethe's poem, be seen for
ever. That substantial mark, surviving and yet a mark of death, of
what is past, gone, irrecoverable, is a peculiarly fitting symbol for the
failure of the whole undertaking.

The tomb on the headland is more potent even than Helen's
cloak and veil. They dissolve into clouds, you remember. The headland survives, out of the age of the Ideal into our modern times. The
tomb is the focal point of modern longing. What the Homeric form
was unable actually to incorporate—a story of unhappy love—may be
felt around the tomb of Achilles and Patroclus like a ghost. The failure, the falling short, has a quite peculiar poignancy. But it is also in
its very nature the spur to production. Out of the sense of loss and
absence starts the will to re-possess. In terms of poetic composition it

is the gap between conception and execution. Beauty intensely conceived and imagined—in execution, in the poem, only partially realized. Robert Graves speaks of the writing of poetry as an act of
recovery. Not the whole of the poem can always be brought to light.
That image is peculiarly apt to the endeavours of poets (and scholars)
in Goethe's day. Think of the broken statuary then coming to light in
Italy and Greece.

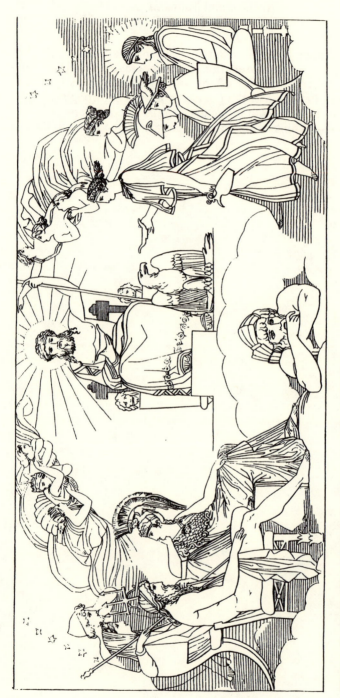

Figure 8. Council of the gods. Flaxman (*Iliad* series).

# Of Chapman's Homer and Other Books

*Bernice Slote*

Much have I travell'd in the realms of gold,
   'And many goodly states and kingdoms seen;
   Round many western islands have I been
Which bards in fealty to Apollo hold.
  Oft of one wide expanse had I been told
    That deep-brow'd Homer ruled as his demesne;
    Yet did I never breathe its pure serene
Till I heard Chapman speak out loud and bold:
Then felt I like some watcher of the skies
    When a new planet swims into his ken;
Or like stout Cortez when with eagle eyes
    He star'd at the Pacific—and all his men
Look'd at each other with a wild surmise—
    Silent, upon a peak in Darien.

To Keats, books were life. What a poet made and how a man lived were all a part of the same adventure to worlds unconfined and beautiful. One vivid example of how books and men behave together is the story of his sonnet, "On First Looking into Chapman's Homer." Readers of Keats know it began on the October night in London in 1816 when he joined his friend Charles Cowden Clarke for some reading, even as the two had enjoyed many books together in the years since Keats was a student in the Enfield school of Clarke's father—books like Spenser's *Faerie Queene*, which had led Keats to a career as a poet.[1] Clarke now had been lent a "beautiful copy of the folio edi-

---

[1] For Clarke's account of Keats, books and the evening with Chapman's Homer, see Charles and Mary Cowden Clarke, *Recollections of Writers*, pp. 120-157;

tion" of George Chapman's Elizabethan translation of Homer's *Iliad* and *Odyssey*. They had read Homer in Pope's translation, but Chapman was a book both famous and rare.

From 1611 to 1616, various editions and combinations of Chapman's translations of Homer had been printed. A good many of the copies now in rare-book collections are slightly different in details, but one "Chapman's Homer" in the Henry E. Huntington Library will serve as a model of the kind of book Keats explored that night in Clarke's rooms. It is a folio of heavy paper, clear type, wide margins. The title pages and section headings are richly decorated with sharp, detailed engraving (both pictures and formal designs of geometric figures, scrolls, motifs). The title page reads: "The Whole Works of Homer; Prince of Poetts. In his Iliads, and Odysses. Translated according to the Greeke, by Geo. Chapman. London: printed for Nathaniell Butter." The introductory pages include a picture of Chapman, who has two moles on the left of his nose, a beard, and bald head fringed with curly hair; a dedication to Prince Henry; a knightly picture of the Prince holding a spear, with helmet and plumes at the lower left side; and other dedications, compliments, and Prefaces to the reader in which Chapman extols Homer's universal greatness: Even among the Indians, when "they used any divine duties according to the custome of their households and hospitalities, they invited ever, Apollo, and Homer." But what Homer was, "his workes shew most truly; to which (if you please) go on and examine him." Certainly Keats and Clarke did go on, and no doubt read one of the dedicatory sonnets which Chapman had placed at the end of the "Iliads," for the poem to Robert Cecyl, Earle of Salisburye, anticipates the general pattern of imagery Keats would use in his sonnet:

> So, none like Homer hath the World enspher'd;
> Earth, Seas, & heaven, fixt in his verse, and moving . . . .

"We read through the night," said Clarke, sampling the passages they knew best: from the *Iliad*, the conversation of the Senators and Helen on the wall of Troy and Antenor's description of Ulysses as orator (Book III), the description of the shield and helmet of Diomed (Book V). Clarke, writing years later, remembered the Keats of that night: "How distinctly is that earnest stare, and protrusion of the upper lip now present with me, as we came upon some piece of rough-

---

and *The Keats Circle*, ed. Hyder Edward Rollins, II, pp. 146-150, 169.

hewn doric elevation in the fine old poet. He sometimes shouted." They read late, but the next morning a messenger brought Clarke Keats's new poem of personal discovery, "On First Looking into Chapman's Homer."

What was so vividly alive and exciting about this reading of Homer? Chapman's lines *are* virile and bold, and the stories themselves exciting; but in addition, *the poetry was read aloud.* This was nothing unusual for the two friends. Clarke said that he *had read to Keats* the "Epithalamion" of Spenser, and Keats had responded physically—"his features and exclamations were ecstatic." Keats read aloud, too: in *Cymbeline*, his eyes filled with tears and his voice faltered at some of Imogen's lines. During the night of Chapman's Homer, Clarke must have read many of the passages, which he knew better than Keats. Clarke was a big man and he had a big voice that would have filled the room. Something of his presence can be guessed by the description of Boythorn in Dickens' *Bleak House*, a character that in later years his wife and friends laughingly thought must have been taken directly from Clarke.[2] Boythorn is an impetuous, loud, hearty, sturdy man with great lungs—"Talking, laughing, or snoring, they make the beams of the house shake." Boythorn (and no doubt Clarke) had a great laugh and a booming voice, and uttered every word with "roundness and fullness." Even by such an indirection we can picture the scene—Keats, slight and compact, listening to the big Clarke pounding away at heroes and seas and shipwrecks. No wonder Keats heard "Chapman speak out loud and bold." The poetry to Keats was not an intellectual maneuver; he was deeply and physically involved, with delighted stares when some passage struck him with a fresh surprise. And remember, *he sometimes shouted.*

Many who have read neither Pope nor Chapman may wonder what there was to shout about in Chapman's version of Homer. Pope's translation was, of course, in the ten-syllable line of the heroic couplet, each two lines making a finished or closed segment. Chapman wrote in couplets, too, but the *Iliad* is put into longer lines of fourteen syllables and the couplets are not always closed. Therefore the breath is longer, more irregular, more racy. The *Odyssey* is in ten-syllable lines, but again the couplets are generally free and open. In addition, Chapman's language is usually more colorful, more imaginatively exciting. For example, Chapman's description of Ulysses as orator throws us into a storm:

2 Richard D. Altick, *The Cowden Clarkes*, pp. 79-80.

But when out of his ample breast he gave his great voice passe
And words that flew about our eares like drifts of winter's snow,
None thenceforth might contend with him . . . (III, 242–244)

Pope puts us neatly into the schoolroom:

But when he speaks, what elocution flows!
Soft as the fleeces of descending snows
The copious accents fall, with easy art;
Melting they fall, and sink into the heart!

Keats liked Chapman's vivid phrases: Neptune's "immortall moving feet" (XIII, 19), and (of Ulysses shipwrecked) "The sea had soakt his heart through" (V, 612), which was limply handled by Pope as "And lost in lassitude lay all the man." Chapman's Homer was a poet whose world was brilliantly alive. And now Keats knew for himself.

Part of Keats's excitement about Homer was tied up with a happy fusion of two other general imaginative experiences in literature: history and exploration, and Greek mythology. In school, Clarke said, Keats had "devoured rather than read" all the school library, "which consisted principally of abridgments of all the voyages and travels of any note" as well as a number of histories. The books that attracted him most, however, were those on mythology: Tooke's *Pantheon*, Lemprière's *Classical Dictionary*, and Spence's *Polymetis*. We could add Ovid, too, for his knowledge of myth. The metaphor of Keats's sonnet was principally the union of these two streams: imaginative discovery seen as geographical discovery in Apollo's world.[3]

All the high adventure and desperate undertaking of the early voyagers, explorers, and discoverers must have appealed to Keats. One of the books he studied was William Robertson's *History of America*, and in it we can trace the geographical-historical framework of the sonnet.[4] Robertson tells mainly of certain "realms of gold," the treasure lands of the Portuguese and Spanish explorers, who sought and eventually found Mexico and Peru, passing literally the "western islands" on the way. One map in Robertson's *History* shows most prominently the range of islands from Cuba and the Caribbean

---

[3] Only these primary influences are considered here. They do not, of course, exclude the addition of other sources that have been suggested for the images of the sonnet. See especially B. Ifor Evans on John Bonnycastle's *An Introduction to Astronomy* (Essays and Studies of the English Association, 1931).

[4] I have used the fourth edition of William Robertson, *The History of America*, (London, 1783), 3 vols. Page references are in the text.

westward through the Gulf of Mexico to Darien, in Central America, and the lands north of it. The question of why Cortez, instead of Balboa, seems to be discovering the Pacific from a peak in Darien has not been answered to everyone's satisfaction. Some critics have argued that Keats simply made a mistake. Others have sensibly pointed out that the metaphor of discovery does not need to mean "the first by anyone" (for Keats had read Homer before, and others had known Chapman's translation).[5] But we also recognize the inescapable parallel of the scene in the poem and Robertson's account of Balboa on a mountain in Darien. Searching for the golden land of Peru, Balboa with tremendous difficulty crossed the marshes and mountains of the Isthmus of Darien:

> At length the Indians assured them, that from the top of the next mountain they should discover the ocean which was the object of their wishes. When, with infinite toil, they had climbed up the greater part of that steep ascent, Balboa commanded his men to halt, and advanced alone to the summit, that he might be the first who should enjoy a spectacle which he had so long desired. As soon as he beheld the South Sea stretching in endless prospect below him, he fell on his knees, and lifting up his hands to Heaven, returned thanks to God, who had conducted him to a discovery so beneficial to his country, and so honourable to himself. His followers, observing his transports of joy, rushed forward to join in his wonder, exultation and gratitude. (I, 250–251)

Another view is that Cortez was taken (consciously or unconsciously) as a blend of all the conquistadors, even as the heroes of legend and myth take on the feats of lesser figures.[6] It is most likely that Keats was thinking of the total story of Robertson's New World, in which Cortez was clearly the principal actor, and he simply used the most dramatic single scene he remembered to embody the act and the emotion of discovery.

---

[5] See Charles C. Walcutt, "Keats' 'On First Looking into Chapman's Homer,' " *Explicator*, V (June 1947), 56; and the more complete discussion in C.V. Wicker, "Cortez–not Balboa," *College English*, 17 (April 1956), 383-387.

[6] See Joseph Warren Beach, "Keats's Realms of Gold," PMLA (March 1934), 246-257.

However, several other passages in Robertson, not usually noted, have some bearing on both the factual problem and the symbolic direction of Keats's poem. For one thing, Cortez had the *type* of experience Keats describes as he first saw Montezuma's Mexico.

> In descending from the mountains of Chalco, across
> which the road lay, the vast plain of Mexico opened
> gradually to their view. When they first beheld this
> prospect, one of the most striking and beautiful on
> the face of the earth; when they observed fertile
> and cultivated fields, stretching farther than the eye
> could reach; when they saw a lake resembling the
> sea in extent, encompassed with large towns, and
> discovered the capital city rising upon an island in
> the middle, adorned with its temples and turrets;
> the scene so far exceeded their imagination, that
> some believed the fanciful descriptions of romance
> were realized. (II, 276)

Furthermore, according to Robertson, Cortez *did* see the Pacific, and from Darien. Going on in Robertson to the close of the extensive account of Cortez's conquest of Mexico, we read that his last schemes were to find some strait to afford easy passage between the Gulf of Mexico and the Pacific, and in 1530 he searched, though unsuccessfully, through the Isthmus of Darien. Eventually he crossed to the pacific side of the isthmus and made his further voyages from ports on the other side of Darien. From there he discovered another land of gold of which he had often heard—the peninsula of California—and surveyed the gulf of the Vermilion Sea between it and New Spain (II, 393–394). Moreover, Pizarro in 1529, financed by Cortez, had also marched across Darien to Panama and from there made the conquest of Peru, that really golden land of the fabled Incas (III, 16–19). Just how the scenes were shifted we do not know, but in one moment, one man, Keats did focus all of the long and difficult search that found its dream made possible. For it was not the ocean alone but the lands beyond––California, Sonora, Peru––that made such a discovery supreme. Chapman was, after all, the *way* to the world of Homer.

Keats had suggested that the world of the imagination had its own geography to explore. With this figure he combined the myth of Apollo as god of poetry and therefore the ruler of its lands. But he had also learned from the textbooks of mythology he had studied (Lemprière, Spence, Tooke) that no god is one thing alone. Apollo is also associated with the sun, light, growth, and life. The realms of gold are in harmony with him. Spence in *Polymetis*[7] describes Apollo's shining face, the brightness beaming from his eyes, the crown of twelve rays on his head. His chariot of gold has a rose-colored harness studded with precious stones. In Tooke's *Pantheon*[8] he is pictured with a halo of light, and it is said that he "shines in garments embroidered with Gold." Apollo the Sun "by his Light makes all Things manifest." In his own "Ode to Apollo" a year before (1815) Keats had already combined Apollo's gold with the poet Homer. In the god's "western halls of gold" bards strike their lyres, "Whose chords are solid rays, and twinkle radiant fires." One bard is Homer who "with his nervous arms / Strikes the twanging harp of war." Another characteristic of Apollo, according to Tooke, is the "Perspicuity and Sharpness of his Eyes" that "do most fitly represent the Foresight of Prophecy." Even if the "eagle eyes" in the sonnet were suggested by Titian's picture of Cortez, as many think, the effect of the two comparisons in the sestet of the poem is to put the "watcher of the skies" and the explorer gazing seaward from the mountain peak into harmony with the visionary quality of Apollo's view. The hawk, after all, was favored by Apollo because he "has Eyes as bright as the sun." Neither Cortez nor the watcher of the skies *is* Apollo, but the discoverer in the world of poetry may well have sight that is suitable to Apollo's realm. Finally, Apollo is the god of harmony, growth, and life. The images of Keats's poem do trace the great cosmic circle of earth and ocean and the planets of the sky, and the vision that might contain it, even as Keats had described the epic itself in his "Epistle to Charles Cowden Clarke" (September, 1816) as king of all, "Round, vast, and spanning all like Saturn's ring." The sonnet on Chapman's Homer joins both history and myth, both human understanding and godlike vision.

Among the books Keats owned at the time of his death (less than five years after he wrote the sonnet) was listed "Marmontel's *Les Incas*, a history-romance of the Incas of Peru, which first appeared in Paris in 1777, with a later English translation published in Dublin, 1797. There is no indication whether Keats had the French or English version, or when it came into his possession. But whether he read it early or late (as cause or continuation of an idea), this book, too, joins

---

[7] Joseph Spence, *Polymetis* (London, 1747), p. 185.
[8] Andrew Tooke, *The Pantheon* (London, 1774), pp. 29-30, 87.

in the fused worlds of the sonnet—Apollo's realms of gold. The Incas, Robertson said in his *History*, were called "children of the Sun" and were sent by their parent, "who beheld with pity the miseries of the human race, to instruct and to reclaim them" (III, 22). The central theme of Marmontel is that the Incas were indeed the children of the sun, and much of the book is devoted to accounts of the temples and rituals of sun-worship. Their sun-god—Apollo, in other lands—pours forth "in one great stream of light, the principles of warmth, of life, and of fertility."[9] The sonnet, "On First Looking into Chapman's Homer," is a motif for the finding of such illumination: it is not so much about reading as about the stirring of life. Certainly Keats's personal quest under Apollo ended before it should, but as his poem records, he knew well how the creative imagination—in reading as well as in writing—could make life outreach space and time.

---

[9] *The Incas* (Dublin, 1797), I, 4.

Figure 9. Leucothea saves Odysseus on the raft. Flaxman (*Odyssey* series).

# The Homeric Competitions
# of Tennyson and Gladstone

*Gerhard Joseph*

In December 1865 the sculptor Thomas Woolner gave a memorable dinner party which, in a Victorian version of the Homeric games, generated a sportive clash between two of the age's heroes. The guests included William Ewart Gladstone, Alfred Tennyson, William Holman Hunt, and the Bristol physician John Addington Symonds. The son of this last entered later in the evening (as did F.T. Palgrave), and it is from the letters of the younger John Addington Symonds that we have a detailed, lively account of the stormy proceedings. The major feature of the evening was the persistency with which Tennyson and Gladstone gravitated toward polar attitudes whatever the topic of conversation, whether the issue under discussion was political or literary. As the younger Symonds entered the dining room, the assembled company had just begun to consider Governor Coote Eyre and his brutal suppression of the Jamaican uprising in which twenty Europeans had been killed and over 600 natives killed or executed. As Gladstone condemned the slaughter with the moral passion and oratorical skill by which he dominated Parliament, Tennyson kept interrupting not with counter-arguments but with *obbligato, sotto voce* prejudices: "We are too tender to savages, we are more tender to a black man than to ourselves. . . . Niggers are tigers, niggers are tigers." Repeatedly the two men differed over this and other matters, "Gladstone with his rich flexible voice, Tennyson with his deep drawl rising into an impatient falsetto when put out, Gladstone arguing, Tennyson putting in a prejudice, Gladstone asserting rashly, Tennyson denying with a bold negative, Gladstone full of facts,

Tennyson relying on impressions, both of them humorous, but the one polished and delicate in repartee, the other broad & coarse & grotesque."

When the company joined the ladies in the drawing room, Woolner gave Gladstone a manuscript book of Tennyson's unpublished (at the time) translations from the *Iliad* (now in the Pierpont Morgan Library), which Gladstone perused in silence. At Tennyson's entrance Woolner asked him to read aloud from the book. " 'No I shant' said Tennyson, standing in the room with a pettish voice & jerking his arms & body from the hips." And then he realized that Gladstone had been looking over the manuscript of the *Iliad.* "This isn't fair—no, this isn't fair," he cried, snatching it away. Tennyson in his nervousness now began to dominate the conversation totally, pontificating upon such matters as the nature of God and size of the universe, the puzzling quality of matter, the value of prayer, and the dependence of moral systems upon the idea of the immortality of the soul. Gladstone was unusually quiet during the long, windy monologue. At last Tennyson consented to go back to the dining room to read his translations to Gladstone and the elder Symonds, the two guests whose Greek he trusted, while the others agreed to remain behind. Young Symonds, however, followed, unperceived by Tennyson, who began to read "in a deep bass growl" the passage about Achilles shouting over the trench. Gladstone, who had held his fire for some time, now continually broke in upon Tennyson with criticisms of individual phrases. In his most "combative House of Commons mannerism, wh[ich] gives him the appearance of thinking too much about himself," Gladstone knew exactly how to break up Tennyson's recital most effectively. Naturally, Tennyson's ill-concealed annoyance at the repeated interruptions only served to egg Gladstone on. In short, the reading—if not the party itself, which finally broke up at 1:00 A.M.—was a disaster.[1]

Now, in the older biographies of both the Prime Minister and the Poet Laureate, these two highly egocentric personalities who dominated their respective spheres in the later nineteenth century are usually characterized as "friends" whose lives touched on many social occasions after their initial meeting in 1837. To be sure, differences in temperament and politics, the ever deepening Liberalism of Gladstone and the increasingly rigid Toryism of Tennyson, made for a certain amount of intellectual sparring and advice-mongering over the

---

[1] *The Letters of John Addington Symonds 1844-1868*, ed. Herbert M. Schueller and Robert L. Peters, 3 vols. (Detroit: Wayne State University Press, 1967-69), 1, 591-98.

years concerning such matters as Gladstone's handling of the Alabama affair reparations in the early 1870s, the various attempts on the part of the Liberals to extend the franchise, and, perhaps most bitterly, Gladstone's Irish policies in the 1880s. But the two landmark biographies of Tennyson—Hallam Tennyson's *Memoir* of 1897 and Sir Charles Tennyson's *Alfred Tennyson* of 1949—suggest that such differences never got in the way of a fundamental mutual affection and respect: "I love Mr. Gladstone, but I hate his policy," Sir Charles quotes Tennyson as saying in summation of his essential attitude.[2] One of the original emphases in Robert Bernard Martin's fine new biography of Tennyson, however, is the extent to which the petulance and compulsive rivalry exemplified by their behaviour at Woolner's party frequently soured the meetings of Tennyson and Gladstone, even if publicly they were deferential and spoke well of one another for the most part. Such intermittent, imperfectly suppressed hostility continued to the very end of their acquaintance: after a last, apparently congenial meeting in 1892, Tennyson's final recorded outburst was to the effect that "I never said anything halfbad enough of that damned old rascal." For his part Gladstone, though invited by the family to be a pallbearer, could not even spare the two hours it would have required to *attend* Tennyson's funeral at Westminster Abbey.[3]

It is appropriate (in light of the present argument, at any rate) that the strictly literary disagreements alluded to in the biographies had to do with classical civilization—and the specific character of Homer's achievement therein. For the source of Tennyson and Gladstone's continuing irritation with one another, as well as of the mutual respect that surely complemented it, was a residual competition over the memory of the "Achilles, whom we knew," as Tennyson referred to Arthur Hallam in "Ulysses." Sixty years after Hallam's death in 1833, there remained an odd undercurrent of jealousy in relations between the two great men of the age, which turned in Palamon and Arcite fashion upon the question of which could claim first place in Hallam's affection. Gladstone had reputedly been Hallam's "most intimate friend"[4] at Eton, a position which Tennyson usurped a few

---

[2] Sir Charles Tennyson, *Alfred Tennyson* (New York: Macmillan, 1949), p. 479.

[3] Robert Bernard Martin, *Tennyson: The Unquiet Heart* (Oxford: Clarendon Press, 1980), pp. 575. 582-83, and *passim*.

[4] Such a characterization by Philip Magnus in *Gladstone: A Biograplly* (London: John Murray, 1954) P. 6 is seconded by T. Vail Motter in his notes to *The Writings of Arthur Hallam* (New York: Modern Language Association of America, 1943). But as Jack Kolb's recent edition of *The Letters of Arthur Hallam* (Columbus: Ohio State University Press, 1981) makes clear, the matter was more complicated. Whatever Gladstone's strong affection, Hallam's closest friend at Eton was not Gladstone

years later at Cambridge and which he secured once and for all in the
public mind, if not necessarily in Gladstone's, with the publication of
*In Memoriam*. (Relevantly enough, although Tennyson circulated tri-
al-run copies among his friends and other interested parties, he specifically did not send one to Gladstone, who on the basis of his acquaintance with Hallam would have seemed an appropriate recipient.) Not that there was anything consciously homosexual in the relation of either friend with Hallam—or for that matter in their conception of Greek male bonding. Hallam, the "Achilles, whom we
knew," was for both merely the noblest of beings; and Gladstone in
his Homeric studies went to rather desperate lengths to argue that
there was nothing sexual about Plato's apologies for homoerotic love
and that the bond in the *Iliad* between Achilles and Patroclus was no
more than the idealization of chaste and manly camaraderie, precisely
the kind of affection that both Gladstone and Tennyson claimed to
have had for the charismatic Hallam. Such *amicitia* also bound together the knights of Arthur's Round Table in the *Idylls of the King*,
Gladstone's favorite Tennysonian work. For while Gladstone had his
reservations about some of Tennyson's poetry, he was so taken with
the *Idylls* that he carried the 1859 version about in his pocket.[5]
    Whatever the complicated source of Gladstone's enthusiasm, he
had been an ardent Homerist from his student days at Eton onward.
And once he was driven out of office after his First Ministry in 1874,
seemingly for good, that enthusiasm became an obsessive cause for
the rest of his life. "There are still two things left for me to do," he
told Mrs. Humphry Ward as late as 1888. "One is to carry Home
Rule—the other is to prove the intimate connection between the
Hebrew and Olympian revelations!"[6] That connection he had already
adumbrated in a three-volume, 1700-page *Studies on Homer and the
Homeric Age*, published in 1858, and he proceeded to elaborate upon
it in a series of books and papers written between 1874 and his return

---

but James Milnes Gaskell. And as Gladstone's tortured draft of a letter dated June
1830 (letter 90a, pp. 368-70) accusing Hallam of having abandoned whatever intimacy
there was suggests, relations between the two were already strained by that time,
however much Hallam in reply tried to reassure Gladstone (letter 91, pp. 37,-73). Perhaps the immediate cause of Gladstone's pain, according to Kolb (p. 370, n. 1), was
Hallam's sonnet entitled "To A. T." ("Oh, last in time, but worthy to be first"), dated
May 1829 (Motter, *Writings of Hallam*, pp. 45-46).

    [5] Martin, p. 423.

    [6] Mrs. Humphry Ward, *A Writer's Recollections* (London: Collins, 1918), p.
238; as quoted in Richard Jenkyns, *The Victorians and Ancient Greece* (Cambridge:
Harvard University Press, 1980), p. 200.

to power in 1880. Altogether, between 1847 and his death in 1898 he composed seven volumes and a very large number of articles to create "the single most extensive body of Victorian Homeric commentary."[7]

The many conversations he had with Tennyson over the years, such as the exchanges at Woolner's party, touched on various technical matters—the meaning of specific Homeric phrases or the question of whether Homer is most naturally translated into English through the hexameters that Gladstone (and, incidentally, Matthew Arnold) favored or in the blank verse iambic pentameter that Tennyson preferred in the "Achilles over the Trench" fragment he read at Woolner's. But the most fascinating biographical allusions are to their discussions concerning the larger meaning of the Olympic system itself, although strangely the *contents* of those discussions have not, as far as I can discover, been recorded. It might therefore be useful to speculate about the positions on the matter that Gladstone and Tennyson, foils for each other in so much else, might have taken.

In this context the two most recent treatments of Gladstone's "Homerology" (his coinage) are worth comparing. It is easy to make light of Gladstone's *idèe fixe*, his dispensational reading of Homer, as Richard Jenkyns has done, dead-pan fashion, in *The Victorians and Ancient Greece*. But one of the ways in which Frank M. Turner's account of the same material in *The Greek Heritage in Victorian Britain* seems both fuller and more discriminating is in his willingness to explore the conviction of Homer's historical realism that allowed a dedicated amateur like Gladstone to particularize a dynamic, evolving Homeric society with a sophistication that prefigured the work of later archeologists and anthropologists, the discoveries of Schliemann and the scholarly views of Jane Harrison and Gilbert Murray. It is only after a thorough discussion of these sensible elements that Turner moves on to Gladstone's more questionable thesis concerning Homer and revelation, first enunciated in the second volume of *Studies on Homer and the Homeric Age* and rather obsessively developed thereafter.[8] An extension of his 200 sermons for the edification of the household staff at Hawarden, this monumental work posits the notion of God's revelation of Himself to the Greeks in the works of Homer prior and as a complement to the revelation accorded the children of

---

[7] Frank M. Turner, *The Greek Heritage in Victorian Britain* (New Haven: Yale University Press, 1981), p. 160. Among the other virtues of Turner's account is a full bibliography of Gladstone's Homeric writings (p. 160, n. 38).

[8] Jenkyns, pp. 199-204; Turner, pp. 159-70; *Studies on Homer and the Homeric Age*, 3 vols. (Oxford: Oxford University Press, 1858).

Abraham in the Old Testament. As God had used the Jews to teach man how he should behave toward Him, so he had employed the Olympian system archetypally expressed in the *Iliad* and the *Odyssey*, a "secular Bible," to teach man how to behave toward his fellow man. Indeed, since Gladstone's orientation was primarily political, he tended to subordinate the Hebrew revelation, which could teach us little about the nature of human community, to the Greek dispensation, which could teach us much. In purposeful transposition, he thus put the Greeks where writers of the Gospels had put the Jews and Homer where they had put the Old Testament, as precursors of Christian revelation in such matters as the existence of a triplicated Godhead, the presence of an Evil One, and the concept of a Redeemer born of woman.

Such an attempt to Christianize Hellenism and canonize Homer by ingenious argument is perfectly representative of syncretist tendencies in the late nineteenth century. Under the impact of German comparative criticism, an increasingly professionalized scholarship sought to emphasize the common elements in all religions rather than the uniqueness of the Judeo-Christian system, and Gladstone was only one of many to try his hand at such mythographic games. As George Landow and Herbert Sussman have recently shown in complementary books,[9] the Victorian period witnessed the wholesale revival of typological thinking, whereby the details of classical and Hebrew story were read as "shadows" or types of Christian antitype, and it is within the context of the revival of such earlier hermeneutic procedures that Gladstone's typologizing of Homer is most respectably comprehensible. To be sure, such methods provoked annoyance in some readers and bemusement in others. Benjamin Jowett, for instance, said that anyone who claimed to have found the doctrine of the Trinity foreshadowed in the Homeric conjunction of Jupiter, Neptune, and Pluto (Gladstone insisted upon the Roman names) must be out of his mind. But if Gladstone's syncretism is not particularly impressive even in terms of nineteenth-century academic scholarship, the moral fervor with which he gave himself over to its elaboration is nevertheless totally representative of the age's search for a synoptic vision that would integrate the Hebrew, Hellenic, and Christian dispensations.

---

[9] George Landow, *William Holman Hunt and Typological Symbolism* (New Haven: Yale University Press, 1979); and Herbert Sussman, *Fact and Fiction: Typology in Carlyle, Ruskin and the Pre-Raphaelite Brotherhood* (Columbus: Ohio State University Press, 1979).

Tennyson's classical vision, if there is such a thing, is harder to get at, since he never gave it the kind of full-blown discursive form that we find in Gladstone. Although some of Tennyson's finest poems are on classical subjects, we are not accustomed to think of "The Hesperides," "Oenone," "The Lotos-Eaters," "Ulysses," "Tithonus," "Tiresias," "Lucretius," and "Demeter and Persephone" (to name the major works) as components of a single design. Nor is Tennyson's classicism as determinedly Homeric in emphasis as Gladstone's. Certainly, Tennyson's interest in Homer extended from the time when as a boy he lay on the beach at Marblethorpe, fighting the Trojan War in his imagination, to the composition late in life of "Demeter and Persephone," based upon the Homeric *Hymn to Demeter.* But while adaptations and echoes of Homer are scattered throughout his work, such poems as "Ilion, Ilion," "The Lotos-Eaters," and "Ulysses," for instance, are rarely Homeric in spirit or style. They lack the forthright ease and directness of Homer (the qualities of "manliness" that Gladstone so admired); their more languorous movement, the more involved and sophisticated language and syntax of Tennyson, are precisely those qualities that make Tennyson seem the most "Virgilian" of English poets. For as Douglas Bush has suggested in his description of Tennyson's classicism, in spite of a fondness for Greek poetry and specifically Homeric themes, Tennyson's craftsmanship was primarily Roman rather than Greek, and like most Roman poets he was essentially Hellenistic.[10] Hence his preference for the Alexandrian idyll over the older Homeric epic mode. But whatever the purely formal inclination, his subject matter had to do with the Olympic system, with a sense of man's relation to divinity ultimately derived from Homer or, alternatively, from Lucretius. And it is in the framework of Tennyson's lifelong intellectual competition with Gladstone that the Homeric element accentuates itself within our mind. For Tennyson's classical poems taken as a body may be said to imply a mythology no less coherent than Gladstone's Homerology—a system, however, not spelled out in didactic certitude but rather implied elliptically in the elegiac dignity, allusiveness, and sensuous detail we associate with a major poet.

Briefly, that dispensation is one in which divinity is essentially hostile to a human race whose champions are forever trying to wrest a sacred "wisdom" from it.[11] Heracles in "The Hesperides" is the first

---

[10] Douglas Bush, *Mythology and the Romantic Tradition in English Poetry* (New York: W. W. Norton, 1963), p. 226.

[11] For a fuller exposition, see Gerhard Joseph, "The Idea of Mortality in Tennyson's Classical and Arthurian Poems: 'Honour Comes with Mystery'," *Modern*

in a line of classical figures who challenge a divine or semi-divine agent in an attempt to discover its "ancient secret." To the extent that such classical poems are parables concerning poetic aspiration, the "wisdom" the classical hero attempts to win from the gods may allude to the poet's "vatic nature, the qualities of the poetic charism."[12] Yet the term achieves a wider metaphysical reach—the ancient secret can assume such various forms as the heavenly Beauty that Paris takes as his deadly gift in "Oenone," the classical "knowledge" that Tennyson's Ulysses is determined to follow beyond the utmost bound of human thought, the passionless bride "divine Tranquility" who lures Lucretius to his doom, the divine knowledge associated with Pallas Athene in "Tiresias," or the immortality for which a human lover negotiates in "Tithonus."

Each of the heroes is doomed to frustration whether he gains the object of his quest or not, because the Olympian deities are able to fend him off or betray him through mystery. With the single exception to be mentioned below, the classical deities are never unambiguously legible to man—Tennyson never considers the possibility of a Promethean sympathy. The Hesperidean Sisters may serve as paradigm: they know that "Honour comes with mystery; / Hoarded wisdom brings delight" (ll.47–48),[13] and that honor depends upon the ability to wrap their "wisdom of the West" within the enigma of numerical symbol (they sing of the "awful mystery" of a tantalizingly suggestive but ultimately impenetrable "five" and "three") so as to preserve their monopoly upon immortality. Elsewhere in his poetry Tennyson claims for his own uses the "quiet gods" of Lucretius' De Rerum Natura, deities who, "careless of mankind," take their nectared ease above a suffering humanity, smiling in secret,

> looking over wasted lands,
> Blight, famine, plague and earthquake, roaring deeps and fiery
>     sands,
> Clanging fights, and flaming towns, and sinking ships, and
>     praying hands.
>           ("The Lotos-Eaters," ll.114–16)

Philology 66 (1968), 136-45; and "Tennyson's Concepts of Knowledge, Wisdom, and Pallas Athene," Modern Philology 69 (1972), 314-22.

12 G. Robert Stange, "Tennyson's Garden of Art: A Study of 'The Hesperides'," PMLA 67 (1952), 732-43; reprinted in John Killham, Critical Essays on the Poetry of Tennyson (London: Routledge and Kegan Paul, 1960), pp. 99-112. The quotation appears on p. 102.

13 Quotations from Tennyson's poetry follow The Poems of Tennyson, ed. Christopher Ricks (London: Longman, Green, 1969).

When Tennyson's classical deities are not such non-Homeric, indifferent "quiet gods," they become the mocking Aphrodite who bestows Helen upon Paris only to bring an entire civilization to ruin, the Eos whose careless gift of eternal life without eternal youth reduces her beloved Tithonus to despair, or the Pallas Athene who blinds Tiresias for the audacity of searching her out. The poem "Lucretius" considers the alternative possibilities that a Venus who oversees the disintegration of the questing poet-philosopher is *either* one or the other, either one of the aloof, quiet deities of the *De rerum* or a jealous Homeric goddess intent upon revenge for his slighting of her in her several mythic guises. Tennyson's classical goddesses are thus supernatural versions of his Viviens and Ettarres, the various fatal women of the poetry. When such divinities touch the human world, they do so like the Zeus of Yeats's "Leda and the Swan"; their ravaging gifts are too terrible for man to bear; the price they exact for the power they offer or are forced to relinquish is catastrophic to the individual and to entire civilizations. For if we compare Tennyson's fastidious quiet gods who take their ease above a struggling humanity with a Pallas Athene who in Homeric fashion actively meddles in the affairs of man, we can see that the differences are not as important as the similarity of their affects upon humankind. Both Tennyson's Lucretian and Homeric deities, even when not actively hostile (as, for instance, the Eos of "Tithonus" is not), are ruinous.

To summarize, then, what might have gone on in the conversations between Tennyson and Gladstone, had those conversations been recorded: if Gladstone would probably have insisted to the end of his days upon the continuity between classical and Christian dispensations, upon a typological connection between Homeric type and Christian antitype,[14] Tennyson would probably have argued for a fundamental irreconcilability of the two mythic systems. The single classical poem in which those systems touch, "Demeter and Persephone," is appropriately enough the Homeric exception that proves the rule. In that work the Mother Goddess, as she comes to understand mortal pain by its analogy to her divine despair at the loss of Persephone, refuses to take part in the feasts of Tennyson's harsh or indifferent gods. She commits her allegiance instead, as Earth Mother, to a suffering humanity. As she does so, she becomes a type of the "younger kindlier Gods" (l. 129) who will displace the hard avengers of the

---

[14] Turner (p. 164, n. 49) describes notes for a long study Gladstone was working on at the end of his life which was to present his final view of the Olympian system. These notes (British Library Add. Mss. 44711-13) suggest that he was still intent upon linking Homer and primitive revelation.

Homeric and the indifferent divinities of the Lucretian systems. She becomes a classical anticipation of the God of Love who, as the *Idylls of the King* demonstrates, periodically sends an Arthur, "the King / In whom high God hath breathed a secret thing" ("The Coming of Arthur," ll.499–500), to redeem the wastelands of the earth. For Tennyson, at the end of his life, one sign of the race's emerging spiritual maturity is its ability to metamorphose classical deities who hoard their ancient wisdom from man into a beneficent God who sends surrogates into the world to bring the race intimations of the soul's immortality. With such a suppositious evolutionary view Gladstone would hardly have quarreled. But even in agreement the old competitive impulse might have reasserted itself. For to Gladstone evolutionary progress was a firm, unassailable certainty (witness his elaborately deferential attack upon the pessimism of "Locksley Hall Sixty Years After" in the *Nineteenth Century* of January 1887[15]). But for Tennyson such typological optimism would have been ringed with doubt. It would have been only one of his two contending voices, merely a faint trust in the larger hope of even "Demeter and Persephone," where the vision of a future "worship which is Love" sinks back into what is finally most powerful in the poem—"The Stone, the Wheel, the dimly-glimmering lawns / Of that Elysium, all the hateful fires / Of torment" that blast the silent field of Asphodel (ll.147–51).

---

[15] To be sure, both Sir Charles Tennyson (p. 494) and Robert Martin (pp. 560-61) cite the political motivation of a Gladstone who felt that "Justice does not require, nay rather she forbids, that the Jubilee of the Queen be marred by tragic notes."

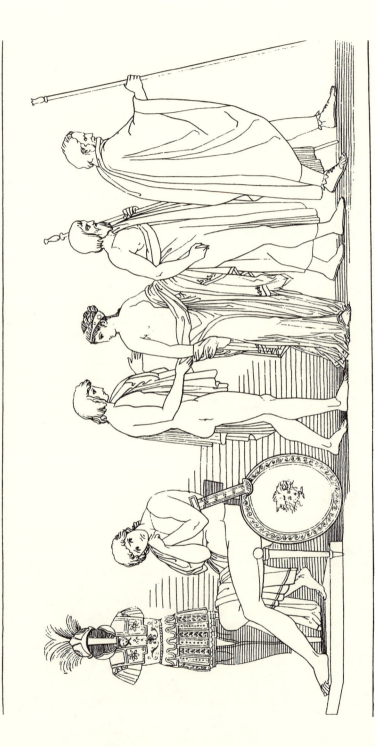

Figure 10. Departure of Briseis from Achilles. Flaxman (*Iliad* series, 1793).

# Tolstoy and Homer

*F.T. Griffiths & S.J. Rabinowitz*

*Tolstoy claimed that "Without false modesty,* War and Peace *is like the* Iliad.*" In the first six pages of their article, Griffiths and Rabinowitz examine what Tolstoy could have meant by that. After disposing of the idea that it might have been narrative unity, they sketch a tradition from Virgil through Statius, Dante, Milton, and Joyce of poets' use of the "doubleness of the Homeric model": tragedy succeeded by comedy, war by peace, and suggest that this is what Tolstoy had in mind.—Ed.*

\* \* \* \* \* \*

Of the innumerable influences on *War and Peace* Tolstoy openly invited comparison only to Homer, with whom consideration of the work as an epic structure must therefore begin.[1] Some of the parallels may, of course, be fortuitous; some may be subconscious; at least some must be printed and deliberate. We might begin by noting the gross movements of Homer's and Tolstoy's pairs of heroes as they leave and reenter society. Achilles begins the *Iliad* as the consummate

---

[1] Formal parallels between Homer and Tolstoy are briefly outlined by Rosemarie R. Ulis, "Has the Historical Novel Replaced the Epic?" *Classical Bulletin,* 40 (1964), 50-52, and George Steiner comments on thematic and philosophical similarities throughout *Tolstoy or Dostoevsky* (New York, 1959), esp. pp. 71-83. Two recent works deal with *War and Peace* as epic, although without any detailed attention to structure: Harry J. Mooney Jr., *Tolstoy's Epic Vision: A Study of* War and Peace *and* Anna Karenina (Tulsa, Okla., 1968), and Laura Jepsen, *From Achilles to Christ: The Myth of the Hero in Tolstoy's* War and Peace (n.p., 1978).

insider: the best warrior at Troy, a better fighter than Agamemnon is a king and politically not much less powerful, son of a goddess and therefore entitled to prerogatives not granted to other mortals. Feeling insufficiently rewarded for his valor, he abandons the Greek siege of Troy and dooms it to failure by his absence as well as by the gods' connivance. The mirror of this tragic tale of withdrawal is the myth of return: Odysseus' decade lost in fairyland shows him to an equal and opposite extent the outsider trying only to get home, and even in Ithaca he must reenter society slowly and from the margins dressed as a beggar to dupe and destroy the far more numerous suitors of his wife. At Anna Scherer's soirée at the start of *War and Peace*, Prince Andrei is the supreme insider who only wants out. Scornful, aloof, remote, he is an Achillean malcontent holding a teacup. He, too, will hear the growing claims of inward and private concerns and, like Achilles, confuse them with some call to cosmic and glorious attainment. At the same party, Pierre, a great clumsy bear of a man "like a child in a toy shop" (p. 10),[2] is making his debut in that same society. Like Odysseus, his final destiny will be the family happiness from which Andrei is in flight. While Achilles and Andrei in their wild swings between paralytic self-involvement and cosmic assertion rarely pause in between, Odysseus and Pierre show more profound connections with earth and with life as it is lived moment by moment. They are comfortable in the human community. Pierre, despite his foreign name, proves the very embodiment of Russianness, while Andrei spends much of the end of his life in voluntary withdrawal (for health, to be sure) in Switzerland. That Pierre marries Andrei's fiancée and beguiles his orphaned son is only the most concrete symbol of the extent to which the two men have exchanged places in the course of the narrative as the outsider gravitates to the center. Achilles and Odysseus embody a parallel contrast of self-immolation and homecoming.

Homer, no more than Tolstoy, cannot negotiate this radical turning without an element of contradiction, as emerges most disconcertingly when the *Iliad*'s heroes reappear as somewhat different characters in the *Odyssey*. The sympathetic Helen of the *Iliad* seems unmistakably witchy in her later years (*Odyssey*, Book IV), and the same Achilles who in the *Iliad* threw away his life without a second thought now reports from Hades (Book XI) that life is worth clinging

---

[2] The translations of *War and Peace* are those of Louise and Aylmer Maude as printed in Leo Tolstoy, *War and Peace*, ed. George Gibian, Norton Critical Edition (New York, 1966).

to at any price. But, then, it is not really the same Achilles. And the Odyssean report (not anticipated in the *Iliad*) that what finally took Troy was not Achillean brawn but the ruse of the Trojan Horse is to adherents of Iliadic values somewhere between revisionism and defamation. Similarly, the latter parts of *War and Peace* no longer sound like quite the same author: Tolstoy opens the work in earnest pursuit of certain premises, only to end it by demonstrating their opposite. We can overlook Andrei's crankiness at the start since he is the only honest and thoughtful voice among the chorus of hypocrites that Anna Scherer has gathered in her salon. History looms large on the horizon; only Andrei has the courage to confront it. And what can be said against a man proving his manhood? The acrimony between those who adore Napoleon and those who fear him gives no hint that the ultimate heroes of the tale are those who at this point scarcely grasp the issue, types like the pregnant Princess Lise or Pierre, who will finally prove true manhood as doting father of Natasha's children. Beyond the convulsions of European history looms the yet larger specter of natural history, whose deities are all goddesses. Against this initially unsuspected touchstone of nature, the great hypocrite of the piece will be Andrei for constantly and variously deluding himself about his ability to see the Truth, when one must instead, like Pierre and Natasha, live it. Since war impends, on first reading one naturally sorts Anna's guests into tragic classifications: heroes, choral bystanders, victims. Lise and Pierre are natural victims. Once familiar with the peaceful idyll that lies beyond 1812, one can trust hindsight to spot the apparent fools as comic heroes (Pierre) and the celebrities as impostors. Andrei is such an *alazon.* But one must visit this landscape, like the Mount of Purgatory (*Inferno* I and *Purgatorio* I), twice to realize that it is not tragic. Paradise, not Golgotha, hides at the top. And the right people are going to find all of this woe therapeutic. Already the *Aeneid* uses such stratifications of outlook by beginning with a happy ending (of much wandering) which turns out to be the start of much woe. What was "Venus saves Trojans" (Book I) on first reading retrospectively becomes "Juno traps Romans." The epic leap *in medias res*, which *War and Peace* so faithfully makes, entails action so straightforward that it may begin at once and a perspective so complex that the only sufficient prologue is a preliminary reading of the whole work.

The individual parallels between Tolstoy and Homer continue in far greater detail than can be pursued here. Pierre's seven years with the temptress Helene replicate the seven years that Odysseus spent in captivity (initially willingly, then, like Pierre, less so) with Calypso.

Years of wandering in fairyland have left Odysseus' wits a bit addled, and it takes the swineherd Eumaeus, whom he first visits in Ithaca, to put him in touch with the realities of his own land. For Pierre, confused by Freemasonry and similar distractions, the peasant Platon plays the same initiatory role. Odysseus customarily penetrates enemy territory disguised as a beggar--so once at Troy (Book IV), as in Ithaca; Pierre will finally be crafty enough to do much the same in Moscow. Neither Odysseus nor Pierre is much given to radical redefinition of social roles: they strive only to be given the chance to fulfill them in the normal way. In both of their protracted and dangerous homecomings the heroic quest is for the attainment of the ordinary.

The prizes are as similar as the heroes, most conspicuously in that both Penelope and Natasha are such paragons of resilient chastity. Both writers have found deft, if provocative, ways of letting these women experience life richly and in ways parallel to their future or returning husbands, but without losing their virtue in the process. Penelope and Natasha spend years being courted and learn much thereby without ever being won. Penelope faces her own Scylla and Charybdis between being too easy with her suitors (and losing everything) or rigidly resisting, thereby getting herself raped and Telemachus killed. Natasha must tack a similarly perilous course between disgrace, narrowly averted with Anatole Kuragin, and the sterile self-righteousness which leaves Sonia an old maid. The couples united or reunited at the end of the *Odyssey* and of *War and Peace* have used hardship and separation to grow more alike, while the unions which had prosperous and easy beginnings (Helen and Menelaus in the *Odyssey*; Helene and Pierre in Tolstoy) have collapsed from within. Tolstoy's Helene is in fact an unmistakable imitation of that Helen of Troy, and her entrance into Anna Scherer's soirée reenacts Helen's entrance onto the walls of Troy in the *Iliad* (Book III). Neither author attempts the details of a beauty which surpasses description; both rely instead on the crowd's reaction ("Surely there is no blame on Trojans and strong-greaved Achaians / if for long time they suffer hardship for a woman like this one" [III. 156–57].[3] "How lovely! said everyone who saw her" [p. 11]) along with the great beauties' gestures of diffidence, which make them even more irresistible.[4] Both Helens have three

---

[3] The translation is that of Richmond Lattimore, *The Iliad of Homer* (Chicago and London, 1951).

[4] Cf. Georg Lukács' comparison of Homer's treatment of Helen to Tolstoy's Anna Karenina, *Werke*, Vol. VI: *Probleme des Realismus* III: *Der historische Roman* (Berlin, 1965), p. 377.

husbands and pay for their scandal with childlessness (by barrenness and abortion, respectively).

Achilles and Andrei resemble each other in nothing so much as in their irreducible contradictoriness. As noted above, both have almost preternatural vision about the universe and their inner selves, but react erratically to the claims of society: that is, both can oscillate from petulant infant to selfless savior without any steady grasp of the manhood in between. Achilles begins Book I trying to save the Greek army at whatever cost to himself, and ends it tearfully begging his goddess mother to have it destroyed to salve his wounded pride. Andrei we see first as a man too big for small talk in Anna's parlor, but then not sufficiently mature to be decent to his pregnant wife. Both men alternate between periods of almost unbelievable heartlessness and of sublime moral perception. It is the same Achilles who can will his friends' death for his own childish reasons and then (as no other Greek could) accept Priam, not as the enemy king but as a grieving father like his own grieving father and as something like an extension of his own self (Book XXIV). Likewise, Andrei can abandon his own family and find Napoleon as an embodiment of greatness more important than the Russians who must die to establish that greatness, then after the battle of Borodino forgive the even more unlucky Anatole simply out of his love for all mankind—even though (or because?) he realizes that "now it is too late" (p. 908). Much can be read simply from the face, as we see in one of his animated moments with Pierre: "Every muscle of his thin face was now quivering with nervous excitement; his eyes, in which the fire of life had seemed extinguished, now flashed with brilliant light. It was evident that the more lifeless he seemed at ordinary times, the more impassioned he became in these moments of almost morbid irritation" (p. 28). Andrei's passions and sympathies, which can be overwhelming when they are not completely absent, direct themselves primarily in retrospect. Only his son's near death wrenches from Andrei the immense love he feels for this child whom he has earlier ignored. Life becomes beautiful for Andrei, as for Achilles, only in those moments (sometimes misleading) when he feels that he is leaving it. Indeed, epiphany becomes Andrei's standard response to extreme pain, as when in the example just given he learns from the agony of Anatole that the meaning of life is in loving others and embracing the common mortality. Since his visions tend not to survive his recoveries, only the deathbed brings irreversible spiritual progress—and that a bleak turning inward that reverses earlier visions of Love. Similarly Achilles realizes his commitment to Patroclus only after he has thoughtlessly dispatched his companion to fight and die in his own armor. It is only after Achilles dooms Patroclus, Hector, and himself that he becomes the great and expansive humanitarian of Book XXIV. When we see him finally at ease with himself and with the enemy king, it is because both are in their last days. For both Achilles and Andrei, nothing in their troubled life becomes them so much as leaving it. Conversely, the *Odyssey*, the grandfather of all Baedekers, is memorable for all its introductions to new and exotic places; the poet tends to be much less interested in leavetaking and, indeed, ends the narrative simply by a bolt from the blue when the gods have seen enough. What we see of Pierre, for all the false turns along the way, is a protracted process of arrival: into society, into married life, into Freemasonry, into war, finally into true marriage and fatherhood.[5]

Apart from the steady habit of pursuing what is lost and resisting what impends, Achilles and Andrei are self-consistent only in living their lives in harmony with higher principles, while Odysseus and Pierre are mostly trying to get through the next hour. The higher principles, of course, tend to keep changing. In withdrawing from the siege, Achilles rejects the all-important esteem of his peers because he feels that he is "honoured already in Zeus' ordinance" (*Iliad* IX.608), that is, that he, unlike other men, has some claim to absolute status in the universe. Yet after Patroclus is killed, vengeance becomes the only absolute. When Priam arrives to reclaim Hector's body, even vengeance has given way to a transcendent sense of humanity which supersedes the difference of Trojan and Greek. Similarly, Andrei has no patience with mortals but worships the superhuman Napoleon; when even he disappoints, the wounded Andrei fixes on the epiphany of the eternal sky. After his visit to Natasha, the blossoming of the oak tree symbolizes the absolute triumph of the life force, with which he willingly puts himself in harmony. Yet it is only the long process of dying that places him, like Achilles, substantially and finally in contact with any absolute principle. Only the proximity of death allows either hero any measure of serenity.

Both authors use the progressive disillusionment of the heroes to demonstrate at once the appeal and the hollowness of military glory. For the Greeks Achilles was the warrior par excellence, and yet it is

---

[5] On Andrei, see especially John Hagan, "A Pattern of Character Development in *War and Peace*: Prince Andrej," *SEEJ* 13 (1969), 164-90, which, however, argues that the work "culminates in the great spiritual quest of Andrej and Pierre, who emerge at the end and from their inner warfare to achieve the peace that passes all understanding."

from his lips that we hear that Menelaus' private grudge about the rape of Helen scarcely warrants the leveling of Troy; that aggression itself "swarms like smoke inside a man's heart / and becomes a thing sweeter to him than the dripping of honey" (XVIII.109–10). Similarly, Andrei can convey Tolstoy's larger point about the futility of militarism because he had once believed in it with almost religious fervor. The same Andrei who announced to Pierre at the outset, "I am going to war, the greatest war there ever was" (p. 28), learns by the end that "war is not courtesy but the most horrible thing in life; and we ought to understand that and not play at war" (p. 865). By contrast, Pierre and Odysseus can fight or not as circumstances demand because they have little coveted military glory for its own sake. To revert to Archilochus' terms, Andrei, like Achilles, is the fox who sees many things at once—too many; the nearsighted Pierre like the hedgehog, sees only what is at hand. But that is what matters.

Finally, the heroes have quite different sorts of relationships with women and, by parallel, with the land itself. While Achilles' career is greatly affected by various women (Helen, then the prized concubine taken from him by Agamemnon, then his mother), he plays very few scenes with them. Similarly Andrei's scenes with women are somehow peripheral to his experience and are often instances of noncommunication, as in his failure to appreciate Lise, Mary, and finally Natasha. By contrast, Odysseus has his best scenes mostly with women: Calypso and Circe, Helen, the princess Nausicaa, his old nurse, Athena, finally Penelope herself. Helene and Natasha similarly demarcate Pierre's spiritual odyssey. Nearly alone among epic heroes Pierre shows little susceptibility to male influence. He acquires and loses a real father, a spiritual brother (Andrei), a council of elders (the Freemasons), and admiring military comrades without much sign of permanent effect. His rebirth comes at the hands of the peasant Platon, whom he perceives, rather curiously, from his first words as an "old Russian peasant woman" and who embodies nonjudgmental mother love more purely than any other character in the work.[6] But then the earliest and greatest mystery about Pierre—glaring in a work so rich in the details of family life—is omission of any mention of his mother, a figure who retrospectively comes to seem the goal of his quest. The magic princess, Helene, certainly was not; Natasha is, but not in the aspect of the alluring maiden. Quite beyond her notable capacity to embody the spirit of motherhood and, indeed, of Russia itself, Natasha starts be-

---

[6] For a discussion of the attendant religious symbolism, see Robert Louis Jackson, "The Second Birth of Pierre Bezukhov," *CASS,* 12 (1978), 535-42.

coming more than a friend to Pierre when as Andrei's widow, she lives in the same state of abandonment in which Pierre would always have known his mother.

With both sets of heroes, their relationship to the land parallels their dealings with the women who so often embody its spirit. Pierre and Andrei, often as their paths cross, seem to travel through different landscapes. For Andrei the path from the salon and the study to the battlefield is straight and unobstructed. He allows himself to be surrounded by only as much landscape as he can confer symbolic meaning on, as is characteristic of tragic heroes: For Oedipus there is only the wild Mount Cithaeron; for Lear, the stormy heath; for Macbeth, Birnam Wood; for Hamlet, the graveyard; for Achilles, only the dust with which he befouls his guilty self. Even the great flowering oak that symbolizes Andrei's awakening love for Natasha functions as a symbol in the text only because Andrei invites epiphany. As a well-read man of his century, he knows the redemptive powers of nature and, bored with his own emotional isolation, chooses to exercise this option. The object that he has picked as a symbol of regeneration is of the tritest: the Tree of Life or Tree of the World familiar already in the context of enchanted forests, golden boughs, and lairs of nymphs and dwarves to be found in everything from nursery tales to epics. Does a thoughtful adult identify himself with the barrenness of a great oak in mid-April without the anticipation that it will be verdant by June? The baleful,then the hopeful voices that Andrei projects onto the tree simply provide a supportive chorus for a scenario that he has mostly plotted out for himself. And what is there in the sky at Austerlitz but the meanings Andrei reads into it? The sky remains the same as always, only now Andrei's self-consciousness has need of it.

Similarly, there is no landscape for the Greeks at Ilium except as the poet or Achilles imports it in similes. And Achilles like Andrei, is the character who most closely parallels the narrator's usual function of drawing parallels and imposing meanings. All of the other Greeks at Troy accept the scepter as a symbol of regal authority, but when Achilles hurls that symbol down in his petulant withdrawal from the camp (Book I), he imposes a new set of meanings on the scepter: He sees it rather as a lifeless branch that will never bear leaf again, as barren as the society over which Agamemnon presides. In speaking, Homer's characters rarely use that repertory of comparisons— charging lions, rushing rivers,cowering lambs—by which the poet makes the movement of battle precise and vivid. Only Achilles regularly shows that command of the language of simile, as for example to the cowering Hector: "As there are no trustworthy oaths between men and lions, nor wolves and lambs have spirit that can be brought to agreement but forever these hold feelings of hate for each other, so there can be no love between you and me, nor shall there be oaths between us" (*Iliad* XXII.262–66). Achilles and Andrei are conspicuous in their respective tales as the characters who speak and think most like the narrator, who are more often found perceiving their settings than being perceived within them. The landscape through which each travels is primarily in his own head: The dark chamber in which Andrei dies should be sufficiently confining, but it is less threatening to him than the dark chamber of which he dreams.

Where Andrei tends to *see* the landscape around him—and mostly in his own terms—Pierre, more passively and more responsively, hears and smells and touches as well. Andrei hears little in nature but the conflicting voices within him, as in the important meeting with Pierre on the raft at Bald Hills: "Prince Andrew felt as if the sound of the waves kept up a refrain to Pierre's words, whispering: 'It is true, believe it' "(p. 422). Pierre, by contrast, can sense mystical and quite unexpected messages even in smell and taste, as in the potato which Platon offers him. Pierre, too, can see symbolism in nature, as when the comet of 1812 symbolizes regeneration for him as the oak had for Andrei, just as the two men earlier voiced their despair in virtually the same words. Yet Pierre has not staged this epiphany, and there is nothing private or calculated in the comet's symbolism. Where the oak evokes Andrei's large and orderly repertory of epiphanic memories (the heavens at Austerlitz, the dead Lise's reproachful face, Pierre on the ferry, Natasha in the moonlight), the comet prompts Pierre instead to forget a painful past and, shedding a few tears, to conceive a hope which he will pursue. Pierre tends not to read meanings into nature closer at hand because he lives too close to it to see it in those terms. He is more a creature of earth, as his name already suggests (Pierre from the Greek *petros* 'rock'). He is compared to a bear at the outset, eats too much and drinks too much.

Similarly, Odysseus uses his eyes carefully in approaching new stops on his voyage, but only to ask the question, "Friend or foe?" Otherwise he is unself-conscious about his proximity to nature, even when he buries himself in leaves to survive the night cold or hides in a ram's fleece to escape the Cyclops. On land, he confronts godhead exclusively and quite variously in its feminine aspects: nymphs, witches, a flirtatious Athena. Likewise, the presiding deity of Pierre's ultimate felicity will be Mother Russia, especially as incarnated in Natasha—a spiritual presence inaccessible to those like Andrei who hear in nature no voices but their own. Through most of the work no

note is made of Pierre's perceptions of nature. In the pivotal raft
scene at Bald Hills, we hear only Andrei's perceptions, even though
the setting is rich with symbolic overtones of boundaries and the
crossing of them, the juncture of two worlds in this twilight, between
light and darkness and perhaps even between life and death. Are we
to be reminded of the raft of Charon in the classical underworld,
where Odysseus and the dead Achilles meet a final time? Yet Pierre,
as he rambles on about the Masonic Truth, grasps none of this. The
earliest and most persuasive sign of his spiritual rebirth after the
debacle at Borodino and his imprisonment is that we start seeing
scenes through his eyes as he grows increasingly aware of his own perceptions. The progression recalls Dante: First, Pierre must be led
through the infernal fires of a devastated Moscow and witness execu-
tions so horrible that they deprive him of his old consciousness: "He
lost the power of thinking or understanding. He could only hear and
see" (p. 1069). Gradually in the Virgin's Field a new and heightened
perception begins to dawn, but not simply from within, not—as was
always the case with Andrei—by an act of will but by the mysterious
workings of Grace: "These bells reminded Pierre that it was Sunday
and the feast of the Nativity of the Virgin" (p. 1066). The first prompt-
ings of this new and redemptive intuition are not conscious: "In place
of the Russian order of life that had been destroyed, Pierre unconsciously felt that a quite different, firm, French order had been established in this ruined nest" (p. 1066). In place of Dante's emergence on
Easter, Tolstoy has used the birth of the Virgin—or is she Mother
Russia, whose minion, Platon Karataev, ministers to Pierre with a
ritual based not on body and blood but on the smell and taste of the
humble potato—a ritual as sensual and mystical as the eucharist, one
(despite Platon's impending death) more purely bound up with growth
and regeneration, and, above all, purely Russian.[7] The scene is an
abandoned church, a manger-like structure, and Platon himself, who
speaks largely proverbs and instructs through ritual, stands apart from
the other characters of the work, almost in the realm of myth, an
avatar of the Natural Man who precedes, initiates, or baptizes so
many returning kings: the swineherd Eumaeus, who initiates Odysseus
back into the life of Ithaca; the *Aeneid*'s King Evander; John the Bap-
tist. Yet the childless and doomed Platon is also reminiscent of a

---

[7] Cf. Jackson: "Platon emerges here as the source and symbol of renewal: as
earth-mother, mother Russia, the people—the indestructible reality of the matrix.
Pierre's 'resurrection' is accompanied, appropriately, by a sense of rebirth of the
world, an experience of movement of the universe" (p. 541).

Christ delegating a mission to a founder like Peter/Pierre; the French soldiers in misnaming Pierre "Kiril" from his patronymic remind us of a further step in the Apostolic succession to St. Cyril and hence to the Slavonic rebirth of Christian Witness, of which Tolstoy here gives a moving example. Moreover, Platon is and is not Plato, and his shed with the light of a surrounding reality breaking through at the cracks is and is not like Plato's Cave. In that analogy lurks much of Tolstoy's creative ambivalence to classical culture. As Platon is to Plato—more unprepossessing, closer to earth, altogether Slavonic—so is Pierre to Odysseus or any of the canonical heroes.

* * * * * *

*War and Peace* attains a synthesis of heroic modes when Pierre attains by grace what Andrei sought by force of will. For Pierre ends up not only with the domestic and affective side lacking in Andrei but also with that participation in Larger Principles which Andrei had wanted so desperately. He has that much desired oneness with nature, though more as gardener than Romantic. And he has the heroism possible in his age: indefatigable zeal for the ordinary. In much the same way, Odysseus merges at the end of his epic the skills of Achillean warrior (though on a reduced scale) and family man. Yet the fragility of Pierre as a synthesis of virtues becomes apparent in Epilogue One when the possibility of yet a fuller synthesis emerges in Nicholenka— born of Andrei; reared by that family among families, the Rostovs; intrigued by Pierre, though increasingly susceptible to the phantom image of his heroic father. Can one read Epilogue Two without wondering how Pierre could ever wade through these heady and important thoughts? The fragility of Odysseus as a combination of father and fighter similarly emerges from the unanimity of sequel writers in making his son his father's next adversary.

Tolstoy does not let his readers long forget that epics are what the great monsters of history carry around with them: Alexander carried his copy of the *Iliad* to India; Napoleon has his text of Ossian with him at Moscow. Some tyrants have written their own, as we are reminded when before their first conversation Pierre leafs through Andrei's copy of Caesar's *Commentaries*. When Napoleon first views Moscow, the perversity of his intentions emerges in nothing so much as his use of the extended comparison: for him, the city is a maiden waiting to be ravished. As we have already seen with Andrei, the calculated application of such elaborate comparisons—since Homer, the hallmark of epic style—tends to be a form of self-delusion, just as Platon's habit of spewing parables without much worrying about how they apply is a sign of spiritual health. The use of simile itself embodies just those qualities of suffocating traditionalism, glory-mongering, and artificiality which Tolstoy most resents, as we sense already when Anna Scherer is linked by a Homeric simile to the foreman of a spinning mill keeping "the conversational machine in steady, proper, and regular motion" (p. 10). Homer's similes of men charging like lions or rocks falling like snow epitomize vitality and energy usually beyond the reach of indecisive and often timorous mortals. Tolstoy turns the device quite oppositely to the mechanistic and life-denying activities he most detests, leading up to the climactic image (developed from *Aeneid* I.430–36) of Moscow as a queenless and doomed hive, an image paired with Napoleon's sick fantasy of the city as waiting maiden. Style itself, it is suggested, can glorify and justify the basest forms of human aggression.[8] The simile can figure the human in animal or mechanical terms (and justify carnage), as well as personify the inert and thereby turn empty abstractions (glory, honor, nationhood) into cruel deities. Similarly, to be susceptible of characterization by a fixed epithet—la belle Hélène, le charmant Hippolyte—no longer signifies heroic attainment, but rather viciousness. Just as these characters' faces are masks, the fixity of their epithets communicates the fixed depravity of their natures.

Like the landscape, the similes come to be used quite differently after Pierre's spiritual rebirth. The healthy clan of saved characters which we see at the end has, of course, no use for them, and the narrator uses extended metaphors about these characters only to figure the liberation from mechanistic perspectives, as when Pierre "threw away the telescope through which he had till now gazed over men's heads, and gladly regarded the ever-changing, eternally great, unfathomable, and infinite life around him" (p. 1227). Only the scientist—or the scientific historiographer—should be using this potent tool of analogy and in ways that point up the largest and inglorious patterns of collective life. Tolstoy uses the simile of ants returning to a ruined heap to explain how Moscow, purged and perfected, begins to be reborn (p. 1231). Such an affirmation of the instinctual life of the race contrasts diametrically with the generation of individual *gloire* and the precise delineation of private psychology which epic similes had originally served. The process by which this literary device is parodied, rejected, then transformed and reapplied parallels the deflation and

---

[8] On the similes, see especially James M. Curtis, "The Function of Imagery in *War and Peace*," *SlavR*, 29 (1970), 460–80.

reconstitution of heroism accomplished by the shift from Andrei to Pierre. That the starting points for these reworkings of heroic values are so very traditional—returning to the first notes sounded in European literature—emphasizes all the more strongly how the final triumph of collective values, the slaying of the dragon of heroic solipsism, is a new departure for mankind. Thereby the Russian order consolidated in these events has all the stronger claim to being a new thing under the sun. But that dragon, of course, had been slain quite a number of times before. As the father of the European sensibility, Homer is a fitting guide for this second birth of Europe—as he had been for Virgil in proclaiming the new Roman dispensation, as Virgil had been for Dante in proclaiming the new Christian order, as all three had been for Milton in proclaiming a new Puritan order. All of these writers, like Tolstoy, proclaim their resistance to the epic style as they inherit it; that gesture of rejection (followed in every case by ceaseless cribbing from the same oppressive antecedents) is one of the surest markers of the genre.

We must also allow that Pierre ends up very much further from Odysseus than Andrei does from Achilles. The *Odyssey* does not imply that the meek shall inherit the earth in quite the way that Tolstoy means the parable; indeed, much the opposite is suggested. The deceptiveness of appearances in Homer counsels caution and guile more than humility. While Odysseus is profoundly unaffected by the disguises he wears, Natasha's strength lies in her ability to be transformed by wearing the peasant shawl at "Uncle's," just as Pierre's tattered disguise in prison allows the French-educated aristocrat to be reborn as Russian peasant. Though mythologically Pierre belongs with Odysseus among the ranks of unlikely saviors, that fatiguing operation of proceeding complexly under the guise of simplicity had hitherto called for an ironist: Socrates and Christ, no less than Odysseus. Now Andrei may at some moments (as in his retreat to being a country gentleman) flirt with the possibilities of such pastoral irony; Pierre, though steadily threatened and tempted by subtlety, emerges at the end unscarred by intellectual progress and no more guileful than when he began. Spared finally the Andreian thoughts that wander through eternity, he grows like a tree, imperceptibly and irreversibly. And where the ironists in the tradition repress, postpone, or outgrow their appetites, Pierre—self-indulgent in profoundly harmless ways—walks fatly through a thin man's role, lumbering where we have seen only artful dodgers and agile saints. Such heroes who triumph through passivity operate in the mode of paradox; Pierre is quite alone in being a staunch literalist.

Yet in all of the epics which show some form of bipolar heroism,
the obsolescent (i.e., Achillean) mode is the closer to everything that
precedes, while the more resilient (Odyssean) heroism that supplants
it makes stronger claims of belonging to the writer's own time and
place. The obsolescent mode tends, among other things, to recapitu-
late the concept of heroism as it has developed in cycle. Aeneas at
Troy could have been a Homeric character; the later Aeneas could
exist only in Italy. Dante-pilgrim with Virgil as guide could be one of
Virgil's own characters; in Paradise he exists and perceives in ways
never articulated in Latin. Milton's Satan is pointedly classical; his
Christ wears the pagan trappings far more lightly.[9] All of these epics
take up from and summarize the cycle that precedes, then advance us
to quite different destinations. Tolstoy, then, is entirely typical in
ending on a note that seems furthest from the tradition. He may have
felt that in conferring something of the common touch on his surviving
band of characters he was bringing the epic full circle. The historical
role he assigns to Homer in "What is Art?" is alongside the Bible as
the last "good, supreme art" still accessible to the masses.[10] In slough-
ing off, layer by layer, the tradition's accreted sophistications *War and
Peace* may aim at an art "comprehensible to everybody."

What unites the major epics is not where they end but that they
almost cannot.[11] Comedy and tragedy have their respective principles
of closure, as war and peace have their separate periodicities; but that
epic synthesis which comes closest to the flow of history itself may,
like the historical record, lack real and conclusive stopping points.
Only the *Iliad* has the fully satisfying conclusion that later epics would
seek and fail to replicate. When Achilles and Priam, enemy chieftains,
break bread together and then simply stare at each other as "an out-
right vision of gods" (XXIV.630–31) in the first moment of silence
and first moment of full human recognition in the epic, the roles of
warrior and family man become fully coincident for the first and only
time in the *Iliad*: The men can accept each other as father and son
because they will finally be implicated in each others' deaths; and
those deaths, once foreseen with cold horror, begin to take on a rich

---

[9] The traditional view that Milton's heavenly host is emphatically nonclassical
has recently been challenged by Francis C. Blessington, Paradise Lost *and the Classical Epic* (Boston, London, and Henley, 1979), pp. 19-49.

[10] *"What is Art?" and Essays on Art*, trans. Aylmer Maude (London, 1929), p.
178.

[11] *In medias res* then, is one way to describe the whole of an epic not just its
beginning. It is a narrative, a story, yet it begins in the middle and never concludes"
(Joan Webber, *Milton and His Epic Tradition*, Seattle, 1979, p. 91).

and almost seductive meaning. Translated to a new level of significance war and peace somehow reconcile themselves in the privileged sympathies of the doomed. However, the narrative irreconcilability of military and domestic values surfaces already at the end of the *Odyssey*, and so gravely that it provoked ancient scholars to surgery. Though the *Odyssey* has consistently maintained that it takes the same process (and maybe more wit) to wear a beggar's rags convincingly in the midst of one's enemies as to carry Hephaestus' glorious shield against Hector, the epic also wants to reassure us that Odysseus is equally good with his fists. Paradoxically, where we last saw Achilles at his most humane and tolerant playing a son-figure to Priam, Odysseus ends his epic as a warrior more ruthless than any seen at Troy. The scene of his slaughtering his wife's contemptible suitors in his own hall offers one particularly grisly reconciliation of devoted husband and serious warrior; likewise, he lovingly initiates his son into bloodthirstiness. Penelope thereafter accepts him only after he has lost (for the first time in the epic) a quite unexpected battle of wits, and as the grammarians Aristophanes and Aristarchus (3rd century B.C.) indicated by (apparently) ending the text here, we have at this point a full and satisfying conclusion to the Odyssean mode of the *Odyssey*.[12] Loose threads in the plot remain, hence Book XXIV (surely written last and perhaps much later and conceivably even by other hands) tries to pick them up, thereby ending all of the *Odyssey* (its late-emerging Iliadic themes as well), and indeed providing a conclusion to all preceding forty-eight books, partly by circling back to the beginning of the *Iliad*, as well as repeating some of the format of that epic's final book. These several structural intentions lead to a disjointed and often lifeless text: The bickering of Achilles and Agamemnon started the *Iliad*; a detour into Hades shows them reconciled at the end of the *Odyssey*. But it is only a detour. A family man may be devoted to his wife; a real warrior must be far more concerned about his father, and so Odysseus must slip away from his reunion with Penelope to visit Laertes, who has withdrawn to the country. This final meditation on fathers and sons rehearses much of what we have seen with Achilles and Priam at the end of the *Iliad*; in both cases the son-figure rejuvenates the old man into his lost heroism. The local

---

[12] The grounds for seeing everything after *Odyssey* XXIII.296 as later and inferior are forcefully summarized by Denys Page, *The Homeric Odyssey* (Oxford, 1955), pp. 101-36. See, however, the counterarguments of Hartmut Erbse, *Beiträge zum Verständnis der Odyssee* (Berlin and New York, 1972), pp. 166-244; John H. Finley, Jr., *Homer's Odyssey* (Cambridge, Mass., and London, 1978), pp. 200-08; and Dorothea Wender, *The Last Scenes of the Odyssey* (Leyden, 1978).

families, having lost older sons at Troy and younger sons in Odysseus'
hall, take arms and allow Odysseus, with his heroic father and heroic
son, a final glorious moment on the battlefield. But where will it all
end? The gods are apparently as bored as the audience by this point,
so Zeus sends a bolt from the blue to suspend a narrative that is proving itself incapable of concluding. Whatever hand was in fact responsible for this final disappointment, the compositional problems
are evident: If Penelope is at the very end, then Laertes is not. If the
epic at the last justifies itself as a worthy heroic sequel to the *Iliad*, it
betrays the pacific Odyssean values. Having shown how twenty years
of history, that is, twenty years of hardship and separation, can lead to
one perfect moment between Odysseus and Penelope, the poet cannot
finally abandon the momentum that that larger historical narrative
has accumulated. It looks as if the narrative has such irrepressible life
that it cannot be stilled; in the wake of literary triumph, the author
cannot stop writing epilogues.

Should we be surprised, then, that Tolstoy, having replicated the
vitality and scope of Homer's narrative so remarkably well, suffers the
same inability to decide on the final moment? The first ending of *War
and Peace*, like that of the *Odyssey*, presents the single perfect moment
of a reunion that is all the richer for the years of postponement and
trial. Natasha and Pierre, like Penelope and Odysseus, have had to
suffer and grow to deserve this moment, and the author will not risk
its perfection by lingering on it. The reader will sigh, turn out the light,
go to sleep, and, awaking the next morning, remember that Natasha
and Pierre are themselves so convincingly flesh and blood that they,
too, will wake up the next day. To be sure, Andrei's life could be
resolved in such a moment of romantic epiphany, but Natasha and
Pierre are capable lovers because they inhabit the real world. Nor is
Tolstoy's larger and absolutely vivid historical canvas so easily forgot-
ten. Epilogue One satisfies our curiosity as far as 1820, thus continuing and concluding the less intimate mode of the narrative that has
been family and historical chronicle. Again the shift from romance to
heroism directs attention from men and women to fathers and sons.
This epilogue, like the final books in both the *Iliad* and the *Odyssey*,
focuses finally on the connection between heroic generations. The
young Nicholas learns his heroism, rather impractically, from Plutarch
here at the end of the tale just as it was Caesar's *Commentaries* that
first came to hand in his father's library at the start of the book. It is
doubly appropriate to use these classical texts here to effect the classical compositional device of *Ringkomposition*. Young Nicholas has
been visited in sleep by a dream of his father; so Achilles by Patroclus,

Aeneas by his wife and later by the shade of his father in Hades. Nicholas still represents the possibility of reconciliation of modes by being born of Andrei, but taken with nothing as much as with Uncle Pierre. Where his father apparently contemplated the idea of Caesar (as of Napoleon—both involving war with the French, one might note) as conqueror, Nicholas is taken rather by figures of heroic self-sacrifice, like Scaevola.[13] Yet in the midst of Pierre's and Natasha's, Mary's and Nicholas', bland happiness and their children, who are rather faceless compared to Nicholenka, Andrei's son seems to suggest the reassertion of Andrei's principles and thereby the possibility of continuing the oscillation of heroic modes. To the extent that Andrei dominated the start of *War and Peace*, this reassertion of his values structurally binds the end (like the end of the *Odyssey*) to the earliest phase of the narrative cycle.

By a final step toward generality, Epilogue Two tries to integrate the sprawling diversity of what precedes by the voice of the philosopher of history.[14] This voice, too, strongly recalls Andrei. To the extent that Andrei expressed Tolstoy's own speculative and restless side (as Pierre does the physical and affective), his death leaves the author without a spokesman. It is as Andrei fades from the scene that the disquisitions on the meaning of history emerge into the text as a counterpoint to characters like Pierre who are living it moment by moment. Andrei's death, at the end of Book XII, is sandwiched between the final emergence of the two voices in the novel (Pierre's and the narrator's) which may be said to be heir to his own. For Andrei's final epiphany and death come in the midst of Pierre's spiritual rebirth presided over by Platon. The immanence of rebirth which Platon intuits in parable ("Lay me down like a stone, O God, and raise me up like a loaf," p. 1076) anticipates the terms of Andrei's characteristically intellectualized and specious reaction to his own dream of death: "Yes, it was death! I died—and woke up. Yes, death is an awakening!" (p. 1090). The darkened room of which Andrei

---

[13] Therein lurks one of Tolstoy's childhood memories as he reported them to his biographer Birukov. His favorite "Aunt" Tatyana Alyexandrovna Yergolskaya had herself as a girl imitated Scaevola's courageous act in burning himself. See Chauncey E. Finch, "Tolstoy as a Student of the Classics," *CJ* 47 (1952), 205.

[14] Cf. Ralph Matlaw's speculation that Tolstoy composed the second epilogue in 1886 from material originally located in the main body of the text "because he wanted the final impression to be didactic rather than novelistic, or to impose some final generalization in his massive work, a generalization that would raise the ending to a more universal meaning" ("Mechanical Structure and Inner Form: A Note on *War and Peace* and *Doctor Zhivago*," *Symposium* 17, 1962, p. 291; rpt. in Gibian [note 2 above], p. 1420).

dreams is an unmistakable reminder of Platon's shed in the preceding scene. Platon's great spiritual strength derives to some extent from his inability to articulate his values, values which Pierre appreciates and assimilates without analyzing.[15] The narrator is left to point the moral: "His words and actions flowed from him as evenly, inevitably, and spontaneously as fragrance exhales from a flower" (p. 1079). Or, in Biblical terms: "Consider the lilies of the field . . . they toil not, neither do they spin" (Matt. 6.28). Andrei remembers his epiphany, at Austerlitz in precisely these terms "when he came to himself after being wounded and the flower of eternal, unfettered love had instantly unfolded itself in his soul" (p. 1087). Yet the metaphor here is self-elected and applied not to the self, as Tolstoy uses it of Platon, but to an abstraction of Love. Andrei's adduction of texts on his deathbed finally reveals the extent to which his self-images follow literary models: "The fowls of the air sow not, neither do they reap, yet your Father feedeth them" (p. 1086; cf. Matt. 6.26). This insight has nothing, of course, to do with Andrei's life and everything to do with "the little falcon," Platon. Impending death has liberated Andrei into the realm of pure theory without the hindrance of a continuing life that works otherwise. Only Natasha proves distracting: Love for her, too strong to be entirely lost, somehow does not mesh with universal, impersonal Love. The details do not fit. The rhythmic clicking of her knitting needles is comforting just as Platon's regular snoring is for Pierre. But where Pierre will let that humble sound embody a sense of order for the moment, Andrei is soothed but unenlightened by the clicking and staunchly looks within for his vision of an Ordering Principle. But at least the theory has finally consolidated itself for Andrei. His final service to the reader in supplying the explanatory texts for a reality being lived by the prisoners in the preceding chapter makes him finally and purely the Word of which Platon is the Flesh, the prophet of a truth increasingly to be incarnated in Pierre.

Now, for Pierre the loss of Andrei as spiritual advisor is a great liberation. The philosophizing voice does not vanish from the text, however, but is instead institutionalized, starting with the next chapter, where the Historian makes his first full affirmation of the Andreian vision of true causes perceptible only with the abandonment of self: "The discovery of these laws (sc. directing events) is only possible when we have quite abandoned the attempt to find the cause in

---

[15] Tolstoy will repeat this situation at the end of *Anna Karenina* (Part VIII, Chs. xi and xii) when, through the tutelage of a peasant named Platon, Levin comes to identify reason as a stumbling block to truth.

the will of just one man, just as the discovery of the laws of the motion of the planets was possible only when man abandoned the conception of the fixity of the earth" (p. 1096). As the earth is no longer the center of the universe, neither should the individual be. The reader may recoil at the analogies drawn between mechanics and morals, but they could not be more Andreian, for he, too, similarly deduced spiritual destiny from atomic theory: "To die means that I, a particle of love, shall return to the general and eternal source" (p. 1089). In transforming Andrei finally into pure theory, Tolstoy discredits him as a character, perhaps, and distances him from our sympathy, but thereby brings him all the closer to himself as author. Andrei's heroic immolation in renouncing life to become pure text unmistakably replicates on another level the author's own creative process and openly acknowledges the contradictoriness of writing books to affirm the virtues of living life without them. Andrei's final epiphany, surely not lost on the hand that wrote it, is that the ultimate virtue of insight is to establish its own futility: "Is it possible that the truth of life has been revealed to me only to show me that I have spent my life in falsity?" (p. 1089). Tolstoy knows perfectly well that people who face the end saying things like this have almost always been saying them all along: Andrei's vision of futility was complete already at Austerlitz. One wonders, then, if the young Tolstoy who so acutely diagnosed the syndrome did not anticipate that he would spend his latter decades as one of this desolate tribe. It is only at the start of Book XIII, immediately after Andrei's death and Pierre's rebirth, that Tolstoy's theoretical panoply—deterministic historiography, Newtonian mechanics, desacralized Christian ethics—is fully revealed: the astronomical analogy here first adduced will also end Epilogue Two. And just as the *Odyssey*, after working us away from the Achillean values for many books, leaves us by an odd turn uncomfortably stranded at the end in Iliadic territory, out on a battlefield, so in *War and Peace* the progress from Andrei to Pierre turns in this second epilogue to a final reassertion of the Andreian side of Tolstoy himself, who, like Andrei, was to be cured of philosophizing only by death. With every successive ending, the Andreian mode creeps back more and more into the text to the point that many readers have the uneasy sense that Tolstoy himself has caught the diseases of which he has cured Russia as reborn in 1812. In any case, these three successive endings in *War and Peace* allow the reader the choice of seeing the work end as novel, as chronicle, or as tract, but prevent him from reading the work as any one of these forms to the exclusion of the others. If the reader, having entrusted his sympathies to the narrative, feels betrayed, distanced, and compelled to decisions when he might prefer merely to carry away a feeling, his reaction may come close to that of the spectator of Brecht's epic theater, who "steht gegenüber, studiert."[16] Indeed, ruptured closure may be the only narrative means for Tolstoy, as for Brecht, to maintain "der Mensch als Prozess," not "als Fixum." In any case, the door is also left open for *Anna Karenina,* even as the fumbled ending of the *Odyssey* accommodated further tales, both the lost *Telegony* and Kazantzakis' modern sequel. A proper epic must allow the cycle to continue.

* * * * * *

. . . one notes the indestructibility of the Achillean-Satanic hero. These firebrands, aloof and self-destructive, all exist to be deflated, made obsolete, and replaced. Yet after we move on to the new heroism—from Achilles to Odysseus, from the Trojan Aeneas to the Roman, from Dante necromantic student of Virgil to Dante the lover of Beatrice, from pagan Satan to Puritan Christ, from Andrei to Pierre—the old heroism tends never to be quite as dead or as boring as the author's piety and pacifism would have it be. Tolstoy's own final reversion to his own more Andreian side must remind us of the pagans, Homer and Virgil, who lapsed in that more vivid direction at the end of the *Odyssey* and the *Aeneid*, as well as Dante and Milton, who seem to have averted such lapses into Satanic territory at the cost of ending on a high, hollow note. However the axis is drawn—war and peace, damnation and salvation, solipsism and community—the larger drift of the texts toward edification and redemption never quite manages to carry most readers with it. Tolstoy is only the latest to discover that having first described an earlier more fallen, more colorful world—a world (like Virgil's Troy and Carthage, Dante's Inferno, Milton's lively Hell and lapsing Paradise) still open to the incursions of older and rawer forms of heroism, the author cannot at will shepherd the reader into the happier and duller vision of his conclusion.

---

[16] Bertolt Brecht, "Anmerkungen" to "Aufstieg und Fall der Stadt Mahagonny," *Stücke* III (Berlin, 1955), p. 267.

Figure 11. Iris tells Priam to ransom Hector's body. Flaxman (*Iliad* series).

# Cavafy and Iliad 24:
# A Modern Alexandrian Interprets Homer

*Seth L. Schein*

"Άλγος ἐν τῇ 'Ιλίῳ κ' οἰμωγή.
         'Η γῆ
τῆς Τροίας ἐν ἀπελπισμῷ πικρῷ καὶ δέει
τὸν μέγαν "Εκτορα τὸν Πριαμίδην κλαίει.

'Ο θρῆνος βοερός, βαρὺς ἠχεῖ.         5
         Ψυχὴ
δὲν μένει ἐν τῇ Τροίᾳ μὴ πενθοῦσα,
τοῦ "Εκτορος τὴν μνήμην ἀμελοῦσα.

'Αλλ' εἶναι μάταιος, ἀνωφελὴς
         πολὺς         10
θρῆνος ἐν πόλει ταλαιπωρημένη·
ἡ δυσμενὴς κωφεύει εἰμαρμένη.

Τ' ἀνωφελῆ ὁ Πρίαμος μισῶν,
         χρυσὸν
ἐξάγει ἐκ τοῦ θησαυροῦ· προσθέτει         15
λέβητας, τάπητας, καὶ χλαίνας· κ' ἔτι

χιτῶνας, τρίποδας, πέπλων σωρὸν
         λαμπρόν,
καὶ ὅ, τι ἄλλο πρόσφορον εἰκάζει,
κ' ἐπὶ τοῦ ἄρματός του τὰ στοιβάζει.         20

Θέλει μὲ λύτρα ἀπὸ τὸν τρομερὸν
                            ἐχθρὸν
τοῦ τέκνου του τὸ σῶμα ν᾽ ἀνακτήσῃ,
καὶ μὲ σεπτὴν κηδείαν νὰ τιμήσῃ.

Φεύγει ἐν τῇ νυκτὶ τῇ σιγηλῇ.                           25
                            Λαλεῖ
ὀλίγα. Μόνη᾽ν σκέψιν τώρα ἔχει
ταχύ, ταχὺ τὸ ἅρμα του νὰ τρέχῃ.

Ἐκτείνεται ὁ δρόμος ζοφερός.
                            Οἰκτρῶς                      30
ὁ ἄνεμος ὀδύρεται κ᾽ οἰμώζει.
Κόραξ ἀπαίσιος μακρόθεν κρώζει.

Ἐδῶ, κυνὸς ἀκούετ᾽ ὑλακή·
                            ἐκεῖ,
ὡς ψίθυρος λαγὼς περνᾷ ταχύπους.                         35
Ὁ βασιλεὺς κεντᾷ, κεντᾷ τοὺς ἵππους.

Τῆς πεδιάδος ἐξυπνοῦν σκιαὶ
                            λαιαί,
καὶ ἀποροῦν πρὸς τί ἐν τόσῃ βίᾳ
πετᾷ ὁ Δαρδανίδης πρὸς τὰ πλοῖα               40

Ἀργείων φονικῶν, καὶ Ἀχαιῶν
                            σκαιῶν.
Ἀλλὰ ὁ βασιλεὺς αὐτὰ δὲν τὰ προσέχει·
φθάνει τὸ ἅρμα του ταχύ, ταχὺ νὰ τρέχει.


Pain in Ilion and wailing.
                            The land
of Troy in bitter despair and fear
weeps for great Hektor, the son of Priam.

The dirge resounds, loud, heavy.                         5
                            No soul
remains in Troy ungrieving,
neglecting the memory of Hektor.

But futile, useless is
the great
lamentation in the suffering city;        10
hostile destiny turns a deaf ear.

Hating the uselessness, Priam
brings out
gold from the storehouse; he adds        15
cauldrons, rugs, and cloaks; and in addition

tunics, tripods, a pile of robes,
shining,
and whatever else seems suitable,
and on his chariot he heaps them up.        20

He wishes with ransom from the terrifying
enemy
to regain his son's body,
and with a reverent funeral to do it honor.

He departs in the silent night.        25
He speaks
little. The only thought he now has
is that his chariot should run fast, fast.

The road stretches out in gloom.
Pitifully        30
the wind laments and wails.
A raven croaks from afar, repulsive, ill-omened.

Here, a dog's barking is heard;
there,
a hare passes swiftfooted like a whisper.        35
The king goads, he goads his horses.

On the plain shadows awaken,
inauspicious,
and wonder why, in so great a hurry,
the son of Dardanos flies toward the ships        40

of the murderous Argives and the rude
Achaeans.

But the king ignores these things;
it's enough that his chariot runs fast, fast.

In this essay I discuss "Priam's Night-Journey," an early poem by
the modern Greek poet, Constantine Cavafy, who lived from 1863 to
1933. "Priam's Night-Journey" was composed in 1893 but was never
published in Cavafy's lifetime; it first appeared in print only in 1968.[1]
I'm interested in this poem as an example of Cavafy's work from a
time when he was just finding his distinctive voice, partly through
adaptation of Homeric and other ancient mythological "sources." I'm
also concerned with the interpretive light its deviations from the
Homeric text can throw on relevant passages of the *Iliad*.[2]

In my title, I refer to Cavafy as a "modern Alexandrian." By this I
mean not only that he was born in Alexandria and lived most of his
life there, and that many of his poems are set in the city's streets,
shops, and buildings, while others refer explicitly to, or evoke, its distinctive style, culture, values, and almost mythical status.[3] I also

---

[1] On Cavafy's unusual way of "publishing" (or not publishing) his poems, see
G.P. Savidis, Οἱ Καβαφικές Ἐκδόσεις *(1891-1932)* (Athens, 1966); E. Keeley and G.
Savidis, "Introduction" to C.P. Cavafy, *Passions and Ancient Days*, transl. E. Keeley
and G. Savidis (New York, 1971), pp. ix-xiii, with references; G. Jusdanis, *The Poetics
of Cavafy: Textuality, Eroticism, History* (Princeton, 1987), pp. 58-63.
   I translate the text of "Priam's Night-Journey" ("Πριάμου Νυκτοπορεία" in
Κ.Π. Καβάφη Ἀνέκδοτα Ποιήματα *1882–1923*, ed. G.P. Savidis (Athens, 1968), pp.
51-53. My translation, for which I claim no poetic merit, tries to be literal and to
preserve Cavafy's word order wherever possible.

[2] According to D.N. Maronitis, Πίσω Μπρός· Προτάσεις καὶ ὑποθέσεις γιὰ
τὴ νεοελληνικὴ ποίηση καὶ πεζογραφία (Athens, 1986), p. 40 n.4, "Priam's Night-
Journey" is the earliest of only ten poems by Cavafy on ancient mythological subjects–a small portion of his 153 published and 154 either unpublished or "renounced"
poems. The others are "Oedipus" (1895), "The Horses of Achilles" (1896), "The
Funeral of Sarpedon" (renounced version, 1896; published version, 1908), "When the
Watchman Saw the Light" (January, 1900), "Interruption" (May, 1900), "Trojans"
(June, 1900), "Disbelief" (1903), and "Ithaca" (1910). Maronitis comments (p. 62,
n.6): "Generally I believe that the ancient mythological poems of Cavafy are composed not only with the intermediacy of a translation but after careful reading of the
original too." Recently, D. Ricks, *The Shade of Homer: A Study in Modern Greek
Poetry* (Cambridge, 1989), has objected to this statement (p. 86) and argued that
"[f]rom childhood Cavafy . . . was rather more familiar with English than with Greek
poetry, ancient or modern" (p. 87). Ricks claims that Cavafy's Homeric poems,
including "Priam's Night-Journey," were influenced in their tone and diction by
Pope's translation of the *Iliad*, a copy of which Cavafy is known to have owned. Ricks
denies the direct influence of the Homeric text, but he himself notes (p. 90, n. 21) that
"some words from Homer are repeated *verbatim* in "Priam's Night-Journey" (which
he unaccountably considers as "essentially an unfinished poem").

[3] Cf. E. Keeley, *Cavafy's Alexandria: Study of a Myth in Progress* (Cambridge,
Mass., 1976)

mean—-and this is more important for my argument—-that Cavafy's relation to the *Iliad* resembles that of Callimachus and other Alexandrian poets of the Hellenistic Age (ca. 300–31 B.C.E.). Like the Alexandrians, his versions of Iliadic scenes, with their shifts of perspective, focus, characterization, and emphasis, show him to have been an attentive reader and creative reinterpreter of Homeric poetry. These poems cannot be adequately understood unless a reader constantly has in mind the relevant passages of the *Iliad* and can recognize Cavafy's overall recasting of the Homeric scenes, as well as the details he omits, alters, or adds. Perhaps the best word for Cavafy's artistic enterprise is "imitation," if by this one means not a translation or an attempt to copy the Homeric original, but something like Robert Lowell's *Imitations*—new poems that take off from earlier poetic texts to which they maintain a palimpsestuous relation that colors their identities as independent works of art. Many of Cavafy's poems throughout his career are inspired by and represent events, people, and art from various stages of ancient, medieval, and modern Greek civilization, but his early Homeric imitations seem to me in a class by themselves as readerly reworkings of poetic texts that demand simultaneous attention to themselves and to these earlier texts in order to be understood.[4] "Priam's Night-Journey does not revise or subvert its "source" quite as drastically as do some of Cavafy's other poems on mythological themes, such as the well-known "Ithaca." Rather, it departs from the earlier text to concentrate on a particular character and state of mind, and to develop in greater detail feelings that are merely mentioned in the "source."

In "Priam's Night-Journey," for example, Cavafy simply leaves out everyone and everything mentioned by Homer in Book 24 of the *Iliad*, except for Priam and the dead Hektor, and concentrates attention on the king, his actions, and his thoughts.[5] There is no mention of sleepless Achilles dragging Hektor's corpse around Patroklos' tomb; no gods on Olympos, no Iris or Hermes assisting Priam on his way, no Thetis urging Achilles to return the corpse and restore himself to human life; no transcendent meeting between Priam and Achilles; not even the actual ransoming of Hektor's body and its return to Troy for the lamentation and burial with which the *Iliad* closes. Instead, the

---

[4] D.N. Maronitis, "Κ.Π. Καβάφης· ένας ποιητής-άυκγνώστης," in M. Πιερής (ed.), Εισαγωγήστην Ποίηση του Καβάφης (Rethymna, 1985), pp. 451-75, comments (p. 451): ". . . reading perhaps constitutes Cavafy's constantly developing poetic method from his first to his last moment."

[5] See Maronitis, Πίσω Μπρός, pp. 45-49.

desperate and futile sorrow of the city at Hektor's death is a foil for Priam's urgent activity, his "Night-Journey" into the darkness not only of the Trojan plain but of his own mind. His interior thoughts and wishes are the real subject of the second half of Cavafy's poem.

In focusing his poem on Priam alone, Cavafy eliminates other details of Homeric action. At *Iliad* 24.248-64, after bringing the ransom out of his storeroom, Priam rebukes his nine surviving sons as good-for-nothing "disgraces" (κατηφόνες, 24.253), "causes of blame and shame" (ἐλέγχεα, 24.260), "liars, dancers who excel at beating rhythm in the dance," but plunder their own community," (24.261–62), and orders them to prepare his chariot so he can be on his way to Achilles. In Cavafy's poem, Priam simply "hates the uselessness" (τ' ἀνωφελῆ ὁ Πρίαμος μισῶν, 13) of the Trojan grief and the dirge for Hektor, and takes action in the face of "this uselessness," bringing out the ransom and piling it on his chariot (14–20). Cavafy mentions almost all the same components of the ransom that Homer mentions: gold, cauldrons, rugs, cloaks, tunics, tripods, and robes, but he omits the "very beautiful drinking cup that Thracian men gave Priam when he came on an embassy, a great possession" (24.234–35). Mention of this cup is the climax of Homer's catalogue of Priam's ransom; Cavafy eliminates both the cup and the distracting reference to Priam's having gone on an embassy to the Thracians sometime in the past.

Indeed, for Cavafy this distraction would exist even at the grammatical level: from line 13 to line 27 he concentrates attention on Priam by making him the subject of every verb, until, in the subordinate clause constituting line 28, his chariot is the subject of νὰ τρέχῃ, "that it should run." On the other hand, Homer makes "Thracian men" the subject of "gave" in 24.234, and the mention of Priam's embassy to the Thracians, an occasion on which he received a very beautiful, valuable cup as a possession, heightens by contrast the representation of the present embassy to Achilles, an occasion on which the king does not spare even the cup (24.235–36) in his effort to retrieve his son's corpse.

The effect of this contrast between past and present, former prosperity and current misery, is further intensified by the reference in 24.236 to Priam as "the old man" (ὁ γέρων), who is the subject of the verbs οὐδέ . . . φείσατο ("didn't spare") and ἤθελε ("wished") in 24.235–36. Cavafy, on the other hand, never refers to "the old man," only to "Priam": the pathos of Homer's ὁ γέρων--noted in his Commentary by Macleod, who points out that Πρίαμος would have been metrically possible[6]--would draw attention away from the king's

---

6 C. Macleod (ed.), *Homer: Iliad, Book 24* (Cambridge, 1982), p. 108.

desperate burst of activity, which is the main effect in this part of Cavafy's poem. The nature of this activity is suggested by Cavafy's making the "twelve very beautiful robes" (24.229), which are the *first* item in Homer's list of the items Priam takes from his coffers for the ransom, into a "pile of robes,/shining" (17–18), which is the *final* item specified in Cavafy's list (apart from "whatever else seems suitable," 19), and which, like the rest of the ransom, "Priam heaps up on his chariot" (κ᾽ ἐπὶ τοῦ ἅρματός του τὰ στοιβάζει, 20). Here "pile" (σωρὸν) and "heaps up" (στοιβάζει) both suggest a desperate, indiscriminate piling on rather than the measured activity of Homer's king.

Both Homer and Cavafy conclude their catalogues of items in the ransom by saying that Priam wished to ransom Hektor's corpse, but they express this desire differently. Homer says, plainly but with understated depth, "He wanted very much in his heart / to ransom his dear son," 24.236–37), while Cavafy offers more--and more superficial--detail: "He wishes with ransom from the terrifying / enemy / to regain his son's body, / and with a reverent funeral to do it honor" (21–24). Here "from the terrifying enemy" (ἀπὸ τὸν τρομερὸν / ἐχθρὸν) and "with a reverent funeral" (μὲ σεπτὴν κηδείαν) seem to me to admit us, as it were, into Priam's thoughts: I think these phrases are to be understood as his own formulations and show how he carries the city's fear with him (δέει ["fear," 3] τρομερὸν "terrifying," 21]). In the same way the verbs "regain" (ἀνακτήσῃ) and "do honor" (τιμήσῃ), each governing as object "his son's body," make Priam's motivation more explicit than does Homer's "to ransom his dear son" (λύσασθαι φίλον υἱόν, 237), which does not, for all its understated depth, provide access to the specific content of Priam's desires.

Up to this point, Cavafy's poem has more or less followed the story as told in *Iliad* 24, though Cavafy borrows certain details from elsewhere in the Book: for example, lines 6–8, "No soul / remains in Troy ungrieving, / neglecting the memory of Hektor," are adapted from 24.707–708, which describe the Trojans flocking around Priam and Idaios as they return with the corpse of Hektor.[7] Nevertheless, as I've said, Cavafy has eliminated all other characters and their speeches and actions, in order to concentrate on Priam and the dead Hektor, the only two figures mentioned by name. But from line 29 on, when Priam "departs in the silent night," "Priam's Night-Journey"

---

[7] As noted by Maronitis, Πίσω Μπρός, p. 50.

leaves Book 24 behind (though, as I shall show, it evokes other Iliadic passages).[8] Cavafy endows the night-time and the night-journeying king with a symbolic and psychological depth in a way that can only be called lyrical and "modern" (or "Alexandrian"), in contrast to Homer's traditional epic manner.

In line 29, there is an obvious shift from the series of active verbs, mostly transitive, with Priam (and then his chariot) as subject in 13–28 to the passive ἐκτείνεται ("stretches out") in 29 and ἀκούεται ("is heard") in 33. I read 29–32 as, in effect, taking place in Priam' s mind: though the subjects of the verbs—"the road" and "the wind"—are not human, the actions of the these verbs are imagined, so to speak, from the king's viewpoint. But ἐκτείνεται is ambiguous: it suggests something that occurs both outside and within Priam's mind: the road "stretching out" and the king straining with tension. Similarly, the wind, a force of nature, "laments and wails" (ὀδύρεται κ' οἰμώζει, 31), and in so doing recalls the city and land of Troy weeping and lamenting in the opening three strophes. Once again, Priam takes with him the feelings he tries to leave behind.

From line 32 through the end of the poem, most of what is described as occurring on the plain, as Priam passes by, refers not to the earlier strophes but, by intertextual echoes, to the *Iliad*. Thus, the raven (or crow) that "croaks from afar" (32) is "repulsive and ill-omened" (ἀπαίσιος, 32) because its sound is that of the birds of prey which, in the *Iliad*, are said to scavenge like dogs on the unburied corpses of dead warriors (1.4–5, 13.831–32)—including the dogs to which Achilles threatens to feed Hektor's body (22.354–55). The dog's barking heard by Priam (33) similarly suggests his son's potential mutilation.[9]

The "hare [that] passes swift-footed like a whisper" (35) recalls the *Iliad* in a more complicated way. Ταχύπους ("swift-footed") is a rare word in modern Greek; it occurs only here in the entire corpus of Cavafy's poetry, and in this context it must suggest the Homeric Achilles who is repeatedly described as "swift-footed," (πόδας ὠκὺς

---

[8] Perhaps, as Maronitis, Πίσω Μπρός, p. 51, suggests, Cavafy derived the division of his poem into what takes place in light and what in darkness from *Iliad* 24: there, all the action, from the assembly of the gods to the departure of Priam and Idaios, apparently takes place on the twelfth day after the death of Hektor (cf. 24.31); darkness falls (24.351) just before the herald notices Hermes, then it is night until Hermes departs for Ólympos and dawn breaks (24.695) just as Priam and Idaios return to the city.

[9] On dogs and birds in the *Iliad*, see J.M. Redfield, *Nature and Culture in the Iliad: The Tragedy of Hector* (Chicago and London, 1975), pp. 168-69, 184-86, 199, 200.

and πόδας ταχύς). Yet mention of the "hare" does not recall Achilles in a straightforward way. Rather, it evokes the scene of Hektor's death at his hands in *Iliad* 22, where, in a curious "reverse simile," Hektor charges Achilles, sword drawn, "like a high-flying eagle, / who plunges (εἶσιν) toward the plain through dark clouds / to snatch a tender lamb or a cowering hare" (22.308–310). On the one hand, the effect of the Homeric simile is to make Hektor's death more glorious, because he dies charging forward like an aggressive bird of prey rather than like the "cowering hare" he resembled in his earlier flight from Achilles (22. 136–75, 188–207)--though there he was actually compared not to a hare but to a dove fleeing a hawk (22.139–44) and a fawn unable to avoid the pursuit and tracking of a hunting dog (22. 189–93). On the other hand, Hektor's charge at Achilles is, as he realizes, doomed from the start, merely an effort to "do something great for those in the future to learn of" (22.305). His comparison to an eagle helps his death exemplify an important aspect of the tragically self-destructive nature of the heroic enterprise in the *Iliad*: that the very activity—aggressive killing—that leads to honor and glory necessarily involves the death not only of other warriors but eventually, in most cases, of the conqueror himself.

All this, I would suggest, is latent in Cavafy's line, "A hare passes swift-footed, like a whisper" (35). I also would like to suggest that the words ". . . like a whisper" (ὡς ψίθυρος) refer to Priam's interpretation of the sound he hears; therefore Priam would be the imaginer of the swift-footed hare, as well as of the wind's lamentation and wailing in line 31. Through an unusual kind of intertextual empowerment, by which a character in one text is familiar with the details of another text, he draws the image of "a hare passes swift-footed" (λαγὼς περνᾷ ταχύπους) from *Iliad* 17.676, where, in a simile like that of 22.308–310, Menelaos is compared to an eagle "whom, even when he is aloft, a swift-footed hare does not escape the notice of." Cavafy, however, makes Priam recall this image and hear a sound in the night in language that brings to mind not Book 17 but the death of Hektor in Book 22, along with the entire meditation on heroism of which this death is a part. It is characteristic of Cavafy's poem that, unlike Homer's epic, which represents Hektor's death and the contradictions of heroism objectively, it subjectifies these matters by making the intertextual allusion a product of Priam's mind.[10]

---

[10] Such intertextuality, in which a character in one text, not its author, recalls narrative details of another text, is relatively unusual. One thinks of Dante, but that is a special case.

This interpretation may seem problematic: for how is one to know that Priam is making subjective, intertextual allusions—or even that he is in any way aware of the sounds and movements that take place as he rushes toward the ships? I would like to read 36, "The king goads, goads his horses" ('Ο βασιλεὺς κεντᾷ, κεντᾷ τοὺς ἵππους), as Priam's urgent response to his own association of the night-sound with his son's death. But this line, with its repeated κεντᾷ, κεντᾷ, obviously echoes 27–28, "The only thought he now has / is that his chariot should run fast, fast" (Μόνην σκέψιν τώρα ἔχει / ταχύ, ταχὺ τὸ ἅρμα του νὰ τρέχῃ), and looks forward to the final line of the poem, "It's enough that his chariot runs fast, fast" (φθάνει τὸ ἅρμα του ταχύ, ταχὺ νὰ τρέχει). But in both these places there is no indication whatsoever that the king is at all aware of the sights and sounds mentioned by the poem's speaker. Indeed, "The only thought he now has" and "It's enough that" may be thought to rule out such awareness and to suggest, instead, a figure so entirely absorbed in his own desperation and in the pain and lamentation he brings with him from Troy, that he is, so to speak, impervious or immune to other stimuli and in no way able to associate them with Hektor's death.

Verses 37–41 are similarly problematic: "On the plain shadows awaken, / inauspicious, / and wonder why, in so great a hurry, / the son of Dardanos flies toward the ships / of the murderous Argives, and the rude Achaeans." It seems likely that these awakening shadows (σκιαὶ) are the ghosts of the dead warriors lying on the plain of battle—their ψυχαί, to use the Homeric term. Neither *Iliad* 24 nor Cavafy's text explicitly mentions these corpses in the description of Priam's journey, but Homer's account of Hermes preparing, at Zeus' command, to escort Priam, mentions that "he took the wand with which he charms the eyes of men / whom he wishes [to charm], and in turn awakens those too who are sleeping," (24.343–44). I would suggest that "those . . . who are sleeping" (ὑπνώοντας ἐγείρει) is the "source" of Cavafy's ἐξυπνοῦν σκιαὶ (37). 'Εξυπνοῦν clearly corresponds intransitively to ἐγείρει; similarly, the use of σκιαὶ to describe ψυχαί in Hades at *Od*. 10.495 and of σκιή in a simile speaking of an insubstantial corpse at *Od*. 11.207 might have prompted Cavafy's use of the word in line 37.[11]

---

[11] In the Homeric text, Priam's family and friends (φίλοι) escort him out of the city "as if he were going deathward," (24.328), and, as C.H. Whitman suggested (*Homer and the Heroic Tradition* [Cambridge, Mass., 1957], pp. 217-18), Hermes meeting Priam "in the darkness, by the tomb of Ilus, a sort of terminus between the two worlds [sc. of the living and the dead]," and escorting him across the river to the shelter of Achilles, suggests a journey to the land of the dead, of which Achilles symbolically "fills the role of the king . . ." On such a journey it would be appropriate for

Maronitis suggests that "the *aporia* of [these lines], which Cavafy attributes to the inauspicious, spectral shadows, transcribes the equivalent *aporia* of Hermes" in the *Iliad*, "when in disguise he encounters Priam 'with amazement' (στῆ ταφών, 24.360)" and inquires " 'where [he] is directing [his] mules and horses / through the divine night, when other mortals are sleeping' " (24.362–63).[12] Maronitis is wrong to speak of Hermes' ἀπορία: στῆ δὲ ταφών describes Priam, not Hermes; it comes as the climax of the description of the king's response to Idaios' pointing out the approach of a man who turns out to be the god: "The old man's mind was confused, and he was deeply afraid, / and the hairs stood straight on his bent limbs, / and he stood amazed," 24.358–60. But Maronitis is correct in drawing attention to this part of *Iliad* 24 as the text Cavafy has in mind in 37–42, though the Alexandrian poet has, characteristically, switched around almost every textual echo to refer to a different character: 1) as I already have pointed out, the awakening shadows of line 37 derive from 24.343–44, where Hermes is said to awaken sleepers with his wand, though in the *Iliad*, as Hermes points out (24.361), it is Priam and Idaios, not "inauspicious shadows," who are awake while other mortals sleep; 2) Hermes, who comes out of the night, is first feared as threatening (24.355) but eventually welcomed by Priam as an "auspicious wayfarer" (ὁδοιπόρον . . . αἴσιον, 24.375–76), as opposed to Cavafy's "repulsive and ill-omened raven" (κόραξ ἀπαίσιος, 32); 3) Hermes, not "shadows," pretends to wonder where Priam is going and isn't he afraid of the "Achaeans who breathe fury" (24.365), whom he further characterizes as "hostile and unfriendly," (24.365). Together, these phrases are the source of Cavafy's "of the murderous Argives, and the rude Achaeans," (41–42); this suggests that Cavafy took "unfriendly" (ἀνάρσιοι) in its etymological sense and transformed it into ακαιόν, which in modern Greek means "rude" or "unmannerly"; 4) Priam is called "son of Dardanos" (Δαρδανίδης) in 40, just as Idaios addresses him as Δαρδανίδε in 24.354.[13] When, in 39–42, the inauspicious shadows "wonder why, in so great a hurry, / the son of Dardanos flies toward the ships / of the murderous Argives and the rude / Achaeans," Cavafy once again calls attention to Priam's urgency. This is signalled by the striking enjambment between 40 and

---

Priam to encounter *psuchai* in the form of the uncomprehending *skiai* that wonder at him in Cavafy's poem.

[12] Maronitis, Πίσω Μπρός, p. 53.

[13] Four of the ten occasions on which Priam is called "son of Dardanos" occur in Book 24: 171, 354 in direct speech; 629, 631 in the narrator's voice.

41–an enjambment bridging the poem's two final strophes and paralleled in the poem only at 16–17, between the fourth and fifth strophes, where, with the help of κ'ἔτι (16), it imitates metrically Priam's indiscriminate piling up of the ransom. One may think in terms of Priam's subjective urgency in the face of Night's threat, through its movements and noises, to block or distract his concentrated mind; or of his total unawareness of the movements and noises, owing to his desperate concentration on his own feelings. In either case the effect is strengthened by the poem's final lines: "But the king pays no attention to these things;/it's enough that his chariot runs fast, fast" (Ἀλλὰ ὁ βασιλεὺς αὐτὰ δὲν τὰ προσέχει· φθάνει τὸ ἅρμα του ταχύ, ταχὺ νὰ τρέχει, 43–44). Here the word φθάνει, "It's enough," produces a slight ambiguity: the normal meaning of this verb in modern Greek is "arrive," and it seems in the first half of 44 that Priam's chariot "is arriving," as in the *Iliad*, at the Greek camp and the shelter of Achilles. But the final words of the line and the poem, νὰ τρέχει tell us to understand φθάνει as part of a special idiom, and insist, in light of the foreclosed meaning "arrive," that Cavafy's poem, unlike the *Iliad*, provides no closural "arrival," no resolution of Priam's agony and of the action to which it prompts him.

In this way, "Priam's Night-Journey" reverses the poetic thrust of the text in reference to which and against which it was composed. This intertextual effect is Callimachean, almost Vergilian, in its demand on a reader to have read and to have in mind the relevant passages from Homer, but Cavafy's mode is modern rather than ancient in its almost symbolist evocation of lamentation and sorrow, Night-terrors and Night-distractions.[14] These, like the "Walls" ("Τείχη") and "Windows" ("Παραθύρα") of Cavafy's poems by those names (also early poems, dating from 1896 and 1897 respectively), present barriers of enclosure or resistance, against which, as Maronitis comments, every movement is futile because the barrier moves along with the one trying to move beyond it—who in this case actually brings his despair and lamentation with him from Troy.[15] Cavafy's Priam is

---

[14] On the symbolist qualities of the poem, see M. Pieris, " Κ.Π. Καβάφης· ἔφορος στο σκοτάδι (η εξελικτική πορεία)," Το μικρό Δέντρο 6 (Athens, 1982), repr. in M. Pieris (ed.), Εισαγωγή, pp. 357-427, esp. pp. 372-89. Cf. Maronitis, "Κ.Π. Καβάφησ," p. 458, on "the symbolist objective and intention" of the poem.

[15] Maronitis, Πίσω Μπρός, p. 55. Jusdanis, *The Poetics of Cavafy*, p. 71, discusses the symbolist qualities of "Windows" and refers to a letter from Cavafy to his brother John in which he says, in Jusdanis' words, that in composing this poem "he sought a vague, enigmatic mode so as to create an effect rather than to describe concrete objects. The aim of the poem was to evoke a mood of pessimism and desperation. . . ." A similar mood is evident in "Priam's Night-Journey."

a figure of such futility; he fails to break through the Night, despite the hatred for the uselessness of the lamentation that impels him to do so. The end of the poem freezes him running away from himself. As far as we know from this poem, Hektor may never be ransomed: "It's enough," for the king, "that his chariot runs fast, fast."[16]

[16] This essay is based on a paper presented at the University of California at Los Angeles and The Graduate School of the City University of New York. I'd like to thank members of both audiences, especially Mary Depew and Michele Hannoosh at UCLA and Constance Tagopoulos and Marina Kotzamani at CUNY, for their helpful criticism, suggestions, and encouragement. I'm especially grateful to Katherine C. King for editorial improvements of both style and substance.

Figure 12. The Sirens. Flaxman (*Odyssey* series).

# Kafka and the Sirens:
# Writing as Lethetic Reading

*Clayton Koelb*

Near the beginning of book 12 of the *Odyssey*, Circe gives Odysseus some famous advice:

> Your next encounter will be with the Sirens, who bewitch everybody that approaches them. There is no homecoming for the man who draws near them unawares and hears the Sirens' voices; no welcome from his wife, no little children brightening at their father's return. For with the music of their song the Sirens cast their spell upon him, and they sit there in a meadow piled high with the mouldering skeletons of men, whose withered skin still hangs upon their bones. Drive your ship past the spot, and to prevent any of your crew from hearing, soften some beeswax and plug their ears with it. But if you wish to listen yourself, make them bind you hand and foot on board and stand you up by the step of the mast, with the rope's ends lashed to the mast itself. This will allow you to listen with enjoyment to the twin Sirens' voices. But if you start begging your men to release you, they must add to the bonds that already hold you fast.[1]

---

[1] Homer, *The Odyssey*, trans. E. V. Rieu (Baltimore: Penguin, 1946), 190.

The hero carries out these instructions exactly, and he is able to experience the marvelous enchantment of the Sirens' song, to let himself in fact be overwhelmed by it, without having to suffer the terrible consequences that befell those who went before him: "The lovely voices came to me across the water, and my heart was filled with such a longing to listen that with nod and frown I signed to my men to set me free."[2] Instead of setting him free, the men do as they have been instructed and tighten his bonds while the ship continues past the islands. Only when they are well out of earshot do they release their captain.

Franz Kafka wrote his own story based on this famous adventure, apparently in late October of 1917, but he never published it. Max Brod, Kafka's friend and literary executor, found it in one of the octavo notebooks Kafka had left and included it in a collection of fiction from Kafka's *Nachlaß* which appeared in 1931. Kafka had not given it a title, and Brod evidently thinking to draw attention to the story's most surprising feature, called it "Das Schweigen der Sirenen" ("The Silence of the Sirens"). In Kafka's version, the Sirens indeed do not sing: "Now the Sirens have a still more fatal weapon than their song, namely their silence."[3] This is the weapon that they use against the wily hero from Ithaca.

Kafka's Odysseus overcomes this formidable enemy, however, because he "did not hear their silence."[4] In Kafka's story of the encounter with the Sirens, not only had Odysseus had himself bound to the mast, but he, too, has stopped his ears with wax, as the second sentence of the narration tells us: "To protect himself from the Sirens Ulysses stopped his ears with wax; and had himself bound to the mast of his ship."[5] This alteration of Homer's story, this wax in Odysseus's ears, is, I contend, a far more significant change than the substitution of silence for singing. It is possible to write a story about the Sirens' silence that is on the whole faithful to the spirit of the Homeric original and can be read as a version of the adventure from the *Odys-*

---

[2] Ibid.

[3] I cite Kafka in English from Franz Kafka, *The Complete Stories*, ed. Nahum N. Glatzer (New York: Schocken, 1971), abbreviated as *CS*; and in German from Franz Kafka, *Sämtliche Erzählungen*, ed. Paul Raabe (Frankfurt a.M.: Fischer, 1970), abbreviated as *SE*. In most cases, as here, I will give a translation in the text and the original in a footnote: *CS* 431, *SE* 305: "Nun haben die Sirenen eine noch schrecklichere Waffe als den Gesang, nämlich ihr Schweigen."

[4] *CS* 431, *SE* 305: "hörte ihr Schweigen nicht."

[5] *CS* 430, *SE* 304: "Um sich vor den Sirenen zu bewahren, stopfte sich Odysseus Wachs in die Ohren und ließ sich am Mast festschmieden."

*sey*. As soon as you put wax in Odysseus's ears however, you leave the Odyssey completely, you forget it, as it were, and embark on a different narrative project altogether.

Homer's story has two essential features. First, it tells how the Greek sailors were able to pass the island of the Sirens without falling victim to the deadly song, and, second but equally important, it explains how Odysseus was able to accomplish the feat of both hearing the Sirens and escaping them. This section of the *Odyssey*, we remember, is not narrated directly by the poet but is part of a long quoted discourse by Odysseus to the Phaeacian king Alcinous and his court. The story of the Sirens is therefore part of a first-person narrative embedded in the poem, where the point of view belongs exclusively to the hero. He can tell us only what he has experienced. Odysseus is able to recount to the Phaeacians exactly what the Sirens sang to him as his ship passed and to make their song a part of his story only because he heard it himself. Odysseus's unstopped ears are an essential feature of the tale, then, not only because of what is revealed about the hero's character but also because they are the absolute narrative prerequisite of the story.

Odysseus plays the role of witness. If the story does nothing else, it establishes him as the single mortal authority on the Sirens. He alone among living men knows what the Sirens sing and what effect their song has. The central section of the *Odyssey*, wherein the most fantastic of the tales are related, depends entirely upon the witness role of the hero and is in a sense *about* nothing so much as this role. The poet does not ask us to believe *him*; he gives us an eyewitness whose stature within the fiction is such that it encourages, though it does not guarantee, belief. Everything we know about the Sirens comes from Odysseus; we must either accept what he says or reject it and, if we reject it, reject along with it a substantial portion of the entire poem.

The most fundamental feature of the Homeric version of the tale, then, is the unique authority it ascribes to the narrating voice of Odysseus himself. One could change various elements of the story and still be true to the basic Homeric structure, so long as Odysseus himself retains his position as unique witness. One could even change the Sirens' song into silence and still remain within the basic tradition established by Homer, as long as it was Odysseus himself who testified to their silence. This is exactly what Rilke did in the poem "Die Insel der Sirenen" ("The Island of the Sirens"), written one decade before Kafka's story, in 1907:

Wenn er denen, die ihm gastlich waren,
spät, nach ihrem Tage noch, da sie
fragten nach den Fahrten und Gefahren
still berichtete: er wußte nie,

wie sie schrecken und mit welchem jähen
Wort sie wenden, daß sie so wie er
in dem blau gestillten Inselmeer
die Vergoldung jener Inseln sähen,

deren Anblick macht, daß die Gefahr
umschlägt; denn nun ist sie nicht im Tosen
und im Wüten, wo sie immer war.
Lautlos kommt sie über die Matrosen,

welche wissen, daß es dort auf jenen
goldnen Inseln manchmal singt—,
und sich blindlings in die Ruder lehnen,
wie umringt

von der Stille, die die ganze Weite
in sich hat und an die Ohren weht,
so als wäre ihre andre Seite
der Gesang, dem keiner widersteht.[6]

Although Rilke revises the Homeric account in a surprising way here, he remains faithful to the basic structure of the classical version. The danger is still the Sirens' song, but now that song is perceived only indirectly: the sailors know that singing is sometimes heard coming from these islands, and the expectation of song conditions their experience of silence so that it is transformed into "the other side" of an irresistible singing. More important than this, though, is Rilke's

---

[6] Quoted from *Der Neuen Gedichte Anderer Teil* (Leipzig: Insel, 1919), 6. Here is a prose translation with no pretensions but which seeks to reproduce the ambiguities and syntactic complexity of the original: "When he quietly reported to those who were hospitable to him, late, after their day was done, since they asked about his journeys and dangers: he never knew how they frighten or with what abrupt word they turn, that they, like him, would see in the blue, becalmed sea of islands the gilding of those islands whose appearance makes the danger shift; because the danger is not in ranting and raving, where ever it was. It comes soundlessly upon the sailors, who know that singing is sometimes heard on those golden islands—and they lean blindly on their oars, as if surrounded by the silence that has all fullness in it and that blows about their ears, as if its other side were the song that none can resist."

reliance on Odysseus as the reliable witness. It is through Odysseus that the reader learns about the island of the Sirens and about the silence that is the other side of song. Like the story from the ancient epic, Rilke's poem focuses as much on the situation of the telling as on the story itself. The first stanza, for example, has nothing at all to do with the Sirens but rather is taken up with setting the scene of Odysseus's report, with explaining why and how he delivered himself of it. One might even suspect that the poem is meant to be as much about the storyteller himself as about the matter of his story. This suspicion is confirmed when we notice that the word *still* is used to describe how the hero "reported" (*berichtete*), the very same lexeme that appears later in substantive form (*Stille*) to describe wherein lies the danger of the islands. Odysseus's "song" is thus no different from whatever it is that emanates from the island of the Sirens. It is a form of "quiet" that contains vast spaces ("die die ganze Weite in sich hat") and that may be as dangerous to the hospitable (*gastlich*) Phaeacians as any tales full of "Tosen und Wüten" (ranting and raving).

Rilke's poem essentially uses the authority of the Homeric text to authorize the alterations it makes in that text. We are not asked to take the word of some unknown, faceless narrator that the Sirens did not actually sing: Odysseus himself, whom Homer has told us was actually there and actually heard whatever it was that came from that island, Odysseus the eyewitness, revises the story. Rilke remains well within the main current of the tradition, even while he questions one of the prominent features of the tradition, because he accepts the fundamental structure of the Homeric narrative situation. One could even say that Rilke basically accepts the central point of the classical story by retaining Odysseus as narrator and sole medium through which we learn what it was the Sirens did; for that central point is not that the Sirens sang this or that song or that they sang at all but that, whatever it was they did, Odysseus was able to observe it and yet come away alive.

For these reasons, then, I would call Rilke's poem an alethetic reading of the Homeric story. An alethetic reading, as I have detailed elsewhere,[7] is one that assumes that the text being read essentially tells the truth, no matter how incredible or full of error that text may appear to be. Such reading assumes that texts have an outside and an inside, or a surface and a depth, and that an incredible surface can be opened up to disclose a depth worthy of belief. Rilke's "Die Insel der

---

[7] See Clayton Koelb, *The Incredulous Reader* (Ithaca: Cornell University Press, 1984), 32-40.

Sirenen" reads the *Odyssey* alethetically in that it assumes that the basic import of the epic is true and correct, even if its surface has been distorted by the replacement of an "actual" silence (as the revision would have it) with the imagined song which is its "other side." Homer's story of the Sirens matches Rilke's version if it is read as a certain kind of allegory wherein the song that Odysseus reports hearing is understood as the mythic fleshing out of the vast space (*Weite*) encompassed by the mysterious silence. In this reading, the words that Odysseus ascribes to the Sirens—words full of flattery ("flower of Achaean chivalry") and promises ("we have foreknowledge of all that is going to happen")[8]—are his own desires projected into the emptiness around him. There is no incompatibility between Rilke's and Homer's accounts as long as we presume that texts do not always say directly what they mean, a presumption fundamental to all alethetic reading.[9]

When we turn to Kafka's story, however, we are faced with a radically different situation. The narrator is no longer Odysseus himself but instead a nameless and characterless voice whose chief claim to authority is his knowledge of tradition, but now a tradition in which Odysseus has no role as witness. This narrator knows things that Odysseus does not and cannot know, including the potential meaning or meanings of the adventure. Odysseus's role as witness is erased from the outset with the announcement that he not only bound himself to the mast but stopped his ears with wax as well. With that announcement the story detaches itself completely from the tradition and sets off on a course entirely its own.

Kafka's "The Silence of the Sirens" is therefore a "lethetic" (that is, forgetful or oblivious) reading of the epic tale.[10] Lethetic reading takes place when the reader acts as if he or she does not believe the text being read and thus deliberately ignores what the text seems to be trying to say. It is not a naive misunderstanding but an intentional radical reshaping of the materials out of which the text is made; it

---

[8] Homer, *The Odyssey*, 194.

[9] For another imaginative and extremely rich alethetic reading of the Homeric story of the Sirens, see Maurice Blanchot, "The Sirens' Song," in *The Sirens' Song: Selected Essays by Maurice Blanchot*, ed. Gabriel Josipovici (Bloomington: Indiana University Press, 1982), 59-65. Blanchot's sketch, first published in 1959 in *Le Livre à venir*, is in many ways very relevant to the topic of my essay, not only because it almost certainly derives in part from Blanchot's reading of Kafka but because it deals as well with one of Rilke's themes, the transformation of "the real song into an imaginary one" (64). Only considerations of space prevent me from treating Blanchot's piece in the body of this essay.

[10] For more on oblivious reading, see *The Incredulous Reader*, 143-57.

assumes, in fact, that the text being read is nothing more than a gathering of such materials, a storehouse of signifiers to be exploited at will. Reading in the lethetic mode is not interested in what a text means, only in what it says—or rather *that* it says. Where alethetic reading sees the text as, say, a house whose structure is sound and whose organization of internal space is excellent, even if its external appearance makes it look shabby or grotesque or even unstable and in need of substantial repair, lethetic reading finds in that same house a supply of building elements—windows, doors, staircases, valuable things of craftsmanship or materials perhaps no longer available—that can be used to make a new house with a completely different structure and internal organization. Rilke is an alethetic reader who does a brilliant alteration of the façade of Homer's magnificent old house; Kafka is a lethetic reader who plunders the old building for its scarce, virtually irreplaceable, ready-made architectural elements.

Before examining Kafka's lethetic reading of the *Odyssey* in detail, it is instructive to look at another text where we find elements Kafka has plundered from his reading of a classic. The short prose sketch that Max Brod published under the title "Das Stadtwappen" ("The City Coat of Arms"), probably written in late 1920, displays in its first sentence the characteristics of a text produced by lethetic reading: "At first all the arrangements for building the Tower of Babel were characterized by fairly good order; indeed the order was perhaps too perfect, too much thought was given to guides, interpreters, accommodations for the workmen, and roads of communication, as if there were centuries before one to do the work in."[11] The first few words, with their reference to the "building of the Tower of Babel" (in the original, "babylonischen Turmbau," that is, "Babylonian tower-construction") conjure up the biblical story with which we are so familiar. And, lest the reader suspect that this "babylonischer Turmbau" might refer to some other construction project undertaken by the Babylonians, Kafka later clarifies the matter definitively: "The essential thing in the whole business is the idea of building a tower that will reach to heaven."[12]

It is hardly necessary to glance back at Genesis 11 to recall the central issue of that story of the Tower of Babel, announced in the

---

[11] *CS* 433, *SE* 306: "Anfangs war beim babylonischen Turmbau alles in leidlicher Ordnung; ja, die Ordnung was vielleicht zu groß, man dachte zu sehr an Wegweiser, Dolmetscher, Arbeiterunterkünfte und Verbindungswege, so als habe man Jahrhunderte vor sich."

[12] *CS*. 433, *SE* 306: "Das Wesentliche des ganzen Unternehmens ist der Gedanke, einen bis in den Himmel reichenden Turm zu bauen."

introductory phrases: "Once upon a time all the world spoke a single language and used the same words." The Genesis narrative presents the building of the tower to heaven as the origin of the many, mutually incomprehensible human languages. Whatever else it is doing, it is unquestionably explaining why, if Adam gave the proper names to all things in the Garden of Eden (Gen. 2) and thus created the perfect language, there are now so many different languages in the world. That is the fundamental meaning of the story, what orders all the other elements.

Kafka shows in his first sentence that he is not interested at all in what the biblical narrative means. He has not failed to understand that meaning—how could one miss it?—but rather has ignored it, acted as if it were not there. If one were to take the story in Genesis seriously, one would suppose that there was one profession that did not and could not exist prior to the building of the tower: interpreter (*Dolmetscher*). By introducing interpreters into the work force of the tower builders, Kafka demonstrates that his story is not simply a different version of the biblical narrative, it is a different story altogether. His story takes place in a different world from the one presented in *Genesis*: this world is already fallen, already thoroughly secularized, and already so full of division and disagreement that no divine intervention is necessary in order to bring about confusion.

For all its obliviousness to the intention of the story from the Old Testament, "The City Coat of Arms" is still recognizably made out of various elements taken out of the old tale and reordered into a new structure. Kafka has not merely taken the notion of building a tower to heaven and pasted it onto a story that has no relation to the biblical one; on the contrary, he has taken many important features from the Old Testament and fit them together in a surprising way. One of the key features of Genesis 11, for example, is its opposition of order to disorder: the project begins with order but, because of divine intervention, ends in confusion. Kafka takes this fundamental opposition and, in typical Kafka fashion, makes it into a paradoxical unity. The order that exists at the commencement of the construction is *already* disorder; it is an order so complex that it is indistinguishable from chaos. The planners are so concerned with thoroughness in all their preparations that they never actually get around to working on the tower, while the preparations become chaotically complex. The chaos manifests itself quickly in the rivalries that develop among the various groups, engaged not in building the tower itself but in the preliminary work, building the construction workers' city: "Every nationality wanted the finest quarter for itself, and this gave rise to disputes, which developed into bloody conflicts. These conflicts never came to an end."[13] Kafka suggests the paradox in the very language of the opening sentence, where he refers to the order as "tolerable" ("in leidlicher Ordnung"). The word *leidlich* contains the morpheme *leid*, which carries a lengthy burden of negative meanings: "painful, disagreeable, unpleasant, bad," and so on. Thus the word Kafka has selected to inform us that the order was, as the Muir translation puts it, "fairly good," tells us at the same time that this order was fairly bad, painful, disagreeable, and unpleasant.

Another element of central importance to the Genesis narrative, divine intervention, is vital in Kafka's story as well. But Kafka has completely transformed the role it plays in his story, moving from the center of the reported action to a kind of appendix placed at the end of the description of the city, where it is cited as part of an apocalyptic prophecy: "All the legends and songs that came to birth in that city are filled with longing for a prophesied day when the city would be destroyed by five successive blows from a gigantic fist. It is for that reason too that the city has a closed fist on its coat of arms."[14] The role of divine intervention in "The City Coat of Arms" is thus radically different from that in the Old Testament story. In the Bible, God intervenes by introducing disorder for the purpose of halting a project that has, from the divine point of view, all too great prospects for success: "Here they are, one people with a single language, and now they have started to do this; henceforward nothing they have a mind to do will be beyond their reach" (Gen. 11:6). In Kafka's story, the project to build the tower has absolutely no prospect for success, since "the second or third generation had already recognized the senselessness of building a heaven-reaching tower."[15] Divine intervention, if it were to come, would not put a stop to a dangerous effort to achieve something like equal status with divinity; it would, on the contrary, bring a merciful end to a sick organism that is unable to put itself out of its own misery.

---

[13] *CS* 433, *SE* 307: "Jede Landsmannschaft wollte das schönste Quartier haben, dadurch ergaben sich Streitigkeiten, die sich bis zu blutigen Kämpfen steigerten. Diese Kämpfe hörten nicht mehr auf."

[14] *CS* 434, *SE* 307: "Alles was in dieser Stadt an Sagen und Liedern entstanden ist, ist erfüllt von der Sehnsucht nach einem prophezeiten Tag, an welchem die Stadt von einer Riesenfaust in fünf kurz aufeinanderfolgenden Schlägen zerschmeltert werden wird. Deshalb hat auch die Stadt die Faust im Wappen.

[15] *CS* 434. *SE* 307: "schon die zweite oder dritte Generation die Sinnlosigkeit des Himmelsturmbaues erkannte."

"The City Coat of Arms" is unquestionably a text that derives from Kafka's reading of the Old Testament, but his reading has been quite untouched by the meaning discoverable by any "serious" reader. To use one of Kafka's own metaphors of reading derived from the Old Testament, his reading has passed "through the midst of the book . . . as once the Jews passed through the Red Sea."[16] Just as the Jews following Moses were able to go through the very center of the Red Sea without being flooded by it, "through the sea on dry ground," as it is reported in Exodus 14, so does Kafka pass through this and other monumental texts of the tradition without being "influenced" (i.e., "flooded") by them. There is no doubt that he can do it quite as well with Homer as with the Old Testament.

As Kafka's oblivious reading of the tower story announces itself most directly in the introduction of the "interpreters," so is his lethetic reading of Homer most evident in the matter of the wax in Odysseus's ears. This is certainly an important feature of the classical version, but it is pointedly attached quite firmly to the ship's crew and not to Odysseus. Kafka takes this element from the epic, detaches it from its original context (as if it were some kind of free-floating signifier), and recombines it with another element, the hero, formerly the one character to whom this feature was forbidden. From the structuralist point of view, the *Odyssey* sets up a binary opposition between captain and crew on the basis of the presence or absence of wax in the ears, an opposition which Kafka quite cheerfully obliterates. Instead of allegorizing the Homeric tale, as Rilke does, Kafka simply treats it as a random collection of elements which can be realigned into new narrative units. We still recognize it as deriving from the *Odyssey*, of course, but it is no longer a version of the same story.

Kafka has reconfigured the elements found in the epic, but he has not taken all the elements that were available. The ship's crew plays a crucial role in the *Odyssey* but disappears altogether in Kafka's story. The only indication in "The Silence of the Sirens" that Odysseus is not completely alone comes in the most indirect manner with the declaration that the hero "had himself" ("ließ sich") tied to the mast. In all other ways Kafka's narrative assumes that a solitary Odysseus goes forth to meet the Sirens, and imagining the presence of a crew can

---

[16] *CS* 75, *SE* 251: "mitten durch das Buch, wie einmal die Juden durch das Rote Meer." For more on this and other metaphors of reading in Kafka, see my " 'In der Strafkolonie': Kafka and the Scene of Reading," *German Quarterly*, 55 (Nov. 1982), 511-25; and especially my "The Margin in the Middle: Kafka's Other Reading of Reading," in *Franz Kafka and the Contemporary Critical Performance: Centenary Readings*, ed. Alan Udoff (Bloomington: Indiana University Press, 1987).

only complicate and weaken one's reading. One would have to wonder if the other sailors were also chained as well as deafened with wax; if they, too, failed to hear the silence but did see the throats, breasts, and eyes of the Sirens as Odysseus does; and if they shared his feelings of "bliss" at the prospect of overcoming the singers. All these issues are irrelevant to Kafka's story, where the focus of interest is entirely upon the confrontation between Odysseus and the Sirens. The Homeric tale, on the other hand, reminds us not only that the crew is present during the encounter but that they are a set of individuals whose lives hang in the balance and whose actions are essential for the stratagem to succeed. When Odysseus, overwhelmed by the power of the song, signals the men to set him free, "they swung forward to their oars and rowed ahead, while Perimedes and Eurylochus jumped up, tightened my bonds and added more."[17]

The only remnant of the Homeric crew in Kafka's story is precisely the wax in the ears. By some kind of conservation of narrative energy, however, all the importance that had attached to the crew in the epic tale now inheres in the wax, which becomes the central element around which all others revolve. The story told by "The Silence of the Sirens" derives entirely from the situation created by putting this wax in the ears not of the now-vanished crew but of Odysseus himself. It is the wax that makes it possible for the hero to fail to hear the silence of the Sirens and to make the erroneous judgment (i.e., that the Sirens are singing but that he cannot hear them) which, paradoxically, saves him from experiencing their power and suffering destruction. The wax thus transforms Odysseus from the reliable witness he was in both the *Odyssey* and Rilke's poem into the fortunate beneficiary of a set of circumstances of which he is himself blissfully ignorant. This change in turn necessitates the change in narrative format introducing the authoritative voice of an unknown reporter who, while not exactly omniscient, possesses far more knowledge of what occurs than the hero does.

This placement of Odysseus within someone else's narrative frame has important consequences for the reader's reception of the story. The Homeric strategy of making Odysseus the teller of his own story (in this central section of the poem) creates an effect of immediacy that has been long recognized and justifiably admired. The reader[18] is placed, as it were, among the Phaeacians, hearing the

---

[17] Homer, *The Odyssey*, 194.

[18] I use the term *reader* to refer to Homer's audience as well as Kafka's in order to maintain the comparison. That this audience was originally a set of listeners rather than readers has been well established by the Parry-Lord proposal, and I do

adventures at first hand, from the lips of the adventurer himself. The epic admits to and acquiesces in the necessity of narration while it overcomes to a great degree the distancing effect of narrative intervention. Kafka, on the other hand, urgently wants this distancing effect. He wants readers who are acutely, even painfully aware of the process of mediation that stands between them and the events reported and who realize that the narrator may not have the last and best word on the subject. Not only do we not have the eyewitness Odysseus telling the tale; we do not have a witness of any kind: the narrator, by mentioning the existence of a "codicil" ("Anhang") that has been "handed down" ("überliefert"), places himself at the end of a tradition ("Überlieferung") that is not necessarily consistent or complete and of which he is only the latest compiler. Thus, while Odysseus of the stopped-up ears could never be in a position to accurately tell what happened, no one else has any much greater claim on possession of the "true" story. One potential set of witnesses, the crew of sailors, has vanished from the scene, and the narrator, for all his assumption of authority, unmasks himself as a latecomer far removed from events he describes.

Paradoxically, Kafka has inserted into his story another set of characters who might have been in a position to understand and accurately relate what happened: the Sirens themselves. In the *Odyssey*, it should be remembered, the Sirens do not appear except insofar as their song reaches the hero's ears. We know no more about them than what Odysseus knows, which is the words of their song. Kafka reverses the situation: his Sirens do not sing, but they do appear. Odysseus sees them and the narrator describes both their appearance and their feelings: "But they—lovelier than ever—stretched their necks and turned, let their awesome hair flutter free in the wind, and freely stretched their claws on the rocks. They no longer had any desire to allure; all that they wanted was to hold as long as they could the radiance that fell from Ulysses' great eyes."[19] Kafka was apparently familiar with the traditional depiction of the Sirens in painting and drawing, where they often "are represented as half women and half birds,"[20] and one could therefore say that his depic-

---

not intend my usage to connote any conflict with this widely accepted theory.

[19] *CS* 431, *SE* 305: "Sie aber–schöner als jemals–streckten und drehten sich, ließen das schaurige Haar offen im Winde wehen und spannten die Krallen frei auf den Felsen. Sie wollten nicht mehr verführen, nur noch den Abglanz vom großen Augenpaar des Odysseus wollten sie so lange als möglich erhaschen."

[20] *The Oxford Classical Dictionary*, 2d ed. (Oxford: Clarendon Press, 1970), 993.

tion of them follows classical precedent. But it is a precedent foreign to the *Odyssey*, where they are never described at all. In typical fashion, Kafka transforms a physical quality of these mythical creatures into a figure of desire: birds have claws capable of grasping (*erhaschen*) prey, and this grasping (the Muir translation uses the rather colorless word *hold*) is what they want to do with the "radiance" they see in Odysseus's eyes.

These Sirens, quite fully fleshed out as characters in Kafka's story, are in the best position of anyone to comprehend fully what is happening, and they would be ideal witnesses, save for one thing: they are not conscious beings. The lack of consciousness, the narrator tells us, is the only thing that saves them from being destroyed by Odysseus's escape: "If the Sirens had possessed consciousness they would have been annihilated at that moment. But they remained as they had been; all that happened was that Ulysses had escaped them."[21] This quality that saves them—another absence, be it noted—also renders them useless as witnesses. *Bewußtsein* means not only "consciousness" but also "knowledge" and "conviction." The Sirens are no more aware than Odysseus of what has occurred. They appear to experience it, but their lack of *Bewußtsein* cancels the experience in the very moment it takes place.

While Rilke found in the *Odyssey* a story of an experience so immediate, vivid, and penetrating that it nearly escapes language altogether, Kafka creates out of the broken shards of the epic a story that questions the possibility of immediate experience. Rilke tells of sailors who are "surrounded" ("umringt") by a silence so palpable that it "blows about their ears" ("an die Ohren weht"). They experience this stillness so intensely that it seems like the inversion of a powerful form of speech, a "song that none can resist" ("Gesang, dem keiner widersteht"). The silence of Rilke's poem is "Stille" (cf. also "still" and "gestillt"), a calm or quiet that is presented as a kind of presence, indeed a plenitude that contains something vast within it ("die die ganze Weite / in sich hat"). Kafka's story is about a different kind of silence, not "Stille" but "Schweigen," not the positive silence of "peace and quiet" but the negative silence of the withholding of speech, not a presence and a plenitude but an absence and a void. "The Silence of the Sirens" presents this negativity as the most powerful weapon the sirens possess, but this negativity is in turn negated by the wax in Odysseus's ears. He fails to hear their failure to speak. The

---

[21] *CS* 432, *SE* 305: "Hatten die Sirenen Bewußtsein, sie wären damals vernichtet worden. So aber blieben sie, nur Odysseus ist ihnen entgangen."

hero emerges from his meeting with the Sirens unscathed, but he remains ignorant of what actually happened. What he believes he has experienced—his victory over the Sirens by means of his wax and chains—has not happened: "He thought they were singing and that he alone did not hear them. For a fleeting moment he saw their throats rising and falling, their breasts lifting, their eyes filled with tears, their lips half-parted, but believed that these were accompaniments to the airs which died unheard around him." And what has happened remains far beyond his experience: "When they were nearest to him he knew of them no longer."[22]

This skepticism about the possibility of immediate experience is only partially modified by the "codicil" appended to the body of "The Silence of the Sirens": "Ulysses, it is said, was so full of guile, was such a fox, that not even the goddess of fate could pierce his armor. Perhaps he had really noticed, although here the human understanding is beyond its depths, that the Sirens were silent, and held up to them and to the gods the aforementioned pretense merely as a sort of shield."[23] The story's conclusion thus restores some credibility to the notion of genuine experience by holding out the possibility that Odysseus somehow knew all along exactly what was happening. At the same time, however, the narrator confesses that, in this interpretation, Odysseus's behavior is not comprehensible by human understanding ("mit Menschenverstand nicht mehr zu begreifen") and thereby in a sense withdraws what the codicil offers. If Odysseus did know and did indeed merely pretend not to hear the silence of the Sirens, his ability both to know (how could he, with his ears full of wax?) and at the same time to resist (how could he, when "no earthly powers can resist" it?) passes beyond the human into something else. The narrator calls him a fox, obviously a commonplace trope for a particularly crafty person, but in Kafka's fiction such tropes never quite lose their literal meanings. It is also said that Odysseus possessed an "innermost self" ("Innerstes") into which the goddess of fate herself could not penetrate, a quality that would put him on a par with, or perhaps even

---

[22] CS 431, SE 305: "er glaubte, sie sängen, und nur er sei behütet, es zu hören. Flüchtig sah er zuerst die Wendungen ihrer Hälse, das tiefe Atmen, die tränenvollen Augen, den halb geöffneten Mund, glaubte aber, dies gehöre zu den Arien, die ungehört um ihn verklangen." CS 431, SE 305: "gerade als er ihnen am nächsten war, wußte er nichts mehr von ihnen."

[23] CS 432, SE 305: "Odysseus, sagt man, war so listenreich, war ein solcher Fuchs, daß selbst die Schicksalsgöttin nicht in sein Innerstes dringen konnte. Vielleicht hat er, obwohl das mit Menschenverstand nicht mehr zu begreifen ist, wirklich gemerkt, daß die Sirenen schwiegen, und hat ihnen und den Göttern den obigen Scheinvorgang nur gewissermaßen als Schild entgegengehalten."

above, the Olympian gods. Odysseus is inhuman on the side of the animals or the angels, and maybe it does not matter which. If he has had a genuine experience in his encounter with the Sirens, it would seem to be of a kind and in a form unavailable to us in our daily lives.

And yet this encounter with the Sirens as interpreted by the codicil does look very much like a kind of experience Kafka has discussed before, the experience of a certain kind of reading:

> I was only going to say books are useful in every sense and quite especially in respects in which one would not expect it. For when one is about to embark on some enterprise, it is precisely the books whose contents have nothing at all in common with the enterprise that are the most useful. For the reader who does after all intend to embark on that enterprise (and even if, as it were, the effect of the book can penetrate only as far as that enthusiasm), will be stimulated by the book to all kinds of thoughts concerning his enterprise. Now, however, since the contents of the books are precisely something of utter indifference, the reader is not at all impeded in those thoughts, and he passes through the midst of the book with them, as the Jews passed through the Red Sea, that's how I should like to put it.[24]

This passage from the relatively early fragment "Hochzeitsvorbe-reitungen auf dem Lande" ("Wedding Preparations in the Country") (1907–1908), which I have already cited in part, presents an interesting analogue to the story of Odysseus and the Sirens as presented in the last paragraph of "The Silence of the Sirens." Once we realize that Odysseus has in fact passed untouched through a "text"—since the song/silence of the Sirens is presented as a particularly powerful

---

[24] *CS* 75, *SE* 251: "ich meinte nur, Bücher sind nützlich in jedem Sinn und ganz besonders, wo man es nicht erwarten sollte. Denn wenn man eine Unternehmung vorhat, so sind gerade die Bücher, deren Inhalt mit der Unternehmung gar nichts Gemeinschaftliches hat, die nützlichsten. Denn der Leser, der doch jene Unternehmung beabsichtigt, also irgendwie (und wenn förmlich auch nur die Wirkung des Buches bis zu jener Hitze dringen kann) erhitzt ist, wird durch das Buch zu lauter Gedanken gereizt, die seine Unternehmung betreffen. Da nun aber der Inhalt des Buches ein gerade ganz gleichgültiger ist, wird der Leser in jenen Gedanken gar nicht gehindert und er zieht mit ihnen mitten durch das Buch, wie einmal die Juden durch das Rote Meer, möchte ich sagen."

form of utterance—with the potential to penetrate ("dringen") and to overwhelm him, the analogy becomes clearer. Odysseus is a man embarked on an enterprise with which the Sirens, their island, and their song, have nothing in common. To become involved with their text would be a disaster to his enterprise, and so, either because he does not perceive or, more interestingly, because he ignores that text, he sails through the danger quite obliviously.

This story must inevitably remind us of another, however: the story of Kafka's encounter with the Sirens' text, the old epic tale of the Sirens as found in Homer. Kafka, the writer embarked on an enterprise altogether different from Homer's, has passed through Homer's text just as obliviously as Odysseus through the Sirens' silence or the Jews through the Red Seas. The Homeric tale, like the biblical narrative of the Tower of Babel, penetrated Kafka only as far as his enthusiasm to write; it stimulated him to many thoughts concerning his own project of writing and furnished certain materials he could use in furthering that project. But its point, its meaning, left him quite untouched. Kafka's writing of his story of the Sirens, a story that concludes by proposing Odysseus's oblivious reading of the potentially devastating text of silence, is the result of Kafka's lethetic reading of the *Odyssey*.

It remains only to indicate briefly why Kafka turned to lethetic reading, a mode so contrary to our usual notions of "good" reading that it has existed for the most part only as a minor subversive tendency within the orthodox tradition of alethetic reading. The most satisfactory explanation is to be found in Kafka's extraordinary sensitivity to some of the disquieting implications of that orthodox tradition. When, for example, in a famous letter to his friend Oskar Pollak in 1904, he tries to describe what "good" books and "good" reading are like, he has recourse to image after image of violence. He says that one does not read books in order to be happy but rather in order to be opened up, to be "wounded" and "stabbed" by books whose effect is like a natural catastrophe ("like a disaster," "like . . . death," "like being banished"). He concludes by insisting that a book ought to be an "axe" to break through the "frozen sea" within the reader.[25] This language may sound extreme, but it only carries through the logical implications of a rhetoric of alethetic reading which, since Plato, has insisted that a "good" reader let himself (or actually more frequently, "herself") be opened up by the text so as to

---

[25] *Letters to Friends, Family, and Editors* (New York: Schocken, 1977), 16.

receive its imprint. Although Kafka always maintained a deep respect for this sort of alethic reading, he obviously found it frightening as well.[26]

Kafka developed his own theory and practice of lethetic reading as a less violent alternative to the orthodox tradition. While he continued to practice and value alethic reading, there were evidently times when he wanted to read only in furtherance of his own thoughts and projects, without being torn open and made into a vessel to be filled by the concepts of another. And when it came to reading that was to form the basis for writing, an author as stubbornly original as Kafka could not help but make use of the lethetic mode.

---

[26] I have summarized very briefly in this paragraph a discussion carried out in detail in my "The Margin in the Middle."

Figure 13. Descent of Athena to Ithaca. Flaxman (*Odyssey* series).

# Homer's Sticks and Stones

## Hugh Kenner

### I

We all, although we all know better, say "Homer" as though sure what the word means; worse, as though sure what some dead writer understood by it. Homer? Keats knew at least two, invented one by Chapman, one by Pope, and so different that to hear the first after having read the second was like winning through to an ocean once merely inferred, or like the sumptuousness of a new world moving into view amid the rigid stars.

Yet the example does not admonish; it seems "romantic." Between Pope and Chapman the difference, we feel, is stylistic: adjectival: whereas Homer's poem, present beneath both versions, is substantive. Adjectives change, the noun abides, and we tend to believe in an underlying commonsense Homer, whose name we can utter as we do the word "elephant," obscurely convinced that under challenge we could always have an elephant brought into the room. Surely to settle the meaning of a noun we have only to produce its referent? A Greek book?

But the noun, and *a fortiori* "Homer," does not abide. Even "elephant" mutates as the centuries pass. Thus the Shorter *Oxford English Dictionary* (1933) offers "A huge quadruped of the Pachydermate order, having long curving ivory tusks and a prehensile proboscis." The key word is "Pachydermate"; it tells us that an elephant is something to classify. Samuel Johnson's Dictionary (1755) has a considerably longer treatment which begins, "The largest of all the quadrupeds, of whose sagacity, faithfulness, prudence, and even understanding many surprising relations are given." Here the key words say that an elephant is something to learn virtue from; Johnson also tells us of the elephant's delicacy in mating, when "such is his pudicity, that he never covers the female as long as any one appears in sight." Since the Oxford lexicographers do not mention this, we may say that during 200 years either the elephant's sensibility has grown blunter, or opinion in England has changed concerning which of his attributes are really important. At Oxford they will say that they know more about him than Johnson did: but ability to assign him to the Pachydermate order need not derive from ampler knowledge, especially when the same dictionary tells us on another page that the system of classification underwriting such an order is "now discarded." And the Oxford writer knows so little of elephants that he calls the Indian species, rather than the African, "the largest of all extant land mammals." No, it is not know]edge that has enlarged, but values that have altered. Each age invents the elephant that corresponds to its needs. The need of Johnson's age was to exemplify conduct, the need of ours is to order phenomena: hence their moral elephant, hence our taxonomic elephant.

With the properties of elephants so elastic, those of literary works, even Greek ones, will hardly be stable. T.S. Eliot instructed us fifty years ago that when *we* change our entire literary heritage changes, but what he said, though widely admired for its subtlety, has been dismissed, like the subtleties Einstein was expounding at about the same time, as one of those interesting arguments that make little practical difference. So we talk on about Joyce and his use of Homer without feeling obliged to specify *which* Homer, as though "Homer" were an immutable constant like pi and not a mental possession as subject to redefinition at need as any other mental possession, for instance the elephant.

As a boy Joyce read Charles Lamb's *Adventures of Ulysses.* About 1908 he wanted to write a story set in Dublin and called "Ulysses." Eight years later he was at work on what he had rethought as a huge book, its structural principle a parallel with the *Odyssey*, its hero moving around a single city as Homer's had moved around the Mediterranean.[1] If we are going to extract meaning from this information we should surely ask which Homer he had in mind, which *Odyssey*, which Odysseus. Had he known Greek the answers would be shut away in his unrecorded intercourse with the text; but since his Greek

---

[1] For a convenient summary of the facts see A. Walton Litz, *The Art of James Joyce*, 1961, 1-3.

(like his later Swahili) was a magpie's hoard of details, sufficient to entertain Greek etymologies but not to write out the first line of the *Odyssey* accurately,[2] let alone read with comfort, he was thrown back, luckily for us, on translations and commentaries, each one a delimited Homer, one time's cross-section. For as lexicographers invent their elephants, every commentator, every translator, invents the Homer of a time and place, closed, self-sufficient. It is easy to particularize a few.

Socrates confronted a Homer whose word on all moral questions was virtually final, though vulnerable to sly Socratic dissent. (The Republic will do better without him.) The Stoics made up a Homer of encyclopaedic attainments, who carefully worked into his two poems all that one might need to know about geography, history, medicine, strategy, and other curriculum subjects. Numerous Renaissance minds found him a paradigmatist of glory. For others he was a writing-master. Early in the 18th century the great Richard Bentley invented a less formidable Homer, composer of "a sequel of songs and rhap-sodies, to be sung by himself for small earnings and good cheer"; this description was written within 15 years of *The Beggar's Opera*, a fact which suggests some correlation between the Homer an age invents and its other modes of expression. Thus the next Homer, sponsored by Friedrich Wolf in Germany, was nobody in particular but rather an editorial committee assembling scraps uniform in style but of miscel-laneous authorship, quite as the game of anonymity played by Augustan poets, whose style was so impersonal it could conceal almost anyone's identity, facilitated the expedience, or amusement, of letting readers guess who had written what. Purchasers of Pope's *Odyssey* in fact held in their hands a work of multiple authorship, for though Pope's name was on the titlepage of the English, as Homer's is on the titlepage of the Greek, large portions of the text had been supplied by two subcontractors. Since it predated by 70 years Wolf's suggestion that the Greek had been cobbled together in the same way, we may remark both that Pope was the most prescient of poets, and that German scholarship had not the advantage of a German Augustanism to speed its perceptions.

Each of these Homers was accessible to Joyce, and interesting to him; each is remote enough to be readily characterized, and we shall

---

[2] See the facsimile opposite page 433 of Ellmann's *James Joyce*; Joyce scat-ters accents at random, writes *ennepa* for *ennepe* and *malla* for *mala*, and apparently wrote *hos* with an omega. Not that his Greeklessness needs laboring: he never con-cealed it. For the curious case of the Swahili words see Jack Dalton's article in *A Wake Digest*, Sydney, 1968, 43-47.

find that the imprint of each on the text of *Ulysses* is discernible with corresponding ease. But we should not expect the Homer of Joyce's own time to leave anything as delimitable as an imprint: being in the foreground, he ought to fill the book. And being the epiphenomenon of a time of transition (as all times are, Mr. Eliot once noted) he ought to be in process, unlike the Homers long gone who seem stable. We shall have to look at several decades' transactions with the *Odyssey*.

## II

It is convenient to start with the Homer Joyce's Homer supplanted, the Homer of Butcher and Lang's 1879 translation, who was still in 1930 sufficiently assertive to mislead Stuart Gilbert. When Dr. Gilbert compiled his book-length exposition of Joyce's Homeric parallels he used that translation not because Joyce had necessarily used it but because Mr. Gilbert found it (Lord forgive him) usable: it catches, he said, "the spirit of the original." One can feel sure that Joyce looked at Butcher and Lang, because he wrote into the text of *Ulysses* passages like

> And lo, as they quaffed their cup of joy, a godlike messenger came swiftly in, radiant as the eye of heaven, a comely youth and behind him there passed an elder of noble gait and countenance. . . .[3]

which is a fair approximation to the rhetoric of

> But the daughter of Cadmus marked him, Ino of the fair ankles . . . and sat upon the well-found raft and spake: "Hapless one, wherefore was Poseidon, shaker of the earth, so wondrous wroth with thee?

A Homer capable of asking wherefore the mightiest of the gods was so wondrous wroth seemed to Joyce simply material for parody, and it is not surprising to find that Butcher and Lang's *Odyssey* was already out of date when it was issued: issued with an acknowledgment to the authority of Matthew Arnold.

Arnold in 1860, in his famous three lectures *On Translating Homer*, had thought it urgent that some vernacular cadence be found

---

3 *Ulysses*, 298 (Vintage edition).

which might be adequate to the Homeric moral qualities: Homer, he said, is rapid, Homer is plain-spoken, Homer is plain-thinking, Homer is noble. Arnold had invented the Victorian Homer. Like the Victorian God, he may well not exist, but it does us good to talk as if he did. And like the Victorian God, he does not so much create his universe as invest it with edifying qualities. For the making of the cat and the caterpillar it is very likely not a person we must hold responsible, but an obscurely majestic force called Evolution. In the same way the story of Adam and Eve has much to teach us even if (especially if) we refrain from asking whether they or their garden ever existed; and the story of Hector and Achilles is told in a rapid, noble, plain-speaking, plain-thinking way that does them credit even though they perhaps never existed either, nor Troy, nor its walls, nor the river Scamander; and does the author credit whether the story has an author or not; and does us credit too, since we are sufficiently responsive to the rapid, the noble, and the plain to take an interest. Very likely, if one insisted in going into it (as Arnold did not, the story had crystallized out of a primitive solar myth, some analogy between the defeated but edifying Hector and the obscured but resurgent winter sun. I caricature, but not much; Sir John Myres describes how "Aryan myths took over the minds of Victorian Homerologists, starting with

> the discovery that among Aryan-speaking peoples there was a large common stock of stories, in part explanatory of natural occurrences such as the courses of the heavenly bodies and changes of the seasons and weather, in part, like the tales of early wars in the *Iliad* and the Mahabharata, neither so clearly aetiological nor so closely parallel. Scholars brought up in the contemporary schools of romantic literature found little difficulty in detecting myth and symbolism in such stories and fitting them, as the Romanticists of the Hellenistic Age have done, into cosmologies and theogonies based on the common stock of more obvious nature-myths. Thus Achilles, Jason and Penelope, with Lycurgus and Codrus, on the one hand, and Minos, Cadmus and Helen on the other, passed over from history to philosophy and ceased to need archaeological commentary at all. Old-fashioned amateurs might "believe in the Trojan War," as old-fashioned par-

sons might "believe in the Exodus," but the seats of
the mighty were occupied by critics and sceptics,
masters of the comparative method.[4]

Arnold went into none of this, no more than contemporary clergymen
went into the view that there had been no Adam nor no Eden; his job,
like theirs, was to salvage something of value, mere qualities, of plain-
ness, and rapidity, and nobility. Accordingly, the Butcher-Lang translation, with one eye on the book of the clergy and the other on the
book called the *Odyssey*, addressed itself to the plight of both these
books by attempting so evident a nobility (though the plain and the
rapid were intractable) as to keep anyone from asking whether all
those verbs had ever had real breathing subjects, or all those adjectives real sticks and stones to substantiate them. And it was lost labor;
because in 1870 one of those "old-fashioned amateurs" Sir John
Myres spoke of had struck a spade against the very walls of Troy.
Heinrich Schliemann, of course; and the scholars' cosmos altered.

A century later one need not retell his story: he had heard Homer
read as a boy and believed what he heard, and amassed a fortune on
which to go and verify his fundamentalist belief. Yet he was justified.
There had been such a city. It had been destroyed, and by fire. Stones,
as well as fables, persisted. And "golden Mycenae": it had indeed
worked gold, and its tombs (bee-haunted; ringed with huge red pop-
pies) yielded golden cups and a mask of gold which Schliemann
thought Agamemnon's, as Troy yielded jewelry he called Helen's
when he hung it on his wife Sophie for a photograph. (A photograph!
It is like a photograph of the True Cross.) So Marion Tweedy Bloom
in 1904 (the phrases set down about 1921) was to don and doff garments we are to think of as Penelope's: ". . . a pair of outsize ladies'
drawers of India mull, cut on generous lines, redolent of opopomax,
jessamine and Muratti's Turkish cigarettes and containing a long
bright steel safety pin":[5] with no less of a cataloguer's exactness, now,
could Achaean splendors be plotted.

After Schliemann, the word "Troy" meant some place in particular. As his discoveries persisted, more and more Homeric words
came to mean something producible, something belonging to the
universe of the naturalistic novelist. Each such word is salvage from
the vortex of mere lexicography, where we learn little more of words

---

4 Sir John L. Myres, *Homer and His Critics*, 1958, 95-6.
5 *Ulysses*, 730.

than what company they keep. When Alice in Wonderland's father Henry George Liddell D.D. collaborated on the Greek Lexicon in the reign of Victoria, the word *euknemides* meant only "well-greaved," which is not really English, and nothing more could be said about it except that another word *Achaoi* (of comparably uncertain scope) tends to draw it into the text, as "sea" draws the word they render "wine-dark," and "Hera" draws "oxeyed." "Oxeyed Hera," we read in Butcher and Lang, and "wine-dark sea," and "well-greaved Achaeans." But by the reign of the second Elizabeth *euknemides* has acquired particularization from a painted vase, a stele, two sherds of pottery, a frieze from the megaron of Mycenae, a fresco at Pylos and an ivory relief from Delos, "all of the third late Helladic era":[6] whoever encounters the word in Homer today has reason to know that it designates something in particular, shinguards, of unspectacular appearance, leather perhaps, and distinctively Achaean, never Trojan. Homer says *euknemides Achaoi* as we might say "sandalled Peace-niks," to certify the designation's authenticity.

Schliemann had dug through Troy and moved on to Mycenae by the time Butcher and Lang were at work, and when their *Odyssey* appeared in 1879, with its bow to Arnold's authority, their Homer and Arnold's was already a ghost. By 1900 Schliemann's successor Dörpfeld was rapping his staff on the soil, he affirmed, of Ithaca, with a persuasiveness pilgrims (German professors and schoolmasters) tended to remember. "Few things were as convincing as a piece of Greek landscape . . . when Dörpfeld explained it to you," recalled Sir John Myres, and "It was probably . . . to Dörpfeld's 'troubling of the waters' that we owe the very copious output of literary criticism of the *Odyssey* in the years from 1903 to 1910."[7] In those years Victor Bérard's readers were being convinced that Odysseus' whole voyage had been at last mapped out, among real rocks, real shores. His *Les Phéniciens et l'Odyssée* (1903) was a book James Joyce found useful.[8]

For the Homer of Joyce's time was the archaeologist's, turning gradually during Joyce's young manhood into a namer of things, no longer a mere arranger of words nor a manifestor of salutary qualities. The things he named, moreover, were producible. Not only was it

---

[6] Denys L. Page, *History and the Homeric Iliad*, 1959, 245.

[7] Myres, 191-2.

[8] Gilbert's ample data on Joyce's use of Bérard is well indexed and need not be summarized. Myres (p. 192) dismisses Berard very quickly. Of course the rightness or wrongness of anyone's detail is irrelevant to our argument: Schliemann's most spectacular conclusions tended to be wrong. What is important is the kind of attention Homer's text was receiving in Joyce's lifetime.

growing clear that if you dug at the sites he designated you found things, it was also clear that reference to his text helped you understand the things you found. His world, when Joyce came to think about it seriously about a decade into the twentieth century, was as real as the bricks brought in to Dublin by the three-master *Rosevean*, and when Joyce eventually told Frank Budgen that he wanted his presentation of Dublin to be complete enough to document a reconstruction of the city,[9] it seems clear that he was thinking of a Dublin one day gone the way of Troy, to be visited by some long future Schliemann, *Ulysses* in hand.

### III

Much of the detail with which he filled the text is either topographical, so that a careful future reader might tell which street intersects with which, and some day be able to put names to the bridges and quays and traces of paving in a ruined townsite, or else minutely domestic, as if to help with the identification of fragments in a kitchen midden. We may notice for instance how carefully he itemizes Bloom's dishes, including the moustache cup.[10] Elsewhere he goes so far as to specify a particular two-shilling piece with three notches in the milled edge, which someone, finding it perhaps between two paving-stones amid the rubble of O'Connell Bridge, may one day know was notched and returned to circulation by Mr. Leopold Bloom in the summer of 1898.[11] By their lost coins, their broken dishes, their eating implements, we deduce much of what we know about the lives of such people as Homer's: they were turning very domestic in men's imaginations during the era of archaeology. It is not surprising that domesticity is the note of Joyce's equivalents.

He was especially careful with the interior of Bloom's house: the arrangement of the rooms and their use, the placing of the furniture and the water supply and the cooking facilities, the location of the area railing outside the measurement of the drop from its crosspiece to the area paving below. Here again he was on up-to-date ground: the layout of the house of Odysseus had been a focus of scholarly contention since 1886, when Schliemann published his account of the

---

[9] Frank Budgen, *James Joyce and the Making of 'Ulysses,'* Midland edition, 67-68.

[10] *Ulysses*, 675.

[11] *Ulysses*, 696.

palace he excavated the previous year at Tiryns. Literature in the sub-sequent decades was filled with floorplans, as proponents of the old "Hellenic" and the new "Mycenaean" archetypes arranged and rear-ranged doors, hearth, courtyard, women's quarters.[12] One such floor plan in particular there is reason to believe Joyce studied carefully. It is on page 16 of the book with which Samuel Butler accosted classical scholarship in 1897: *The Authoress of the Odyssey.*

Butler derived it not from a Hellenic or a Mycenaean house (though his notes indicate that he was aware of that controversy) but simply, he said, from the poem, to each word of which he insisted on assigning a definite meaning, thought out in the process of making a new kind of translation which appears abridged in the *Authoress* and was published intact in 1900. Pondering one adjective (*hypselos*, lofty) near the end of the first book (I.426) when Telemachus goes to his bedchamber, Butler perceived a difficulty which had eluded everyone, not least Butcher and Lang.

Butcher and Lang replace Greek words with English ones from the lexicon, and tell us that the chamber was "builded high up in the fair court, in a place with wide prospect." But Butler insisted on imagining such things clearly, and having reconstructed the "court" as no more than an open space surrounded by a cloister, he saw the need to specify a structure for Telemachus' room to be at the top of. He places it, therefore, "in a lofty tower," and marks "the tower in which Telemachus used to sleep" on his plan. Butler has more to say about this tower: it has, for instance, a trap-door through which one could get out onto the roof. We may be in the presence of the very phrases which suggested to Joyce the placing of his Telemachus in the tower onto the top of which he and his associate mount on the very first page of the book.

It is true that Joyce built experiences of Stephen's on his own, and that he had himself lived for a while in the Martello Tower. It is also true that he had in mind as well the opening of *Hamlet*, high on the battlements of Elsinore. But only with Butler's help can we discover a clear Homeric correspondence at the very beginning of *Ulysses* where the correspondences ought to be plain if they are going to work. And Butler has more for us than this one interesting detail. If we investi-gate his book further we may wonder how far it may have helped sug-gest Joyce's whole enterprise.

Butler's was simply the first creative mind—Joyce's was the second—to take the archaeologist's Homer seriously: to consider what

---

[12] For a convenient summary see Myres, 163 ff.

it might mean to believe that the *Odyssey* was composed by a real person in touch with the living details of real cities, real harbors, real bowls and cups and pins and spoons, real kings, real warriors, real houses. His book is the first about the *Odyssey* to be illustrated with photographs: of the actual Trojan walls, or of an actual cave that might have been the Cyclops'. Such grounding in the actual brought new criteria to the ancient problem of details that don't fit. Horace had believed in a real Homer, making things up; there were slips because he sometimes nodded. Wolf had believed in a number of bards, making things up; there were inconsistencies because they didn't check one another's work. Butler, in the age of the novel, worked from a different psychology of creation: the poet using knowledge of an immediate and experienced world, and making errors when he got beyond his knowledge and had to guess. He noticed for instance an Odyssean ship with the rudder at the front, and concluded that the writer was guessing about the sea.[13] About other details the writer was not guessing at all, and Butler concluded that the poem had been composed by a Sicilian city-dweller familiar with courts and noble houses. The author was, he went on to argue, a woman, and herself the model for the Princess Nausicaa, a hypothesis Joyce seems to have been acknowledging when he put his Nausicaa episode into the idiom of a lady novelist, and tying knots in when he made it easy for readers of *Ulysses* to conclude that its author in turn had modelled on himself a different secondary character, Telemachus.

Had it not obtruded that unacceptable female Homer, Butler's book might have been taken rather seriously. He knew the Homeric text as only a man can know it who has worked over its meaning word by word. He knew the archaeological literature, and took pains to inspect the relevant sites at first hand; he even visited Hissarlik to photograph the Trojan walls uncovered by Schliemann. In quest of likely sites for Odysseus' voyagings he pored over Admiralty charts ("things of recent date," he remarked, in generous extenuation of his predecessors' blindness, "and I do not think anyone would have been likely to have run the 'Odyssey' to ground without their help"),[14] and having fixed on Sicily he went twice to the island for extensive inspection of likely details. With the information available at the turn of the century scholars would have been hard put indeed to refute him; indeed he undercuts so many difficulties that the will to refute might

---

[13] Samuel Butler, *The Authoress of the Odyssey*, 1922 reprint, 9-10.
[14] Butler, 263.

have dwindled, and left him in a position like Bentley's or Wolf's, inventor of the Homer of his age. Instead he chose to be the man with the silly bee in his bonnet about a poetess, and his most serious reader, it may be, was James Joyce.

For anyone who will look at Butler's eighth chapter can imagine its effect on a man perhaps already thinking, or perhaps about to think, about Ulysses in Dublin. In that chapter he described what he found out once he had fixed his attention on Sicily, and identified the Scherian harbor with that of Trapani on the west coast of the island. Not only is Scheria, where Nausicaa lives, drawn from Trapani, Ithaca as well, where Penelope waits, is drawn from Trapani; and the Ionian islands of the *Odyssey* are simply islands off Trapani. The very Cyclops' cave can be found near Trapani. All the poem's urban topography, in short, has been elaborated from familiarity with a single city, and all the rural topography, and all the nautical, from the country and the waters around that one city. There is one remote place, Pylos, in Homer's book, and one remote place, Gibraltar, in Joyce's. Otherwise, both books (if we follow Butler's account) create an illusion of epic sweep and scope while contriving to stay closely in touch with the author's home. Trapani and its harbor and environs; Dublin's streets, Dublin strand, Dublin bay. It is impossible to prove, but attractive to guess, that Joyce related the Homeric world to one city as a consequence of the fact that Butler had. If on Butler's showing the vast sweep of Odysseus' travels had been built out of familiarity with the town of Trapani surely those travels could be concentrated once more into the town of Dublin: like Trapani, a seaport on an island.

More: Butler was moved to make a plain prose version of the *Odyssey*, the first such version in history. There had been cribs, of course, but a crib is not English prose: it is a map of the Greek words. Butler's purpose was to make his reader understand how the poet's mind had grounded itself on actualities: Telemachus' shirt hung on a peg by his bedside, pieces of sucking pig roasted on skewers in the embers. Plain prose requires that its writer imagine clearly what he is writing about: we have seen how Butler's acceptance of this discipline produced Telemachus' tower. It gives the texture of a naturalistic novel, the same texture a reader of Joyce encounters.

Butler, in short, brings the archaeologist's Homer to a focus, and a very Joycean Homer this proves to be: an observer and ingenious transposer of actualities, and a writer whose useful experience was that of a single city. The characters, Butler thought, had been drawn from known people[15] (as were Joyce's), and though he detects evidence of the poet's inexperience, Butler in the age of the novel finds it natural that a masterpiece should have been produced by someone who (like Joyce) "did not like inventing," but was "richly endowed with that highest kind of imagination which consists in wise selection and judicious application of materials derived from life."[16] For "no artist"—here Joyce would have explicitly concurred—"can reach an ideal higher than his own best actual environment. Trying to materially improve upon that with which he or she is fairly familiar invariably ends in failure. It is only adjuncts that may be arranged and varied—the essence may be taken or left, but it must not be bettered."[17] That was written not when Joyce was 45, by a commentator on *Ulysses*, but when Joyce was 15, by a commentator on Homer. The effect of Schliemann's discoveries on a creative mind which knew at first hand about novel-writing was to compel such a characterization of the mind from which the *Odyssey* proceeded: a mind like the one that drafted the letter of 5 May 1906 to Grant Richards about *Dubliners*, remarking that "he is a very bold man who dares to alter in the presentment, still more to deform, whatever he has been and heard."[18]

Despite the suggestive detail of the tower, and the correspondence between Trapani and Dublin, the question of Joyce's direct use of Butler would remain sheer speculation had not another Dubliner, W.B. Stanford, wondered in the 1950's what nobody had thought to wonder previously: on which books about Homer did James Joyce depend? And happily Stanislaus Joyce was ready with a list: "Virgil, Ovid, Dante, Racine, Fénelon, Tennyson, Phillips, d'Annunzio, and Hauptmann, as well as"—voilà!—"Samuel Butler's *The Authoress of the Odyssey* and Bérard's *Les Phéniciens et l'Odyssée*, and the translations by Butler and Cowper."[19]  Butler's book, Butler's translation (and no mention of Butcher and Lang): the translation and the eccentric book which between them characterize the Homer of Joyce's time, a Homer legitimately derived from the archaelogical discoveries that had rendered the Victorian Homer obsolete, a Homer with an almost naive sense of fact. Parallels between *Ulysses* and such

---

[15] Butler, 200-201, 205.

[16] Butler, 202.

[17] Butler, 208.

[18] *Letters*, II-134.

[19] W.B. Stanford, *The Ulysses Theme*, second edition, 1964, 276, note 6.

a Homer's *Odyssey* give rise to none of the strain we intuit if we approach Joyce's text with some less relevant Homer in our minds than Schliemann's and Butler's. It is when we attempt to hold in one mental act Mr. Bloom's plain prose Dublin and Butcher and Lang's high-falutin' Mediterranean that we find ourselves trying to explain the parallels away: Joyce put them in to amuse himself, they were more useful to him than they can be to the reader, he needed an intricate structure for his chaos. But the schemata which writers draw up for their own convenience they commonly try to hide, and Joyce on the contrary drew from this one the very title of his book. He found it, evidently, easy and natural and helpful to the reader, and if we concentrate on the right Homer we may be on the way of finding it easy and natural too.

## IV

But the right Homer, Joyce well knew, is not the only one, and he took his usual pains to incorporate the others as well. As one chapter of *Ulysses*, The Oxen of the Sun, is a museum of styles, so is the whole of *Ulysses* a museum of Homers. The Homer of Joyce's own time, the Homer of molecular actualities, is as pervasive as the air, or as Dublin. That is why he is the hardest to recognize until he is pointed out; Homers, like styles, are the more recognizable the more remote they are from us in time. The next most recent Homer, the one of comparative mythology, is more plainly discernible, though not being very distant he presents very large outlines, as throughout Joyce's book the *Odyssey* and two later works, *Hamlet* and *Don Giovanni*, turn out to be all of them versions of the same story. (The text has even one reference to solar myths, in the inventory of the World's Twelve Worst Books.) Behind him we find the Homer of multiple authorship, who corresponds to the fact that *Ulysses* would seem on stylistic grounds to have a number of different authors, one of them a woman. The Homer of Stoic exegesis moreover has obviously been at work, strewing the pages with systematized lore, not only the treatise on how the water reaches Bloom's tap or the mnemonic for the colors of the spectrum, but also appropriate Arts, appropriate Symbols, appropriate Bodily Organs. Perhaps the intricate scaffolding that has occupied and irritated readers since Mr. Gilbert first disclosed it in 1930 is best realized as a way of furthering the Homeric motif: a compendious ordering of the various sorts of things the Educator of Greece was supposed to have known. The way they are worked into Joyce's text has been called arbitrary, but it corresponds to the way exegetes once got them out of Homer's.

In the details and infrastructures of *Ulysses* we can find whatever Homers we like. They are visible, all of them, through the Homer that had been invented in Joyce's early lifetime by men who read kitchen-middens as Sherlock Holmes or Flaubert could read a room and as Joyce's readers are expected to read his book: a book, and a Homer, made not of mere sonorous words which neither hurt nor nourish, but of cups and saucers, chairs and tables, sticks and stones.

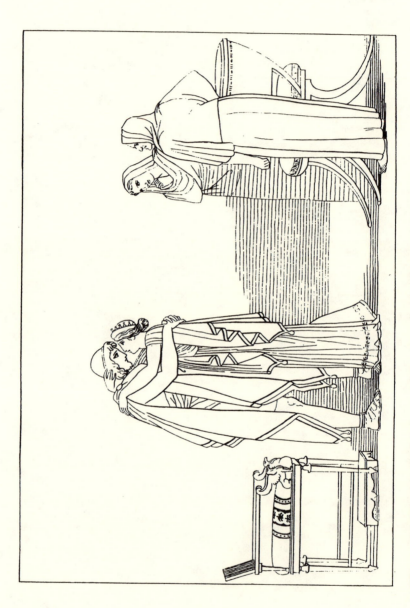

Figure 14. Reunion of Odysseus and Penelope. Flaxman (*Odyssey* series).

# An Approach To The Homeric Content Of Joyce's "Ulysses"

*Vivienne Koch*

If the general analogy about the *Odyssey* and *Ulysses* is to mean anything at all, it must mean more than the set of correspondences in characters and story which has been exhaustively explored and annotated up to this point. It must mean more, even, than the painfully recondite tracking down of allusions, of place names—in short, the etymological study to which much of the scholarship surrounding Joyce's *Ulysses* reduces itself. Investigations on these levels are far from fruitless as the erudite, suggestive exegesis compiled by the pioneering Stuart Gilbert proved. It is precisely, however, the fact that Gilbert had aesthetic insight as well which made his James Joyce's *Ulysses* stand head and shoulders above comparable commentaries.

It seems that the qualitative aspects of *Ulysses* in relation to its three thousand year old model can best be suggested in terms of their *differences*. By *differences* I mean not merely the obvious facts of language and content (the world-wandering, for example, as opposed to the Dublin-trotting) although these, too, have their indubitable significances, but rather those *shifts* in value which occur because of consciously planned or unconsciously executed divergences from the prototype. For example, it is not the *order* of events as it bears on the *Odyssey* which is important in *Ulysses,* but rather the *kind* of relationship suggested either through likeness or difference.

On the conscious level, we have a rich store of material in Frank Budgen's *James Joyce and The Making of Ulysses* regarding Joyce's own intentions as narrated to Budgen. Of the structure Joyce said "The *Odyssey* serves me as a ground plan." And, from the sophisti-

cated and self-conscious viewpoint of the modern scholar, he wished
to give a picture of Dublin so complete that "if the city one day disappeared from the earth it could be reconstructed out of my book."
Joyce's ambitious goal is obviously tied in with his awareness of the
role of the Homeric poems in the reconstruction of the Aegean civilization. For the Homeric poems are acknowledged as the major
source of historic considerations of early Greek culture by most students of that epoch. With an artistic arrogance that is at once amusing
and admirable, Joyce hoped to do in *Ulysses* what five hundred years
of story-telling had crystallized into the Homeric epics!

But there are differences in value between the Greek epic and
Joyce's 20th century novel which are implicit in the very simple fact
that they are separated by centuries in time and by at least three civilizations in texture. Let us examine some of the distinctions which flow
from these factors: Take, for example the elementary facts that Odysseus traveled about for ten years after the Fall of Troy before returning to Ithaca, whereas our modern Ulysses, Leopold Bloom, confines
his crucial explorations to a single day (approximately 20 hours on
June 16, 1904) in Dublin. That there has been an enormous shift in
philosophical and physical concepts of the meaning of time from the
Greek world to the modern scientific world is something immediately
apparent in *Ulysses* even were this knowledge not public. As a matter
of fact, Joyce took a particular delight in the "definitions" of time and
space which he permitted Stephen to expound: Time is the
"ineluctable modality of the audible." And Space "the ineluctable
modality of the visible."[1] Joyce's peculiarly twentieth century,
relativistic approach was further indicated by the differentiated perceptions of time assigned to Bloom and to Stephen. Of Bloom, Joyce
said: "Time is the time the movement takes." And of Stephen: ". . .
hates past time because it would bind him with present duties." And
to this, Budgen adds his own acute comment that Bloom and Stephen
are opposites in the sense that Bloom is while Stephen is becoming.
This characterization of Stephen rings with greater authority, when
viewed in the light of Joyce's own sardonic remark that "Some people
who read my book 'A Portrait of the Artist as a Young Man' forget
that it is called 'A Portrait of the Artist as a *Young Man*'." The
Stephen of *Ulysses* is the Stephen who was *becoming* that one in the
earlier novel. But he is becoming still another Stephen.[2]

---

[1] Joyce said to Budgen, "My definitions of space and time are good. What?"

[2] This view of Stephen is not held by all students of Joyce. J.W. Beach in his
*The Twentieth Century Novel* charges both Stephen and Bloom with "a paralysis of the
will to action" and implies that both characters are in a state of stasis. Harry Levin in

It is clear, then, that Joyce does not worship his source blindly, although accusations of grecophilism have been heaped fiercely upon him. His point of departure, analogically, is that Dublin, a small city of 150,000 people in 1904, is a cosmos in itself comparable in variety, occurrences and people to the whole world of the wandering Greek. The compression of modern life, its enormous range within an urban, microcosmic structure like Dublin, say, permits for Joyce a scope as wide as was the whole Greek cosmogony for Homer. From these enormous differences in modern experience as opposed to what the ancient world knew, as well as from our own relativistic time concepts, derive the totally different narrative methods of the Greek and the Irishman.

Recognizing this *a priori* opposition between the *Odyssey* and *Ulysses*, the opposition between two worlds, it is curious that so little comment has been made on the artistic and technical disparateness flowing from it. Homer's narrative method leans heavily on a third person outer shell with occasional first person interpolations as that of Odysseus's stories at Alcinous' court or Telemachus' plea at the court of Nestor. Joyce's interlacing use of every traditional type of written discourse (rhetoric, narrative, drama, catechism, etc.) plus his own development of the subjective soliloquy or "monologue intérieur" makes the method of *Ulysses* lean heavily in the direction of a first person subjectivity. What this ultimately results in is a density of psychological pressures on the characters in *Ulysses*, which (whether they were present or not in the "real" Greek originals is not relevant) has very little connection with the liberated, objectively-rarefied atmosphere created by the motivation-structure of the *Odyssey*. To point the case: When, in the *Odyssey*, Telemachus expresses a doubt as to his paternity, saying that our fathers are the ones our mothers say they are, we are somewhat startled at this more oblique, subjective intrusion which clouds the essentially direct Telemachus-Odysseus relationship: the son in search of the (not *a*) father.

Stuart Gilbert skirts the whole problem of aesthetic weight of the interior monologue or "silent monologue" as he prefers to call it. From one point of view he is within his rights to do so. For he takes the purely operational and entirely sound view that "it hardly matters whether the technique ('silent monologue') is veracious or not; it has

---

*James Joyce* seems to subscribe to Mr. Beach's view when he says: ". . . his characterization is static because his characters are paralyzed." One might legitimately question–were one to grant Mr. Levin's assumption–whether the *dynamic* characterization of "paralyzed" characters is not, at least, a possibility.

served him as a bridge over which to march his eighteen episodes, and, once he has got his troops across, the opposing forces can, for all he cares, blow the bridge sky-high." Although it is important to recognize that the basic validity of the stream of consciousness technique lies in the pragmatic fact that *it works,* it distorts the total emotional impact of *Ulysses* to conceive of this method as a mere *device* separate from the "episodes" for which it acts as a skeletal bridging. For it seems to imply, first, a separation between content and method; and, second, to adduce a primary significance to the "episodes" as opposed to *what they mean* to the characters. I would be inclined, rather, (if such a dichotomy does not, in itself, constitute a wrenching of the organism) to see the "episodes" as the bridge and the "interior monologues" as the chain of islands it connects.

In reality, of course, even this rearrangement is not wholly satisfactory. For, in *Ulysses,* the episodic movement is so tied up with the psychological progression that a separation is not only difficult but also undesirable. For example in the "Gertie McDowell" episode (which corresponds, but very roughly, to Odysseus' encounter with Nausicaa on the shores of Phaeacia) all that "happens" overtly is that Leopold Bloom gazes upon and is moved by the charms of the modern seaside cuddle-bunny, Gertie McDowell, who, in turn, desires the "dark foreigner" sitting on a near-by rock-ledge. Actually, however, there is tremendous subjective activity, both mental and physical, in Leopold Bloom and Gertie too. An activity which on Gertie's part, at least, ranges over the most salient facts of her literal and emotional biography. Thus, the net weight of the so-called Nausicaa episode is that of a self-contained novelette.

Joyce's handling is so different from Homer's treatment of Nausicaa that it hardly seems to need comment. All we know about Nausicaa in the *Odyssey* are the immediate facts pertinent to her encounter with Odysseus. We know she is the King's daughter, prudent and orderly; prompted by a dream, she secures permission from her father to do the family washing on the pretext that one of her bachelor brothers may marry. We see her washing the white garments, playing ball with her maidens, and then, still poised but moved, somehow, assisting the stormtossed hero back to her father's palace. The very real sexual encounter which takes place in the Gertie McDowell episode is quite different both in intensity and meaning from Nausicaa's vague admiration for the handsome stranger whom her father vainly wishes he could marry her to, or her worshipful absorption in the stranger's tales. For Gertie and Leopold Bloom never exchange a single overt word or touch and yet Bloom, at least, actually consummates the equivalent of a physical encounter, while Gertie visualizes herself in all the minutest details as the "wifey" of the "dark foreigner." The very language of this *third person* interior monologue is Gertie's; that is, the terms of the True-confession magazines from which she seems to have sprung full-grown but, unlike the denizens of its pages, *alive.* Joyce wrote of it "Nausicaa is written in a namby-pamby jammy marmalady drawersy (alto la!) style . . ."

As a matter of fact, in Homer, too, the Nausicaa episode is curiously namby-pamby. A beautiful young maiden and the naked protagonist meet on a white beach; their association continues at her father's house; there is some interest indicated on the young woman's part, at least. Yet, nothing happens. From Odysseus's first response on viewing Nausicaa—he coyly drapes himself with reeds and rushes—a complete decorum is maintained. Joyce employs his source by abstracting the quality of namby-pambyness from the *events* and applying it to the *style* of his own Nausicaa episode. Thus, a strangely fresh effect is secured by a likeness in difference.

At any rate, the thing to bear in mind is that the "Hellas ridden" Joyce, as represented by Stephen Dedalus, is aiming at Ireland through Greece and not at Greece through Ireland. Gertie McDowell, the amateur flapper of the Dublin of 1904, is sister-under-the-skin in only the most superficial characteristics to the Princess Nausicaa Apart from Gertie's youth in relation to Leopold's middle age, her actual inexperience in relation to his "world-weariness" (both factors resembling Nausicaa's situation in relation to Odysseus), the deepest connection between the girls three thousand years apart is Gertie's, like Nausicaa's, intuitive acceptance of Leopold-Ulysses as "different," a "foreigner" but nevertheless with some indefinable, romantic superiority accruing to him just because of this very "foreigness."

It is equally misleading and far-fetched to talk about the "unity of time and place" in *Ulysses* as if there were any unity of time or place in the *Odyssey.* If *Ulysses* has unity of time and place it is a *principia* derived from the Greek theatre and Aristotle's summary of it in his *Poetics.* Pragmatically, it is far more meaningful to see the cyclical movement of the twenty hours described in *Ulysses,* just as it is useful to recognize the cyclical movement of the *Odyssey* which covers six weeks of Ulysses' actual experience but ten years of his adventuring.

But these cycles are far from identical. It is true that the first section of *Ulysses,* devoted to Stephen Dedalus, corresponds roughly to the *Telemachia* of the *Odyssey.* In the *Telemachia,* Athena conceives of sending off Telemachus on a search for Odysseus, "to ask those he meets for news of his dear father's return: not that he will hear any-thing, but his zeal will earn him repute among men." Thus, Tele-machus' fruitless journey is conceived by Athene as a kind of educa-tional apprenticeship, a means of preparing him (in reputation) for his eventual kingship. That Telemachus "finds" his father is an illusory factor; for in reality, he never does. Odysseus merely returns. But Stephen's search is clearly of another order: it is a search for a father *in principle*; the Father-Principle, in short, denied to him (whom Pater-Bloom intuitively identifies with the changeling, fairy boy) by nature, and by his own nature.

Thus, Stephen's search, unlike that of Telemachus, is not merely a discipline, *for-the-sake-of*; it is rather a self-generated and self-con-suming drive for self-discovery or selfhood. For it is only through the father that the son can know himself. In a certain sense, of course, the Greek notion of kingliness is self-knowledge so that Telemachus and Stephen Dedalus are not entirely separate in their goals.

The clue to Joyce's conception of the father-son relationship is to be found in the brilliant Scylla and Charybdis chapter which deals largely (on its literal level) with Shakespearian criticism and the character of Hamlet. It is generally felt that Stephen's views here are satirical, gymnastic, and intended as ironic tongue-in-cheek-comment on "scholarship" for the benefit of his high-minded (always excepting Buck Mulligan!) audience at the Dublin Public Library. But it is more than that. It contains, first of all, that essential anchorage to reality (here, a set of values) which gives the bite to all irony; and it provides, like all play-acting (*vide* the play within the play in *Hamlet*) the thing with which to prick the conscience of the king: here, the king, by his own analogy of the father-son principle as "apostolic succession," is Stephen himself.

Gilbert recognizes that there is more to Stephen's discourse on fatherhood than an ingenious and witty tour de force at Shake-speare's, or history's, expense. He says: "The mystery of paternity, in its application to the First and Second Persons of the Trinity, to King Hamlet and the Prince, and by implication, to the curious symbiosis of Stephen and Mr. Bloom is ever in the background of Stephen's Shake-spearian exegesis. All through this chapter he is capturing in a net of analogies, is *symbolizing* (in the exact meaning of this word: *throwing together*), the protean manifestations of the creative force (one of whose dynamics in the animate world is the rite of procreation, pater-nity). God (Father and Son)—Shakespeare—Stephen Dedalus: all are vehicles of a like energy."

"Fatherhood," says Stephen in the now famous passage, "in the sense of conscious begetting, is unknown to man. It is a mystical estate, an apostolic succession, from only begetter to only begotten. On that mystery and not on the madonna . . . the church is founded and founded irremovably because, founded like the world, macro- and microcosm upon the void. Upon incertitude, upon unlikelihood . . . Paternity may be a legal fiction." It is this passage so central to an understanding of Stephen's personality, to the very structure of *Ulysses* itself, which has served as the focus for attacks on Joyce's *Weltanschauung,* as a "metaphysical nihilism." We can entertain such a charge only if we evaluate Stephen Dedalus as the significant figure in *Ulysses;* only if we naively identify the point of view of the creator with his own creation.[3] And to do that we must ignore Molly Bloom's positive and passionately affirmative impact, as well as the sceptical but understanding acceptance of Leopold Bloom. That seems to be too large a price to pay.

Indeed, the very nature of the father-hunt in which Telemachus and Stephen engage themselves provides for different conclusions. In spite of what T.E. Shaw would undoubtedly call Telemachus' "priggish" doubts about his paternity (that is to say, his mother's honor), the Greek son sought for, did not discover, but eventually regained his own father or, if we are to be "priggish" too, the only father his mother would credit. For Stephen, the conclusion was not so happy. There is a bare touch and go in his spiritual union with Bloom. Yet the *paternity* is strongly felt by the Dublin Ulysses. Stephen can feel his sonship only on a considerably more remote plane. For two reasons: Bloom, unlike Stephen, has been haunted during his Dublin Odyssey by fragmentary memories of little Rudy, the son who died in infancy. Rudy has been a part of his conscious thought processes, and the incidents in the brothel, where he has followed Stephen to protect him, merely serve to crystallize for him the analogical base in his protective feelings toward the strange, but familiar, young man. But the realization takes place, as it must, metaphorically. After they leave the

---

[3] It is true that there is a heavy autobiographical weighting to Stephen. Joyce himself has gone on record for that: "I haven't let that young man off lightly have I? Many writers have written about themselves. I wonder if any one of them has been as candid as I have?" Yet the transmutation of the artistic process clearly affects the nature of the Stephen-Joyce relationship. It is revealing that when *Ulysses* was appearing serially in *The Little Review* Joyce received letters from readers (much as the Victorian novelists did) urging more of Stephen and less of Bloom; His reaction was: "Stephen no longer interests me to the same extent. He has a shape that can't be changed." Despite Joyce's intention, it might well be worth considering who actually establishes himself as hero in *Ulysses,* Leopold Bloom or Stephen.

brothel Stephen is struck down by the pugnacious Private Carr and as Bloom leans over him holding his hat and ashplant and thinking " . . . Well educated. Pity . . . Not hurt anyhow."

> *"Silent, thoughtful, alert, he stands on guard, his fingers at his lips in the attitude of a secret master. Against the dark wall a figure appears slowly, a fairy boy of eleven, a changeling, kidnapped, dressed in an Eton suit with glass shoes and a little bronze helmet, holding a book in his hand. He reads from right to left inaudibly, smiling, kissing the page.*
>
> Bloom
>
> (*Wonderstruck, calls inaudibly.*) Rudy!
>
> Rudy
>
> (*Gazes unseeing into Bloom's eyes and goes on reading, kissing, smiling. He has a delicate mauve face. On his suit he has diamond and ruby buttons. In his free left hand he holds a slim ivory cane with a violet bowknot. A white lambkin peeks out of his waistcoat pocket.*"

Thus the union of the Stephen image with the Rudy image is accomplished most delicately and with a tender magic.

But Stephen, unlike Telemachus, and like Rudy, never acknowledges on any conscious level his sonship; rather, like Rudy "he gazes unseeing into Bloom's eyes." For Stephen had earlier in "the feast of pure reason" at the public library humorously stated his own unconscious dilemma: " . . . if the father who has not a son be not a father can the the son who has not a father be a son?" The answer is clear in Episode 17 which is equated with Ithaca. For it is here that Bloom makes his "proposal of asylum" for the night to Stephen which "Promptly, inexplicably, with amicability, gratefully . . . was declined." There is, in Stephen, an ambivalence toward the idea of sonship which expresses itself touchingly but "inexplicably" (to himself, too, no doubt) in his refusal of the fatherly offer. For in spite of his human needs for sonship there is in Stephen, the exile in his own land, as Bloom is the exile in a strange one, a hard core of *use* for his own estrangement from such love. It is Stephen the artificer-heir of the Artificer-Dedalus who clings to this emotional dispossession, or unpossession, if you will, for what, he recognizes intuitively, he can later, as artist, do with it. This, then, is Stephen's real difference from Telemachus whose needs were simple, direct, and once met easily satisfied: Essentially, Stephen cannot be a son. And, seen in his role as artist, maker, the reason for this becomes apparent. For if the Father principle is the procreative principle, it is the principle Stephen seeks only to *use*. That is Stephen's tragic situation: He wants a father and almost finding one, he cannot be a son.

There are two basic and somewhat humorous antagonisms between the ancient and the modern Ulysses: the former is uniformly and consistently successful in love; the latter is successful only partially:–by remote control (*vide* the ocular rape of Gertie-Nausicaa, and the transports, via postal service, of Miss Martha Clifford) and, ultimately, with Penelope-Molly for the first time in ten years and then only after her voluptuous afternoon with her current lover, Blazes Boylan. In another matter, there exists a satiric breach (as wide as the gap between the two cultures themselves) between the Greek "adventure-suffering and adventure-seeking man" and the Dublin canvasser–his spiritual descendant: Ulysses is tested, "tried" by the gods; Ulysses-Bloom is tried and tested mostly by his wife. It is true the objectionable "Citizen" taunts him for his race; it is true the medical students try to pull his leg; but we never feel that Bloom has been singled out for persecution, for *trial*, as was *Odysseus*; that is, by anyone except Molly herself. The change in our deities has indeed been considerable!

As a matter of fact, apart from Molly Bloom there is a huge imbalance between the men and women in Joyce. How different from Homer where, if Palmer's evaluation is correct, the women are the dominant forces in the story. None of the supporting cast of women in *Ulysses* have stature as at least three of the men do: Bloom, Stephen, and Buck Mulligan (the latter as the goatish, comic muse). Or perhaps, it is that they all become dwarfed in comparison with a female colossus like Molly, the type, the symbol, the Mother of them all. Yet, as a social fact, apart from aesthetic considerations, this difference in the status of Joyce's women has import. In Ireland, certainly the Ireland of 1904, woman's place was in the home. The Church still sees to that–at least in principle. The women we find abroad in Bloom's peregrinations are streetwalkers, barmaids, or servant girls on errands. Adolescents like Gertie and her tom-boy friend Cissy Caffrey are only auxiliary nursemaids to their mothers, doing the family marketing or minding the younger children. It seems not at all atypical that Stephen, the University scholar and gentleman, should have a little ragamuffin sister, Dilly, who starving for a bun, spends her penny for a French primer she cannot read! It is Molly and a dead woman, Stephen's mother, who are the female powers.

As in Joyce's *Portrait of the Artist as a Young Man*, the background of *Ulysses*, unlike that of the *Odyssey*, is one of a grinding lower-middle-class poverty: stale, threadbare, malodorous. Joyce's Dublin is a city whose fetid odors of human filth and horse dung, whose garbage-bearing Liffey, seem very far from Ithaca, that rocky, windswept island of the blue Aegean. Yet even these implied and unstated contrasts create an ironic counterpoint which is an ever-present though muffled beat of doom. Take, for example, the measure of the kind of itemization of the household economy of Penelope's, Nestor's or Menalaus' establishments as compared with Bloom's domain at 7 Eccles Street or the Martello tower of Stephen and Buck Mulligan. When Athene first appeared to Telemachus with the "look of Mentes, a chief in Taphos,"

> "he spread smooth draperies over a throne of cunning workmanship and seated her upon it. For her feet there was a foot-stool, while for himself he drew up a painted lounge-chair . . . A maid came with a precious golden ewer and poured water for them above its silver basin, rinsing their hands. She drew to their side a gleaming table and on it the matronly housekeeper arranged her suore or bread and many prepared dishes . . . A carver filled and passed them trenchers of meat in great variety, and set on their tables two golden beakers which the steward, as often as he walked up and down the hall, refilled for them with wine."

The wine, by the way, Telemachus elsewhere describes as "stuff with the glint of sunlight in it."

At Menelaus' "marvellous" house Telemachus is repaid in kind although the splendor exceeds that of his own kingly home and he and his party "stared around, feasting their eyes." Later,

> "Helen . . . came out from her high-coffered, incense-laden room with her women; of whom Adraste carried the graceful reclining chair for her mistress while Alcippe had her soft wollen carpet and Phylo a silver basket given the queen by Alcandre . . . The basket was mounted on a wheeled carriage also of silver and the rims of it were carried out in gold. It was heaped full of the smoothest yarn

and across it, at the moment, lay the distaff wound
with wool of a wood-violet blue."

It is against this luxurious background, rich and stately, that we must
place the basement kitchen in which Ulysses-Bloom receives his
Telemachus-Stephen.

> "What did Stephen see on raising his gaze to the
> height of a yard from the fire towards the opposite
> wall?
> Under a row of coiled spring housebells a cur-
> vilinear rope, ... from which hung four small sized
> square handkerchiefs folded unattached consecu-
> tively in adjacent rectangles and one pair of ladies
> grey hose with lisle suspended tops and feet ..."

> "What did Bloom see on the range?
> On the right (smaller) hob a blue enamelled
> saucepan: on the left (larger) hob a black iron
> kettle."

> "What lay under exposure on the lower middle
> and upper shelves of the kitchen dresser opened by
> Bloom?
> On the lower shelf five vertical breakfast plates,
> six horizontal breakfast saucers on which rested
> inverted breakfast cups, a mustache cup, unin-
> verted, and saucer of Crown Derby, four white gold-
> rimmed egg cups ... and a phial of aromatic violet
> comfits. On the middle shelf a chipped egg cup con-
> taining pepper. A drum of table salt, four con-
> glomerated black olives in oleaginous paper, an
> empty pot of Plumtree's potted meat ... a small
> dish containing a slice of fresh ribsteak. On the
> upper shelf a battery of jamjars of various sizes and
> proveniences."

And so the differential persists all though the modern voyaging.
Yet it is precisely the kind of *tonal* differentia which many commentators ignore, so busy are they exploring the overt correspondences or inventing absurd ones where they do not exist; and, in both
instances, with the accent always on the literal significations. Yet to

fail to see the margin for bitter and humorous comment provided, for example, by the physical *goods* of the Greek prototypes over against the impoverished, mean array of the hero of a quantitatively-oriented culture is to miss an enormous range of implication. Of course, the Homeric collater, too, was performing an act of memory, was succumbing to a nostalgia for a way of living that was no longer known to the Aechaen city-states by which he was surrounded.

In *Ulysses*, interestingly, it is Buck Mulligan, the Rabelaisian medical student, who verbalizes the Hellenism, which infects many of the characters, most frequently and self-consciously. In the early pages of *Ulysses*, Buck, bantering with Stephen, introduces himself to us: "My name is absurd too: Malachi Mulligan, two dactyls. But it has a Hellenic ring, hasn't it? Tripping and sunny like the buck himself. We must go to Athens. Will you come if I can get the aunt to fork out twenty quid?" Later, again to Stephen, he grandiosely proposes: "God, Kinch, if you and I could only work together we might do something for the island. Hellenise it." And looking out over Dublin Bay: "God, he said quietly. Isn't that what Algy calls it: a grey sweet mother? The snotgreen sea. The scrotum-tightening sea. *Epi oinopa ponton*. Ah, Dedalus, the Greeks. I must teach you. You must read them in the original. *Thalatta! Thalatta! . . .*" It is in this sense rather than in the more obvious role which has been assigned to Buck as Antinous, the most likely of Penelope's suitors, that Stephen is being robbed of his inheritance. Gilbert confines this usurpation to Buck's "lording it" in the Martello Tower for which Stephen pays the rent and to which Buck keeps the key. Yet, Stephen's real disinheritance seems more significantly to lie in his being cut off from the Hellenic roots to which the ribald, cynical Buck has the key (i.e. the *language*) for Stephen has to rely on translation from the Greek. When Gilbert adds somewhat speciously "Like Antinous and the other suitors, Mulligan and his like would despoil the son of his heritage or drive him into exile" it is not clear to what order of patrimony he refers for he does not document his statement. It must be remembered that, in reality, Antinous, had he succeeded, would have been the usurper of Ulysses; he was, in so far as he swilled and lived on his estate, the usurper only of Telemachus's *goods*. The inheritance of which Buck would deprive Stephen is of another order. As a matter of fact, Stephen, ultimately, himself rejects his real "inheritance"; this rejection, flowing, as I have tried to show, from his essential inability to accept "sonship."

The central fact, then, about the correspondences existing between the *Odyssey* and *Ulysses* in terms of structure, event, dramatis personae and so on is that Joyce's emphasis was always on deriving the essential quality from his model rather than on literal, easy, or even ingenious, parallels. There is abundant testimony as to his intent; there is even more abundant corroboration as to its successful realization in the text of *Ulysses* itself. For example, when working on the *Oxen of the Sun* episode, Joyce confessed to Budgen that he had struggled to resolve his own conflicts about the meaning of that episode in the *Odyssey*. He finally concluded: "The companions of Ulysses disobey the commands of Pallas. They slay and flay the oxen of the Sun god and all are damned save the prudent and pious Ulysses. I interpret the killing of the sacred oxen as the crime against fecundity by sterilising the act of coition and I think my interpretation is as sound as that of any other commentator on Homer." (It is worthwhile to note that Joyce terms himself "commentator.") Another controversial parallel which Joyce resolved by characteristically free treatment was the slaughter of the suitors which he said "always seemed to me un-Ulyssean." And, as Budgen adds, "Appropriately, it is in the bedroom that Bloom meets and disposes of the suitors. From this base he takes the salute of the host of his wife's admirers. With bloodless thought Bloom banishes his rivals to nonentity . . ." And if thee is any doubt about the fullness of Bloom's triumph it is the final chapter of the book, Molly Bloom's soliloquy, which settles it. For Molly's interior monologue is what, as Joyce said, gives "the indispensable counter-sign to Bloom's passport to eternity."

What emerges from these considerations, then, is that any approach to an evaluation of the relationship which *Ulysses* bears to the *Odyssey* must be premised on an ungrudging acceptance of the heretical nature of the creative process. We have the "ground plan"— the *Odyssey*. We have the working notes of the architect—Joyce's notes and conversations as well as some Mss. versions. We have, finally, the edifice itself—*Ulysses*. And, richly and strangely, something has happened which none of these historical facts will explain. It is what has gone *in between* that makes for "history with a difference."

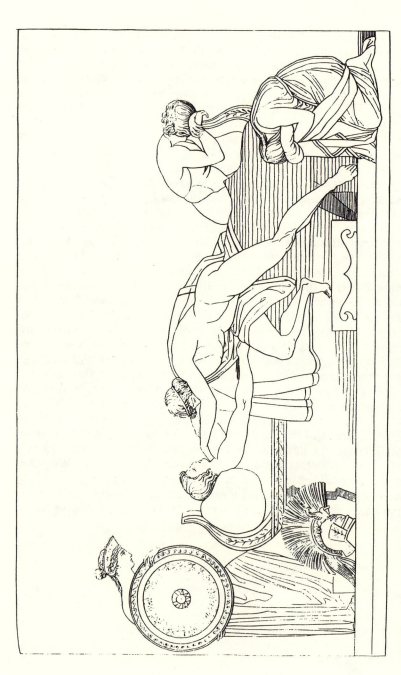

Figure 15. Achilles laments over Patroklos. Flaxman (*Iliad* series).

# Achilles Awash in Sexual Politics

*Katherine Callen King*

Marguerite Yourcenar, the woman chosen to end the French Academy's 300 years of male exclusivity, vehemently denied that she was a feminist, and her most famous work focuses on male heroes. It comes as no surprise, then, that Yourcenar introduces *Feux* (*Fires*),[1] an early less famous work that does largely focus on women, with the assertion that its nine startling revisions of classical myth were intended only "to glorify . . . or perhaps exorcise" ("glorifier . . . ou peut-être exorciser") an intense love relationship.[2] Yourcenar turned to ancient myth not to perform feminist revision of the conscious type Alicia Ostriker discusses,[3] but because it represented for her "une approche de l'absolu. Pour tâcher de découvrir sous l'être humain ce qu'il y a en lui de durable, ou . . . d'éternel" ("a way of approaching the absolute, a way of delving beneath the human surface to discover what was durable, or . . . eternal").[4] Nonetheless, what is *éternel*

---

[1] Written in 1935 and published in 1936. The title of this collection of nine stories and *pensées* was originally the title of the *pensées* published separately in 1935: "Feux," *Revue de France* 4 (1935) 491-98.

[2] *Feux* (Gallimard, Paris, 1974), 26. All page references will be to this most recent edition. All translations are my own unless otherwise noted. *Feux* has been translated into English by Dori Katz with the collaboration of Yourcenar (*Fires*, Farrar Strauss and Giroux: New York, 1981), but the reader should be warned that there are places where the English version differs significantly from the French.

[3] "The Thieves of Language: Women Poets and Revisionist Mythmaking," *Signs* 8 (1982) 68-90.

[4] *Les yeux ouverts*: *Entretiens avec Matthieu Galey* (Centurion, Paris, 1980) 92-3. WITH OPEN EYES: CONVERSATIONS WITH MATTHIEU GALEY trans. Arthur Goldhammer, Beacon Press, Boston, 1984, 67. She intensifies the sense of eternality she sought by fusing past and present with striking anachronisms: for example, Thetis, Achilles' prescient goddess mother, sees in the eyes of Jupiter a *film*

emerges from her 1930's female consciousness remarkably altered
from its appearance in centuries of male tradition: Yourcenar's
gender-charged transformations of traditional plot-detail and imagery
infect "the absolute" with festering feminist questions.

I will examine here the production of these feminist questions
through analysis of the classical and modern elements in the second of
a pair of short stories, "Achille ou le mensonge" and "Patrocle ou le
destin," that were originally published together in 1935 as "Dédamie"
and "Penthésilée" under the general title "Deux amours d'Achille"
("Two Loves of Achilles").5 The *Iliad*, western culture's originary war
poem, is of paramount concern to these stories' exploration of gender-
identification and violence, but as the original subtitles indicate,
Yourcenar approaches her heroic absolute circuitously through
Achilles' pre- and post-Iliadic relationships with women: Deidamia,
whom he loves and leaves, and Penthesileia, whom he kills and loves.
Yourcenar weaves these disparate works together on a loom of current events6 and psychoanalytic theory, shuttling back and forth
between war as literal social event and war as an image for conflict
between  male and female in society, masculine and feminine in the
psyche.7

*       *       *

Patroclus's corpse may be lying on the beach covered with blue
flies, or it may be lying next to Achilles in his shadow-strewn tent, or it
may be already burned and buried. The only thing that is totally clear
about this seemingly ubiquitous corpse is that it and death are the
only things that have any reality for Achilles. The living world has dis-

---

of Achilles' death [42]; Paris is disfigured by a *grenade* [63].

5 "Deux amours d'Achille" was published in *Mercure de France*, 263 (1935)
118-27. Aside from the loss of the subtitles (and consequent shift of emphasis in the
second part from Penthesileia to Patroclus) there are few major alterations. Changes
other than punctuation will be indicated in footnotes.

6 1935 was the year Mussolini invaded Ethiopia. The stories were written
before the invasion, but as Yourcenar says in *Les yeux ouverts*, "Le sentiment du
danger, accru aussi par la guerre d'Espagne, et par ce que je savais des dessous du
fascisme italien, était très fort chez moi en ce temps-là [118] ("In those days I had a
very strong feeling of imminent danger, heightened by the war in Spain and by what I
knew of the underside of Italian fascism" [*With Open Eyes*, 88]). In the preface to
*Feux* she says that the ballet-like duel between Achilles and Penthesileia in "Patrocle"
reflected the "atmosphère de jeux angoissés" of the times (16-17).

7 I examine "Achille" in the longer version of this essay published in *LIT* 2
(1991), 202–09.

appeared along with "cet ami qui tout à la fois avait rempli le monde et l'avait remplacé" ("this friend who both filled the world and replaced it" [63]), which is a re-casting of the Homeric Achilles' assertion that he "valued Patroclus above all other companions, equal to my own self" [18.81–82].[8] This and several other re-castings of Achilles' grief and martial valor distill the *Iliad*'s meditation on mortality into the question of how heroism relates to bodies, specifically dead bodies and female bodies, and thus continue in "Patrocle"/"Penthésilée" the exploration of masculinity and aggression begun in "Achille"/ "Dédamie."

In "Achille" Achilles' simultaneous embrace of Patroclus and heroism had involved adopting categorical distinctions (between truth and falsehood, male and female). Now, on Yourcenar's Trojan plain, ten years of war have produced a landscape in which both heroism and distinctions have been lost. The story opens in an eternal twilight in which the creations of culture—towers, lipstick—seem to merge with the products of nature—mountains, blood [61–62]. People have settled into a "routine rouge où la paix se mélangeait à la guerre comme la terre à l'eau dans les puantes régions" ("red routine, in which peace blended with war like earth with water in stinking swamplands" [62]). This "red routine" with its "stinking" absence of demarcation between war and peace represents the third stage of war: an age of heroes mowed down by scyth-chariots and an age of dutiful self-sacrificing soldiers have both passed, and all that is left are suicidal "joueurs" ("players") whom the invention of tanks has reduced to the function of "ramparts" [62]. This list of ages recapitulates a progression from individualistic Homeric through civic Roman to modern impersonal and overtly meaningless warfare. But the violent anachronisms of the passage that follows—Iphigeneia shot for abetting a mutiny, Paris disfigured by a grenade [63]—discourage readers from nostalgically privileging the first type of warfare; they draw all warfare throughout literary and factual history into one long continuum of War—war for war's sake.

It is in this un-distinguished war setting that Yourcenar's martial hero confronts the corporeality of his friend. Like Homer's Achilles, who in his initial grief "lay stretched all his huge length in the dust" [*Iliad* 18.26–27], Yourcenar's Achilles makes his appearance "nu,

---

[8] This sentiment also recalls Achilles' wish in *Iliad* 16.97-100 that all Greeks and Trojans, that is the whole world, might perish and leave him and Patroclus alone. See Cedric Whitman's interpretation of these lines in *Homer and the Heroic Tradition* Norton (New York, 1965) 199.

couché à même la terre comme s'il s'efforçait d'imiter ce cadavre,"
["naked, lying on the bare earth as if he were trying to imitate this
corpse,"]. The Homeric line is commonly read as imaging Achilles'
own death, as indicating that he is as good as dead already.[9] Yourcenar gives it a new twist: her supine Achilles "se laissait ronger par
la vermine de ses souvenirs" ["allowed himself to be eaten away by
the vermin of his memories" 63]. Memories—history, movement
through time—invade and waste the "self" just as death wastes the
body. Subsequent text reveals that Achilles judges the former destruction as worse than the latter; the fixity of death, in fact, comes to be
seen as an heroic corrective to the always potential putrefaction of
life.

The product of Achilles' death-like grief in "Patrocle" is the
opposite of the indiscriminate homicidal rage that it engenders in the
*Iliad.* Yourcenar's Achilles comes to believe that death is "comme un
sacre dont seuls les plus purs sont dignes: beaucoup d'hommes se
défont, peu d'hommes meurent" ("like a sacrament of which only the
most pure are worthy: many men cease to exist, few men die" [63]).
He creates an arbitrary distinction to fill his empty world with meaning, and with the words "sacre" "pur" and "digne" he gives death—a
certain kind of military death—abstract cultural value. The unsettling
melange of war/peace nature/culture that opened the story is thus
partially corrected.

Homer's Achilles vowed to take vengeance on the man who "having killed Patroclus stripped off his armor" [*Iliad* 18.82–83]. Yourcenar's Achilles, on the contrary, envies Hector for being the one to
have stripped the veils of life from his friend:

> La haine inavouée qui dort au fond de l'amour
> prédisposait Achille à la tache de sculpteur: il
> enviait Hector d'avoir achevé ce chef-d'oeuvre; lui
> seul aurait dû arracher les derniers voiles que la
> pensée, le geste, le fait même d'être en vie inter-
> posait entre eux, pour découvrir Patrocle dans sa
> sublime nudité de mort. [64]

> [The unavowed hate that lies at the base of love
> predisposed Achilles to the sculptor's task:  he

---

[9] *Iliad* 18.71, in which Thetis takes her son's head in her hands as a mother
would do at a funeral, reinforces this interpretation. See especially Johannes Kakridis
*Homeric Researches* (Lund, 1949) 72.

envied Hector for having completed this masterpiece; he was the one who should have stripped off
the last veils that thought, gesture, the very fact of
being alive had interposed between them, in order
to uncover Patroclus in the sublime nudity of
death.]

This metaphor of killer as sculptor resonates with imagery in an
earlier passage: Achilles' memories of Patroclus had focused on his
*pallor*, his *rigid* shoulders, his *cold* hands, his *stone*like heaviness while
he slept—"comme si Patrocle n'avait été vivant qu'une ébauche de
cadavre" ("as if Patroclus living had been nothing but the sketch for a
corpse" [64]). The sculptor's work, which displaces warm ruddy flesh
in favor of putrefaction-proof cold colorless stone, appears to be this
story's analogue to Homeric *kleos*, the immortal glory in epic song that
was the goal of Iliadic heroism. But how different these products of
warfare—the one, a narrative shaping and re-creation of action, the
preservation of *existence* in collective memory; the other, a chiseling
down to a hard human *essence* that is proof against the most voracious
of personal memories.

The aggression of Yourcenar's Achilles and Hector seems to have
a single object: the pursuit of death as the pursuit of individuated
human essence. When such essence is achieved in the corpse of his
world-replacing friend, Yourcenar's Achilles withdraws from the fighting. No story of Achilles' would be complete without this withdrawal:
in the *Iliad* it occurs for the sake of heroic *timê* "honor"; in the Middle
Ages it is motivated by love for an enemy princess; in Yourcenar's
strikingly different version, Achilles refuses to kill further "pour ne
pas susciter à Patrocle des rivaux d'outre-tombe" ("in order not to
create rivals for Patroclus beyond the tomb" [64–65]). In his desire to
maintain the distinctiveness of the dead man, Achilles encloses himself in his death ("s'enfermait dans ce mort") and loses all consciousness of living beings except as phantoms ["les vivants ne se montraient
à lui que sous forme de fantômes" 65]. He refuses, that is, to
acknowledge the flesh of existence.

Fleshly beings eventually challenge Achilles' essentialist reality,
force his gaze away from the ideas of purity, distinctiveness, and death
that now constitute his world. Yourcenar employs two important
Homeric motifs, heroic fire and Achilles' battle with the river, to
depict this challenge, opposing the immovable, unchanging essence
that is the goal of warfare/masculinity with a flowing, shape-changing
existence that is eventually associated with femininity.

As Cedric Whitman has so ably demonstrated, in the *Iliad* fire is associated with "death, sacrifice, the fall of Troy . . . rage, destruction, heroic valor, and heroic honor." [143, 132]; it becomes a symbol particularly of Achilles' wrathful prowess.[10]  Water, specifically river water, is associated in the River Fight [*Iliad*. 21.233–380] with the protection of Troy and, in a rare passage that looks beyond the war to the future Trojan landscape, with the obliteration of the Achaean war camp [*Iliad* 12.15–33]. Achilles, in the scene in which he throws Lykaon's body into the river, sees it as a means to deny a dead warrior a funeral [*Iliad*. 21.122–27], and so does his retaliating enemy, the river Xanthus, who threatens to "hide Achilles in mud" and "wrap him in sand" so that the Greeks won't be able to find his bones and give him a tomb [*Iliad* 21.318–24]. Achilles is saved from drowning in Xanthos's great crest of blood-purple water by Hephaistos, god of Fire, who burns first the corpses on the plain and then the river himself [*Iliad* 21. 324–376].  The river under control, Achilles continues his rampage against the Trojans and is himself again associated with destructive fire in a simile that compares him to the wrath of the gods burning a city [*Iliad*. 21.522–25].  Homeric fire, then, images death and the martial heroism that immortalizes one's name in song or tomb; water images both non-heroic life and obliterating change.

Yourcenar transforms the fire-water imagery and the details of this scene, maintaining the fundamental opposition between life and death, obliterating change and immortalizing destruction, but adding a further polarity between feminine and masculine. While Achilles is enclosed in death, there arises from the earth "une humidité traîtresse" ("a traitorous dampness" [65]). This dampness is first associated with marching feet and loosening earth. Next we read: "les deux camps[11] réconciliés luttaient avec le fleuve s'efforçant de noyer l'homme: Achille pâle entra dans ce soir de fin de monde" ("the two camps reconciled struggled against the river that was attempting to harm man: pale Achilles entered into this cataclysmic night" [65]). Mysteriously, both Greek and Trojan armies seem to be united in opposition to this man-hating river. Achilles' rationale for opposing it is given at length:

---

[10] See the chapter, "Fire and Other Elements," in *Homer and the Heroic Tradition* Norton (New York, 1965) 128-153.

[11] The original version has "soldats" instead of "deux camps" [125]. The change makes it clear that it is *soldiery* rather than Greek soldiers or Trojan soldiers that opposes water.

Loin de voir dans les vivants les précaires rescapés
d'un raz-de-mort menaçant toujours, c'étaient les
morts maintenant qui lui paraissaient submergés
par l'immonde déluge des vivants. Contre l'eau
mouvante, animée, informe, Achille défendait les
pierres et le ciment qui servent à faire des tombes.
[65]

[Far from seeing the living as precarious escapees
from an always menacing wave of death, now it was
the dead who appeared to him to be overwhelmed
by the vile flood of the living. Against the moving,
animate·shapeless water, Achilles defended the
stones and cement that served to make tombs.]

For Achilles, water is exclusively an image of life, non-individuated
and therefore "vile" life. He joins battle against what is "moving,
animate, shapeless" on behalf of what is fixed, lifeless and shaped
("pierres" "ciment" "tombes"). The voice of Homer in the background suggests further that this water not only lacks shape but
deprives of shape, obliterates.

As Achilles joins battle against "l'immonde déluge" of life, he is
joined imagistically with fire in a passage that again has its roots in
Homer:

Quand l'incendie descendu des forêts de l'Ida vint
jusque dans le port lécher le ventre des navires,
Achille prit contre les troncs, les mâts, les voiles
insolemment fragiles, le parti du feu qui ne craint
pas d'embrasser les morts sur le lit de bois de
buchers. [66]

[When the conflagration came down from Ida's
forests all the way to the port to lick the belly of the
ships, Achilles took the part of fire against the
trunks, masts, insolently fragile sails: fire that
doesn't fear to embrace the dead on the bed of
their wooden biers.]

Achilles' taking "le parti du feu" creates a striking reversal of his
behavior in *Iliad* 16, where the sight of fire on the ships makes him
anxious "lest there no longer be means of fleeing" [127–29]. A

reader's consciousness of this reversal highlights the fact that Achilles' heroic fire—which is a constant in both works—is here fighting not other fire but water and the organic matter (trunks, masts, sails) that make survival possible. If, as was suggested earlier, all soldiers are united against this common enemy ["le fleuve s'efforçant de noyer l'homme"], then we may read this imagery as implying that the true object of war is, simply, the eradication of life.[12] But we must go further than this simple anti-war inference, for, as this passage begins to make clear, "l'homme" that was the object of the river's enmity does not represent generic humanity. The sexual connotations of "embrasser . . . sur le lit" ("embrace . . . on the bed") suggest that just as sex had in "Achille" substituted for homicide, now homicide—the fire-embraced corpse—substitutes for sex, and they remind the reader that the warrior has rejected the bisexual bed of love in favor of the monosexual field of war. When the implicitly rejected female emerges from the water in the next passage, the reader may substitute "masculine behavior" for "war" and infer that it is *masculinity* that is fundamentally opposed to life.

The maleficent water takes shape as "alien peoples" pouring "out of Asia like rivers" ("D'étranges peuplades débouchaient de l'Asie comme des fleuves" [66]). Achilles slaughters the first flowing aliens like animals "sans même y reconnaître des linéaments humains" ("without even recognizing their human lineaments" [66]). Then come the Amazons, "une inondation de seins" ("an inundation of breasts"), whose closeness to animality in the soldiers' minds is signified by their exciting "odor of naked fleece" ("l'armée frémissait à cette odeur de toisons nues" [66]). The men's enemy is unindividuated bodies, fluid and animal and female, whose only distinguishing mark is the breast, the source and symbol of the most basic life-nurturing flow.

Achilles' enmity now becomes quite specifically misogynistic, hinging on a familiar nature/culture dichotomy which is here expressed as (feminine) instinct versus (masculine) choice:

> Toute sa vie, les femmes avaient représenté pour
> Achille la part instinctive du malheur, celle dont il
> n'avait pas choisi la forme, qu'il devait subir, ne
> pouvait accepter. [66]

---

12 Additional support for this inference comes from the passage in "Achille" which likens Deidamia's expiring life to water dripping from a vase: "la vie de Déidamie s'échapper de sa gorge comme l'eau du goulot trop étroit d'un vase" (50).

[All his life women had represented for Achilles the
instinctive part of unhappiness, that whose form he
did not choose, which he had to endure but could
not accept.]

Women are blamed for inhibition of heroism (Thetis), failure of
understanding (Lycomedes' daughters), and the humiliation of love
(Briseis) [66–67]. Here, again, awareness of how Yourcenar is transforming Homer highlights the masculist workings of her
nature/culture dichotomy. In the *Iliad* Achilles lamented that Thetis
did not marry an immortal, Peleus a mortal, "for you (Thetis) will suffer great grief for your dead son" (*Iliad* 18.86–89). The Homeric passage is ambiguous: we can interpret Achilles' words either as genuine
sympathy for the immanent suffering of his mother or as a complaint
against the gods who forced her (*embalón*) to a mortal bed and
thereby made him, her son, mortal instead of immortal.[13] Yourcenar's re-working of this lament takes the second interpretation but
turns it inside out: Achilles' complaint is against his mother, not the
gods, and against being half *im*mortal, not half mortal:

Il reprochait à sa mère d'avoir fait de lui un métis à
mi-chemin entre le dieu et l'homme, lui ôtant ainsi
la moitié du mérite qu'ont les hommes à se faire
dieux. [66–67]

[He reproached his mother for having made him a
half-cast midway between god and man, thereby
depriving him of half the merit men get by making
themselves gods.]

Thetis has given him ("fait de lui") something that is valuable only if
self-made ("se faire"); her natural gift (divine genes) is negative
because it diminishes the scope of culture (that is, men's struggle to
surpass their nature). Achilles' second complaint against her is
related: she ought not to have bathed him in the Styx, for heroism
consists in being vulnerable:

---

[13] Greek myth stresses the involuntary nature of Thetis's union with a mortal,
forced on her because she was destined to bear a son mightier than his father.
Catullus transformed the relationship into a love match (Poem 64), and this seems to
be the variant Yourcenar is following in *Feux* when she writes that Thetis' only youthful fault was to sleep with Achilles' father "sans prendre la précaution banale de le
changer en dieu" [43].

> Il lui gardait rancune de l'avoir tout enfant mené
> aux bains de Styx pour immuniser contre la peur,
> comme si l'héroisme ne consistait pas à être
> vulnérable. [67]

Her gift of invulnerability deprives him of the possibility of risk and therefore of choice. Heroism, a cultural construct like the godhood that is its goal, involves competing with nature: with the mortality of the body, the instinct to live, the fear of dying. We may note that Thetis's counter-heroic baby-bathing fits perfectly into a pattern of oppositional water/fire life/death imagery, as does the pun on *mère* and *mer* that was consciously meant to evoke "le double aspect de Thetis" [Preface to *Feux* p.23]. Achilles' complaints mark mothering, water, instinct, love, natural divinity as negative; merit, fear, heroism, vulnerability, humiliation, achieved divinity as positive.[14]

Yourcenar here shifts from the male battles of the *Iliad* to the male-female battle between Achilles and the Amazons, whose fullest ancient narrations (in Quintus of Smyrna's *Posthomerica* and "Dictys'" *Ephemeris*) are also marked by misogyny.[15] Representatives of everything negative in Achilles' life, Yourcenar's Amazons are attacked and die specifically as women: through with attempting to understand the "mystery of being a woman" ["Achille" 50], Achilles hacks through the unsolvable puzzle of his opponents' female innards ("trancha des noeuds gordiens de viscères"); the process of their dying is described as "giving birth" through their newly opened flesh ("enfantant la mort par la brèche des blessures"). They end as a heap of "pulpe nue" ("naked pulp" [67]). There is nothing "pure" nothing "sacramental" about these female deaths. The mushy organic heap at the end of the river is the diametric opposite of the "sculpture" in Achilles' tent.

There is one female who is as hard and inorganic as a hero: Penthesileia the Amazon queen. She is portrayed as androgynous, like the character Misandra in "Achille," who, despite her masculine heart, was entombed in the palace, a prisoner of her breasts [53].

---

[14] Note the absence of father in either list: the male must "se faire."

[15] The pseudo-Dictys wrote probably in the first century C.E., but aside from a few Greek fragments his work survives only in a fourth-century Latin translation. Quintus wrote in the fourth century, but his Greek continuation of Homer is not influenced by "Dictys." It is interesting that in Quintus, Penthesileia enters battle "like a wave of the thundering sea" (*Posthomerica* 1.320) and in "Dictys" she ends in a river, dumped there by misogynistic Greeks to punish her for "having dared to cross the natural boundaries of her sex" ("quoniam naturae sexusque condicionem superare ausa esset" (*Ephemeris* 4.3).

Penthesileia is not imprisoned by her breasts, but she is in a sense defined by them: she alone of the Amazons has "consented" to cut one off ("Seule d'entre ses compagnes, elle avait consenti à se faire couper le sein" [68]).[16] The verb *consentir* provokes the question, who or what proposed/demanded this surgery? We are not given an explicit answer, but one is suggested by Yourcenar's subsequent labeling of the "mutilated" chest as "divine": "mais cette mutilation n'était qu'a peine sensible sur cette gorge de dieu" ("but this mutilation was hardly perceptible on her godlike chest" [68]). Divinity was associated with butchers [53] and masculinity in "Achille"; here, consistently, divinity makes the "mutilation" of the female body "hardly perceptible"—divinity, that is, provides cover/justification for those who forcefully eradicate the soft feminine part, who suppress the female in order to pursue male status.

The metal armor this "Furie minerale" wears has a similar function. Hard ["dur noyau" 67] like her fellow divinities Misandra and Achilles, Penthesileia conceals her femininity under armor in order to prevent the softening ("qu'on ne s'attendrit pas") of her opponents [67]. "Masquée d'or" ("masked in gold"), with hair "d'or" and "de l'or" sounding in her pure voice [68], she is on the outside as metallic as the phallic Patroclus in "Achille." Her armor, however, makes her no more successful at becoming the Other than Achilles' dress had made him. Just as swordlike Patroclus had broken the "charme" of femininity in Lycomedes' palace, Achilles' spear "comme pour rompre un charme" breaks through to the feminine body behind the "pur soldat,"[17] subjecting her to a "viol de fer" ("iron rape" [69]) that forcefully reimposes her female status and brings the sexual imagery of the two stories full circle.

"Patrocle" 's story of this godlike soldierwoman felled by an iron rape adds a further dimension to the connection between masculinity, aggression and godhood established in "Achille." Both stories associate divinity with domination of the feminine in the self (body or psyche) and with domination of the female in society. Here Yourcenar suggests that a woman's identification with masculine ideals can mutilate her femininity but cannot eradicate it. She can therefore achieve only lesser divinity (a Fury) and must eventually fall to the superior force of undiluted masculinity.

---

[16] A prominent third-century c.e. Roman sarcophagus in the Louvre depicts all Amazons with breast intact.

[17] In contrast to Patroclus, who *is* a sword, and to Achilles, who wields one, Penthesileia's description nowhere includes this (defining?) weapon.

It was traditional for Achilles to fall in love with the dead Amazon queen upon seeing the beautiful face under the helmet. In Quintus of Smyrna's version, Penthesileia achieved a kind of equality with Patroclus:

> The son of Peleus grieved greatly as he
> looked on the strong girl's loveliness in the dust;
> wherefore baneful sorrow ate away his heart,
> sorrow as great as before when Patroclus was killed.
>
> [*Posthomerica* 718–21]

Quintus's equivalency in grief carries no thematic weight; Achilles' instantaneous sorrow is typical of the universal superficiality of the *Posthomerica*'s characters and tends only to trivialize the hero's feeling for Patroclus. Yourcenar adopts Quintus's version to conclude her own story, but rewrites it to produce yet another profoundly pessimistic suggestion about male-female relations.

It is not discovered beauty that provokes sorrow in Yourcenar's Achilles; it is the revelation that the face behind the metal mask has itself become a mask:

> La visière levée découvrit, au lieu d'un visage, un masque aux yeux aveugles que les baisers n'atteignaient plus. Achille sanglotait, soutenait la tête de cette victime digne d'être un ami. C'était le seul être au monde qui ressemblait à Patrocle. [69]

> [The raised visor discovered, instead of a face, a mask with blind eyes that kisses no longer reached. Achilles sobbed, holding the head of this victim worthy of being a friend. It was the only being in the world who resembled Patroclus.]

The head of the woman who died fighting has attained a fixity that associates her both with the "masque blond" of divinely masculinized day in "Achille" and with the sculptured male essence of Patroclus. This implied shift from feminine existence to masculine essence, which is apparently what leads Achilles to accord Penthesileia a measure of recognition, is reinforced by the gendered nouns in the last two sentences: *victime* is naturally and appropriately feminine, but *ami*, which could have been written as feminine to match the sex of the character to which it refers, is masculine. Yourcenar's choice of masculine gender emphasizes a generic rather than personal quality of friendship, a fixed concept rather than a changeable relationship. It also, by contrast with Quintus, whose Achilles felt pain because he had killed her instead of *marrying* her (*Posthomerica* 1.671–72), emphasizes the non-sexual nature of the bond Achilles is acknowledging: the object of desire, as we saw at the end of "Achille," is seen as female; the rival, the partner in competition (Misandra, Patroclus) is seen as male. In the story's last sentence, *être*, which linked the feminine and masculine nouns in the preceding sentence, becomes a masculine substantive, "le seul être," thus making the shift in gender and abstraction permanent. The *femme* behind the armor is no longer available to be raped; she has disappeared for good into the fixed ideality of masculine culture. It is now that "she" can be mourned.

The shift from feminine to masculine, from personal to abstract, in the last paragraph of "Patrocle" occurs also in the naming of the stories between their original publication and their inclusion in *Feux*. Not only do masculine names replace the female ones that subtitled the two halves of "Deux amours d'Achille," but abstract nouns are attached: *le mensonge* and *le destin*.[18] Do these abstractions add anything to our interpretation? Yes: ambiguity. Readers are forced to ask if "lie" applies to the attempt to become the Other or whether it calls into question masculine claims to Apolline categories? Is it "destiny" to recognize the self in the Other only when it is too late? or is a man "destined" to remake the Other into the self (that is, kill her) before he can love? Yourcenar gives no answers to these questions, but she does suggest that the failure of androgyny, the essential(?) inability of the male to understand and value the female components of the human psyche and of society, his destined(?) devaluing of the real in favor of the ideal, is the cause of individual and global tragedy.

As I said in the beginning, Yourcenar did not set out to write a feminist critique of power relations and cultural ideals. Nonetheless, the critique is there, affirming an involvement with her political and intellectual world that was passionate, discerning, and pessimistic. She focuses on the individual psyche, but the violence she finds there reverberates from and into society. Her concentration on the mental health of the individual (male) human being may thus be seen as an attack on the authoritarian fascism that was beginning to disquiet many in Europe.[19] But her acceptance of the martial bipolar dis-

---

[18] All nine of the stories in *Feux* have abstract nouns attached to their titles, but all but one of the other seven bear female names.

[19] She thus joins the cohort of contemporary women writers Shari Benstock portrays as universally aware of "the destructive possibilities of a masculine ethic of

course that has dominated the psychoanalytic as well as political and cultural theory[20] leads her to impasse, restricts her from imagining any alternatives to the conflictive male-female relations she depicts. With Yourcenar, as with many other unconsciously feminist women writers, we must content ourselves with the negative vision, with one more agonized "report from the battlefield of sexual politics."[21]

---

domination and authoritarianism" (*Women of the Left Bank: Paris, 1900-1940* (Austin, 1987) 124-25.

[20] As Hélène Cixous points out, manhood has paraded "ses métaphores comme des bannières à travers l'histoire..C'est toujours bien sur de guerre de guerre, de combat qu'il s'agit" [Le sexe ou la tête?" *Les Cahiers du GRIF*, no.13 (1976) p.9]. This long tradition has forced even feminists like Luce Irigaray to think in opposi-tional terms: she continues to envision the fluid (real) as feminine, the fixed (ideal) as masculine, but she, unlike Yourcenar, valorizes the former and explicitly names patriarchal culture rather than a masculine principle as the problem. See especially "La 'mécanique' des fluides" in *Ce sexe qui n'en est pas un*, Editions de Minuit: Paris, 1977.

[21] So Annis Pratt describes women's fiction ("The New Feminist Criticisms: Exploring the History of the New Space," in *Beyond Intellectual Sexism: A New Woman A New Reality* (New York, 1976) 193.

Figure 16. Odysseus slays the suitors. Flaxman (*Odyssey* series).

# Kazantzakis' Odyssey
## A Modern Rival to Homer

*Morton P. Levitt*

*The Odyssey: A Modern Sequel* is one of the great encyclopedic works of our time, encompassing the major motifs of our civilization and Homer's, bridging the gap of our common heritage not only for Greeks but for all those to whom Homer is both ancestor and guide. Writing like his predecessor in a period of calm between tumultuous epochs, Kazantzakis endeavors similarly to include all the knowledge and history of his own time, to make of his epic too a symbolic chronicle of the glorious past and a guide for action in the troublesome future. " 'Blessed be that hour that gave me birth between two eras!' " Odysseus proclaims, as if he were himself the epic poet (III, 742).[1] As Homer employed the surviving folk tales and legends of the Mycenaeans to narrate their greatness and fall, so Kazantzakis makes use of Homer to dramatize both those mythic extremes and our own. But his is a far different work, a revolutionary contrast to the conservative Homer, a direct challenge to that earlier *Odyssey*: it was Kimon Friar who added the subtitle "A Modern Sequel" to the later epic; Kazantzakis called it simply *Odyssey*.

Like Homer, he begins *in medias res*, in the middle this time of Homer, as if in the midst of a sentence: "And when in his wide courtyards Odysseus had cut down / the insolent youths. . . ." Soon after, accompanied by his son, as in Homer, the returned king puts down by

---

[1] Introduction to *The Odyssey: A Modern Sequel* (New York, 1958), p. ix. All subsequent references to the text of the poem are to this edition.

guile the revolt of his subjects, the first of many revolts in these new adventures, with implications far more compelling than in the original. For there are commoners at the head of this crowd—more commoners than in all of Homer—and maimed veterans returned from Troy. For them the far-off war, in a cause removed from their interests and needs, is a sign not only of their own king's arrogance but also of an entire society concerned alone with its elite; thus they repudiate also the attitude of Homer, who numbers only nobles and slaves in his social perspective. " 'The guileless gods grant freedom only to earth's masters,' " says Helen, referring at this point not to those most fit but to those most nobly born (III, 1260). But Odysseus can no longer accept such a view, and the revolt in Ithaca is the last in which he will act as tradition demands. Each subsequent uprising will have similar social and political overtones, but his attitude toward each will subtly change, building progressively, until in the end the king will join with the rebels, convinced that not only society but all humanity must be purged and reformed.

In Homer, the revolt of his Ithacan subjects provides one more step in the reconciliation of Odysseus with those who have so long awaited him: with his wife, with his son, with the people he once ruled. Kazantzakis replaces these scenes with an account of the returned king's own alienation. Seeing Penelope for the first time after the slaughter of the suitors, he tries to convince himself that she all along has been his lone goal:

> ". . . she who for years has waited you to force
> her bolted knees and join you in rejoicing cries,
> she is the one you've longed for, battling the far seas,
> the cruel gods and deep voices of your deathless mind."
>
> (I, 30–33)

But he feels only rage at her seeming connivance with the suitors and cannot even bring himself to speak to her. When he does tell her of his travels, it is only of Calypso and Circe and Nausicaa that he speaks, temptations he ultimately resisted not for her sake but for his own, because he was not a god as Calypso would have it, but a mortal; because his essential humanity was threatened by the gross sensuality of Circe; because his need to reach above himself, his potential divinity, would have shriveled in simple home life with Nausicaa. It is hardly a politic tale to tell even to a wife renowned for her patience, and it could hardly have come from the travel-weary, home-loving husband of the original epic; yet it is Homer's Odysseus who unaccountably tells his wife, immediately upon their reunion, of the prophecy that he must travel again to lands and seas beyond the borders known to the Greeks. When, finally, he does leave Ithaca, this new Odysseus has no farewell for his " 'heavy-fated' " (II, 1117), "his luckless wife" (II, 1446); she sees him last at dawn, "treading on tiptoe through the court . . . like a thief" (II, 1462).

Telemachus is appalled by his father's indelicacy, by the demands he makes on those he encounters, both by his grasp for, and his rejection of, divinity:

> . . . shuddering, [he] spied on the hard knees and thighs,
> the hands that could choke virtue, that on savage shores
> brashly could seize yet cast aside the dread Immortals.
>                                             (II, 198–200)

The prince has fought bravely beside his father against the suitors, but now he counsels moderation and quiet acceptance of life in Ithaca. He is precisely the sort of ruler that any reasonable citizen would desire. And with him, we reasonable men might curse his father, who makes it impossible to follow in traditional paths, to live calmly and well:

> "You set all minds on fire, you plague man's simple heart,
> you drive the craftsman from his shop, uproot the plow,
> until the country bridegroom wants his bride no more
> but longs for travel and immortal Helen's arms."
>                                             (I, 1280–83)

An old bard who had known Odysseus' grandfather sings of the ideal monarch, the " 'good man . . . grown old [who] sits like God in the market place' " (II, 1130–32). Laertes has been such a king; his grandson will be another. But Odysseus disdains their ideal, for under such moderate rulers, he knows, men are too easily content, too willing to limit their divine aspirations. It is only when the prince Telemachus endeavors to seize the throne that his father the king elects to abdicate, pleased for once by the initiative of his " 'wretched, well-bred' " conservative son (II, 1122).

Even Ithaca and the symbols of his reign fail the returned king: his people are mundane—" 'a mess of bellies and stinking breath!' " (I, 1069); the assembly he so longed to hold is made up of close-minded and cowardly elders—"was this, by God, the foul fistful his soul desired?" (II, 702). His journey, he has now come to realize, has made him unfit for Ithaca—his goal, paradoxically, more noble than its attainment. To reach it, he had resisted all the faces of death; now, he discovers, "even his native land was a sweet mask of Death" (II, 434).

By the end of the second book of this new *Odyssey*—corresponding in time to the last book of Homer, in which reconciliation is finally complete—the king has collected a new crew of misfits and left Ithaca forever: en route to Sparta, where he carries off Helen a second time, offering her not love but adventure and freedom; to Minoan Crete, where he presides over the fall of its decadent civilization; to Egypt, where he leads a futile, bloody revolt and from which he escapes as Moses leading an army of rebels and misfits. In Africa, at the source of the Nile, he founds a utopian city of craftsmen, warriors, and scholars, a socialist state in which the family is outlawed and the people glorified as a whole, a state destroyed at its birth by a volcanic eruption and earthquake. As he moves further south, now without companions or followers, Odysseus comes increasingly to deny his old worldly concerns, to move away from society and politics, away from his idealism and concern for the flesh. Finally, at the southernmost pole, in a snowy white deathship, his mind and soul leap free of his body, and he becomes free at last even of the need for freedom.

> All the great body of the world-roamer turned to
> mist, and slowly his snow-ship, his memory, fruit
> and friends drifted like fog far down the sea,
> vanished like dew. Then flesh dissolved, glances
> congealed, the heart's pulse stopped,  and the great
> mind leapt to the peak of its holy freedom, fluttered
> with empty wings, then upright through the air
> soared high and freed itself from it's last cage, its
> freedom.
>
> (XXIV, 1387–93)

In his movement from body to spirit, from Ithaca to the Antarctic, Kazantzakis' Odysseus creates a new philosophical complex, one built on a base of Mediterranean archaeology and history, of the fertility myths of Africa and the Near East, fulfilling at last the prophecy of Homer's Tieresias in Hades: that the sailor would travel from his home to a land so far from the sea that its people would mistake the oar on his shoulder for a winnowing fan; that he would experience there new adventures of great moral and intellectual import; that he would eventually die on the sea—" a seaborne death soft as this hand of mist."[2] The oar of Odysseus is a basic symbol of Kazantzakis'

---

[2] *The Odyssey* of Homer, Book XI, trans. Robert Fitzgerald (Garden City,

poem: from it will sprout man's figurative wings, emblem of his spiritual rebirth, of his human potential for godhead. For this man there will be no Mycenaean funeral games, no burial in the *tholos* tombs of his ancestors: Odysseus will indeed die in mist, his flesh dissolved into spirit, into that combination of mind and soul from which, Kazantzakis believes, the ancient fertility figures were sprung and into which we must evolve if we and our civilization are similarly to be renewed.

From the small beginnings provided by Homer and the Cyclical Epics, by Dante's insight into the wanderer Odysseus as symbol of man's everlasting search for forbidden knowledge,[3] by old legends in Herodotus and elsewhere of voyages by Phoenicians and Greeks beyond the Pillars of Heracles, Kazantzakis has created an epic that is rich in myth and in symbol, in speculation about the nature of man and his universe, in plans for expanding the force of our spiritual lives. In many ways, his effort is more daring than Homer's, and in many ways it is more successful. Both poets organize masterfully a vast body of complex and often contradictory material; both attempt in a sense to transmit all the knowledge of their times and to dramatize the universality inherent in seemingly local incidents. Out of the inevitable aftermath to a petty conflict between historically minor kingdoms, Homer was able to fashion in the *Odyssey* a document of universal import—not simply to tell us all there was to know in his

---

New York, 1963), p. 189.

[3] See *The Inferno*, trans. John Ciardi, Canto XXVI.

> not fondness for my son, nor reverence
> for my aged father, nor Penelope's claim
>
> to the joys of love, could drive out of my mind
> the lust to experience the far-flung world
> and the failings and felicities of mankind.

By substituting this "personification of centrifugal force" for the "centripetal, homeward-bound figure" of Homer, Dante "made Ulysses symbolize the anarchic element in those conflicts between orthodoxy and heresy, conservatism and progressivism, classicism and romanticism, which vexed his own time and were to vex later epochs more tragically. When he condemned this Ulysses he condemned what he thought to be a destructive force in society." Yet there is at the same time a "paradoxical feeling of admiration which is evident in Dante's portrait of the doomed hero." W.B. Stanford, *The Ulysses Theme* (Oxford, 1954), pp. 181-82. Giovanni Pascoli's *Ultima Viaggio* (1904), following the tradition of Dante, has Odysseus leave Ithaca after ten years and begin to retrace his voyages. Instead of fond memories, however, he finds no trace that he has passed there before—a most nihilistic conclusion to so active a life.

time about the civilization of Bronze Age Greece, or to suggest its
continued impact on his own era, some four or five centuries later. In
Odysseus he created a character who would stand for future ages as a
relevant symbol of man's enduring intellect—in both its positive and
its negative aspects—what W.B. Stanford has called "the untypical
hero." But Kazantzakis' endeavor is far more comprehensive than
this—more comprehensive because, on the simplest level, we know
more today than Homer did about the Bronze Age in the Aegean,
because in addition Kazantzakis' world is not confined to the Aegean
and the immediately surrounding areas, because there is no longer a
single, unified body of custom and lore that is shared by all readers:
Freud, Jung, Frazer, Marx, Nietzsche, Bergson, and all those others
who have molded our century, and whom Kazantzakis has used in his
*Odyssey*, present together a cultural image that is infinitely more
diverse and far-reaching than is apparent in Homer.

For Homer, a single theme—hospitality and its abuses—can serve
as determinant of all the principal events and provide a kind of continuing norm against which to judge characters and acts. Zeus, after
all, is the god of hospitality, and in this peripatetic, sea-faring society
no principle is more highly valued—and no man is more outcast than
the one who abuses the obligations of guest or of host (Paris,
Polyphemus, the suitors). The rules hold good even today throughout
Greece. So much of Homer is dependent upon the Greek experience
that whatever universality arises from the original *Odyssey* seems a
direct outgrowth of that experience. But Kazantzakis, no less steeped
in the culture and values of Greece—perhaps because the lesson of
Crete gave him no choice—is less limited to insular Greece for his
themes. Moreover, there is an almost picaresque quality to Homer's
great epic; surely there is pattern to the hero's wanderings, yet we may
suspect that certain landfalls at least are largely coincidental, more a
function of plot than of the development of theme. The movement of
Kazantzakis' hero, however—in myth and in symbol as well as in
spiritual development—is an artfully wrought progression that has
about it an air of inevitability, as if the long journey from Ithaca to the
Antarctic were one that all men, symbolically at least, must undertake.
Perhaps, finally, Kazantzakis in his much longer poem does nod somewhat more than Homer, but his narrative on the whole is wonderfully
sustained, as entertaining in general as anything in Homer, often
deeply moving when we hear it read aloud. *The Odyssey: A Modern
Sequel* is derived from Homer, to be sure, but it is not bound to or
intimidated by the original. Kazantzakis is not Homer's imitator but
his rival.

Certainly there is no work in modern times—not even *Ulysses* or *Finnegans Wake*—that more effectively dramatizes the intellectual and spiritual forces that have shaped our era or that gives us a better sense of what we are and what we might yet become. For Kazantzakis' Odysseus is very different from Homer's—different as well from the heroes of Joyce, Dante, Tennyson, and others who have used him as symbol of enduring contemporary man. It is not simply that the literary background to this latest Odysseus is denser than in any of his predecessors, or even that the philosophical overtones emanating from him are more profound and compelling. The difference has to do with the nature of myth: this Odysseus, unlike the others, is both self-conscious subject and creator of myths, as well as, in the end, the destroyer of outmoded mythologies, even of those in which he himself has a part, especially of those in which he is protagonist.

Early in his travels, Odysseus is willing still to play at becoming god. It is a few days out from Ithaca, and his ship has put in to land in search of food and water. There, alongside a stream, "pushing a curly bull-calf in the stream to cool it," a young maiden appears before him.

> "A god has chanced to find me by this stream," she thought;
> "I bend and bow low to his grace, his will be done."
> The swift mind-reader felt the maiden's fear and joy:
> "Yes, you've divined it, lovely lass, I'm a sea-god
> who saw you far off from the waves and leapt ashore
> so that the thighs of god and man might meet in love."

In return, he offers her immortality.

> ". . . in nine months' time, I swear,
> I'll lie upon your lap once more and touch your lips;
> an infant god shall suck your breasts, your house shall shine."

This is pure opportunism, of course, hucksterism almost; yet in this anthropomorphic world, a world so ripe with fertility that any natural object—swan, bull, or falling leaf—may be the source of new life, somehow it works: as the girl follows him back to the ship, "flowers sprang up from sterile sands wherever she passed" (III, 483–547).

By the end of his travels, however, Odysseus is less willing to play at the god-making game, for the gods, he has come to realize, " 'are like countless birds that pass above our heads / and the mind soon confuses their harsh cries and wings' " (XXI, 461–62). Becoming a god is no substitute for being a man. On the south African coast, he learns

of a band of exiled Cretans and the icon of the "great god" (XXI, 445)
that they carry with them, a god whose worship has spread like human
fire among the African tribesmen.

> "... that Cretan demon of the sea
> with all his visible attributes and secret name:
> A sea-cap like an upright prow, a flaming beard,
> a curved bow in his huge hands as he stoops to kneel;
> some in their prayers call him 'Savior,' and some 'Slayer,'
> but in their secret hymns the priests cry out 'Odysseus!' "
> The archer frowned and bit his tongue, that from his lips
> his savage mocking laughter might not burst in peals,
> ..................................
> "I've been reduced to a god and walk the earth like myth!"
>                     (XXI, 467–511)

The man who misuses myth in order to play at divinity is like the
artist who believes in his own false creations. Orpheus the piper,
"wine-dreg of God" (V,424), misleads the Cretan king with his song in
order to keep the rebellion alive; his art is deceptive but useful in the
overall scheme.[4] Later, however, he himself is misled by the rhythms
of his voice, by the miracles that he appears to have called forth, by
the tale he has concocted of a new, healing god; thinking to become
god himself, he forsakes the friends who need him and thus loses his
vale as both artist and man. But no such fate can befall Odysseus, the
artist and mythmaker.

---

[4] VII, 1128. The episode described below is in XIII, 510-700. An earlier scene
on Crete dramatizes the illusory and potentially misleading quality of art. Back from
the charade in the Diktean cave, Idomeneus has ordered a goldsmith to immortalize
the event:

> "God stood on high and I stood straight on earth before him,
> the great sun hung low to my right, the full moon left,
> so that their double beams met in my dazzled eyes.
> God spread his hands and gave into my trust the firm
> round disk of earth with all its souls and mighty laws.
> I did not move, and held the whole world in my palms;
> God questioned, and I stared straight in his eyes and answered.
> I questioned too, and he replied like a true friend.
> Gather your wits, O goldsmith, teach your crafty hands
> how to immortalize this meeting in pure gold.
> Make infinite what lasted but a lightning flash on earth!"
>                                         (V, 1202-12)

The poet's Prologue to the Sun invokes man as artist controlling his own destiny;[5] the final words of Odysseus enjoin us all to follow the difficult path of the man who would be free of the prisons of life and of death alike; the Epilogue, spoken this time by the Sun, mourns the loss of the free-spirited man, commemorates his going:

> Then the earth vanished, the sea dimmed, all flesh dissolved,
> the body turned to fragile spirit and spirit to air,
> till the air moved and sighed as in the hollow hush
> was heard the ultimate and despairing cry of Earth,
> the sun's lament, but with no throat or mouth or voice:
> "Mother, enjoy the food you've cooked, the wine you hold,
> Mother, if you've a rose-bed, rest your weary bones,
> Mother, I don't want wine to drink or bread to eat—
> today I've seen my loved one vanish like a dwindling thought."
>                              (14–22)

Whether he dissolves into mist like Odysseus or remains to deal with the affairs of earth, man as artist can create his own mythology, can control the progress of his life and the life of mankind. Odysseus impels us to be the masters of our own myths, to make of our lives a work of art that is worthy of belief. This is the central theme of *The Odyssey: A Modern Sequel* and indeed of all Kazantzakis' life and art .

---

[5] Prologue, 17-22:
Great Sun, who pass on high yet watch all things below,
I see the sun-drenched cap of the great castle-wrecker:
let's kick and scuff it round to see where it will take us!
Learn, lads, that Time has cycles and that Fate has wheels
and that the mind of man sits high and twirls them round;
come quick, let's spin the world about and send it tumbling!

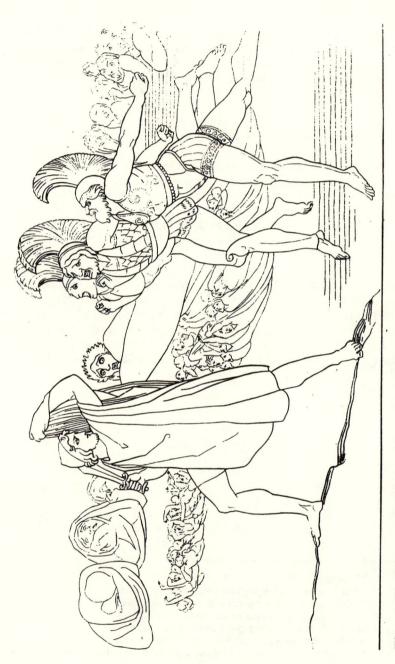

Figure 17. Odysseus in Hades. Flaxman (*Odyssey* series).

# Seferis' Myth of Return and Hellenism's Suspended Homecoming

*Artemis Leontis*

Noon at the archaeological museum. They unearth now—some in crates, some bare to the flesh in the earth—the statues. In one of the big old galleries, familiar from our student years, with the dull façade that somewhat resembled the dreary public library, the workmen excavate with shovels and pickaxes. If you didn't look at the roof, the floor, the windows, and the walls with inscriptions in gold, this could be any excavation <site> (*topos*). Statues, still sunken in the earth, appeared naked from the waist up, planted at random.—It was a chorus of the resurrected, a second coming of bodies that gave you a crazy joy.—Emotion from this sudden familiarity. The bronze Zeus, or Poseidon, lying on a crate like an ordinary tired laborer. I touched him on the chest, where the arm joins the shoulder, on the belly, on his hair. It seemed that I touched my own body.—Crazy <from the *topos*>. Every day carried away more and more by this drunkenness. The sea, the mountains that dance motionless. I found them the same in these rippled chitons: water turned into marble around the chests and the sides of headless fragments. (Seferis, *A Poet's Journal* 28–29, with additions to Anagnostopoulos' translation that reflect a closer translation put in angular brackets.)

This diary entry from the published notebooks of George Seferis, dated Tuesday, 4 June 1946, evokes an emotional moment of cultural return, a "second coming" of Hellenic civilization. Seferis describes the "excavation site" of the Archaeological Museum in Athens, where statues placed in storage at the beginning of World War II for protection from the invading and later occupying German forces are resurrected from their vaults beneath the floors. The "resurrection of bodies," as Seferis refers to the event, becomes a symbol of the poet's return to the light of the Greek landscape as well as a figure for the nation' recovery after World War II.

Yet reconstructive efforts in Greece at this time were set back by a ruthless Civil War encouraged, if not provoked, by leaders in England and the United States who wished to counter possible infiltration into the western bloc by the other emergent super power, the Soviet Union. This is the beginning of the Cold War, and its first theater of operation is Greece. Seferis does not name the historical moment with any precision. Instead, his emphasis on bodies and intense emotions serves to neutralize, or even to repress, the fact that Greece is in the midst of Civil War. Indeed, his powerful juxtaposition of ancient statues, resurrected bodies, and "crazy" feelings deriving from the land bypasses the historical present by crossing through the excavation site of classical Hellas and into a life-bearing, emotion-begetting Greek landscape.

While facing what was for him the unmentionable disarray of the Greek Civil War (and, not much later, Greece's rapid modernization in the Cold War "Reconstruction"), Seferis also began claiming an ever-*deepening*[1] place of origin for Neohellenism.[2] He related his work more explicitly to Greek antiquity and "the literary tradition whose origin is universally attributed to Homer" (Argyros 315). The formal correlative to this decentered *topos* was the familiar literary quotation divested of its material and historical context and identified

---

[1] For Andréas Karandónis, a contemporary Greek critic, "Seferis grows out of the deepest layers of our linguistic existence . . . Seferis' role is to keep clear a road to the deepest depth–and not to the scattered literary successes that remain on the surface of our language's truth" (*Introduction to Contemporary Poetry* 164-65).

[2] The celebrated German critic, E.R. Curtius, too, responded to cultural transformations in the years during and after World War II by turning his attention away from the broad "synchronic" plane of contemporary European literatures to the historical line of classical and medieval Latin texts. See especially his *Essays on European Literature* and *European Literature and the Latin Middle Ages*, where Curtius desribes himself carving a path "deeper and deeper into my chosen field of study; . . . [and], in the end, a new line of continuity in the history of European culture . . . becoming discernible" (502).

with the fragmented spirit, body, and reality of Neohellenism. To this end, he developed the modernist technique of settling disestablished quotations from classical sources into the newly claimed autotelic center of culture, the literary text. Unassimilated quotations connected by meaningful ellipses would signal the hidden circumstances of their distant cultural homeland, the deep structure of Hellenism that continued to shape everyday existence.[3]

Seferis used this technique of the unassimilated quotation with great success in *Thrush*, a poem where he systematically transposed characters and fragments from ancient sources into a modern setting and gave full form to the idea of a *nostos*.[4] Here the modernizing force of appropriation is used to translate "poetry's source"[5] into the confused literary horizon of an elliptical modernist work. The disembodied narrative voice of the Homeric epic is adapted to new purposes and given a new position in the contemporary cultural order.

From its opening lines, *Thrush* faces the problem of blocked access to a sacred center of culture. The Odyssean poetic persona charts the inhospitable forces of modernity in the first section of the poem, "The House by the Sea"; here he contemplates the fragile qualities of home under the conditions of "war, destruction, migration" (I.2) that break down more permanent walls of refuge. In the poem's second section, "Sensual Elpenor," Odysseus overhears the monologue of a mediocre man and records the difficulties of living in the undifferentiated spatial continuum of modernity. As he draws near to "The Shipwreck of Thrush," the third section of the poem, he draws a circle around a calming and stabilizing center surrounded by a throng of chaotic voices. The question looming in the poem's horizon is this: what might home be, and how might one reach it, now that "the world has become an endless hotel" (I.21)?

---

[3] James Longenbach in his *Modernist Poetics of History* provides necessary background for understanding Pound' and Eliot's related notions of history, which appear in their poetic techniques of incorporating "levels" of tradition.

[4] Several critics have discussed Seferis' incorporation of ancient sources, particularly Homer. On *Thrush*, see Mark Davis, "Seferis' *Thrush*"; Dimítris Maronítis, "The Nekuia of *Thrush*"; Dimítris Nikolareízis, "The Presence of Homer in Neohellenic Poetry"; George Thaniel, "George Seferis' *Thrush and the Poetry of Ezra Pound,*" "*George Seferis' Thrush* and T.S. Eliot' *Four Quartets*," and "George Seferis' *Thrush*: A Modern Descent"; Vayenás, *The Genealogy of* Thrush; and Anthony Zahareas, "George Seferis: Myth and History." For an insightful discussion of Seferis as a reader of Homer for whom Ithaca "sums[s] up...the disorder" of present circumstances, see Ruth Padel, "Homer's Reader" 107-21.

[5] The term is from Dionysius of Halicarnassus, *On the Arrangement of Words*, 23.

The horizon of the poem is drawn on two levels, one representational and the other intertextual, both pointing in the direction of an elusive "σπίτι" ("house" or "home")[6] for a contemporary Odysseus. First there is the inhospitable "House by the Sea" on the island of Poros, which offers a window onto contemporary Hellenic reality: its "empty rooms with an iron-framed bed and nothing of my own" (I.25–27) give the representational vantage point of displacement. From this window, the modern Odysseus contemplates the shipwreck "Thrush" that went down sometime in World War II and remained unsalvaged throughout the Greek Civil War.

From here the transient narrative persona, with no stable, responsive center of refuge from the surrounding chaos, reflects on the qualities of lost homes: "The houses I had they took away" (I.1). Houses are endowed with racial properties (*filí*, "race") (I.11), their own age, and feelings reflecting the character of their occupants or circumstances of their abandonment. Under modern conditions, "houses easily become obstinate" and insensitive to habitation "when you empty them" (I.40).

The trait of unresponsiveness is typical of the human condition in modernity. As people lose ground in war, they begin the endless process of exile and migration. They experience a prolonged loss of distinct place and lose their ability to respond to others. Conversations become common property. One "Elpenor" in the poem is a typical case of such a human shipwreck. He is obsessed by voices and images from the past, haunted by "the fragrance of the absence of a youthful form" (II.46).

Because the horizon of the poem is intertextual as well as representational, *Thrush* also underscores the theme of lost homecoming through the citation of older works. By way of indirect references to Circe and Odysseus, direct allusions to Elpenor, and the anticipated appearance of Teiresias (whose presence is eclipsed by Socrates and Oedipus), the poem recalls two well-known episodes from Odysseus' adventures: the encounter with Circe and the journey to "the house of Hades," the best-known *nekuia* in western literature. The "House by the Sea," a sign of the endless inhospitality of the modern "hotel," is identified with the houses of both Circe and Hades (both of which

---

6 Modern Greek does not distinguish between house and home; both are designated by "σπίτι." "Οἶκος", a Homeric word for dwelling-place, also remains in use. Its sense is closer to "house" (specifically the building structure), since it is marked with the greater formality of a word systematically kept in circulation by *katharévusa* (the purist language that sought to replace vernacular words with ancient ones).

are by the sea, as Homer informs us). The poem then links itself intertextually to events that take place between these two limits of Odysseus' adventures and adopts the theme of Odysseus' suspended *nostos* ("homecoming").

The literary connection with the *Odyssey* is vaguely drawn in the first section in the person of the narrator, who leans subtly on the character of Odysseus, the literary figure of instability and *Wanderlust*:

> Let us *imagine* then that the one who says "I" in *Thrush* is an Odysseus. Perhaps this even has the advantage of allowing us to contemplate that people of some instability, of adventures and war . . . always move between the same monsters and the same desires. In this way we hold onto the symbols and names which the myth handed over to us—so long as we recognize that the typical characters have been transformed in accordance with the passage of time and the changing conditions of our world. (Seferis, "Stage Directions for *Thrush*" 31–32).

Now a nameless resident of modernity's endless hotel, the modern Odysseus peers out of his temporary shelter while the contemporary world leaks in. Rather than travel to exotic ports, he waits for others to visit him, hoping that someone might provide the key for return to the lost homeland. To put it another way, Odysseus is the modern topographer who studies the present disarray and attempts to recover the order of another world.

References to the *Odyssey* become more obvious with the appearance of "Sensual Elpenor" in the second section. A brief narration of Elpenor's fate in the *Odyssey* might help establish the connections between the two poems. Elpenor appears in Odysseus' Phaeacean tales (Books 7–12), which include the hero's journey to the underworld and his conversations with the dead. As Odysseus describes preparations for the journey from Circe's halls to Hades, he recalls the circumstances of Elpenor's accidental death. "There was one Elpenor, the youngest of all, not exceedingly valiant in war or well-balanced in his mental powers" (10.552–553). Elpenor gets drunk at Circe's, climbs onto her roof for fresh air, and falls asleep. In the morning rush of preparation for Odysseus' journey to Hades, Elpenor awakens, forgets where he is, springs up suddenly, and "tumble[s] headlong from the roof; so he broke his neck and his spirit went down to Hades" (10.559–560). Odysseus takes no notice of the loss until he encounters a bitter Elpenor at the gates of Hades. Elpenor tells his story and demands a proper burial.

In the first section of *Thrush*, "Odysseus" anticipates the visit of the dead man dressed "in black and white clothes with colorful jewels, / . . . coming to say good-bye" (I.27–29, 32). The flashback in the second part of the poem is devoted almost in its entirety to recording this man's one-sided conversation, overheard by the narrator on the eve of the man's death. Here the unfortunate victim is openly identified with the Homeric Elpenor: "He had the bearing of Elpenor just before his fall and demolition, though he wasn't drunk" (II.4–5).

A mortal Circe-like figure, "μια γυναίκα ελικοβλέφαρη βαθύζωνη" ("a deep-girded, quick-glancing woman") (I.33) is Elpenor's unsympathetic interlocutor. "Returning from southerly ports / Smyrna, Rhodes, Syracuse, Alexandria / cities closed like hot shutters" (I.34–36), she has become versed in the intoxicating possibilities of "fragrances of golden fruit and herbs" (I.37) and immune to the sufferings of men (I.38–39). Seferis' unnamed temptress arouses in Elpenor inexpressible desire.[7]

Elpenor's monologue is an oblique formulation of this desire. Its message rides on the metaphor of fragmented statues becoming lifelike and bending in the light. Reverting to the netherworld of myth, Elpenor seems to lose himself in the thought that fragments of the past might possess a haunting life of their own, more real than the fleeting present. He privileges broken stones with a permanence that the aging body cannot possess. His desire for Circe draws him into the world of the non-rational.

If the spirit of the Homeric Elpenor is unable to enter the house of Hades after his demise at Circe's because his corpse remains unburied,[8] here the modern Elpenor seems to dwell on the threshold between dead and living because he refuses to come to terms with the conditions of modernity that codify the past as ruin. He makes no clear distinction between past and present. For this reason, he can only turn a deaf ear to Circe's persistent reminder that today "The statues are in the museum" (II.26 and 54).

---

[7] In his critical commentary, "Stage Directions for *Thrush*," Seferis claims that Elpenor metonymically represents all the "mindless and satiated" companions of Odysseus (38); he is furthermore a foil to true heroes, typical of the worst "bearers of destruction" (40).

[8] Elpenor's passage out of the twilight zone is contingent on his receiving a proper burial, something he motivates by threats: "Do not leave me behind unwept and unburied when you go back there, / lest I bring upon you the wrath of some god" (*Odyssey* 11.72-73).

The intertextual status of Elpenor reflects his temporal and spatial atopia: the transposed quotation evokes his homesickness. When Elpenor makes his final appearance in the poem's third section, *Thrush* refers directly to the Homeric passage where the ghost of Elpenor offers to Odysseus his life—blood, the oar. Here Seferis' appropriation of Homer becomes explicit. We recall Odysseus' encounter with Elpenor at the entrance to the underworld (*Odyssey* 11.51–54). Elpenor approaches his leader and requests that his corpse be burned with his armor, a burial mound heaped on the grey sea's shore, and his oar with which he rowed alongside his companions planted in the mound of sand (11.77–78). The oar is to be a "σῆμα" ("gravestone/sign") marking a completed life "εξσσομένοισι πύθεσθαι" ("so that future generations may learn of me") (11.76). This passage resonates in *Thrush* when Elpenor offers the narrator "the wood that cooled my forehead" as a sign of his toil during "the hours when midday burned my veins." Like Elpenor's oar, this "wood" (*xílo*) must find its *telos* in the hands of others: "σε ξένα χέρια θέλει ανθίσει Πάρ' το, σού το χαρίζω" ("it will blossom in someone else's hands. Take it, it's my gift to you") (III.1–3). Its destiny, however, is altered, since "the wood" is now to blossom in living hands rather than to mark a resting place for the dead.

The extensive allusion to Elpenor prepares the scene for new literary encounters that first reach into the heart of the *Odyssey*, then suddenly swerve in the direction of other texts. Elpenor receives no recognition or thanks for his gift of "the wood" because the narrator's attention is already drawn elsewhere along the horizon of the *Odyssey*:

> Other voices slowly followed
> one by one; whispers thin and thirsty
> coming out of the sun's dark side;
> you would say they were looking to drink a drop of blood;
> familiar voices, but I couldn't distinguish them.
> > (*Thrush* III.12–15).

Clearly this passage alludes to the description of the ghastly throng that encircles Odysseus at the house of Hades: "there gathered spirits of the dead out of Erebus . . . The throng moved toward the bloody pit from every side / with a deafening shout; and pale fear seized me" (*Odyssey* 11.36–37, 42–43).

As *Thrush* reaches this moment of near convergence with the *Odyssey*, it becomes possible to assess the intertextual relationship of the modern to the ancient poem. Poetic recollection has effaced the distinctive outlines of epic figures and whatever narrative detail might be incongruous with the modern setting. At the same time, it develops features that are especially suited to the tenor of times. The once insignificant character of Elpenor takes center stage. Recognizable Homeric elements—the dark scenery of Erebus ("το σκοτεινό" in *Thrush*), the throng thirsting for blood—are transported almost wholesale into the modern poem, while the narrator's reaction remains muted—appropriately so, perhaps, for the poem's unheroic setting.

With the approach of the thirsty throng, *Thrush* takes a step toward what is arguably the center of the *Odyssey*, the exchange between the hero and Teiresias that is the goal of Odysseus' underworld journey "to the halls of Hades and dreaded Persephone" (10.491). As Circe explains: "you will consult the spirit of the Theban Teiresias / the blind seer whose mental powers are still intact; / for Persephone provided him with a mind even after death / so that he alone has understanding (νόμον), while others flit about like shadows" (10.492–495).

In the underworld, Odysseus discovers that none of the spirits—not even his mother—is capable of recognizing him before drinking his offering of dark blood. The exception is Teiresias who "recognized me and addressed me: Son of Laertes, sprung from Zeus, Odysseus of many devices!" (11.91–92). Teiresias drinks from the blood and forthwith pronounces the crucial word *nostos* (11.100), which he alone can dispatch. Teiresias thus becomes the guide for Odysseus' safe return to the light of home.

Teiresias' oracular procedure is to place "ἐπὶ φρέσι" ("in the mind") of Odysseus the proper σῆμα ("sign"), which should not escape the hero's notice ("οὐ λανθάνειν") (11.126). He points to Poseidon as the god who is detaining Odysseus (11.101–103). He entreats Odysseus to curb the appetite of his companions when he arrives at Thrinacia and finds Helios' fatted flocks grazing there (11.104–114). He describes a woeful state of affairs in Ithaca. He predicts Odysseus' violent revenge against Penelope's voracious suitors. Finally, he describes the subsequent inland journey Odysseus must make and the unmistakable sign (σῆμα . . . μάλ᾽ ἀριφραδές"), the misnamed oar, that will indicate his wanderings are over.

We have already seen that Teiresias retains the power of "νόος" even after his passage into Hades. The gift of interpreting *terata* (another word for "signs") is encoded into his identity as one "having to do with signs" (*teres-ias*).[9] This makes Teiresias the appropriate guide for Odysseus, whose special power is his ability to recognize the "νόος" ("mind," "way of thinking") of others by the power of his own mind, and to act accordingly (cf. 1.3). Teiresias is especially capable of offering Odysseus insight into significant matters, such as the means by which he may gain his *nostos*, the elusive goal of his wanderings (see *Odyssey* 11.100).

Furthermore, *nostos* shares an etymological root with *noos*.[10] As Teiresias delivers the *sema* ("sign") of *nostos* ("homecoming"), Odysseus applies his *noos* ("mind") to decode this sign and thus effect his *nostos*. In "*Sema* and *Noesis*," Nagy describes the process of encoding and decoding *nostos* thus:

> the seer Teiresias is giving a *sema* to Odysseus, and the follow up expression "and it will not escape your mind" raises the expectation that getting the sign is linked with its recognition. The word *noos* is indeed overtly linked with the concept of *sema* here, but the attention is as much on the *encoding* and on the *decoding* of the sign. The narrative stresses that Teiresias, who is giving the *sema* to Odysseus, is exceptional among the *psykhai* in Hades in that his cognitive faculties—or *phrenes*, are intact (10.493): it is because Persephone had given him *noos* (10.494). This *sema*, then, is implicitly encoded by the *noos* of Teiresias—and presumably must be decoded by the *noos* of Odysseus.(44)

Another important modernist poem bears witness to the irretrievable social and cultural context of the exchange of signs between the "original" soothsayer and myth—maker. I refer to Ezra Pound's first *Canto*, which Seferis translated into Greek in 1939.[11] This poem

---

9 Emile Boisacq, Pierre Chantraine, and Hjalmar Frisk all agree that "Teresias" ("Teiresias," in epic poetry, with the first syllable augmented for metrical reasons) is derived from the noun *teras*, meaning "a significant sign or token." Boisacq includes the following interesting gloss concerning the Teresias who appears in Homer: "(Hom), nom parlant d'un devin qui '*interprete les signes*' " (my emphasis).

10 On the etymology of *noos* see D. Frame, *The Myth of Return in Early Greek Epic* 1-5. Frame offers formal evidence that *noos* and *nostos* derive from the same Indo-European root-verb, *nes-, which signifies a "return to light and life." See also his "The Origins of the Greek NOYS."

11 Seferis' translations of Canto I, XIII, and XXX appeared in the journal *Ta Néa Grámmata* (April-June 1939) and are reprinted in his volume of translations,

offers an archaizing English rendition of a Latin version of *Odyssey* 11,
translated by the obscure Andreas Divus in 1538 (Kearns 18). It faithfully recounts Odysseus' descent "to the place / Aforesaid by Circe"
(17–18), his meeting with Elpenor, "pitiful spirit" (26), and his initial
neglect of Anticlea "whom I beat off" (58). When the poem reaches
the interview between the peregrinating hero and "Tiresias Theban,"
however, it takes a significant turn away from its textual source,
though not from Teiresias. The soothsayer appears, gives his sign of
recognition and then asks, "A second time? why? man of ill star, /
facing the sunless dead and this joyless region?" (60–61). Here he
addresses not the hero, who reportedly traveled to Hades in mythic
times, but the 20th-century literary persona who aims at reproducing
this event.

After drinking the blood, "Tiresias Theban" divines a familiar
answer, but in the third person: "Odysseus / Shalt return through
spiteful Neptune, over dark seas, / Lose all companions" (65–67).
With the shift in address, the context of the prophecy also shifts. No
longer does Teiresias address the hero of the Odyssey; instead he
reports his prediction of Odysseus' pitiful homecoming to the suddenly anonynmous narrator, who is himself given no such reassuring
prophecy of return. There follows a series of interruptions, so that the
message of a prospective homecoming reaches the reader only
through a mass of "cultural layering,"[12] that is to say, through
numerous voices that have edited, revised, translated, interpreted, or
in some way appropriated Homer's *Odyssey*. Pound's homesick
modern persona has such great difficulty hearing Teiresias' prophecy
that he immediately registers a complaint to the noisy translator: "Lie
quiet Divus. I mean, that is Andreas Divus / In officina Wecheli,
1538, out of Homer" (68–69). Other voices interject from the Babel-
like configuration.[13] These, too, relay the message that many literary

---

"*Copyings.*" See Thaniel, "George Seferis' *Thrush* and the Poetry of Ezra Pound."

[12] G. Kearns documents these sources and adds: "Once we are aware of all
the voices in the *Canto*–Homer, Virgil, Divus, the Cretan, the Anglo Saxon bard,
Pound–we see more clearly in the structure of the *Canto* one of Pound's essential
methods, 'cultural overlaying' (21). Seferis calls this technique a "mosaic" of words
(*Copyings* 151).

[13] Lines 71-76 are rich in "cultural layering." They refer first to, "The
Cretan," Georgius Dartone, who called himself Cretensis and translated *Homeric
Hymns* into Latin. Aphrodite is then described in both Latin and Greek as *veneranda*
("worthy of worship;) in her *orichalki* ("bronze") form. The "golden bough" plucked
by Aeneas before his descent into Avernus–a descent which echoes the *nekuia* of
Odysseus–is that bough made familiar to an English-speaking audience by Sir James
George Frazer.

voyagers stand between moderns and ancients—so many, in fact, that the scene of pure origins remains hopelessly out of reach. Through the din of literary interjections, the modern poet makes his own voice heard by this seemingly nonsensical addendum, "So that" (76). This is his introduction to the 116 *Cantos* that follow. In an age when poets' too great consciousness of secondariness has blocked passage to the original centers of culture,[14] Pound attempts to project the fresh voice of modern pastiche.[15] He offers songs with deliberate anachronisms and simultaneous readings from Homer to Ovid, troubadour tales to Renaissance history, Chinese calligraphy to ideograms.

Seferis takes a very different approach from that of Pound in his appropriation of Homer.[16] He omits Teiresias' divinations entirely and dangles in their place a literary quotation from another preeminent classical text, Plato's *Apology*: "Κι ἄ με δικάσετε να πιῶ φαρμάκι, ευχαριστῶ· / το δίκιο σας θα' ναι το δίκιο μου· πού να πηγαίνω / γυρίζοντας σε ξένους τόπους, ένα στρογγυλό λιθάρι. / Το θάνατο τον προτιμῶ· / ποιός πάει για το καλύτερο ο θεός το ξέρει" ("And if you condemn me to drink poison, I thank you; your justice will be my justice; it is not for me to go wandering through foreign *topoi*, like a rolling stone. I prefer death; god knows who goes to the better lot") (III.20–25). These words recall the conclusion of the *Apology*, "ὁπότεροι δὲ ἡμῶν ἔρχονται ἐπὶ ἄμεινον πρᾶγμα, ἄδηλον παντὶ πλὴν τῷ θεῷ" ("which of the two of us goes to a better lot is unknown to everyone except the god") (42a).

---

[14] This inconclusive finale may be supplemented by a programmatic statement made by Pound in 1928: "Quite simply: I want a new civilization. It must be *as good* as the best that has been. It can't possibly be the same, so why worry, novelty is enforced" (qtd. in Kearns 23).

[15] Logenbach argues that the full effect of literary quotation in Pound's work is something more than pastiche: it is an "imaginative reconstruction" (18) of the literary past. "Just as Odysseus gives life to ghosts, Pound gives his own life to a dead poet, translating Divus's translation of Homer into English and filtering the result through the ancient rhythms of 'The Seafarer.' . . . Pound's poem including history begins with an invocation of the dead, a séance that reveals how historical knowledge is acquired by infusing the ghosts of the past with the life of the present" (17-18).

[16] One might also consider Eliot's *The Waste Land*, another poem where Teiresias is the presiding consciousness. See especially part III, with Eliot's invaluable commentary on the persona of the poem. Logenbach observes that "Tiresias" (like Pound, Eliot exploys a non-Homeric spelling) "was to function not only as the 'most important personage in the poem' but as an observing consciousness who can penetrate the everyday world...to 'trace the cryptogram' of a higher reality–transforming that everyday reality into a visionary world of myth" (214). The voice of Tiresias "*seems* to be the voice of history itself, an expression of the 'entire past' woven into the texture of the present" (208).

*Thrush*'s turn from Homer to Plato comes at a crucial point, indicating a significant shift in textual strategies. Until this moment, Homeric figures and episodes appear as foils for a modern quest for home. They add literary depth by marking major continuities and ruptures between the archaic order—with its hierarchy of gods and heroes—and the contemporary world—with its overwhelming chaos. The unexpected quotation from another major text, however, complicates the intertextual horizon of *Thrush*, defers the Homeric *sema* ("sign") of *nostos*, and relocates the cultural center of the poem.

One may recall that the virtues attached to the figure of Socrates are *sophia* and *dike*. Contrary to the Homeric value of a quick *noos*, Socratic wisdom is acquired through an ironic profession of ignorance and fearless submission to the unknown. In the *Apology*, Socrates defends his reputation as *sophotatos* ("the wisest of men") by admitting his ignorance, specifically on the subject of death: "To fear death, gentlemen, is nothing else than to think one is wise when one is not; for it is thinking one knows what one does not. No one knows whether death is not the greatest of all blessings to man, yet they fear it as if they know that it is the greatest form of evil" (*Apology* 29a).

When Socrates chooses death as his punishment, he offers "τοῦ θείου σημείου" ("the divine *semeion* [sign]") (40b) as proof that he may meet with a better fate than his accusers: "for the customary *semeion* would surely have opposed me, if I had not been going to meet with something good" (40c). As he submits to Athenian law, Socrates pronounces his final words, through which he derives the ultimate argumentative advantage by claiming that his accusers are no less ignorant than he is about the quality of their future: "ἐμοὶ μὲν ἀποθανουμένῳ, ὑμῖν δὲ βιωσομένοις· ὁπότεροι δὲ ἡμῶν ἔρχονται ἐπὶ ἄμεινον πρᾶγμα, ἄδηλον παντὶ πλὴν τῷ θεῷ" ("I am about to die, while you will continue to live; which of the two of us goes to a better lot is not evident to anyone except the god") (42a).

These are the passages that *Thrush* incorporates into its scene of descent. The modern poem gives prominence not only to Socrates' calm submission to fate ("And if you condemn me to drink poison, I thank you"), his compliance with the ruling system of justice ("your justice will be my justice"), and loyalty to place ("It is not for me to go wandering through foreign *topoi*, like a rolling stone"), but also to his plea of ignorance and deferral to "god" on the subject of unknown destinations ("I prefer death; god knows who goes to the better lot").

One should not overlook the fact, too, that Socrates' modern declaration of agnosticism is heard "from the sun's other side, το σκοτεινό" (*Thrush* III.14). Το σκοτεινό means literally "that which is dark." In Seferis' poetic corpus, this word becomes a figure for the meaningful "void behind the mask"[17] of perceptible existence. It is also set in plain analogy to the *Apology*'s "ἄδηλον" (that which is "not evident," "invisible," "obscure," "inscrutable"), where human language and perception reach a productive stopping point. Even more resonant is the *Republic*'s "dark cave" (Book VII), the realm of illusion where people are imprisoned with their backs to the sunlit exit. One is gradually set free from the bonds of illusion as one comes to recognize the predicament of the senses' bondage and learn first to rely on improved physical perception, then to use the processes of reason, and finally to develop insight into the world of the absolute.

The image of a "dark" or blind side of human existence functions in *Thrush* as a placard for the deeper understanding of things hidden from plain human perception. This understanding can only be claimed by a Socratic turn, that is to say, through a declaration of ignorance about origins and destinations. Indeed, it is a Socratic declaration of ignorance that provides the key for a return to "the light" in *Thrush* rather than Teiresias' *sema* ("sign") of *noos* ("recognition") and *epos* that transform suffering into *mythos* ("story")—bringing closure to Odysseus' journey and instituting learning for others.

In his published supplementary essay, "Stage Directions for *Thrush*" (1950) Seferis offers this explanation of the shift from Teiresias to Socrates:

> I am trying now to understand why there was this replacement of Teiresias by Socrates in *Thrush*. My first answer is this: because I sensed that the *tónos* [tone] of the whole which I was trying to create was elsewhere; I didn't even consider the Theban one. Then—autobiographically speaking—because the *Apology* is a text which especially influenced me in my life; perhaps because my generation grew up and lived in a period of injustice. Third, because I have a very organic intuition which identifies humanity with the Hellenic *physis*. (54)

---

[17] The phrase, "κάτω ἀπ᾽ τὴν προσωπίδα" (void behind the mask") occurs in "The King of Asine," which names the generative void, "ἕνα σημείο σκοτεινό" ("a dark point/sign," line 29). In his deconstructive reading of the poem, Dionisis Kapsális takes this "dark sign" as evidence both of "mythopoeia which demythologizes itself," and "the process of demythologizing which in turn becomes blind" ("Critique of Hellenic Modernism" 45).

The first point that Seferis makes is predictable enough. He reveals that aesthetic criteria concerning the *"tónos* of the whole" bear final weight in the poet's decision to incorporate certain sources and discard others. Seferis' image of the poetic work harmoniously reorganizing literary particles drawn from a synchronically available tradition is indebted to T.S. Eliot's idea of the poetic work as the harmonization of historical layers, in which older layers resonate with the more recent "particles," together forming a new whole.[18] This resonance is what Seferis calls the *tónos* of the poem. Seferis' second point about the substitution of Socrates for Teiresias derives from personal experience. Here he offers the *Apology* as the appropriate antidote to contemporary injustices that remain unnamed (as it is Seferis' custom to avoid specific references to the sordid details of Greek politics).

With his third statement of justification, however, Seferis seems to move in another direction: "I have a very organic intuition which identifies humanity with the Hellenic nature (*physis*)." The connection between "humanity" and Socrates is not explained here, though it may be drawn out of Seferis' earlier claim: "In *Thrush*, the interpreter of homecoming is not Teiresias, but someone whom I feel to be more human than Teiresias: the one who is just" ("Stage Directions for *Thrush*" 52). Then, without warning, Seferis introduces the subject of "the Hellenic *physis*," with its connotations of both geographical and racial determinism. How can one justify this appeal to "the Hellenic *physis*" as a final factor deciding which trait (humanity, say, as opposed to the power to divine the future) should be admitted as the "sign" at the crux of the poem? Even references to "harmony" and "tone"—aesthetic criteria that subject the "particle" to the demands of the "whole"—do not adequately anticipate the requirements of landscape (the nature of the land) and blood (the nature of the people). And what does one make of nature's linkage to specifically Hellenic determinants?

The poem exhibits similar ellipses. Leaping from the agnosticism of Socrates to the narrator's prophetic complaint about place, *Thrush* laments a modern condition in which the qualities of "Man" and "Sun" are not adequately appreciated: "Χώρες του ήλιου και δεν

---

[18] Seferis systematically discussed and translated Eliot's work into Greek. Seferis published his translation of *The Waste Land* in 1936, with a lengthy introduction. His "Introduction to T.S. Eliot" truly introduced the American poet to the Greek cultural scene. "C.P. Cavafy and T.S. Eliot in Parallel" (1941) became another standard work on Eliot. On Seferis' and Eliot's parallel strategies of self-promotion, see Vangélis Calotychos, "The Art of Making Claques."

μπορείτε ν' αντικρίσετε τον ήλιο. Χώρες του ανθρώπου και δεν μπορείτε νάντικρίσετε τον άνθρωπο" ("Lands of the sun, and yet you cannot face the sun. Lands of Man, and yet you cannot face Man") (*Thrush* III.25–26). The two terms, Man and Sun, are bound together under the rubric of "Το Φως" ("The Light," the subtitle of the poem's closing section), which is only experienced properly when one has progressed toward the end of life: "As the years pass / the critics who condemn you multiply; / as the years pass and you converse with fewer voices / you observe the sun with different eyes" (III.27–30).

Passage beyond a devalued modern existence to a real "homecoming," a "return to light and life" (the etymological meaning of *nostos*, as indicated earlier) is, as I have suggested, the *telos* of the poem. The return to light takes the narrator through eminent literary sources to the physical landscape of Hellenism radiating with light. Both culture and nature emanate from this "Light" of Hellenism, as Seferis explains in the essay on *Thrush*. Homeric epics, the tragedies of Aeschylus, the philosophy of Anaximander and Heraclitus all constitute sophisticated, natural reactions to the element of light found in the Hellenic *topío* ("landscape").

If Seferis unequivocally claims to experience "the condition of nonexistence, the abolition of the self . . . when facing the grandeur of certain foreign *topía* [landscapes]" ("Stage Directions for *Thrush*" 54), he also senses a "humanizing function" in "the principally Hellenic natural *topía*" (55) that are filled with light. This light finally merges with the living force that runs through not only "the blood of man," but also the cultural tradition of Hellenism, from Homer to the present: "It's so simple: Imagine that the light of day and the blood of Man are the same thing? *How* deeply can one actually experience this? . . . If the humanizing function which I referred to gave birth to the *Odyssey*, *how* far can we actually *see* the *Odyssey* ?" (55–56).

The conflation of culture and nature is a fundamental feature of *Thrush*. The *topos* of cultural return becomes identical with the physical *topos* of Hellas. This is the major ellipsis that must be elaborated if we are to understand the rhetorical operations of *nostos* in Seferis' work. First, literary quotation from ancient sources lays a "natural" foundation for the site of Hellenism. Next, not only does this modernist technique render the distant past more hospitable to latecomers who suffer from the burden of their ancestors' priority;[19] it also marks

---

[19] I refer to Walter Jackson Bate's influential book *The Burden of the Past and the English Poet*, which argues that tradition only became a burden when a combination of specific cultural conditions occurred. An increase in the means of perserv-

the boundaries of home for a fragmented and scattered tradition. Finally, if the poem defines the condition of modernity as the loss of home, it provides the literary sign of Socratic agnosticism as the key to homecoming. The modern individual must recognize the limits of cultural knowledge if he is to reach Hellenism's natural home, "the light" of the Greek landscape,[20] reflected in the literary tradition of Hellenism.

Like a character in his own poems, Seferis' focus on the light allows him to be blind to the the features of that contemporary landscape, which is typical of the modernist literary approach that chooses not to be "diagnostic"[21] about the effects either of war or of rapid modernization on the social, political, and geographical horizon. In his odyssey, Seferis colors "The light" of Hellenism's physical scenery with a spiritual hue. His reinvention of the sacred facilitates a relatively painless homecoming for Hellenism that bypasses obstacles created by current developments on the national and international front. This is his way of salvaging the post-War shipwreck of Neohellenism.

## Works Cited

Argyros, Alexander. "The Hollow King: A Heideggerian Approach to George Seferis's 'The King of Asine'. " *boundary 2* (Fall and Winter 1986–87): 305–321.

Bate, Walter Jackson. *The Burden of the Past and the English Poet.* Cambridge: Harvard U. Press, 1970.

Bloom, Harold. *The Anxiety of Influence.* Oxford: Oxford U. Press, 1975.

---

ing and distributing literature, which resulted in the expansion of the archive of works available at a given time to a poet, a deepening self-consciousness about the wealth and richness of this legacy, and an imperative that (new) poetry be original combined to create a sense that the possibilities of language were being exhausted and that the (Romantic and Modern) poet had to work against very difficult odds.

[20] Seferis identifies "the light" as the new home of Odysseus, "*his own* home, the home to which Odysseus wishes to return" ("Stage Directions for Thrush" 50).

[21] In "Beyond the Cave," Fredric Jameson criticizes the modernist literary (non-) reckoning with the "bondage" of contemporary ideology. He suggests that a "diagnostic" approach: "Our task—specialists that are in the reflections of things—is a more patient and modest, more *diagnostic* one. Yet even such a task as the analysis of literature and culture will come to nothing unless we keep the knowledge of our own historical situation vividly present to us: for we are least of all, in our position, entitled to the claim that we did not understand, that we though all those things were real, that we had no way of knowing we were living in a cave" (132, my emphasis).

Boisacq, Emile. *Dictionnaire Etymologique de la Langue Grecque.* Paris: Klincksieck, 1938.

Calotychos, Vangelis. "The Art of Making Claques: Politics of Tradition in the Critical Essays of T. S. Eliot and George Seferis." *Modernism in Greece? Essays on the Critical and Literary Margins of a Movement.* Ed. Mary N. Layoun. New York: Pella, 1990, 81–136.

Chantraine, Pierre. *Dictionnaire Etymologique de la Langue Grecque.* Paris: Klincksieck, 1977.

Curtius, Ernst Robert. *Essays on European Literature.* Trans. Michael Kowal. Princeton: Princeton U. Press, 1973.

___. *European Literature and the Latin Middle Ages* [1948]. Trans. Willard Trask. Princeton: Princeton U. Press, 1973.

Dállas, Yánnis. "A Feeling Beyond Cavafy, with *Thrush* as the Key" ("Μιά αίσθηση πέρα από τον Καβάφη. Με το κλειδή της Κίκλης"). Για τον Σεφέρη. Τιμητικό αφιέρωμα στα τριάντα χρόνια της Στροφής. Athens: Ermís, 1981, 292–303.

Davis, Mark. "Seferis' *Thrush*." *Neo-Hellenika* 2 (1975): 280–98.

Eliot, T.S. *The Sacred Wood: Essays on Poetry and Criticism.* London: Faber, 1920.

___. "Ulysses, Order, and Myth." *The Dial* 75 (1923): 480–83.

___. *The Waste Land and Other Poems.* New York: Harcourt, Brace, and World, 1962.

Frame, D. "The Origins of Greek *NOYS*." Ph.D. diss., Harvard University, 1971.

___. *The Myth of Return in Early Greek Epic.* New Haven: Yale U. Press, 1978.

Frisk, Hjalmar. *Griechisches Etymologisches Worterbuch.* Heidelberg: Carl Winter, 1961.

Jameson, Fredric. "Beyond the Cave. Demystifying the Ideology of Modernism" [1975]. *The Ideologies of Theory. Essays 1971–1986.* Volume 2: "Syntax of History." "Theory and History of Literature." Minneapolis: U. of Minnesota Press, 1988, 115–32.

Kapsális, Dionísis. "Critique of Greek Modernism, Part II: In the Shadow of Myth" ("Κριτική του ελληνικού μοντερνισμού, Μερος Β΄. Στη σκιά του μύθου"). Καθημερινός Πολίτης 26 (November 2, 1984): 44–46.

Karandónis, Andréas. *Introduction to Contemporary Poetry* (Εισαγωγή στη νεώτερη ποίηση. Athens: Galaxía, 1958.

Kearns, G. *Guide to Ezra Pound's Cantos.* New Brunswick: Rutgers U. Press, 1980.

Longenbach, James. *Modernist Poetics of History: Pound, Eliot, and the Sense of the Past*. Princeton: Princeton U. Press, 1987.

Maronítis, Dimítris N. "The *Nekuia* of *Thrush*" ("Η νέκυια της 'Κίκλης' "). Η ποίηση του Γιώργου Σεφέρη. Μελέτες και μαθήματα. Athens: Ermís, 1984. 15–28.

Nagy, Gregory. "*Sema* and *Noesis*: Some Illustrations." *Arethusa* 16 (Spring–Summer 1983): 35–55.

Nikolareízis, Dimítris. "The Presence of Homer in Modern Greek Poetry" ("Η παρουσία του Ομήρου στη νέα ελληνική ποίηση") [1947]. Δοκίμια Κριτικής. Athens: G. Féxis, 1962. 209–36.

Padel, Ruth. "Homer's Reader: A Reading of George Seferis." *Proceedings of the Cambridge Philological Society* n.s. 31 (1985): 74–132.

Seferis, George. *Copyings* (Αντιγραφές). Athens: 'Ikaros, 1965.

___. *Days* (Μέρες). Volume V (1 January 1945–19 April 1951). Athens. 'Ikaros, 1986.

___. "Ezra Pound. Three 'Cantos'" ("Ezra Pound. Triva 'Canto.'"). Τα Νέα Γράμματα (April–June 1939): 187–200.

___. *Poetry* (Ποιήματα). Athens: 'Ikaros, 1974.

___. *A Poet's Journal. Days of 1945–1951*. Trans. Athan Anagnostopoulos. Cambridge, Mass.: The Belknap Press of Harvard U. Press, 1974.

___. "Second Prologue to My Book, T.S. Eliot: The Wasteland and Other Poems" ("Δεύτερος πρόλογος· στο βιβλίο μου Θ.Σ. 'Ελιοτ· Η 'Ερημη Χώρα και άλλα ποιήματα") ([1949]. Δοκιμές Vol. II. Athens: 'Ikaros, 1981. 25–29.

___. "Stage Directions for *Thrush*" ("Μιά σκηνοθεσία για την Κίκλη") [1949]. Δοκιμές Vol. II. Athens: 'Ikaros, 1981. 30–56.

Segal, Charles. "Orpheus, Agamemnon, and the Anxiety of Influence. Mythic Intertexts in Seferis, *Mythistorema* 3." *Classical and Modern Literature* 9 (Summer 1989): 291–298.

Stone, James. "A Letter on *Thrush*." *Journal of the Hellenic Diaspora* 7 (1980): 5–26.

Thaniel, George. "George Seferis' *Thrush*: A Modern 'Descent'." *CRCL* 4 (1977): 89–102.

___. "George Seferis' *Thrush* and the Poetry of Ezra Pound." *Comparative Literary Studies* 11 (1974): 326–36.

___. "George Seferis' *Thrush* and T.S. Eliot's *Four Quartets*." *Neohelicon* 4 (1976): 261–82.

___. "The Moon, the Heron, and *The Thrush*. George Seferis, Douglas Lepan, and Greek Myth." *Classical and Modern Literature* 9:4 (Summer 1989): 315–25.

Vayenás, Násos. *Geneology of Thrush* (Η Γενεαλογία της Κίκλης).
    Athens, 1974.
Zahareas, Anthony N. "George Seferis:  Myth and History." *Books
    Abroad* 42:2 (Spring 1968): 190–98.

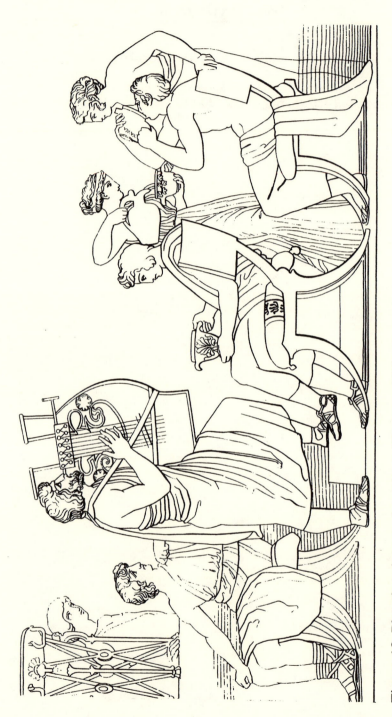

Figure 18. Phemios sings to the suitors. Flaxman (*Odyssey* series).

# Homer, Odysseus, and the "Angel of History"

*Ernest Wichner*
*Translated by Michael Armstrong*
*with Nicholas Vazsonyi*

At the beginning of the 1960s, the "late period" of Erich Arendt's lyrical creativity, the material of Greek mythology, which previously had made only an occasional appearance in his work, became the central component of his poetical language. In the early poems an identification of the author with Odysseus/Ulysses was recognizable—a biographical identification traceable to Arendt's own Odyssey of exile; but now a change of perspective takes place. Uncritical emphasis ("Ulysses' weite Fahrt," ["Ulysses' Far Journey"] 1950) yields to a more distanced and more reflective use of motifs and figures from Greek myth. The two essayistic prose texts, however, which Erich Arendt contributed to two picture-books,[1] retain the earlier emphasis.

This study will investigate poems in which the figures of Homer and Odysseus are central to Erich Arendt's poetics. Since it will appear that even Odysseus, a figure previously conceived in optimistic terms, is now brought to utter collapse, the image of the "angel of history" (from Walter Benjamin), one of the central metaphors of Erich Arendt's lyric poems, will be traced through his works in order to clarify his perspective on history. In addition, the similarity or dissimilarity of the image to Walter Benjamin's Ninth Historical-Philosophical Thesis will be investigated.

---

[1] Erich Arendt and Katja Hayek-Arendt, *Griechische Inselwelt* (Leipzig: VEB, F. A. Brockhaus, 1962, 1967); Erich Arendt, *Säule Kubus Gesicht* (Dresden: VEB, Verlag der Kunst, 1966); see also note 2.

### Homer

The volume *Ägäis* (1967) begins with the poem "Steine von Chios," ("Stones of Chios") as does the 1980 volume of Arendt's collected poems, *Starrend von Zeit und Helle. Gedichte der Ägäis.*[2] Chios, an island in the eastern Mediterranean off the coast of Asia Minor, is one of between eight and twenty islands and cities which claim to have been the dwelling place of Homer. It is certain that Chios was the home of the Homeridae.

A brief exposition, which, despite its brevity, evokes the landscape of Chios with its specific nuances of atmosphere, is followed, in the central position in the first stanza and at the beginning of a quotation, by an (or "the") "I."

> Graurollend:
>                     Salz,
> rundum, die unlösliche
> Öde.—"Ich,
> mein Leib fühlt es
> starren, das
> aufgerissene Auge
> Meer."
>
> (Rolling grey:
>                     Salt
> all around, the insoluble
> bleakness.—"I,
> my body feels it staring, the
> opened eye
> the sea.")

This is a quoted "I," and therefore an earlier "I," a predecessor which says what the "I" of the poem could say, and in all probability wants to say, for its statement refers to the compromised perception and the mood of the one who narrates the present context. It also points to a particular style of perception: the "Leib" ("body") feels the "aufgerissenes Auge Meer" ("opened eye of the sea") staring. The second stanza, made up entirely of the speech of an "I" who is pre-

---

[2] Erich Arendt, *Starrend von Zeit und Helle. Gedichte der Ägäis*, ed. Gerhard Wolf (Munich: Carl Hanser Verlag, 1980). Unless otherwise noted, quotations are taken from this edition.

sently speaking, ends with the exposed solitary word "blind" and gives further information about the figure who speaks with and within the lyrical self: Homer, the blind poet/seer, whose "I" has spoken in quotation in the first stanza, substituting for the lyrical self as a lyrical self. Even the opening metaphor, "Graurollend / Salz . . ." ("Rolling grey / Salt"), part of the immediate perception of the speaker, seems to have been borrowed from Homer: "on the edge of the gray salt flood" (*Il*. 14.30).[3] So begins a journey through the island, of which our poem is a "report." The poet Erich Arendt traveled through the islands of the Aegean and met in words and in stones his predecessor Homer, the poet who had gazed into the abysses of human history and had given an account of what he saw. Arendt, more than 2500 years later, is confronted by the same experience and the same poetical problem. It is natural to hold a dialogue with Homer and thus to be assured of one's own artistic means. What is the power or the impotence of poetry? To whom does it speak, and with what success?

"The 'I' speaks, I think, first to itself, in a process of self-discovery. From compulsions, which desire to pass from unconsciousness to clarity, to formulation" (E. Arendt).[4] The "I" speaks to itself in a process of self-discovery; this cannot mean that the word is spoken to an isolated subjectivity. The "I" is a constructed, a social, entity, and it seeks to reassure itself in language, society's means of transmitting social experience. Only formulation creates clarity.

Arendt is concerned with the effort involved in the process of formulation, as was Homer, according to Arendt. Once more a trace of this effort is embodied in Homer's speech, in direct speech which Arendt perhaps puts in the ancient poet's mouth:

—"Er kennt das Irren,
mein Stab, der
aus dem Stein
das Wort Schlägt . . .
und dann
das innere Echo! Winter
Sommer der Hölle!"

---

[3] Cf. Homer, *Ilias*: Neue Übersetzung, Nachwort und Register von Roland Hampe (Stuttgart 1979).

[4] Erich Arendt in conversation with Gregor Laschen; see *Deutsche Bücher* 1976.2 (Amsterdam).

(—"It knows that wandering,
my staff that
beats the word
from the stone . . .
and then that inner echo! Winter
summer of Hell!")

With the staff (the rhapsode's staff and the blind man's staff) the
blind poet strikes the word from the stone, examines it, notices the
error, and begins anew, until the "inner echo" (process of self-
discovery) temporarily stops the process. "Winter / summer of Hell!"
may be an expression that sounds the "inner echo." The imaginary
comrade is also present at the first moment of sociability; this makes
it possible to speak of "the world." Where sociability appears, even if
it is only in an uncertain "once," the work of poetry may become
"world-possessing" ("welthaltig"); here, with reference to the process
of self-discovery, the world, palpated word for word out of the stone,
passes into the unconscious and the unknown.

With "deep / in the word" begins singing that presupposes the
knowledge of pain and of dust (metaphors for transitoriness as well as
for doctrines and ideologies that despise humanity[5]):

Im Mittag, flugzeug-
durchblinkt,
lauschen die Steine:

Vor Jahren, tausend,
einer ging hier,
vorüber, kannte den
Schmerz, einen Staub,
Wort, tief
im Wort . . . ging
singend, der Stab sang, seine
suchende Hand,
in der andern, aufgelesen
ein Stein, blank,
in der Sprache
des Himmels . . . Brot,

---

[5] Helmut Lethen, "Überlegungen zu Gedichten Erich Arendts," in *Der zerstückte Traum. Für Erich Arendt zum 75. Geburtstag*, ed. Gregor Laschen and
Manfred Schlösser (Berlin and Darmstadt 1978).

sagte er—
    steinglanzzerweht
    sein Lächeln.

(In midday, glittering
with planes,
the stones listen:

Years ago, a thousand,
Someone walked here,
in the past, he knew the
pain, a staff,
word, deep
in the word . . . he went
singing, the staff sang, his
searching hand,
in the other, a stone
was gathered, smooth, bare,
in the language
of the heavens . . . Bread,
he said—
    his smile
    blown away by the stone's glitter.)

Stones become words, become bread; D. Gelbrich calls these gathered stones "poetry's bread of life."[6] Poetic metaphors live, must live, from the fact that they achieve what elsewhere is impossible.

> Then was Jesus led up of the spirit into the wilderness to be tempted of the devil. And when he had fasted forty days and forty nights, he was afterwards anhungered. And when the tempter came to him, he said, If thou be the Son of God, command that these stones be made bread. But he answered and said, It is written, thou shalt not live by bread alone, but by every word that proceedeth out of the mouth of God.
> (Mt. IV:1–4).

---

[6] Dorothea Gelbrich, "Epochenerlebnis und Geschichtlichkeit antiker Landschaft. Besonderheiten der Antikenrezeption Erich Arendts," in *Lyriker im Zwiegespräch. Traditionsbeziehungen im Gedicht*, ed. Ingrid Hähnel (Berlin and Weimar 1981).

It is no accident that the poem "Steine von Chios," written in
1963, stands at the head of the "Ägäis" cycle, preceding poems written
earlier. The identification of the lyrical self with Homer, an identification which penetrates the structure of perception, is poetological
and programmatic. The blind poet with his apparently limited capa-
cities to perceive stands for a new poetic approach. It would surely be
an exaggeration to speak of a new beginning, since this new approach
was prepared by Arendt's "storm" experience, his "odes of flight,"
and—as Arendt himself says—"by a collision with the cantos of Ezra
Pound."[7]

This new approach is defined by the effort to create a poetry in
which "the very greatest attention is paid to formation of words,"
which concentrates "on the sound, rhythm, density, and tension of
words," which conceives of landscape (Aegean) itself as poetry, and
"which communicates itself to the skin's nerve-endings, not only to the
brain."[8]

And—to repeat—Arendt inserts an invented Homeric "I" into the
lyric self, speaks in Homeric metaphors ("Graurollend / Salz" ["Rolling grey / Salt"]), and problematizes the processes of word formation,
which stand at the beginning of European poetry and of all poetry.
"The poet is not concerned with a new image of Homer, but rather
with the evocation of the first of European poets as "model" of the
poetic relationship to the world. The Homer legend, thus understood,
becomes the legend of the nature of the poetical as that of a creative
experience of a world that one has walked through and touched with
all the senses."[9]

If, while penetrating it, Homer serves to guarantee the lyrical self
the possibility of poetic renunciation and "self-discovery" of almost
godlike dimensions in its creativity (the stone-word-bread metaphor),
and if this "act of creation" is reflected as a poetic process (of word-
and self-discovery), this process is transferred, in the elegy "Kouros,"
to a non-linguistic medium (sculpture) and carried further. In contrast to "wandering" (in "Steine von Chios"), which necessarily
accompanies exact denomination, here (in "Kouros") sensuous effort
to the point of physical pain is described as the necessary presupposi-
tion to, as a part of, creative renunciation.

---

[7] Achim Roscher, "Verstehen und Verständlichkeit" (conversation with
Erich Arendt), *Neue Deutsche Literatur* 1973.4 (Berlin–DDR).

[8] "Verstehen und Verständlichkeit," *op. cit.*

[9] D. Gelbrich, *op. cit.*

Aber, unter der Hand,
Meißel und—
die blutet, dem Stein
den Hartglanz Stille entreißt,
wächst wie
Blöße von
    Haut und Meer
das ungesichtige Antlitz.
Zeitengeduld.

(But, under the hand,
chisel and—
which bleeds, tranquility
snatches the solid gleam from the stone,
the unfaced countenance
grows like
a naked space of
skin and sea.
Patient of time.)

Here arises the question of engagement, the addressee of this effort, since "Welt! meint / der Schritt" ("World! the step means") does not remain exclusively inwardly directed.

"The fundamental question posed is 'for what purpose does a poem become engaged?' It becomes engaged for the sake of one's own 'I.' In order to set forth transitoriness, to illuminate it by the word. Or for the purposelessness of history, that is, for the sake of a fundamental and foundation-laying understanding. For knowledge of man's and earth's determination to die, their exhaustion, for what is 'questionable' in political activity. For something philosophical. The portrayal of basic situations. In an essential poem there is, for me, no non-engagement. Every act of making clear—which is of course a poem's aim—is engagement. Although the writer does not aim at an engagement *for* something. But rather merely portrays. Stands only in the effort of the word."[10]

The writer stands only in the effort of the word. Gregor Laschen speaks of a "poetics of the total word;"[11] here—in "Steine von Chios"—engagement is concretized and takes root programatically.

---

[10] E. Arendt in conversation with G. Laschen, *op. cit.*

[11] Gregor Laschen, *Lyrik in der DDR. Anmerkungen zur Sprachverfassung des modernen Gedichts* (Frankfurt/Main 1971).

And it can certainly have reference to objects; in the phrases "foundation-laying understanding--to set forth transitoriness--purposelessness of history" Arendt names them and avoids "the threatening point of antithesis,"[12] in which the often invoked and hostile sisters "l'art pour l'art" and "engagierte Kunst" negate each other and themselves: ". . . engaged art, because, in its capacity as art necessarily disengaged from reality, it eliminates differentiation from the latter; that of *l'art pour l'art*, because in its solipsism it denies that inextinguishable reference to reality, which is contained, as its polemical a priori, in the independence of art vis-a-vis reality."[13]

It remains to remark that Arendt affirms the autonomy of poetry, and not merely that aspect of autonomy, since conceded in the German Democratic Republic, which relates to the personally subjective nuances in the realm of artistic production; rather, he clearly understands the  autonomy of poetry as a condition of the possibility of its influence. "Yes, I plead for the autonomy of poetry, or of art in general.  I believe that whenever art places itself in the service of anything, it exerts no influence and no interaction between the written word and the reader can exist."[14]

This will serve as prelude to our examination of the second great Homer poem, which differently and more clearly than "Steine von Chios" exhibits the concepts of Arendt's poetics (which have now been discussed theoretically) and the function and significance of his reception of Homer and his identification with him: "Stunde Homer" ("Hour of Homer," 1962).

As is almost typical for the "Ägäis" cycle, the poem begins with a terse exposition. It consists of three words: "Feuerbraue / des Mittags!" ("Firebrow of midday!") and describes a moment in time (midday), a climactic condition of burning heat (fire), and the sense experience of this condition (firebrow).  In the word "Braue," (brow) the observer comes, *pars pro toto*, into the picture, which thus speaks of vision in the tormentingly brilliant midday sun.  This can have two different consequences: first, it can unduly emphasize that which is seen; second--as one experiences in harsh light--the contours of the seen object may melt and flow into each other:  that which is seen and that which is imagined are confused.  That only both possibilities together

---

12 Theodor W. Adorno, "Engagement," in *Noten zur Literatur III* (Frankfurt/Main 1965).

13 Th. W. Adorno, *op. cit.*, 110 f.

14 Erich Arendt in conversation with Manfred Schlösser, *Der zerstückte Traum, op. cit.*

result in a poetically viable procedure can be inferred as the text's dialectical structure.

The poem consists of stanzas in two columns, which in order and in tone are differentiated and are variously related to each other. The left column

> Erblindet!
> > blind
> wie der wissende
> Fels, singend
> in deiner Nacht:

> (Blinded!
> > blind
> like the knowing
> cliff, singing
> in your night:)

addresses Homer, identifies him with the knowing cliff, bids him sing. Next, after description of condition and perceptions—"Helmloses Licht! ("helmless light") (the ambiguity of clarity-brightness and defenselessness is again emphasized)—follows an enumeration of what is attributed to the song of the summoned/imagined Homer-figure.[15] Corresponding to the left-hand column of stanzas, and interrupting and accentuating it, are, on the right and in cursive type (which underscores the flowing character of the stanzas), stages of an inner monologue.

The light metaphor, "Helmloses Licht!" picks up the first expository phrase "Feuerbraue / des Mittags!" ("Firebrow of midday")and, like the stones in their capacity as latently eloquent memory ("Steine von Chios"), establishes the union of present time and myth, of lyrical self and Homer. The light is witness of what Homer reported—

---

[15] That this column of stanzas cannot be read as a revocation of what was evoked by Homer in his songs can be seen in the fact that here, unlike in Homer, the myth of Achilles and Penthesilea is added: "... the fate of Penthesilea was treated in the *Aithiopis* by Arctinos of Miletus, a lost poem that was part of the epic cycle. The motif of Achilles' love for Penthesilea may come from Hellenistic poetry": Herbert Hunger, *Lexikon der griechischen und römischen Mythologie* (Reinbek bei Hamburg 1974).

Helmloses Licht! das sah
die hautlose Blöße, gehöhlt
der Herzgang Leid—Schildetosen, hirn-
weiße Sonne! das sah,
im Steinwuchs des Himmels,
zerrissen, das blut, seine Küste
hufezerstampft . . . sah
den entgipfelten Blick . . .

(Helmless light! which saw
the skinless nakedness, the hollowed-out
heart-throbbing pain—shieldroaring, brain-
white sun! it saw
in the stone-shapes of the heavens
the blood, torn, its measured
shore, saw
the lowered gaze.)

—and determines the perception, imagination, and reflection of the lyrical self: the insight into permanence of the story of suffering that Homer portrayed, its validity for the lyrical self, which in its biological and social limitations can only lament and record: "— Zeit Zeit! / grabende unter uns in uns, / klagumklag Stein. Wohin, mein / rasender Zorn, der sang / . . ." ("—Time time! / burying under us in us, / endlessly-lamenting stone. Whereto my / crazed wrath, which sang / . . .").

Homer's hour is the hour of light that actualizes, too sharply emphasizes while simultaneously blinding, and triggers the imagination. Thus does the apostrophized Homer-figure, in the course of the poem, lose its contours, open itself to the reflections of the speaker, become poetically fictionalized. It gains contour and individuality only by losing itself in the text—by the agency of the text.

The dialectical structure of the poem ("almost a dramatic process" according to R. Bernhard[16]) is based on simultaneous evocation of the experience of suffering, which extends from mythical times (Nausicaa, Achilles, Penthesilea, etc.) to their transformation in history (Troy, "Eisenblutende Stunde" ["hour of bleeding iron"]) and from the historical past to the present of the poem and the reader

---

16 Rüdiger Bernhardt, "Das Wort als poetischer Gegenstand in der Lyrik Erich Arendts," *Zeitschrift für Germanistik* 1981.3 (Leipzig: VEB, Verlag Enzyklopädie).

(this in the left-hand column of stanzas), and the lamenting monologue of reflection on this experience (in the right-hand column).
Only when both are complete, when, despite the possible continuation
of the tale of suffering and despite the lamentation of the individual,
both are driven to their highest pitch, does the penultimate left-hand
stanza merge Eros and Thanatos to heighten the evoked suffering in
the single disembodied individual:

> —und sah, unflatvoll
> gierende Mäuler, die fleddernden
> Helden. Schrei—
> aufgerissen den Schoß.
>     Eisenblutende
> Stunde! Tod nur
> Tod, schändend
> begattend Tod den Tod,
> der losläßt
> die Lust seiner Lenden
> —Achill—,
> im geröteten Staub
> seinr Wollust
> Penthesilea.
>     Entleibt.

> —and saw, filthy
> desirous snouts, the plundering heroes. Scream—
> the womb torn open.
>     Hour of
> bleeding iron! Death only
> death, shameful
> death begetting death,
> which releases
> the lust of his loins
> —Achilles—
> in the ruddied dust of his desire
> Penthesileia.
>     Killed.

—-while the right-hand strophe, the end of the chain of reflections,
conceives of history as "Wolfshunger Geschichte" ("Story of wolf-
hunger) and once again unites elements of mythical seeing ("der Mus-
cheläugige" ["the mussel-eyed one"]) with the last imaginable

moment of history, the skeletization of clouds, the last collision of
man against man, and atmosphere,

> *Wolfshunger Geschichte:*
> *Skelett*
> *einer Wolke und vor*
> *den Mauern*
>           *unentwegt*
> *der Muscheläugige.*
>
> *(Story of wolf-hunger:*
> *skeleton*
> *of a cloud and before*
> *the walls*
>           *unflinching*
> *the mussel-eyed one.)*

—only then does song begin. Only when confronted by the pressingly
possible, the visible end of the individual and the probable end of the
species, do lamentation and courage, death (of the individual) and
death (of the species), abandoned and scorned by the gods, find
expression in song. It is the song of the one who, "nachgeschlagen
sein Aug," (his eye strick by night) all too clearly sees what is.

> Da,
> vom Tisch der Götter
> herab, bog das Gelächter
> den Irdischen.
> Einer nur, nacht-
> geschlagen sein Aug,
> hob
> die Träne
>           die wog
> wie Menschenmut und
> Verbrechen, Tod-
> und-Tod. Da erst
>
> begann
> das Singen:
>           Spätfels
>           Geduld!

(There
down from the table of the gods,
laughter distorts
the earthly.
Only one, his eye
struck by night,
lifted
the tear
            that sways
like human courage and
crime, death-
upon-death. Only then
began
the singing:
            belated rock
            patience!)

The song of this individual congeals, in the words "Spätfels /
Geduld!," (belated rock / patience!) into the song of a new Homer,
newly constituted from the text. He is the poet of the twentieth
century who, conscious of his tradition, points to the now visible end
of history and urges a subsequent patience and endurance.

"In contrast to 'Steine von Chios,' 'Stunde Homers' does not deal
exclusively with the problem of reflective images and the poetic mirroring thereof; rather, the poem treats the relation between the concrete historical process and the work of art."[17] This statement of
Bernhardt's is inaccurate because "Steine von Chios" deals not only
with reflective images and the poetic mirroring of reflective images,
but also with establishing the conception of a poet who, beyond the
mirroring of historical and poetic experience, understands himself to
be an authentic and incorruptible witness of genuine realities,
registering them with *all* his senses. "Stunde Homers" likewise deals
not only with the "relation between the concrete historical process
and the work of art"—the concrete historical process, as far as one can
speak of such a thing, is already absorbed in the work of art (left-hand
stanzas)—but also with defining the position of the poet:—"Immersion
in the historical dimension would necessarily unveil what formerly
remained unresolved; not otherwise is the present to be united with
the past"[18]—who, if he indulges in the poetical reproduction of past

---

[17] R. Bernhardt, *op. cit.*, 285f.

[18] Theodor W. Adorno, *Ästhetische Theorie* (Frankfurt/Main 1970) 36f.

epochs, opposes to this the correlative of his own historical and poetical experience (in monologue—the right-hand stanzas[19]) and thus in his own reflections re-examines the tendency of the already formulated experience. Only when "what formerly remained unresolved" is fixed by the evocation of that which was mirrored in the earlier work of art, and when the simultaneous reflection of this experience is fixed by one speaking in the present, does poetry begin.

Against Homeric poetics, comprised in the verses "Das ist der Götter Werk: sie haben den Menschen Verderben / Zugesponnen, daß es den Künftigen werde zum Liede," ("This is the gods' work: they have woven ruin into human life, so that it might become song for future generations."),[20] and against the ancient singer's mimetic attitude to reality, is set here the mimesis of the modern work of art: "the mimesis of works of art is similarity with themselves."[21] It is by this style of mimesis that the relation to each other of the two columns of stanzas (in "Stunde Homer") is determined. The poetological gesture of the poem becomes, by exemplifying this mimetic procedure, almost a didactic gesture and thereby more than "the possibility of a poet."[22]

*Odysseus*

Unlike Erich Arendt's relation to Homer, which is based chiefly on poetic theory, his relation to the figure of Odysseus is primarily "biographical." These pages will not only trace chronologically and interpret Erich Arendt's response to the figure of Odysseus—this has often been done[23]—but will also discuss an aspect of his preoccupation with this character which can be described, but only approximately, as "actualization" and is thus pertinent to Erich Arendt's conception of Homer as well.

The poem "Odysseus' Heimkehr" ("Odysseus's Return") (1962) and its misinterpretation as an "expression of sternest distancing from,

[19] Monologue, because art has lost the social famework that can make possible the certainty of a second person, an other.

[20] Cf. Homer, *Odyssee*, ed. Roland Hampe (Stuttgart 1979).

[21] Th. W. Adorno, *Ästhetische Theorie, op. cit.*, 159f.

[22] Heinz Czechowski, "Erich Arendt," in H. Czechowski, *Spruch und Widerspruch. Aufsätze und Besprechungen* (Halle/Saale 1974).

[23] Volder Riedel, "Homer-Rezeption und poetische Konfession Erich Arendts," in *Weimarer Beiträge* 1981.5 (Berlin und Weimar); cf. Heinz Czechowski, *op. cit.*, 9 ff.; Dorothea Gelbrich, *op. cit.*, 23 ff.

and mordant condemnation of, the figure of Odysseus"[24] lead one to ponder the relation between the speaking figure (Odysseus) and the lyrical self in the poems of Erich Arendt. Th. W. Adorno, in his *Ästhetische Theorie*, begins with the lyrical "I", "which proclaimed itself for centuries and lent an air of obviousness to poetical subjectivity. But it is by no means identical with the 'I' that appears in the poem." In contrast, he discusses the "I" that "speaks latently, through the structure," which posits the grammatical "I" of the poem and concretizes itself within the structure "by the act of its discourse."[25] In this "latently speaking 'I' " the symbolic and figural aspects of the poem come together: Odysseus—if it is he who speaks in the text—and the lyrical self. Like the two columns of stanzas, they become parts of *one* discourse.

It will by now be unnecessary to come back to Erich Arendt's self-identification with the figure of Odysseus in order to demonstrate the actuality of *both* columns of stanzas and their convergence in the discourse of the "latently speaking 'I'," in which the two voices—that ostensibly spoken by Odysseus (in the left-hand column) and the equally ostensible reply of the traditional lyrical self (in the right-hand column)—constitute a single discourse.

Like the poems "Steine von Chios" and "Stunde Homer," "Odysseus' Heimkehr" also begins with a short exposition, which, printed in Roman type, stands at the left, above the column of stanzas printed in italics and thus reveals the influence that it radiates upon each stanza, deciphering and uniting both.

> Hinfällige Stunde
>       und
> das Gedächtnis des Todes
> groß!
>
> (Frail hour
>       and
> the memory of death
> great!)

These words—as in the first stanza of "Stunde Homer," which construct a frame with the concluding stanza, the same essential elements appearing in both—point to the final stanza

---

[24] Volker Riedel, *op. cit.*, 105f.
[25] Th. W. Adorno, *Ästhetische Theorie*, 249f.

> ... dein Segel,
> Scheiternder,
> setz
> schwarz.
>
> (set,
> you foundering one,
> your sail
> black.)

and thus the "dialogue-sections"[26] of the poem lose a certain amount of room for development.

In the poem's two columns, there is ambiguity in the moment of homecoming of the *single* Odysseus, who (as he was in Homer) is a historically and literarily conditioned Odysseus of the poem's present time.

To do justice to the poem, an interpreter would have to proceed step by step to consider each left-hand stanza in the context of the entire left-hand column and to compare it with the subsequent stanza of the right-hand column, which likewise would have to be examined in the context of the entire right-hand column. Here only a few steps will be taken.

> *Muschelleere des*
> *Himmels: Herz, mein*
> *Narbenbau!*
>
> *(The conch-void of*
> *the heavens: heart, my*
> *evidence of scars!)*

---

[26] The "dialogue sections," or rather, on one side (left) a column of stanzas comprising an internal monologue with elements of dialogue, and on the other side (right) a column of stanzas in the second person which nonetheless contains assertion and reply. These sections are each complete in themselves, reflecting their own elements and interrupting their sequence of discourse and that of the corresponding column, and each is also interrelated with the other. The dialogic character becomes more pronounced in the second half of the poem. V. Riedel's insistence on the dialogic character of the poem—"The poem 'Odysseus' Heimkehr' cannot be adequately evaluated if one disregards the dialogic character nor if one considers it apart from Arendt's total *oeuvre* and apart from its literary-historical context" (*op. cit.*, 107)—leads him rashly to disjoin Odysseus from the lyrical self and finally to declare: "Odysseus does not understand what it is all about, . . . a 'defeated' character who was not equal to the demands of history."

begins the left-hand column: the distant gaze into the empty sky and (identical to this) into the heart made up of scars, the movement turning from without (sky) to within (heart); the external emptiness corresponds to the internal scars. The right-hand stanza refers to the exposition in that it picks up the most significant word "Tod" ("death") and also refers to the left-hand stanza, the statement of which it develops: ". . . Herz, mein / Narbenbau! // des Todes—(. . .) ("heart, my / edifice of scars! // of death—")." The right-hand stanza specifies elements from the sphere of experience of the speaker on the left, extends the attempt to survive beyond the *Odyssey* to the present ("legtest legst," [you intended, intend"]) and evokes once more (as in "Steine vom Chios" and "Stunde Homer") the power of stone, the memory of rock, here present as survival and so unanimous.

> (. . .)
> und legtest legst
> zu überleben, (. . .)
> (. . .)
> (. . .)
> das Haupt
> an den bleibenden Fels
> mit dem Gedächtnis
> wie ER.
>
> (. . .
> and you intended intend
> to survive, . . .
> . . .
> . . .
> your head
> on the remaining rock
> with the memory
> as HE.)

The next left-hand stanza, in reference to the first left-hand stanza, concretizes the "Narbenbau Herz" ("edifice of scars"), specifies the wounds that caused the scars; in reference to the preceding right-hand stanza, it can be read as a description of the contents of "Gedächtnis" ("memory"). Thus the stanzas, with their accents on "Narbenbau" and "Gedächtnis," are fused.

*Unrast, hohlgehendes*
*Irren, Blick*
*ohne Vergessen! Iris,*
*Wundhaut, sie läßt*
*nicht vom Aug: dem Erinnerten, Mund,*
*rückwärts sämtlicher*
*Glanz der Verblichnen*
*Blick, der läßt, der*
*verrät—*

*(Restlessness, empty*
*wandering, glimpse without forgetting! Iris,*
*wounded skin, she does not*
*take her eye from: the remembered one, mouth,*
*the backwards glimpse*
*the entire lustre of the pallid one*
*who permits, who betrays—)*

Here the influence of Paul Celan's lyric poems, an influence that
is more obvious in Arendt's later volumes of verse, is already visible.

Augentausch, endlich, zur Unzeit:
bildbeständig,
verholzt
die Netzhaut—:
das Ewigkeitszeichen,[27]

(Optical illusion, finite, till timelessness:
unchanging picture,
the retina
turned to wood—
sign of eternity,)

The poetic conception, shared by the two authors, of the "view
without forgetting," the perspective of the work of art which is constituted only in its gaze at horror in history, which must endure the
sight of horror, survives only in this way. This is different from the
backward glance at the "Glanz der Verblichenen" (luster of the pallid
one") which permits and betrays, and also unlike the forward glance
toward the dream, which merely throws one back once more upon
oneself and paralyzes:

---

[27] Paul Celan, "Nacht," in *Sprachgitter* (Frankfurt/Main 1959).

(...)
und ständig den
Traum ertragen, der sich
ins Gesicht blickt,
erstarrend!

(...
and to bear
the dream continuously, which
gazes into one's face,
paralyzing!)

Just as in Arendt's poems the eye is almost equated with the other
sense organs—H. Lethen speaks of "promiscuity of sense perception
in the poems"[28]—so too it shares with the power of remembrance—
rooted in the archaic, residing in stones, and activated to speech by
the sense of touch—to make memory and memory's objects articulate.
To aid in the understanding of the lines "(...) Iris, / Wundhaut, sie
läßt / nicht vom Aug: dem Erinnerten, Mund, / (...)" ("Iris, /
wounded skin, she does not / take her eye from: the remembered one,
mouth"), here are two passages from the poem "Prager Judenfried-
hof" ("Jewish Cemetery of Prague," 1961), dedicated to Paul Celan:
"Augen ihr Münder / Augen! (...)" ("Eyes you mouths / eyes!") and:

Augen Münder
der Schrift,
Schattenzug eines
Erinnerns, eingegraben,
auglos hier mundlos.
Dem Staub verschwistert
unsere Finger,
lesen den Namen.

(Eyes, mouths
of writing,
shadowtrain of a
memory, buried,
eyeless here mouthless.
Our fingers, sisters
with the dust,
read the name.)

---

[28] H. Lethen, *op. cit.*, 41.

Here the eye becomes the expressive organ of a different sort of memory--recollection's traces, preserved in writing, of historical processes ("die späte Schrift" ["belated writing"], it is called in "Steine von Chios," in contrast to early, pre-historical, orally conceived myth); and if vision is destroyed, the sense of touch takes its place: "unsere Finger / lesen den Namen" ("Our fingers / read the name"). The de-hierarchization of their (near) interchangeability stands for the possibility of the self, however reduced, to articulate protest and resistance, in the name of sensuous and physical integrity, against the possible and indeed already experienced total destruction of humankind (Auschwitz, Hiroshima) and to refuse, though cognizant of its own diminution, to withdraw from the experience of horror. Thus Arendt's confidence in sense perception can also be read as a critical disagreement with Celan, who in his volume of poems *Sprachgitter* (1959) concentrates all the power of the senses, indeed all of man's capacity for sense experience and for understanding, into the metaphor of the eye.[29]

When one continues to read the individual stanzas of the poem "Odysseus' Heimkehr," always with reference to the opposite column and to stanzas above and below, there gradually emerges a texture of despair and longing for flight, of pusillanimity carried to the point of a longing for death,

> *Todstreifenden Segels,*
> *dennoch davon-*
> *kommen! Flut,*
> *die nicht trägt, die*
> *trägt und*
>       *verwirft!*

> *(With the sail striped by death,*
> *nevertheless to*
> *survive! Flood,*
> *which carries not, which*
> *carries and*
>       *rejects!)*

---

[29] See Marlies Janz, *Von Engagement absoluter Poesie. Zur Lyrik und Ästhetik Paul Celans* (Frankfurt/Main 1976), especially *"Sprachgitter:* Wiederherstellung von Leben und ästhetische Stilisation," 63 ff.

> Und dann:
> die Abendspreu, wenn
> überm Randlosen, weitum,
> ein Schmerz hinabwill
> zu allem Schlaf: So
> ausgehöhlt der Mut! (. . .)
>
> (And then:
> the evening chaff, if
> anguish wants to
> go down far over the
> void to total sleep: so
> courage erodes!)

a texture of impossible, but nonetheless imaginable, regression to the un-self-conscious innocence of an animal,

> *Kirke doch! Kirke,*
> *einziger, todlos*
> *tödlicher Kuß, (. . .)*
> *(. . .)*
> *(. . .): Unschuld*
> *des Tiers!—letztes*
> *Vergessen o Nie-*
> *vergessen!,*
>
> *(But Circe! Circe,*
> *the sole immortal*
> *deathly kiss, . . .*
> *. . .: animal*
> *innocence!—ultimate*
> *forgetting oh never-*
> *forgetting!)*

a texture of suffering and collapse, which proceeds through pre-history (i.e., myth) and history (almost becoming a symbol of time itself),

> *Übermaß Zeit! welcher*
> *Himmel nicht*
> *ward begraben! Und*
> *das Rauschen der Schilde?—*
> *schwarz, wie Todesnacht, jedes*
> *Troja umsonst (. . .),*

*(Excess time! what*
*Heaven was not*
*buried! And the*
*rustling of the shields?—*
*black as deathly night, every*
*Troy in vain . . .)*

to the present moment of the return to Ithaca, the return to the German Democratic Republic, and through this again to the "now" of the poem and its reader.

After all the defeat, doubt, and despair, there is no returning home; the arrival beneath one's own roof—"(. . .) die Fahne Rauch / überm Herzen, eine / Schwertspitze Rost, / verblätternd / Ruhm (. . .)" ("the trail of smoke / over the heart, a / rusty sword tip / peeling / fame")—occurs, but it is a failure: "(. . .) Größeres / wollten die Meere! / Nicht das Dach (. . .)" ("the sea would want greater! / Not the roof. . ."); the return becomes part of the story of struggle and defeat, and nowhere opens up a view of Utopia, "das Größere" ("the greater") ("welcher / Himmel nicht / ward begraben!" [what / Heaven was not / buried!"]).

The first left-hand stanza recurs, with slight variations, at the end of the poem:

*Muschelleere des*          *Windleere meines*
*Himmels: Herz, mein*       *ach, ihres*
*Narbenbau!*                *Herzens! Wo?*

*Conch-void of the*         *Wind-void of my*
*heavens: heart my*         *ah, your*
*scarred edifice*           *heart! Where?)*

But now vision reverses its direction. From within, from the windless heart, outward, from "I" to "you." The question "where?" is asked, and (if one reads "black" as the color, *inter alia*, of pirates and anarchists) the answer is given annihilatingly, soberly, rebelliously—with a challenge:

Hier,
        unterm Ausgeträumt
des Himmels, der
die Masten schweigend dir
zerbricht, dein Segel,

Scheiternder,
setz
schwarz.

(Here,
          under the completed dream
of the heavens, which
without speaking breaks your
masts, set,
foundering one,
your sail
black.)

The power that brings about the returning hero's collapse is yet worse than the powers of myth: those were nameable, visible, and perceptible (lightning, thunder, storm, etc.), but this is a power that proceeds in silence. Its consequences are destruction and grief. Arendt's Odysseus—one different from Homer's, who reflects the limitations of possibility and the forms of literary discourse from the side of the lyrical self—stands for one of the central thematic aspects of Erich Arendt's lyric poetry. In, with, and through the figure of Odysseus, Arendt's own political biography, from the flight from the Nazis to his own Odyssey of political exile (Switzerland, Spain, France, Curaçao, Colombia) to the German Democratic Republic of the 50s and 60s, is described and fixed in its present position.

"Only those who conceive of Arendt's poems as apolitical will be astonished at the political precision with which they portray the breach in the years 1960–61," says H. Lethen, and he refers to the "dismantling of the sea-voyage metaphor" which points toward a clear difference between Arendt's view of history and that of Brecht.[30] Lethen's view is supported by reference to the *Buckower Elegien*. Arendt firmly rejects the critical and melancholy tendencies of the poetry of the late 1950s, and (in opposition to Brecht as well as to Celan) he takes over and transforms metaphors and images from the poetry of that period in such a manner as to establish his own political and poetological position. In addition to the sail metaphor, Arendt in the *Buckower Elegien* adopts and adapts the smoke metaphor. To Brecht's melancholy attempt at an idyll in the here and now,

---

[30] H. Lethen, *op. cit.*, 44.

Brecht:        Der Rauch
               Das kleine Haus unter Bäumen am See.
               Vom Dach steigt Rauch.
               Fehlte er
               Wie trostlos dann wären
               Haus, Bäumen und See

               (The smoke
               the small house under trees at the lake.
               Smoke rises from the roof.
               Were he absent
               then how desolate would be
               house, trees, and lake.)

Arendt:        Odysseus' Heimkehr
               Hör, windverworfen,
               geburtenleer
               die einsame Trift! Größeres
               wolten die Meere! Nicht
               das Dach, die Fahne Rauch
               überm Herzen, eine
               Schwertspitze Rost,
               verblätternd,
                           Ruhm (...),

               (Hear of Odysseus's
               return, wind-blown,
               the lonely pasture
               barren of offspring! The seas
               would want greater! Not
               the roof, the trail of smoke
               over the heart, a
               rusty sword-tip,
               peeling,
                           fame ...)

he opposes his own brusque rejection: sail and smoke, metaphors for
movement on a wide scale and for the habitability of the shore that is
gained, are threadbare, devoid of content, and alien. They serve only
as negative images.

## The "Angel of History"

[In the concluding pages of "Homer, Odysseus, and the 'Angel of History,' Wichner demonstrates a clear correspondence between the imagery of two other poems ("Elegie," [1961] and "Im Museum" [1975]) and Walter Benjamin's Ninth "Historical-Philosophical Thesis." This Thesis is a meditation on, a literary image of, Paul Klee's painting "Angelus Novus." Benjamin names Klee's angel the "angel of history, who looks as though he were about to flee from something at which he stares. His eyes are open wide, his mouth gapes, his wings are outspread. . . . He has turned his countenance toward the past. Where we perceive a chain of circumstances, he sees a single catastrophe, continually heaping ruin upon ruin, scattering rubble at his feet. He would gladly linger, wake the dead, and put together what has been shattered. But a storm blows from paradise; it has billowed out his wings and is so strong that he cannot furl them. This storm drives him irresistibly into the future, to which he turns his back, while before him the rubble heap rises up to heaven. This storm is what we call progress."[31]

Wichner argues that Arendt's poetic theory and Benjamin's angel of history share this "gaze at horror in history," Arendt expressing it as the "perplexity of the speaking self that cannot distance itself and is caught in the historical process." He concludes that "Erich Arendt's 'Homer,' 'Odysseus,' and 'Angel of History' are united by the care exercised in the various poems to find the precise word as the fundamental prerequisite for the precise perspective on the existence of the individual caught up in the historical process. In the face of the conceivable and now clearly practicable annihilation of all, this poetic method calls into existence the capacity for clear denomination of that which is; it leads to a poetry free of fin-de-siécle pathos and of the anxiety of gradual speechlessness, and thus once more, patiently, it expresses the possibility of song."]

---

[31] Walter Benjamin, *Zur Kritik der Gewalt und andere Aufsätze* (Frankfurt/Main 1971) 84f.

Figure 19. Aphrodite and Helen. Flaxman (*Iliad* series).

# Derek Walcott's Omeros
# and Derek Walcott's Homer[1]

*Oliver Taplin*

"All that Greek manure under the green bananas"
*Omeros LIV iii*

Homeric Epic may seem to have been dead over 250 years ago, in verse at least, in English at least. Yet one of the greatest works of twentieth-century literature in any language is a kind of Homeric epic, albeit in prose. Derek Walcott's *Omeros* was published in September 1990, and it may seem hasty to nominate it in the same breath as *Ulysses*; yet I am far from alone in feeling that a major new work of literature has just appeared, one that will stand the test of time, of repeated rereading and rediscovery. It presents a narrative that is rich and complex yet accessible, moving, gripping, intensely local yet international in the scope of its sympathies. It dwells with minute observation on the tangible accoutrements of day-to-day life, and yet also delves deep into the anxieties of history, psychology, race, education--and the many other preoccupations of a remarkable

---

[1]This review was not written as a review, but it does not pretend to be a fully garnished academic article either. I have been so stimulated by Walcott's new poem that I want to seize the opportunity to say something about it within a few months of first publication: the resurrected *Arion* (from Walcott's own university) has helpfully given me the ideal opportunity. This means that I have not attempted to draw on Walcott's earlier work, relevant though that is, no doubt–let alone on the secondary literature about it–nor on theoretical writing about allusion and intertextuality, relevant though that may be.

sensibility. And all this is carried along with pace and panache through a poetry expressed in astonishingly luxuriant English.

*Omeros* is profoundly Homeric and undoubtedly epic. Yet Derek Walcott himself has repeatedly denied that his poem is epic and has depreciated its affinities with the *Iliad* and the *Odyssey*. For example, "I do not think of it as an epic . . . that isn't the Homer I was thinking of" (*New York Times*, October 9, 1990); "I've never really read the *Iliad* and the *Odyssey*" (*The Independent*, 10 November 1990); "I'm a very poor classical scholar . . . I don't use my work as a sort of referential this-equals-that, this is supposed to be that in black, or whatever" ("Poetry Please," BBC Radio 4, 22 October 1990). "The theme of the book is not really a parallel, an overlay, putting the *Iliad* or the *Odyssey* over a village in the Caribbean" ("Poetry Please," 29 October 1990). I set out to explore this tension.

First, however, it might be appropriate to give some sort of "description" of the poem; and this may also convey some idea of its richness and texture. In form it is arranged in 64 chapters, and each chapter is divided into three sections which vary from 9 to 99 lines in length (all printed on 320 pages in the first edition).[2] The twelve-syllable lines are basically trochaic ("this thudding metre" *XLIXiii*). They are grouped in threes with intricate interlocking rhymes and half-rhymes—many of them breath-taking—usually between alternate lines. In other words the metre is an adaptation of *terza rima*.[3] It inspires this beautiful progressive pair of images:

> Because Rhyme remains the parentheses of palms
> shielding a candle's tongue, it is the language's
> desire to enclose the loved world in its arms.
>                                    (*XIIIiii*)

To turn to content, pride of place must go to St. Lucia, since *Omeros* is a celebration of the island of the lesser Antilles in the Caribbean where Derek Walcott grew up.[4] She is celebrated in the

---

[2]Hence citations in the form *LIViii* etc. The poem is also divided into seven books of greatly varying length. But it is not clear to me that they reflect the structure more fundamentally than the chapters–I cannot see, for example, why books four and five are not unified, or why book three starts and ends where it does.

[3]A Professor of Classics (who is given to rebuking nonclassicists for their ignorance) unhappily described it as "blank verse" in *The New York Times Book Review* for October 7, 1990. She also mentioned "occasional rhyme" and quoted the one and only section (*XXXIIIii*) which is in an anomalous metre, incantatory couplets (an unsuccessful device to my ear).

[4]Population 120,300, area 616 sq. km/238 sq. miles, according to the reference book.

present, though with warnings about the effects of her degradation by speculators and tourism (see further p. 321 below). She is also celebrated for her past, for the lives of the slaves brought from Africa who were the ancestors of present citizens, and for her place in the colonial wars between France and England, culminating in "the Battle of the Saints" in 1782. This endowed St. Lucia with the title of "the Helen of the West Indies." The main narrative is all set in this one island and its coastal waters, except for one expedition south toward the Grenadines, and for a sunstroke-vision in which the fisherman Achille returns in time and place to the village in Africa where his ancestor Afolabe (renamed Achille) was captured by slavers in the eighteenth century. Otherwise the poem is taken further afield only by fictional characters from the past, and by the first-person narrator, a restless, expatriot traveler, who is seen in New York, Boston, Georgia, Dublin, and London as well as on St. Lucia. More on him in a moment.

The central character is Achille (French pronunciation), a big-hearted but desperately poor fisherman. "I sang of quiet Achille, Afolbe's son" (*LXIVi*), "My main man, my nigger!" (*XXXVIi*).[5] Achille ends the poem reunited with his beloved Helen, who is soon to bear a child (which he wants to give an African name, *LXIIIiii*). Helen is a hot-blooded woman of extraordinary panther-like poise and beauty, a beauty for which men might well die, as they did for "the Helen of the West Indies." It is uncertain whether her child's father is Achille or Hector, for whom she left him. The two men were mates, *compères* (*XLVIi*), but had quarreled. Hector had given up fishing for a more lucrative living driving a minibus-taxi. He crashes his vehicle one day and is killed. A fellow taxi-driver comments:

> A road-warrior
> He would drive like a madman when the power took.
> He had a nice woman. Maybe he died for her.
>                               (*XLViii*)

"For her and tourism, I thought," adds the narrator.

Philoctete is a friend of both the rivals. He was a fisherman too until his shin was injured by a rusty anchor and the stinking ulcer would not heal. He is forced to clean out pig-pens and to grow yams for a livelihood, until he is eventually cured—soon after Hector's

---

[5]Cf. "And I'm homing with him, Homeros, my nigger . . ." *XXXii*.

death (as in the Greek myth). His physician is the huge wise-woman "sibyl" Ma Kilman, who runs the "No Pain Café." Instinct leads her to the medicine of an exotic stinking plant whose seed had been carried from Africa by a migrating sea-swift. Ma Kilman often passes the time of day talking to the last of this cast-list of the significant characters from Achille's village, the blind ex-merchant-seaman Seven Seas. He is a story-teller and is equated with Omeros/Homer. He is also incarnated in the form of the African griot who witnessed the massacre of Afolabe's village (*XXVIIii*), and the Sioux shaman who witnessed similar events in the Plains of the advancing United States (*XXXVi, XLIIIii*). He also turns up as a tattered old bargeman in London hugging a dog-eared manuscript (*XXXVIII, LVIiii*), and even momentarily as James Joyce, "our age's Omeros" (*XXXIXiii*).[6]

There is also a childless white couple who have settled in St. Lucia. (Regimental Sergeant) Major Dennis Plunkett has steadily grown away from England, and come to love-hate the island where he farms pigs, and used to run the school cadet force when it included Achille, Hector and the narrator. He is obsessed "from afar" with the beauty of Helen, and it is partly for her sake that he spends his time researching the history of the Helen Island and its celebrated sea-battle. He discovers intriguing parallels with the Trojan War, and also a casualty of the battle called Plunkett, whom he adopts as a kind of ghost-son.[7] Helen used to be a housemaid for Plunkett's wife Maud, until they quarreled over a yellow dress which was regarded as stolen. Maud, who sews and gardens with great skill, dies of cancer soon after Hector's death. Her death and her funeral, which brings together all the major characters (*LIIIi*), are deeply moving. Though Plunkett has his absurdities—and Walcott especially enjoys playing with his linguistic traits—he is probably the most fully and affectionately painted character in the poem.

One could hardly expect a Professor of English at Boston University in 1990 to have a relationship with his first-person narrator which is narratologically unproblematic. I shall call the narrator "I." Like the real Derek Walcott, "I" returns regularly to St. Lucia, but wanders around the world and spends much of his time in Boston. Walcott dedicates *Omeros* to, among others, "my brother, Roderick";

---

[6]There seem to be echoes of Molly Bloom's closing soliloquy in the memories of Dennis and Maud's courting in *LXIi*.

[7]The story of the young Midshipman Plunkett who died accidentally on his own sword in the Battle of the Saints is told by an omniscient narrator in chapters *XIV-XV*.

"I" tells his mother, who suffers from Alzheimer's disease, that she has two sons and a daughter "their names are Derek, Roddy, and Pam"; and he adds "I have to go back to the States again" (*XXXIIi*). Walcott and "I" seem to have a lot of external biography in common. Whether or not there is any identity with the real Derek Walcott's *inner* life, "I" is suffering from the painful ending of a relationship with a "Circe"-woman (*XXXIXiii, XLIXiii*). This was "the wrong love";[8] and "I" is eventually cured of it at the same moment as Philoctete is cured of *his* wound (*XLIXiii, LIXi*). They were both afflicted with shame and self-hate (*XLVIIIiii*). "We shall all heal" is the poem's optimistic burden (*LXIIIii*).

As with "I," it is calculatedly left open how far most of the characters are "real" people. In the case of the Plunketts, however, their fictionality is explicit. Soon after their introduction we have:

> This wound I have stitched into Plunkett's character.
> He has to be wounded, affliction is one theme
> of this work, this fiction, since every "I" is a
> fiction finally. Phantom narrator, resume . . .
>
> (Vii)

And at Maud's funeral:

> I was both there and not there. I was attending
> the funeral of a character I'd created;
> the fiction of her life needed a good ending
>
> as much as mine . . .
>
> (LIIIii)

Besides Midshipman Plunkett, there is one further character who seems to be explicitly a fiction, a nineteenth-century Boston woman called Catherine Weldon, who moves West and witnesses the near-extermination of the native American tribes. It seems that "I" created her when in a depressed state he was reading a history of the events:

---

[8]"I" 's inner "auto"-biography supplies what are to my perception the most cryptic passages of the poem—and perhaps the least successful. It is unclear (so far as I can see) whether the "Circe" relationship is the same as the broken marriage obliquely alluded to in *XXXiii* and *XLVIIIi*.

So Catherine Weldon rose in high relief

through the thin page of cloud, making a fiction
of my own loss. I was searching for characters,
and in her shawled voice I heard the snow that would be
    blown

when the wind covered the tracks of the Dakotas,
the Sioux, and the Crows; my sorrow had been replaced.
                                          (XXXViii)

                        *   *   *

In the light of this narratological complexity, it is time to return to
the significance of Homer for Derek Walcott and for *Omeros*. First—
of course—there is no Homeric grid mechanically imposed, no straight
parallels or one-to-one correspondences. That is not the way that the
best creative literature interacts with the precedent works that it
draws strength from: that is not how the *Aeneid* or *Télémaque* or
*Ulysses* relate to Homer any more than *Omeros*. Yet Walcott's poem is
still, as I hope to show, infused and suffused with Homer all the way
from its title-page to its final section with "A triumphant Achilles, /
his hands gloved in blood" (*LXIViii*).[9]
    Yet there is a deep ambivalence, a simultaneous embracing and
fending off. This is already there half-suppressed in *IIiii*, the section
which both introduces "I" into the poem and explains "Omeros"—the
modern Greek for Homer, as he is informed by a Greek woman-
friend. That chapter ends:

    And I heard a hollow moan exhaled from a vase,
    not for kings floundering in lances of rain; the prose
    of abrupt fishermen cursing over canoes.

Yet the poem is in verse not prose, and it contains only occasional
snatches of speech in the Antillean *patois*, English and French—and
those are versified. Even the word *prose* is a half-rhyme.
    There is a more explicit "self-contradiction" toward the end of the
poem in *LVIiii*. The marble form of Homer has floated to St. Lucia in

---

[9]Note the final 's' on 'Achilles', and compare the last line of *Iliad* book 20.
This is, however, the blood of fish, not men.

a vision,[10] and guides "I," as Virgil guided Dante, to see the damned in the island's volcanic sulphur-pits. "I" (like the real Derek Walcott) "boasts" that he has never read the *Odyssey* ("not all the way through")—the bard's feelings are understandably hurt! Yet a few lines later "I" confesses that he has always heard Homer's voice in the sea, and that even as a boy "the word 'Homer' meant joy," and he ends up boasting, "Master, I was the freshest of all your readers." He loves Homer, yet denies him.

This ambivalence came out fascinatingly in an interview that Walcott gave on BBC Radio 4 ("Poetry Please," 29 October 1990). He explained how Plunkett searches in history for Trojan parallels, and how "the narrator of the book, the writer of the book" is intrigued by the literary references. "But the book in the end," he added, "turns round and says, 'Well, there's no need to have these associations. Things have to become themselves and stand in their own light without history and without literature before they can be properly named. They have to be their own thing.' " Is there some kind of evasion here? It seems that "the book" turns round and overrules "I," and relegates Homer to a half irrelevance. Where does Derek Walcott come into this?[11]

The allusions and interactions between one work of literature and another can vary enormously in their relative complexity and their degree of explicitness (which is one reason why I am not using the blanket term "intertextuality"). Some of the Homeric elements in *Omeros* are overt, "planted" so to speak, while others are oblique or distant, and more likely to have been drawn from submerged, unconscious levels of response. On the conscious level there is the central idea of the struggle over Helen, who is several times located on the parapet of Troy, as in *Iliad* 3. 139ff., see, for example, in *XVIIIii, iii*. Then there are several references each to, for example, Agamemnon, Menelaus, Myrmidons, Scamander, Paris (especially the *Ville de Paris*, the sunken French flagship). There are also planted allusions to Penelope, Ithaca, Calypso (with her inevitable Caribbean pun), Circe with men turned into pigs, and, most frequently, to the one-eyed Cyclops Polyphemus. He is conjured up as the lighthouse

---

[10]"I" first sees "the floating head" in the sea (*LVIi*)–like the head of Orpheus floating to Lesbos?

[11]According to the reverse of the title page of the London Faber and Faber edition (I have not seen the New York edition by Farrar, Straus, and Giroux), "Derek Walcott is hereby identified as author of this work in accordance with Section 77 of the Copyright, Designs and Patents Act 1988."

(*IIii*), the cyclone (*IXiii*),[12] Plunkett's magnifying glass (*XIXiii*), the tourist's camera (*LIXiii*). Then in the last chapter:

> And Achille himself had been one of those children
> whose voices are surf under a galvanized roof;
> sheep bleating in the schoolyard; a Caribbean
>
> whose woolly crests were the backs of the Cyclops's flock,
> with the smart man under one's belly. Blue stories
> we recited as children lifted with the rock
>
> of Polyphemus.
>
> (*LXIVii*)

I believe that I can trace other deeper buried interactions with Homer, not just the use of names or incidents, but passages which draw strength from a particular touch in the *Iliad* or *Odyssey*. Though dug in like manure, rather than planted, these may be no less telling for readers. Take first the last stanzas of the chapter which introduces the Plunketts. Dennis used to act as the official starter for "the village Olympiad" on St. Peter's Day:

> It wasn't Aegean. They climbed no Parthenon
> to be laurelled. The depot faced their arena,
> the sea's amphitheatre. When one wore a crown—
> *victor ludorum*—no one knew what it meant, or
> cared to be told. The Latin syllables would drown
> in the clapping dialect of the crowd. Hector
>
> would win, or Achille by a hair; but everyone
> knew as the crossing ovals of their thighs would soar
> in jumps down the cheering aisle, in their marathon
>
> six times round the village, that the true bounty was
> Helen, not a shield nor the ham saved for Christmas.
>
> (*Viii*)

---

[12]The cyclone is pictured in terms of a riotous party of the gods, both Greek and African. The word *fête* is used several times, as in "Fête start!" Is this a pun with *fate*? (In the quotation that follows, from *LXIVii*, I must admit that I am baffled by the reference of "blue" stories.)

Six times round the village may bring to mind Achilles' pursuit of Hector three times round the walls of Troy in *Iliad* 22. A closer focus will light on *Iliad* 22.158–61:[13]

> And the one who fled was great but the one pursuing
> greater, even greater—their pace mounting in speed
> since both men strove, not for a sacrificial beast
> or oxhide trophy [i.e. a shield], prizes runners fight for, no,
> they raced for the life of Hector breaker of horses.

The prize in *Omeros* is a woman's love not a man's life; yet this reverberation so near the beginning sounds a warning note that this rivalry will cost Hector's life before the poem is over.

Hector's vehicle is introduced in *XXIIii*:

> The Comet, a sixteen-seater passenger-van,
> was the chariot that Hector bought.

After his death another taxi-driver says, "A good pal of mine died in that chariot / of his called the Comet" (*XLVii*). The use of "chariot" is more than a vague gesture toward Homer: the Iliadic chariot that matters is the one behind which Achilles drags Hector's body through the dust (*Iliad* 22.395ff., 24.14ff. etc.). So Hector's Comet is ominous for him right from its first mention. But the Iliadic resonance also foreshadows an eventual reconciliation after Hector's death (in contrast to Paris and Menelaus): this comes with the burial of Hector in *XLVIi*. Then in the course of the wonderful celebratory chapter *LV*, which makes a kind of first ending to the poem, there are these lines about Helen:'

> The sail of her bellying stomach seems to him [Achille]
> to bear not only the curved child sailing in her
> but Hector's mound, . . .

This refers to the piled conch-shells under which Hector is buried "near the sea he had loved once" (*XLVIi*), but it also embraces, I suggest, the burial-mound at Troy with which the *Iliad* ends:

---

[13]I quote the *Iliad* in the new translation by Robert Fagles (Viking 1990).

> They quickly lowered the chest in a deep, hollow grave
> and over it piled a cope of huge stones closely set,
> they hastily heaped a barrow . . .
> . . . And once they'd heaped the mound
> they turned back home to Troy . . .
> (*Iliad* 24.797–99, 801)

The vital difference is that there is hope for Helen's child in *Omeros*, while we know that, unprotected by his father, Hector's child in the *Iliad* will soon be hurled to his death from the city-walls.

Homer also touches Maud Plunkett with mortality, though in her case the interaction is with the *Odyssey*. Like Penelope she works daily at her tapestry, but unlike Penelope Maud does not unpick hers; and it will provide a funeral shroud, not for old Laertes, but for herself. In the section where it is most fully described Dennis thinks with a shudder "this is her shroud, not her silver jubilee gift" (*XVIii*). Sure enough it is there draping her bier (*LIIIii, iii*).[14] The Penelope association bears strange fruit. "I" meets Plunkett in the bank next day and is filled with anger and contempt for the class-conscious Sergeant-Major whom, by reflex response, he calls "Sir." Yet when Dennis calls him "Sir" in return, his eyes fill with tears (*LIVi*). "I" used to call his own father "Sir" (*XIIi*); and he admits:

> There was Plunkett in my father, much as there was
> my mother in Maud . . .
> . . . there in that khaki Ulysses
>
> there was a changing shadow of Telemachus
> in me, in his absent war, and an empire's guilt
> stitched in the one pattern of Maud's fabulous quilt.
> (*LIIii*)

*          *          *

Whether such well "dug in" affinities with Homer should be attributed to the subtle and well-read mind of "I" or of Derek Walcott, they go far beyond any sort of simple parallel or equivalence, and engender a depth and power which could not have been achieved

---

[14]The sea-swift that she had embroidered links her art to that of "I" whose pen-nib is often imaged as a swift's beak, and to Achille since his vision was led to Africa by a migrating sea-swift.

otherwise. Yet it is not just Walcott who plays down the significance of Homer, the "I" of *Omeros* does so as well. In *LIVii* and *iii*, for instance, he wishes to shake off the Homeric echoes:

> Why not see Helen
>
> as the sun saw her, with no Homeric shadow,
> swinging her plastic sandals on the beach alone,
> as fresh as the sea-wind?

Again in *LXIIii*:

> . . . make all those parallels pointless. Names are not oars
> that have to be laid side by side, nor are legends.

In some places there is a positive distaste expressed for ancient Greece, sometimes rather loosely blended with imperial Rome. There is a scattering of disparaging applications of "marble," "alabaster," "cold," and above all "white." Odysseus himself drives his black crew to war against their will (*XLii*). Athens, paradigm for the slavery of the American South as well as for its architecture (cf. *XXXVi*), is singled out for special contempt:

> eaten with prejudice
> from its pillared base, the Athenian *demos*,
> its *demos* demonic and its *ocracy* crass,
> corrupting the blue-veined marble with its disease,
> stillborn as a corpse, for all those ideals went cold
> in the heat of its hate
>
> (*XLIi*)

Here I suspect that we come close to the root of Walcott's flinching from Homer, his spurning embrace. Ancient Greece stands as the base of European civilization, and as the paradigm for a high culture incorporating slavery.[15] Also Greece is whitewashed with the elitist brush of a "classical education" ("I'm not a good classical

---

15      . . . I could, since the only civilizations
      were those with snow, whiten to anonymity.
      (*XLIIIiii*)
      I suspect that later in *XLIIIiii* I detect a word of special distaste for Oxford–shrouded, as I write these words, with snow!

scholar"). So not even Homer is an unmixed blessing. Yet, in more expansive moments, *Omeros* sees that each new use of the past affects other previous uses—and abuses. *Omeros* will itself do something to diminish the unsympathetic accretions around Homer.

There is one association of Homeric epic which Derek Walcott is particularly keen to dissociate himself from. "I do not think of it as an epic . . . Where are the battles? There are a few, I suppose. But 'epic' makes people think of great wars and great warriors" (*New York Times*, October 9, 1990). "So it's not really that kind of an epic poem with battles" ("Poetry Please," 29 October 1990). The point about great warriors is pretty dubious in the post-Joyce era; and the claim about wars and battles is not true even of the *Odyssey*, much of which is set in the everyday world of everyday things and activities.[16]

It is true that violent death is absent from the main narrative of *Omeros*, except for Hector's crash, which is narrated with a strange and moving calm. But many violent deaths are evoked from the past, at Troy, in Africa, at the Battle of the Saints, and in the American plains. And one is described in gruesome detail: the "ghost" of the future Achille, after witnessing the raid on his ancestral village in Africa, brains one of the slavers with an oar.

> He hid and felt the same
> mania that, in the arrows of drizzle, he felt for Hector.
> (*XXVIIiii*)

Throughout the poem there is the association of oars with weapons, above all at Hector's funeral when Achille places an oar in the canoe-coffin with the words, "Mate, this is your spear" (*XLVIi*). The noun *lance* is everywhere; and again and again rain and drizzle are associated with showers of lances or arrows. "Are they still fighting wars?" Homer asks when he appears to "I" (*LVIiii*). *Omeros* never forgets that men do fight wars and do kill each other.

And perhaps there is a new enemy in the poem, less palpable, more insidious, an enemy that threatens to kill the kind of life on St. Lucia that the poem celebrates. The attackers are the property speculators, developers, factory-fishers, and the tourists.[17]

---

[16] I wonder whether there is a connection between the faithful Eumaeus, who looks after Odysseus' pig farm, and Philoctete, who looks after Plunkett's pig farm.

[17] A more global warning is introduced when Achille suspects from strange climatic conditions that "somewhere people interfering / with the course of nature" (LXi); and XLVIiii seems to point to the destruction of the forests in South America.

> The village was surrendering a life besieged
> by the lances of yachts in the white marina
> . . .
>
> . . . its life adjusted to the lenses
>
> of cameras, that, perniciously elegiac,
> took shots of passing things . . .
>                                    (*LXIIii*)

From the walls of the eighteenth-century English fort the tourists "shot the humped island with its blue horns" (*LXIIii*). Walcott curses the profiteering exploiters to hell in the "Dante" sequence (*LVIII*).

* * *

In the *Odyssey*, Odysseus is praised for telling the story of his adventures as skillfully as a poet (*Od.* 11.368). Yet there is an even better story-teller than Odysseus, and that is Homer, who tells Odysseus' story for him. In the same way there is a poet who tells the story even better than the "I" of *Omeros*—and who has an even more interesting relationship with Homer than "I" has—and that is Derek Walcott. He makes at least one personal appearance in the poem, hunched and silent, when Seven Seas/Homer is lecturing "I" at the sulphur-pits:

> Mark you, *he* does not go; he sends his narrator;
> he plays tricks with time because there are two journeys
> in every odyssey, one on worried water,
> the other crouched and motionless, without noise.
> For both, the "I" is a mast' a desk is a raft
> for one, foaming with paper, and dipping the beak
>
> of a pen in its foam, while an actual craft
> carries the other to cities where people speak
> a different language, or look at him differently . . .
>                                    (*LVIIIii*)

In the end, that figure crouched with pen over desk made the poem. It cannot "turn round" without him. And so, in the end, Derek Walcott knows Homer better than he is willing to acknowledge. And Homer has helped once more to create a new and great epic.

# SELECT BIBLIOGRAPHY

Almeida, Hermione de. *Byron and Joyce through Homer*. London: Macmillan, 1981.

Beni, Paolo. *Comparazione di Omero, Virgilio, e Torquato; ed a qui di loro si debba la palma nell' eroico poema: del quale si vanno anco reconoscendo i precetti; con dar largo conto de'poeti eroici tanto greci, quanto Latini ed italiani, ed in particolare si fa giudizio dell' Ariosto: di Paolo Beni.* (c. 1600). In *Opere di Torquato Tasso colle controversie sulle GERUSALEMME.* Vols. 21–22. Pisa: Nicolò Capurro, 1821.

Bernal, Martin. *Black Athena: The Afroasiatic Roots of Classical Civilization, Volume I: The Fabrication of Ancient Greece 1785–1985*. New Brunswick, N.J.: Rutgers University Press, 1987.

Bien, Peter. *Kazantzakis. Politics of the Spirit.* Princeton: Princeton University Press, 1989

Bleicher, Thomas. *Homer in der deutschen Literatur (1450–1740)*. Stuttgart: Metzler, 1972.

Bolgar, R. R. (1977) *The Classical Heritage and its Beneficiaries*. Cambridge: Cambridge University Press, 1954, rprt. 1977.

Brower, Reuben A. *Hero & Saint: Shakespeare and the Graeco-Roman Tradition*. Oxford: Oxford University Press, 1971.

Burke, Peter. "Italian Literature and Society, 1350–1650" in *The Old World: Discovery and Rebirth* ed. D. Daiches and A. Thorlby. London: Aldus Books, 1974

Butler, E. M. *The Tyranny of Greece over Germany: A Study of the Influence Exercised by greek Art and Poetry over the Great German Writers of the Eighteenth, Nineteenth and Twentieth Centuries.* Cambridge: Cambridge University Press, 1935.

Chapman, George. *The Whole Works of Homer, prince of poets in his Iliads, and Odysses.* London: N. Butter, 1616.

Chiampi, James T. "Tasso's Rinaldo in the Body of the Text." *Romanic Review* 82,4 (Nov. 1990) 487–503.

Chiappelli, Fredi. *Studi sul linguaggio del Tassso epico.* Florence: F. Le Monnier, 1957.

Clarke, Howard. *Homer's Readers: A Historical Introduction to the Iliad and the Odyssey.* Newark: University of Delaware Press, 1981.

Cottaz, Joseph. *Le Tasse et la conception epique.* Paris: Italia, 1942.

Dacier, Anne. *Des Causes de la corruption du goust.* Paris: Imprimerie Royale, 1714.

Dasenbrock, Reed Way. "*Ulysses* and Joyce's Discovery of Vico's 'True Homer.'" *Eiré-Ireland* 20 (1985) 96–108.

Dolce, Lodovico. *L'Achille et L'Enea di Messer Lodovico Dolce dove Egli Tessendo l'Historia della Iliade de' Homero a' Quella dell'Eneide di Vergilio, ambedue l'ha Divinamenta Redotte in Ottava Rima. con Argomenti et Allegorie per Ogni Canto: Et due Tavoli: l'una delle Sentenze; l'altra de i Nomi, & delle cose piu notabile.* Venice: Gabriel Giolito de' Ferrari, 1572

Ellmann, Maud. "Polytropic Man: Paternity, Identity and Naming in *The Odyssey* and *A Portrait of the Artist as a Young Man.*" *James Joyce: New Perspectives.* Ed. Colin MacCabe (Bloomington: Indiana University Press, 1982) 73–103.

*Flaxman's Illustrations to Homer: Drawn by John Flaxman, Engraved by William Blake and Others.* Edited, with Introduction and Commentary, Roberk Essick and Jenijoy La Belle. New York: Dover Publications, 1977.

Forsyth, Neil. "Homer in Milton: The Attendance Motif and the Graces." *Comparative Literature* 33,2 (Spring, 1981) 137–155.

Garnier, Nicole. *Antoine Coypel (1661-1722): peintre du roi.* Paris: Arthena, 1989.

Haskins, C.H. *The Renaissance of the Twelfth Century.* Cambridge: Harvard University Press, 1955.

Hepp, Noémi. *Homère en France au XVII^e Siècle.* Paris: Librairie C. Klincksieck, 1968.

Highet, Gilbert. *The Classical Tradition: Greek and Roman Influences on Western Literature.* New York and London: Oxford University Press, 1949.

Jenkyns, Richard. "Homer and the Homeric Ideal." *The Victorians and Ancient Greece.* Oxford: Blackwell, 1980. 192–226.

Johnson, W. R. *Darkness Visible.* Berkeley and Los Angeles: University of California Press, 1976.

Kates, Judith A. *Tasso and Milton: The Problem of Christian Epic.* London and Toronto: Associated University Presses: 1983.

Keener, Frederick M. "On the Poets' Secret: Allusion and Parallelism in Pope's *Homer.*" *The Yearbook of English Studies* 18 (1988) 159–170.

Kenner, Hugh. "Pound and Homer." in *Ezra Pound Among the Poets.* Edited by George Bornstein. Chicago and London: University of Chicago Press, 1985

King, Katherine Callen. *Achilles: Paradigms of the War Hero from Homer to the Middle Ages.* Berkeley and Los Angeles: University of California Press, 1987.

Kimbrough, Robert. *Shakespeare's* Troilus & Cressida *and its Setting.* Cambridge: Harvard University Press, 1964.

Knox, Bernard. "Achilles in the Caribbean." *New York Review of Books* (March 7, 1991) 3-4

Leadbeater, Lewis W. "Homeric Themes in Jean Giraudoux's Siegfried. *Classical and Modern Literature* 2,3 (Spring, 1982) 147–160.

Levine, Joseph M. "The Battle of the Books and the Shield of Achilles" *Eighteenth Century Life* 96 (1984) 33–61.

*Libro de Alexandre.* Edited and introduced by Jesús Cañas Murillo. Madrid: Editora Nacional, 1978.

Merchant, Paul. "Children of Homer: The Epic Strain in Modern Greek Literature" in *Aspects of the Epic*, ed. Tom Winnifrith and K. W. Gransden. London: MacMillan, 1983. 92-108.

Michael, Ian. *The Treatment of Classical Material in the Libro de Alexandre.* Manchester: Manchester University Press, 1970.

Multineddu, Salvatore. *Le fonti della Gerusalemme liberata.* Torino: C. Clausen, 1895.

Padel, Ruth. "Homer's Reader: A Reading of George Seferis" *Proceedings of the Cambridge Philological Society*, n.s. 31 (1985) 74–132.

Palli Bonet, Julio. *Homero en España.* Barcelona: University of Barcelona Press, 1953.

Parry, Adam. "Introduction," in Milman Parry, *The Making of Homeric Verse: The Collected Papers of Milman Parry.* Oxford: Clarendon Press, 1971.

Pfeiffer, Rudolf. *History of Classical Scholarship: From 1300–1850.* Oxford: Clarendon Press, 1976.

Pope, Alexander. *The Iliad of Homer.* Second Edition. Six Volumes. Bernard Lintot: 1720-1721.

Quint, David. "Political Allegory in the *Gerusalemme Liberata*" *Renaissance Quarterly* 43 (1990) 1–29.

Reynolds, L. D. and Wilson, N.G. (1974) *Scribes and Scholars.* Oxford: Clarendon Press, 1974.

Scherer, Margaret R. *The Legends of Troy in Art and Literature.* New York and London: Phaidon Press, 1963.

Smith, Stan. "Writing a Will: Yeats's Ancestral Voices in 'The Tower' and 'Meditations in Time of Civil War.'" *Irish University Review* 13,1 (Spring 1983) 14–37.

Stanford, W. B. *The Ulysses Theme: A Study in the Adaptability of a Traditional Hero.* Second Edition. Ann Arbor: University of Michigan Press, 1968. Originally published London, 1963.

Steadman, John M. "Achilles and Renaissance Epic: Moral Criticism and Literary Tradition" in *Lebende Antike: Symposion für Rudolf Sühnel.* Ed. H. Meller. (Berlin: Erich Schmidt Verlag, 1967) 139–154.

Stevenson, Catherine Barnes. "The Shade of Homer exorcises the Ghost of De Quincey: Tennyson's 'The Lotus Eaters'." *Browning Institute Studies* 10 (1982) 117–141.

Struever, Nancy S. "Translation as Taste." *The Eighteenth Century* 22,1 (Winter, 1988) 32–46.

Summers, Claude J. "'Or One Could Weep Because Another Wept': The Counterplot of Auden's 'The Shield of Achilles.'" *Journal of English and Germanic Philology* 83,2 (April, 1984) 214-232.

Tasso, Torquato. *Discorsi della poema eroico,* in *Torquato Tasso: Prose,* ed. Ettore Mazzali (Milan and Naples: Riccardo Ricciardi, n.d.) pp. 487–729.

———. *Discourses on the Heroic Poem.* Translated by Mariella Cavachini and Irene Samuel. Oxford: Clarendon Press, 1973.

Turner, Frank M. "The Reading of Homer." *The Greek Heritage in Victorian Britain.* New Haven: Yale University Press, 1981. 135–186.

Wiebenson, Dora. "Subjects from Homer's *Iliad* in Neoclassical Art." *Art Bulletin* 46 (1964) 23–37.

Weinberg, Bernard. *A History of Literary Criticism in the Italian Renaissance.* University of Chicago Press, 1961; repr. 1974.

Westlake, J. H. J. "W. H. Auden's 'The Shield of Achilles': An Interpretation." *Literatur in Wissenschaft und Unterricht* 1 (1968) 50-58.

Wood, Diane S. and Teeta M. Smith. "Anachronistic Elements in Jehan Samxon's *Les Iliades* (1530)." *Explorations in Renaissance Culture* 7 (1981) 47-60.